THE HOME
DECORATOR'S
BIBLE

THE HOME DECORATOR'S BIBLE

Anoop Parikh, Debora Robertson, Thomas Lane,

Elizabeth Hilliard, Melanie Paine

Crown Publishers, Inc.
New York

Published by Crown Publishers, Inc., 201 East 50th Street, New York,
New York 10022. Member of the Crown Publishing Group.

Random House, Inc. New York, Toronto, London, Sydney, Auckland

http://www.randomhouse.com/

CROWN is a trademark of Crown Publishers, Inc.

Commissioning Editor:	Denny Hemming
Senior Editor:	Catriona Woodburn
Art Editor:	Tony Seddon
Picture Researcher:	Rachel Davies
Production Controller:	Mano Mylvaganam
Copy Editors:	Sally Harding, Maggi McCormick, Sarah Sears, Alison Wormleighton
Americanizer:	Eleanor Van Zandt
Indexer:	Hilary Bird
Designers:	Isabel de Cordova, Amanda Lerwill
Artwork Visualizer:	Jean Morley
Illustrator:	Clare Melinsky

Library of Congress Cataloging-in-Publication Data
is available upon request

ISBN 0-517-70373-4

10 9 8 7 6 5 4 3 2 1
First American Edition

First published in the United Kingdom in 1996 by Conran Octopus
Limited 37 Shelton Street, London WC2 9HN

Printed in Singapore

Front jacket photographs: *Above* — Jerome Darblay. *Below from left
to right* — Francis Hammond, Polly Wreford/Homes & Gardens/
Robert Harding Syndication, Tom Leighton/Wedding & Home/
Robert Harding Syndication, Fritz von der Schulenburg
(Richard Mudditt)/The Interior Archive.

Back jacket photographs: *Above* — Todd Eberle. *Below from left
to right* — Verne Fotografie, Antoine Bootz, Eric Thorburn/Abode,
Fritz von der Schulenburg/The Interior Archive.

CONTENTS

DESIGN & DETAILING
8

WALLS
48

▽

FLOORS
122

WINDOWS & DOORS
196

FURNITURE & FURNISHINGS
270

DESIGN &
DETAILING

The greatest thing about decorating your own home is that it allows you to say "I made that," or "I did it myself." In an age when so much daily activity seems pre-programmed or conducted via a computer keyboard without regard to physical distances or borders, there is something inherently precious about this. From the moment when you hit on an idea, through the stages of planning out your changes, gathering tools and materials, preparing the ground, doing the job, and finally standing back to admire your handiwork, decorating requires you to make the decisions, be they budgetary, aesthetic, or just plain practical. The essence of its appeal is that it allows you to take control.

As we all know, however, being decisive is not always easy. In decorating, as in life, issues can become confused by the sheer range of options that seems to be available, fear of what the neighbors might think, and a lack of confidence in your own abilities. It often seems easier to put a room together by

buying odds and ends in a piecemeal and rather halfhearted fashion or to opt for the safest, most familiar solutions. Unfortunately, the former approach can make a room seem unpleasantly "bitty," and the latter all too often results in bland and depressing spaces, devoid of any sign that they might be lived in by real people.

Creating a home with personality, therefore, begins with the question "What do I really want?" You will find this easier to answer if you look closely at rooms that appeal in some way and identify those aspects or details that you like most. It might be the way the color of the furniture contrasts with that of the walls or something as minor as a cute curtain trim. Try also to describe the atmosphere in these rooms. Is it lively or serene? Airy or claustrophobic? Does the decor make you feel calm or jumpy? Identifying the qualities that appeal, as well as those that repel, enables you to focus on how you would like your home to look and feel.

You do not have to limit yourself to looking at other houses for ideas. It may be that a place that features in childhood memories, a favorite item of clothing, or a vacation postcard is equally evocative. Whatever they happen to be, the next step is to collect all your sources together. Spread them out on a flat surface or paste them onto a board and see whether some kind of story begins to emerge. It may be that the colors in front of you form a kind of family or that similar styles of furniture appear in several of the photographs.

These themes provide the perfect starting point, as they can be used as reference material to suggest paint colors, for example, or to guide your choice of furnishings. Use them as a springboard for ideas. A preponderance of coarse, natural textures, for example, might suggest slubbed linen and burlap for upholstery and window treatments. You will probably reject some of these ideas farther down the line and modify others to suit your budget or as a compromise with loved ones, but don't worry. The important thing is that you are no longer stuck at square one.

You will probably also notice that your tastes are more eclectic than you thought. Modern furnishings put in a guest appearance alongside your favorite traditional interiors, or vice versa, and some elements are there just for fun. These should not be discarded when it comes to turning inspiration into reality—quite the opposite, in fact. The most stylish and welcoming interiors are always those that contain intriguing contrasts or one or two surprises.

This chapter aims to provide you with all the information you need to put a basic decorative scheme together. It begins by looking at color, texture, and pattern—the basic building blocks of any decorative scheme—and explains how to interpret a decorative style so that it fits comfortably into your surroundings. The chapter then goes on to tell you everything you need to know about working with architectural detail, lighting, and storage—the three elements of a scheme that pretty much determine how a room is both used and enjoyed.

◀◀ *Simple decor and furnishings allow distinctive architectural character to shine through. Here, attention is drawn toward the beamed ceiling and double-sided fireplace by picking them out in a contrasting color, while the seating blends with the pale floor and walls.*

◀ *Small rooms benefit just as much as their larger equivalents from a bold and consistent decorative approach. Areas of strong color and pattern give this compact bedroom instant character, but it is important that relative proportions be finely judged, so that no one element of the scheme overwhelms the others.*

Color, pattern, and texture

Color and, to a lesser extent, pattern and texture
elicit powerful and sometimes unpredictable
responses in each of us. When we flick through
a paint chart or gather swatches of fabric,
spiritual traditions, gender conditioning, fashion,
and much else come into play. And you can be
sure that no two people will describe a color's
qualities or create a coordinated set of patterns
in exactly the same way.

Color in particular is so much a part of our lives that we often take it for granted—until such time as we are deprived of it. Not so long ago, visitors to the former Soviet Union invariably remarked on how colorless the cities there seemed, thanks to the absence of any street advertising. And in the earth's deserts and at its ice caps it is not just the extremes of temperature that inspire awe but also the seemingly monochrome barrenness of those landscapes.

There is no doubt that using color and ornament is a basic form of creative self-expression. Even those cultures with the most limited resources manage to find ways of decorating their surroundings and possessions, and they do it in ways that are often exuberant and joyful. Yet in the developed world today only children seem to enjoy color and pattern for their own sakes. As we grow older we become self-conscious about using them, perhaps out of fear of ridicule or in conforming to the outdated and inaccurate notion that modern means white and plain.

Although it is not always easy to ignore all those so-called rules for using color and pattern, such as blue always being chilly and mixing no more than three patterns in one room, do try. Be guided by your likes and dislikes, and think about how you and others will be using the room. If it is to be used for relaxing in, and as a foil for your favorite objects, a harmonious color scheme and a relatively plain backdrop are probably in order. On the other hand, a room that is likely to bustle with activity all day, such as a family kitchen, needs to be bright and welcoming, but not so full of decorative distractions that it becomes tiring.

Take note also of the room's position relative to the sun. Rooms that receive sunlight for long periods have a tendency to overheat in the warmer months, so you may want to include a touch of cool color, such as a minty green or ultramarine blue, in your scheme. Those rooms that get very little natural light will need brightening up; white is the most commonly used color, but pale gray-blues and greens work just as well. And don't forget you have other weapons in your

◄◄ *A seemingly simple and uninspiring-sounding arrangement of brown objects against a yellow wall looks anything but dull when it includes pleasing textural contrasts, such as that of the old wood cabinet against the smooth wall, and whimsical found objects which introduce a touch of pattern.*

◄ *Shiny materials, such as stainless steel, not only contrast well with rough textures, such as stone and brick, they also take on and reflect the colors of objects nearby. This is a useful way of softening the cold and hard character of metallic surfaces. It also makes a small amount of intense color go farther.*

decorative armory; a bright rug and strategically placed mirrors will also help to liven up a dingy room.

There is no mystery to mixing colors, patterns, and textures in a decorative scheme; it is all about creating contrasts of scale and proportion. Most coordinated fabric and wallpaper ranges are based on mixing large-scale patterns with small all-over motifs and plain colors, and these work best when one design plays the starring role and the rest are used in smaller quantities. The same applies when creating color combinations. While a small amount of contrasting color can liven up a scheme, living with large areas of competing color soon becomes uncomfortable.

In general, decorative schemes that are composed of different tones of the same color are the most harmonious and calming, while room schemes that contain contrasting colors tend to be livelier. If you bear this in mind, there is absolutely no reason at all why a room filled with both pattern and texture shouldn't be relaxing and easy to live with, or why a room containing just a few carefully chosen objects shouldn't be lively and inspiring. The secret is to experiment and not to be afraid to change your mind as you go along. You may not get exactly the effect you want immediately, but decorating would be no fun if it weren't a little bit unpredictable.

Talking about color

While our perception of colors is entirely subjective, it is useful to have some idea of how colors behave with one another, both in theory and in practice, and to know how to describe their qualities or characters. This makes life easier whether you plan to mix colors yourself or to order special paints to match a favorite object or fabric.

Color spectrum

Modern color theory is based on the spectrum—the series of colors that we see when white light passes through a prism or when sunlight passes through airborne droplets of water to create a rainbow. Although each color blends almost imperceptibly into its neighbor, we tend for convenience to depict the spectrum as six distinct bands of color: namely red, orange, yellow, green, blue, and violet.

The ends of the spectrum can be brought around to form a circle, to create what is known as a color wheel. This shows the relationship of each color to the others more clearly, and it becomes easier to see that there are three pure or primary colors—blue, red, and yellow—and three secondary colors—green, orange, and violet—each created by mixing two primary colors. Mixing equal parts of a primary color and an adjacent secondary color gives rise to a tertiary color: green and yellow, for example, produce lime green; blue and green create turquoise; while violet and red make a bluish red known as crimson.

Descriptive terms

Colors that stand opposite each other on the wheel, and which are therefore as unlike one another as possible, are known as complementary colors. They create the strongest contrasts, and therefore the liveliest color schemes. Adjacent colors, particularly those that sit between two primary colors—for example turquoise, blue, and green—are harmonious, as the eye can travel easily from one to another. Strong, pure colors may be described as saturated. And a color that is said to have been "knocked back" or "dirtied" has had its intensity deliberately weakened. This is a device often employed by professional designers to add a touch of drab color to a bright or pastel scheme to make the main colors seem even fresher in comparison.

The qualities that we most often ascribe to colors are warmth and coolness. The warm colors—reds, yellows, and oranges—seem to come toward you, and this is what makes rooms decorated in these colors seem cozy and welcoming. They also seem to make a room look smaller. In contrast, cool colors—violets, blues, greens, and black— seem to recede and appear to create a sense of space. As with everything, there are plenty of exceptions, however. The color of faded denim, for example, is a ubiquitous and much-loved warm blue, while nature provides more such examples in cornflowers and forget-me-nots. Red—supposedly the hottest color of all—is anything but when it appears as a sugary pink or in crimson pigment.

Tone

A color's tone describes its darkness or lightness. Darker tones—also known as shades—are created by adding black to a saturated color, while light tones—sometimes called tints—are created by adding white. Two of the easiest ways to create a harmonious scheme are to put together colors that are similar in tone or to combine several tones of a single color.

A color scheme based on combining more than one tone of a single hue is often called monochromatic, and when it is based on a neutral color, such as beige, the shades blend to create a muted and subtle backdrop. Sometimes, though, the different tones vary so much that it is hard to believe they are all derived from one color. An example would be a scheme based on an orangy red, which might deepen to chocolate brown and lighten to a rosy pink.

Contrasting color

We tend to think of single-color schemes as being the easiest to live with, but they can look flat and uninspiring until small amounts of subtly contrasting color are added. Living with strongly colored surroundings is easier than you might think. Painting one wall of a room in a deeper color creates an instant focal point, and if the color is based on warm reds and yellows it will provide a wonderful backdrop for wooden furniture.

A designer I know paints each wall of a room with a different color; one might be inky blue, another terra-cotta, the third oxblood, and so on. The scheme works because all the shades have a similar tonal value and are more or less as strong as each other. Instead of being knocked out by

◀ *When using more than one strong color in a room, give each one the same amount of space. Alternatively, use colors of similar intensity. It is worth remembering that when light bounces off a wall, it transfers the color of that wall to objects nearby. This is easy to see when deep or saturated shades are used, as here.*

▲ *In a nineteenth-century Parisian apartment, details such as door panels and baseboards have been played down by the blanket application of deep colors, in order to focus attention on the custom-designed furniture and the plaster ceiling decoration. This is a good quick fix when walls and woodwork are in less than perfect condition.*

This all sounds rather academic, but is useful to bear in mind when you are working around an existing feature, such as a fireplace or carpet, in a nondescript color. A dull, reddish-brown carpet, for example, will spring into life if it is teamed with walls painted in aquamarine, an intriguing color that hovers between blue and green, and perhaps one or two accessories in a yellowy green such as lime.

Acquiring color sense

Hardly anyone is born with great color sense, so when it comes to choosing colors it is natural to hesitate. Since an understanding of how color works is gained only through familiarity and practice, there is nothing wrong with settling for a neutral background at first then adding color to it by degrees. You might, for example, begin with off-white walls and wooden furniture, then add some decorative interest in the form of colorful pictures and add more color, if you feel that the room needs it, in the form of pillows and displays. Try to create specific areas of interest, which will give coherence and greater impact to displays, rather than just scattering accessories at random around a room.

Color and light

Unless you use a room only at night, it is a good idea to check that your color scheme works in both natural and artificial light. Because daylight in a room is usually directional, it highlights those objects nearest the window, leaving the rest in progressively deeper shadow as you move away from the window. If the room is not too deep and contains only one window, the wall facing it will be brighter than the side and window walls. At night, however, the room is likely to be more evenly lit, with several light sources insuring that all the surfaces, and hence the colors and textures, are seen more clearly.

You may have noticed that colors change in artificial light. Halogen and low-voltage halogen bulbs emit a bright white light, which renders colors more true, while common incandescent bulbs emit a

the color when you enter the room, you feel welcomed and cosseted. Because your eyes are not constantly straining to distinguish between lighter and darker shades, the overall feeling is relaxed.

That is not to say that strong tonal contrasts are a bad thing. The classic black-and-white tiled floor laid in a checkerboard pattern gives hallways, and any other area where you don't spend much time, a graphic and efficient appeal. When one of the colors predominates, however, the result is more subdued and easier on the eye, without being any less smart or crisp.

Mixing lighter and darker tones also helps to balance complementary colors, such as orange and blue. You might, for example, place bright orange glass vases on a pale blue shelf or windowsill.

Subtler contrasts can be created by putting together a split-complementary scheme. Here, a color is teamed with those that sit on either side of its complementary color on the color wheel. Orange, for example, may be combined with green and violet—the shades that are found on either side of blue—or with turquoise and violet blue, which are more closely related to blue.

◄ An apartment's industrial origins are revealed by picking out structural elements such as the steel beams in scarlet and black. Later additions to the space, such as the kitchen, are made to blend in by painting them in similarly strong shades. The pressed metal ceiling panels help to direct the light downward.

yellowish light, which tends to make most colors warmer. The latter isn't always the blessing it seems, as pale yellows tend to disappear, terra-cotta becomes orange, and reddish-purples turn brown. But there is something reassuring about the familiar glow. It is worth remembering that a colored lampshade will also tint the light shining through it.

The texture of a surface also affects how we see a color. In general, matte or rough surfaces, which absorb light, look darker than glossy or shiny ones, which reflect it. It is especially important to bear this in mind when choosing fabrics, as there is a great deal of difference between how a color will appear say, on a nubby cotton and on silk satin. Extremely shiny surfaces, such as those made from chrome, seem to have no color of their own, as they reflect those around them. Even the texture of a paint finish affects the colors we see. Some new paints are formulated without light-reflecting plastics, which has the effect of making the colors appear softer and chalkier than those of synthetic paint finishes.

▲ The color and surface variation found in natural building materials may be all the "decoration" you need. However, it is important to get the details right. The planking used on the floor and ceiling runs in the same direction, and at right angles to that used on the walls and the floor in the hall, so that each area remains clearly defined.

Choosing and using pattern

Pattern can be bought off the shelf as fabric or wallpaper, or it may be created when a decorative element is repeated several times, as in the slats of a blind or a row of candlesticks on a mantelpiece. It can be something that you apply by hand, by using a stencil or a simple printing block perhaps. Our nineteenth-century forebears loved pattern and layered it over every available surface, but few of us today would feel comfortable with such an approach. Instead, we tend to use it as a focal point, in the form of a row of pictures perhaps or as the decorative equivalent of cake frosting, to make a plain interior feel more homey and special.

Scale

However you choose to use pattern, the most important factors to consider are scale and color. Large-scale patterns are like warm colors (see pages 14–15) in that they appear to come toward you. They create a lively and stimulating atmosphere, and they can make a large space seem cozier. In small spaces, however, they need to be handled with care. Unless they are used as a focal point, in the form of a rug perhaps, they can easily swamp a scheme and make walls and other surfaces appear to close in.

Like cool colors (see pages 14–15), small-scale patterns appear to recede, making small spaces seem bigger. They can be used as an effective form of camouflage – awkward angles and corners will be played down if you use a subtle, non-directional patterned wallpaper. Unfortunately, small-scale patterns applied over a large area can be bland, unless vibrant colors are used, and when viewed from a distance they may "read" as a single color and so blur into insignificance.

For this reason, it is often a good idea to match the scale of the pattern to that of the area over which it is to be used. A large sofa will obviously display a grandiloquently patterned damask better than would a simple dining chair with an upholstered seat. Similarly, a small spriggy stencil looks charming when used to define the edges of a tabletop, but would simply look lost on an expanse of wall or ceiling. This is a far from hard and fast rule, however, and sometimes

a small-scale pattern is used as a backdrop instead of a plain color. Patchwork effects are actually enriched by the use of both large- and small-scale pattern fragments.

When you are applying pattern to a three-dimensional object, such as a table or a sofa, consider using designs that enhance the form in some way. A boxy chair, for example, can be made to look even more rectilinear by covering it in a geometric pattern, or it can be softened by using a rambling floral. Creating a sense of balance and symmetry also matters. When using a boldly patterned fabric to cover a sofa or chair, make sure that you have enough material to center the design on the chair back and seat. If the pattern has a clear direction, such as a stripe, it should also follow

through over the back, seat, and front, and the arms should mirror one another as far as possible.

Mixing patterns

As you gain confidence in your own tastes, try experimenting with simple pattern mixtures. Many types of geometric pattern have a natural affinity for one another. Stripes, for example, look good not only with checks but also with plaids and dots. Mixing geometric and non-geometric designs also works well. A traditional *toile de Jouy* pattern, for example, looks more modern when teamed with a check or stripe in harmonizing colors.

Mixing patterns is easier when they have one or more color in common and there are contrasts or harmonies of scale and design.

Thus a leafy print might be mixed with a check that picks up a color in the motif, or the zigzag pattern of a tribal fabric could be echoed by a subtle patterned weave.

Mixing patterns becomes even more satisfying when you include your own designs. This is not as difficult as it sounds. You could, for example, use patterned wallpaper below a chair rail and paint a stripe that is based on one or two of the colors in the paper above. Or you could create a simple coordinating stencil by tracing a suitable motif from a print that you plan to use in the same room. An image can be turned into a pattern by experimenting with a photocopier (see pages 98–99). In time, it will no doubt be possible to create customized and highly sophisticated patterns using computer-aided design.

◀▲ *A scheme based on a single color is far from monotonous when it includes touches of pattern in harmonious shades. In this living room, patterned accessories in cool reds provide visual relief from the expanses of warm pink, yet remain in keeping with the room's cozy and inviting character.*

▲ *A paper frieze of Matisse-inspired figures and a checkered tile floor add personal touch to a functional kitchen. At first sight the frieze appears to consist of random flowing shapes, but it is in fact made up of repeated panels for easy application. Space has been left around the frieze to make its design open and appealing.*

Surface effects and textures

▶ The highlights and shadows on partitions made from woven metal strips are an intriguing source of pattern, and complement the graphic use of wood and color in the room that they enclose. A room divider such as this would have to be custom-built, but it has the advantage of taking up less floor space than a conventional wall.

up for any absence of color or pattern. Too much softness, however, in the form of fussy curtains or accessories perhaps, can make a room seem overdecorated and stifling.

A material's texture also suggests its suitability for a particular purpose or environment. For example, smooth, polished wood and laminates are usually chosen for kitchen countertops, because they are considered to be easy to clean. By contrast, damasks are usually reserved for formal or grand rooms, partly because they look expensive and delicate but also because they catch the light in interesting ways and so lend sparkle to rooms that are mainly used in the evenings.

Decorative use

Using texture as a decorative tool is all about creating pleasing contrasts. For example, the spartan feel of a featureless room can be tempered by hanging draperies that fall into deep folds by the windows. Or an expanse of polished wood floor could be broken up with rag rugs or dhurries. An eclectic

Textures do not always register as strongly as colors and patterns do. A red sofa or a green wall, for example, is just what it appears to be to most people until they look more closely and see that in fact the sofa is velvet or the wall has been stippled. Nevertheless, textures play a central role in any decorative scheme. If you visualize the walls of a room painted in a flat color, for instance, and then imagine them treated with a paint effect based on the same colors, you will "see" the difference. Certain textures also give greater depth to patterns. A print that looks crisply detailed on smooth cotton will be softly blurred on nubby chenille.

Smooth and coarse textures

As with color and pattern, it is convenient for the purpose of definition to divide textures into two camps. The first consists of

shiny or smooth surfaces and includes many metals, glass, gloss paint, and silky fabrics. These reflect light and can, therefore, be used to brighten a room or make it seem larger. Like warm colors and bold patterns, they also stimulate the senses, which makes them a useful addition to work spaces and other activity areas. However, a room with too many shiny surfaces can be chilly and will get on your nerves after a while.

In contrast, coarse textures such as natural floor coverings, burlap, rough-hewn wood, and wool tweed absorb light so they seem duller, but with more subtle variations in color. Natural materials also have the advantage of aging better than synthetics. Rough or soft textures create a feeling of intimacy and absorb sound, which makes them perfect for living spaces and bedrooms. The tactile pleasure they provide can more than make

approach to furnishing also helps. You might mix a cotton-covered sofa with wooden chairs upholstered with woven cloth tape or place well-worn leather chairs around a pristine glass table.

Textural mixes can be theatrical as well as subtle, and nowhere is this easier, or more appropriate, than at the dining table. Rather than setting smooth porcelain and glass on a plain white tablecloth, try placing them on folksy crocheted mats. Or mix rustic earthenware with a psychedelic fabric print. Besides creating a sense of occasion, this approach allows you to experiment with decorative effects without having to commit yourself to living with the results for any length of time.

Changing the look

It makes a great deal of sense to be able to change the look of a room to suit your mood or the occasion, not least because most rooms need to serve more than one purpose. It is also pleasing to be able to reflect the changing seasons. Few of us have the means to

◀ *Naturally striped beech veneer creates a pleasingly irregular pattern on the fronts of kitchen cabinets and on the sides of the breakfast bar. The asymmetric vertical stripes help to soften the overall geometric feel of the kitchen by providing a contrast to the grid-like patterns of the slate-tiled floor and bottle rack.*

◀◀ *A feeling of opulence is conveyed by basing the scheme on a patinated oak herringbone parquet floor. Its color is echoed in the walls and moldings, which have been painted with layers of tinted glaze. The walls and floor are able to play a more important role as distracting clutter has been kept to a minimum.*

completely redo a room at whim, but well chosen finishing touches, such as armfuls of fresh flowers or adding a new accent color in the form of accessories, can make a surprisingly large difference.

Changing the look will be even easier if some of the latest developments in textile technology become more widely available. Fabrics that change color with temperature already exist, so in theory it should become possible to buy fabric that changes from a warm color in winter to a cooling tint during the summer months.

Some textiles can even be used as building materials. Tensile roofing structures made from fiberglass cloth keep the wind and rain out as effectively as a conventionally built roof, but they let in light and can be rolled back at the touch of a button. Such innovations are currently found mainly on top of large buildings, such as sports stadia and factories, but are beginning to be used on a smaller scale.

Perhaps more importantly, textile designers are creating useful, and in some cases highly sophisticated, materials from refuse. For example, plastic soft drink bottles and other household containers can now be recycled on a commercial basis to make a strong and colorful sheet material that can be used in much the same way as man-made boards; while yarns have been developed with quick-drying and solar heat converting properties, with obvious implications for energy consumption in the home.

No one can be sure when developments such as these will become widely available but certainly the potential uses of contemporary textiles in interiors are limited only by our imagination.

Interpreting a style

▶ A cool color palette
and simple yet punchy
patterns are combined
to create a particularly
sophisticated country
style. Slipcovers and
a layered window
treatment provide
softness and a sense
of welcome in what
might otherwise have
been a rather austere
room scheme, and the
use of natural and
washed-out greens as
accent colors helps to
refresh the eye without
upsetting the calm and
muted feel of the room.

▶▶ A sample board
allows you to preview
and make adjustments
to a scheme before it is
completed, helping
to avoid unnecessary
heartache and expense.

The whole point of decorating is to create more pleasant surroundings for yourself and your loved ones—perhaps even (and we could be talking heresy here) to have some fun. It is not about being slavishly faithful to a historical period or imitating a look in a photograph down to the last detail, both of which are impossible. Rather it is about gathering and interpreting information to suit your budget, your surroundings, and, not least, your lifestyle.

The easiest way to do this is to take your color scheme from a source of inspiration. For a period look, you may be able to locate the right paint shades in one of the "historical" ranges. Alternatively, look for colors that are evocative of the time:

in colonial America, for example, muted shades of green, blue, and rose were popular. Trying to match a color to a magazine picture is rarely simple, for the way the room was lit to take the photograph greatly affects the colors shown. However, it can be done by laying paint samples next to details of a room.

Materials can be highly evocative of period themes, but it is often more appropriate to adapt an idea than to copy it exactly. For example, if you love stone floors, but laying one in your apartment is not an option, try incorporating the material in the form of decorative accessories, or perhaps by choosing a soft flooring in a similarly neutral color; alternatively you could

lay plywood squares and paint them in imitation of flagstones (see pages 144–145).

Careful choice of seemingly minor elements, such as light switches and door handles, will add character and period flavor, making the difference between a room that feels stylishly pulled together and one with a vaguely halfhearted feel.

Once you have a look that you like, you can use elements of it throughout your home. You might, for example, use colors with similar tonal values in each room or include a favorite material. This establishes connections between different parts of the house and gives you the chance to enjoy it as a whole rather than treating it as a set of unrelated boxes.

This is not to say that each room should look the same. Homes are divided into rooms because human beings have a need for both private and communal space, and the demands we make on our surroundings vary according to whether we are alone or in company, even according to the time of day or year. That some rooms will get more sun than others, for instance, must be taken into account. Your decorative vocabulary also needs to be able to express changes in mood as you move through your home and reflect the fact that each space has different uses.

Making a sample board

The first step toward converting a collection of samples and color references into a three-dimensional room is to mount them on a sufficiently large piece of paper or board, known as a sample board.

Think of it as a miniature version of the room, and try to keep samples in proportion. If, for example, the color of the flooring is to provide a neutral backdrop, try to get hold of a sample that is large enough to allow you to place fabric and paint swatches on top of it. If you plan to use a certain fabric for decorative piping only, place only a fragment next to the upholstery or pillow fabrics. Use the board to check that paint and fabric colors match, if that is what you intended.

Over a few days, look at the assembled board in the room that you are planning to change to get an idea of how the scheme will alter on sunny and overcast days as well as at night. Ask yourself whether you would be happy to wake up in such a room or to walk into it at the end of a long and tiring day. Look at the scheme as a whole and at individual contrasts of color, pattern, and texture, and use your reactions as a guide to where changes might need to be made.

Sample boards do not stop being useful once the room is decorated and furnished. Any stylistic references that you have collected may suggest ideas for finishing touches such as display arrangements. When you are decorating more than one room in the house, it is a good idea to look at all the sample boards together to see how and where themes can be carried through.

Architectural details

The term "architectural detail" encompasses
all the fixed features that you might
find in a building. In the home, this includes
decorative moldings such as ceiling rosettes,
baseboards, chair and picture rails, crown
moldings or their humbler cousins coves,
fireplaces, and door and window architraves.
Similarly, stair balusters and handrails can also
be termed as fixed architectural details.

Ornamental plasterwork

Although wood has been fashioned into architectural details for centuries, the use of ornamental plasterwork is relatively recent. It first became common in the mid-eighteenth century, when it would have been molded on site by craftsmen. Increased demand led to the development of mass-produced ornaments made from cast plaster, papier-mâché, and even cast iron, and the patenting of fibrous plaster in the 1850s made it easier to produce large and complex designs in one piece. By the end of the nineteenth century plasterwork had come to be regarded as just another building trade, and the end of World War I marked the beginning of a long and gradual decline in its popularity.

Architectural moldings

Anyone who lives in an old building where the original architectural details have been lost knows that they have a much greater impact than the word "detail" implies. Their main practical purpose is to neaten the joints where two surfaces meet. Crown moldings and baseboards, for example, help to conceal the cracks and rough edges that invariably occur where walls meet respectively the ceiling and floor. In addition, they create a visual link or "bridge" between the two surfaces, to make it easier for the eye to travel from one to another.

Moldings also help to add a sense of scale, and improve proportions. Architraves make doors and windows, in particular, seem more imposing, while chair and picture rails help to break up expanses of wall.

If you are lucky enough to live in an old house or apartment that retains its original features, you only have to decide on a suitable decorative approach and the extent to which you wish to highlight them. In rooms where you are likely to notice a decorative ceiling, such as bedrooms and bathrooms, it can be fun to draw attention to moldings by picking them out in a contrasting color. This has the added advantage of making a high ceiling seem lower. Elsewhere you may want to blend them into the background, so that the effect is that of a relief pattern.

Restoration

Replacing broken or missing details is a straightforward matter, unless you plan to install a mantelpiece. If you are starting from scratch, there are plenty of books that will tell you which styles are appropriate to the age and scale of your home.

Reproduction moldings, which are available in various styles and materials, are easy to install. Those made from synthetic

▲ *An open staircase creates a dramatic focal point in any hall or circulation area, and as it is partly transparent, it can help to make a small space seem bigger. It should, however, be good to look at from every angle, so it is not necessarily the cheapest option, and any items stored under the stairs will need to be attractively organized.*

◀ *You don't have to live in a castle or château to indulge a taste for paneled walls: a relief grid pattern made from wood strips looks good in any moderately high-ceilinged room. Painting them the same color as the walls, as in this case, allows attention to be focused on both the fireplace and the furnishings.*

materials, such as vinyl, are virtually indistinguishable from the real thing once they are fixed and painted, but do check that they exactly match any existing moldings in profile and scale. If the range at your local store is limited, you can combine simple moldings and rails to imitate grander effects. A baseboard, for example, can be made deeper by topping it with a profiled molding. Or, it may be possible to cast replacements from broken examples or from items that have survived in the home of a friendly neighbor.

Modern style

In modern buildings—that is, anything built after the 1920s—architectural details need to be added with great sensitivity. Houses in a self-consciously modern style were designed to be free of moldings and ornament, because this was thought to reduce the places where dirt could collect, and it is perhaps best to keep them that way.

However, such single-mindedness seems inappropriate for a modern house that emulates traditional building styles, or one with a smattering of "period" features. In such cases, perhaps the safest option is to forget historical accuracy, and add ornament only where it serves a practical purpose. You might make a narrow room seem wider by dividing the walls with chair and picture rails, or install a fireplace in a room to provide a focal point. If the fireplace works, and you can comfortably arrange seating around it, it is much less likely to look out of place. Similarly, hanging paintings from the picture rail will make it look like a planned decision rather than an afterthought.

Whatever the age or style of your home, it is vital to use details that correspond in scale. Their size should reflect the height of the room, or the ceiling area in the case of rosettes and crown molding. It can be fun to exaggerate their proportions slightly when creating a themed or theatrical scheme. For example, you might widen the door and window architraves in a modern house so that they "go" better with period furnishings, but they should not be so large that they become visually distracting.

Crown moldings and coves

Crown moldings and coves are fixed at the point where the walls meet the ceiling. A crown molding is a projecting ornamental molding, while a cove is a plain molding with a concave profile. Both are manufactured as long lengths that can be cut to size. Wood and vinyl are popular materials for these and other moldings.

Like all plasterwork, they do not last forever. In houses that are divided into apartments, sections are often hacked away to make space for partition walls; intricate cast detail can be submerged under layers of paint or chipped; and if your building has ever suffered from severe damp, the bond between the molding and the wall may have come loose. However, they are easy to replace or repair (see pages 96–97). Walls and ceilings should be dry and free of dust before starting work, and wallpapers should be removed.

▲ Like any other work of art, an intricately patterned ceiling deserves to be properly framed. Here, the job is carried out by a crown molding that echoes the stepped profile of the plasterwork. These are ideal for breaking up a large expanse of wall, and most rooms will benefit from this prominence of detail.

▶ A cove with curved edges normally requires special casting in order to match the curvature of the walls. Creating a step between the straight and curved sections of the walls, as shown here, makes it a great deal easier to conceal imperfect joints. Notice that a cove gives an unadorned ceiling and wall a sense of interest.

Architraves and ceiling rosettes

Architraves

The molded or carved part of the frame surrounding a door or window opening is known as an architrave. Besides making the opening more imposing, it serves to hide the join between the structural part of the frame and the walls. It can be made from profiled softwood or man-made boards such as medium-density fiberboard (MDF).

Most modern architraves are relatively plain, although historical designs are also available. To draw attention to moldings in good condition, or a fine example, try painting it in a color that contrasts with, or complements, that of the door.

Ceiling rosettes

A ceiling rosette is an ornamental motif, usually circular or oval, with a pattern that radiates from the center. It creates a focal point for the ceiling plane and acts as a suitably impressive foil for a hanging lamp or chandelier hung from its center. It can be fixed against a plain background, or form the centerpiece of a richly patterned surface.

Traditionally rosettes were made of plaster; and if you are lucky enough to know a plasterer who does decorative work, you could have the real thing. A more likely option is to buy a reproduction rosette, made of synthetic material. These come in a wide range of designs and sizes, both round and oval, to suit Colonial, Federal and Victorian houses. The larger ones look best in rooms with fairly high ceilings. Look for casts with crisp details and neatly finished edges.

Ceiling rosettes are easy to install. If a hanging lamp is to be fixed in the center, make sure there is a pre-formed hole for the cord or that it will be easy to create one.

▲ A standard-sized door opening is given a touch of grandeur by fitting an architrave with a small pediment on top. Here, this consists of a plain inner molding that has been cut to shape and painted to match the walls, surrounded by a more detailed design in a contrasting color.

▶ Even where a ceiling rosette no longer serves its original purpose, which was to draw attention to a chandelier, it is well worth retaining as a purely decorative feature. This is especially true of rooms where you spend any time seated or lying down, as the ceiling occupies a large part of your field of vision.

Picture rails, chair rails, and baseboards

Because they are commonly made from low-grade softwoods, plastic, or plaster, picture rails, chair rails and baseboards are relatively inexpensive, and can be found in a variety of patterns. To fit picture rails, chair rails, and baseboards, see pages 120–121.

Picture rails

Placed a short way from the top of the wall and immediately below a frieze, picture rails were originally used, as the name suggests, for hanging pictures. A groove or channel was formed along the top edge of the molding to hold picture hooks securely; if this was made deep enough, it could also be used to display plates. Like chair rails (below), picture rails can make a large difference to the way we perceive space. By dividing the wall into smaller areas, they help to establish a visual rhythm which the eye reads as an improvement in the proportions of the room.

Chair rails

Chair rails are usually placed about one-third of the way up the wall. Their original function was to prevent chair backs from being pushed up against the wall and damaging it. They were also used to signal the division between a hardwearing finish or paneling used on the lower part of the wall, known as the dado, and the finer finish used on the upper part. Late eighteenth-century examples would have been decorated with Neoclassical motifs made from gesso or carved wood, and those in grand Victorian hallways were sometimes made from ceramic tiles. Modern examples tend to be made from humbler materials, such as softwood, or are replaced by wallpaper borders.

Baseboards

Although the line created by a baseboard is regularly broken by doorways and fireplaces or obscured by furniture, it nevertheless plays an important decorative role. It draws attention to the floor by framing it, and when used in conjunction with a chair rail and a picture rail it can be used to create bands of color and texture on the walls. Baseboards are usually about 4 or 5 inches (10–12cm) deep. In some old houses you will find deeper ones, often fashioned from two or more moldings joined together. Baseboards are frequently absent in minimal or rustic interiors and may be replaced by a band of painted color or flawless plastering. Although architraves are not, strictly speaking, wall moldings at all, because they are fixed to the outer rim of the door frame, it is usual for the architrave and baseboard patterns to match.

▶ *Moldings in a room need not all be painted the same color. Here, a white cornice helps to brighten up a dark background of teal green, while a gold painted picture rail provides a decorative theme and, like the lines painted on the sides of expensive cars, conveys a sense of luxury.*

Plaques, columns, corbels, and friezes

The material also lends itself well to being colored or decorated. Traditionally, this took the form of gilding or painting, but plaster can also be tinted with pigments before casting. This is surprisingly easy to do yourself and worth considering, for paint effects never achieve quite the same depth of color.

Friezes

The band of decoration along the upper part of a wall, immediately below a crown molding, is known as a frieze. In recent years, this area seems to have been reserved for stenciling or embossed wallpapers, if it is decorated at all, but in the late eighteenth century it consisted of interlocking pieces of plasterwork covered in a mixture of classical patterns. The inaccessibility of the moldings made them an obvious dust trap, so it is perhaps not surprising that they are no longer popular. But the idea is worth considering in boxy rooms, as a frieze would visually expand the ceiling and make the room seem bigger.

Plaster moldings

Large eighteenth- and nineteenth-century houses were often embellished with a variety of plaster ornaments, including plaques, columns, and corbels. Plaques were placed like pictures on the wall, while columns and corbels provided support for arches, beams, and crown moldings. (For mounting, see pages 96–97.) Plaster was also molded, and later cast, into wall alcoves and emblems such as anthemions (a stylized honeysuckle leaf shape), lion heads, urns, and acanthus leaves. Ornamental plaster has enjoyed something of a revival in recent years, thanks to its cool yet matte finish when left bare. This time around, however, castings play a purely decorative role. They may be hung on the wall, propped on a shelf, or made into accessories such as vases, lamp bases, and picture frames.

Staircases

▶ *While it is often desirable to make a feature out of a staircase, a bold decorative treatment is not always the answer, as it can seem out of character. Here, a limed wood effect and subtle distressing soften the appearance of a traditional wooden staircase, and echo the subtle pink tint of the surrounding walls.*

▼ *In a double-height living space, a galleried walkway allows the full height of the walls to be used for storing books and gives the seating area a more human and intimate scale. The perforated metal staircase is not set at an angle purely for dramatic effect—it also maximizes the amount of clear living space.*

A staircase is almost always the largest item of joinery or cast detail in a house and usually dominates the space in which it is contained. Yours may not have the sweeping curves of those found in the grandest houses, but it is unlikely to be an eyesore either, so it makes sense to play up its features. In older houses, these may well include ornately turned balusters (the upright posts that join the handrail to the beam that supports the outer edge of the stairs, known as a string) and newel posts (the thicker post found at each end of a flight of stairs). These are mostly made of wood, so lend themselves well to painting and staining.

The stairs themselves are almost always made from cheap wood or concrete—they were seldom meant to be left on show. Wood treads and risers that are in good condition can be stained or decorated with painted patterns, but avoid polishing or covering them in gloss paint, as this makes them slippery and dangerous.

Carpet or matting is the most popular choice, because it deadens noise. Look for densely woven materials with a short pile, as these are less likely permanently to trap dirt and dust and are easier to maintain. Seagrass and sisal are perhaps the most suitable of the natural mattings currently available. If you prefer carpet, it is best to go for a level-looped carpet, which has the sturdiest construction. For a stairway that will be subjected to heavy traffic, consider using a commercial-weight carpet.

Hallways in modern buildings often consist of a double-height space in which the staircase makes an attractively sculptural shape, or it may simply be placed in a large living area. To prevent the staircase from overwhelming its surroundings, builders and architects may choose materials that help to create a feeling of transparency, such as barely-there metal handrails, open-tread stairs, and wire balustrading. Here too, however, safety is of paramount importance. The stair treads should be covered in, or made from, a material with a suitable texture, such as perforated metal and rubber. And it should not be possible for children to slip through the balustrading.

Fireplaces

▲ *The ideal fireplace would look wonderful and serve a useful purpose, whatever the weather or time of year. This fine example approaches perfection by acting as a support for the staircase that runs immediately behind it and also by offering a variety of levels and surfaces on which to sit or display favorite possessions.*

overall character of the room in mind, as well as your property. If your budget won't stretch far enough for a readymade mantelpiece, you could consider making one from MDF (medium-density fiberboard) or lengths of architrave and molding.

It may be that the mantelpiece is let down by the interior of the fireplace, in which case a new grate could be installed. If you prefer to avoid the mess that a real fire entails, you can buy a gas fire that mimics the real thing, complete with imitation logs.

If the entire fireplace is a total eyesore, the surrounding firebricks can be pulled out along with the mantelpiece, to create a deep recess, which is then lined with a heat-proof material such as bricks, slate, or tiles, and the same material can be used for the hearth. The recess can then have a grate, stove, or perhaps a gas log-effect fire installed.

▲ *Fireplaces for small rooms are often delicately shrunken affairs. If this doesn't appeal, a custom-built mantelpiece with a more assertive outline may be the answer. This one is made from rough-hewn sections of tree trunk arranged in a way that evokes the order and symmetry of Neoclassical architecture.*

Almost all fireplaces consist of three elements: a grate where the fuel is burned; a mantelpiece, usually made from marble, stone, or wood; and a hearth which protects the floor from ash.

The mantelpiece can do much to animate a room and provide a focal point, but all too often a fireplace has a rather forlorn and unloved look. It may be too large or too small, or finished in an unsympathetic material. The grate may have been removed or boarded up. However, there may well be redeeming features. The fireplace may have a pleasing shape or finish, or an attractive detail hidden behind paint or boarding. A fine wood mantelpiece can be cleaned and polished, while poor-quality wood can be customized with paint effects or applied decoration. Cosmetic repairs, such as removing scratches in wood, are easy enough to do yourself, but larger repairs, such as replacing a broken section of a marble fireplace, should be left to experts.

An inappropriate mantelpiece can be replaced. The replacement must suit the scale of the room: in particular, make sure the distance between the ceiling and mantelshelf is neither too small nor too large. And bear the

Lighting

Because lighting determines how you use your home and feel about it at night or when it is dull outside, it is difficult to overestimate its importance. The subject can be made needlessly complex, with much bandying-about of technical terms such as "lumens" and "kelvins," but fortunately it is easy to distinguish between good and bad lighting. Good lighting relaxes and warms you, blending into the background and leaving you free to enjoy spaces and the people within them. Bad lighting competes for your attention, making you jumpy and tense.

The right lighting can reveal space that was formerly hidden. It can make rooms look bigger and turn awkward or unused areas into intimate corners. It can enhance architectural details and decorative fixtures, reducing the need for additional furnishings and clutter. It can even alter colors and textures.

Lighting needs to be considered from the earliest stages of planning a room. In fact, the position of the major light sources should be determined at the same time as the furniture layout. A scale plan of the room and the main items of furniture is invaluable, as it allows you to work out the best positions for built-in sources, such as recessed down-lights. And it suggests where you might safely and usefully locate plug-in fixtures, such as reading lamps and floor-standing up-lights. Since many rooms are multipurpose, a key requirement of any lighting system is that it be flexible.

Most lighting needs can be met by a combination of three different types of lights. Ambient or background light, from up-lights or wall-washers perhaps, helps you to move around a room and creates a little extra brightness on dull days. Task lights, such as desk lamps, bump up the brightness level in those areas where you work, read, or pursue hobbies. You may also need display lighting to draw attention to favorite objects. Fixtures that are more beautiful than useful, such as chandeliers and candelabra, are sometimes referred to as decorative lighting.

It also helps to vary the direction and intensity of light fixtures. A desk lamp with a pivoting head, for example, can be used as a small up-light or wall-washer when it is not required for task lighting. Dimmer switches are ideal for changing the mood of a room from bright and businesslike to softly relaxing, and most designers regard them as essential.

There are plenty of ways to improve the quality of existing lighting without having to endure the mess and upheaval caused by running cables into walls or running them above ceilings. If your current arrangements consist simply of a central pendant fixture, try replacing the existing cord with a longer piece, so that the fixture can be moved to

where it will be most useful, perhaps over a dining or display table. Alternatively, for greater flexibility, replace it with spotlights on a track system.

The range of plug-in fixtures includes picture lights, clip-on spots and wall-washers, as well as floor and table lamps. Of course, the cord is usually exposed, but some modern designs turn it into a feature. In many cases it may be possible to play down the cord by running it along a baseboard, around a corner, or behind furniture. There should never be any danger of someone tripping over it, however; and if there are no outlets nearby, compromises may have to be made.

If there are several light sources in a room, but you are still unhappy with the effect, check the bulbs. They may simply be too bright, or dim, for their surroundings, or glare could be reduced by replacing a standard bulb with a reflector type.

Changing shades also makes a big difference. Dark colors glow softly when the light is turned on, while translucent materials allow more light into a room and thereby help to make the space seem brighter. Those with a spreading shape cast a wider pool of light than upright examples. Repositioning a shade in relation to the bulb can help: the closer the bulb to the bottom edge of the shade, the larger the pool of light.

If adding extra outlets or re-routing cables and conduits is inevitable or if you think the wiring system in your home might need to be updated, call in a qualified electrician. The installation of electrical systems and the use of fixtures near water are governed by safety regulations. You may also be prevented from using certain types of fixture in very old buildings if the heat they emit cannot be sufficiently well isolated from the surroundings.

◄◄ *When several examples of a simple light fixture are grouped together, they create an attractive rhythmic pattern. The light produced is less tiring—the pool of light from each bulb overlaps with the others, so the contrast between bright and shaded areas decreases, and your eyes no longer need to adjust.*

◄ *Candles and votives are highly evocative, if sadly inefficient, sources of light, and well worth considering for situations where creating the right atmosphere matters more than providing safe levels of illumination. A chandelier such as this makes a stunning focal point, as long as it can be lowered for easy lighting.*

Designing with light

▲ *Timeless and relatively inexpensive, paper lampshades look good whether or not they are lit. The range of shapes, sizes, and colors of paper shades is now enormous, but they all have one thing in common: none should be fitted with a bulb that exceeds the manufacturer's recommended wattage.*

▶ *There is seldom room for a whimsical approach when lighting a kitchen. Sources should be placed so that work surfaces remain shadow-free, and where they illuminate the contents of open cabinets. It is also extremely helpful if they can be recessed out of dirt's way, or at the very least be encased in easy-to-clean fixtures.*

Besides working out which types of light fixtures would best suit your needs, you must make sure that they are correctly positioned. If you adhere to the principle that good lighting is efficient yet unobtrusive, it follows that fixtures should be placed where they can do their job without casting unwanted shadows or creating glare.

Indirect lighting

One way to do this is to shine light indirectly into a room by using an up-light to bounce it off the walls and ceiling. To do this effectively, the light source needs to be far enough away from the ceiling to create a broad glow yet high enough to be above the eye level of anyone standing in the room. Most floor-standing models are tall enough to satisfy these requirements, but the more elongated designs can look awkward in low-ceilinged rooms. If you plan to use wall-mounted fixtures, try holding them about 67 inches (170cm) from the floor to begin with, and adjust the height from there.

When used on its own, however, indirect lighting can make a room look flat and uninteresting. Visible sources of light, such as ceiling spots, some hanging fixtures, and even candles add sparkle and life; perhaps

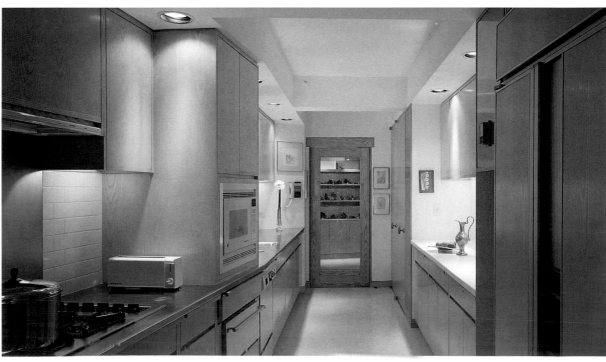

◄ If you plan to use a room for more than one purpose, several types of fixtures will be necessary. These need not match; instead choose fixtures that do their job properly. Hanging lamps mounted close to the ceiling are fine for background illumination, but task lights should be placed so that they keep work or display areas free of shadow.

they remind us of man's original light sources, the sun and fire. But they need to be carefully controlled to avoid glare, which can be done in a number of ways: by reducing the size of the fixture's opening, as in an eyeball fixture; by using reflective material around or inside the bulb; or by making them appear less bright, by using low-wattage bulbs and dimmers.

Softening the light

Local pools of glare-free light can also be produced by fixtures that encase the bulb in a translucent material, such as frosted glass or paper, or by lamps with conventional shades. These are best used in places where you can get away with low levels of background light, such as bedrooms or dining rooms. They are not really suitable for lighting your path through a space or for use as task lighting.

Direct lighting

Special care needs to be taken with task and display lamps, as the bulb is more than likely to be exposed. When a table or floor lamp is being used as a task light, the bottom edge of the shade should be positioned high enough to allow light to fall on your work area or lap, but not so high that the bright inner surface of the shade can be seen.

Light distribution

The distribution of light around a room matters too. The areas where you are likely to sit and relax or work should obviously be brighter than the background, so that you are drawn into a pool of light. And displays need to be highlighted, but not to the extent that they become distracting. In general, it is best to avoid over-dramatic contrasts of light and shade, especially in a space where you are reading or working, as this causes eyestrain.

Of course, compromises will have to be made, especially if you are furnishing on a tight budget or find your options severely limited by a lease. If the only source of light is a centrally placed bulb on a cord, consider replacing it with a surface-mounted track; this allows you to use several smaller light sources to wash the wall, and perhaps highlight an item of furniture such as a dining table. You will need to run a longer piece of cord from the center of the ceiling to your new fixture, but this can be concealed in a channel painted to match the background.

Make the most of plug-in fixtures, too. Look for designs that will take tungsten or halogen bulbs, as they can be used with dimmer switches. Consider also whether you can improve on existing or inherited lamps; replacing lined fabric lampshades with examples made from a light-diffusing material, such as paper, does much to brighten up a gloomy room, and don't forget that a simple change of bulb—from pearl to a reflector bulb, for example—can do wonders for the efficiency and attractiveness of a lamp.

Selecting fixtures

Finally, consider the style of the fixtures. Choosing all the fixtures from a single range or made in the same material can help give a coordinated look to a room scheme. But there is no reason why you shouldn't select lamps and fixtures individually, especially if they are attractive objects in their own right. However, bear in mind the overall look and feel of a room, as well as the uses to which the fixtures will be put. While a table lamp with a pleated silk shade may look cozy and elegant in a living room, it will seem incongruous, to say the least, in a busy, steam-filled kitchen. Think about proportion, too; a table lamp should be of a size suitable for the table.

Directory of lighting

Task lights

Task lighting is a must in any area where you plan to read or do close work. It can be provided by a desk lamp, a floor-standing lamp with an adjustable head, an industrial-style lamp that clamps to a desk or shelf, or a rise-and-fall pendant fixture. Whichever design you choose, position it so that your work area is kept free of shadow, without exposing the bulb to the extent that it causes glare. Lamps with a long reach are useful where the light source needs to be moved closer for detailed work, such as over a craft bench, or if you simply like to read while sitting in the middle of your sofa. **2**

Display lighting

Besides drawing attention to objects and pictures, display lighting subtly adds sparkle to interiors. Picture lights and cabinet fixtures are two of the fixed or built-in options, but a plug-in mini-spot or clip-on lamp often works just as well if you do not want to go to the trouble and expense of permanent fixtures. To light a picture, the lamp should be angled toward the image to minimize awkward reflections and glare. Decorative objects are best lit from above or the front to accentuate their shape and texture. Large areas of displayed books or CDs should be evenly lit, so that their covers can be read easily.

Pendant fixtures

Because they are often to be found hanging from a single central point on a ceiling, pendant fixtures echo the old-fashioned practice of lighting rooms with chandeliers. Unfortunately, a single overhead fixture produces a directional light that is both difficult to adjust and unflattering to faces and should not, therefore, be relied upon as the main source of light in a room. Instead, fit it with low-wattage bulbs so that it merely glows decoratively

and add extra background light with wall lights or free-standing fixtures. Simple pendant lamps and lanterns look best when they are grouped in some way. Try hanging two or three in a row over a kitchen counter, desk, or dining table. **3**

Down-lights

Compact and unobtrusive, down-lights can be mounted directly on the ceiling or partly or totally recessed. If they are attached to a track, they can be removed or repositioned, which is an advantage in areas where the furniture is regularly moved around. A row of down-lights may be used to provide a wash of background light, while individual lamps can be turned into display lights with the help of lenses and cowls (half-cylinder shades). It is easy to recess down-lights into a ceiling: fixtures are supplied with a template for cutting the hole and the wiring is the same as for a pendant lamp. Apartment dwellers may not be allowed to install these types of fixtures. **1**

Table lamps

Modernists may well sneer, but old-fashioned table lamps are among the most versatile fixtures available. They are portable, need little room, provide a useful mixture of task and ambient lighting, and elegantly underpin the style of your decor. The shade is the business end of the lamp, as the material from which it is made diffuses and colors the light, and its shape dictates how much light is cast below it: those with a spreading shape cast wider pools of light. When combining shades and bases, aim for a well-proportioned and balanced look. Candlestick-style bases suit shades with a small diameter, while solid bases go better with wide-angle examples.   **5**

Wall lights

Wall lights have obvious advantages in areas where floor space is limited and need not involve running cables into the wall if the cord is attractive. The output of wall lights is usually directed up at the walls and ceiling, which makes them a good source of ambient light. As they are on display, their visual impact can be significant. A sconce can be used to give a bare patch of wall a sense of purpose, while a row of lamps in a hallway adds rhythmic pattern.   **4**

Floor lamps

Since much of the furniture in a room tends to have a strongly horizontal feel, the vertical lines of floor lamps often add a welcome contrast. They vary enormously in style and function, and range from traditional styles, which provide both ambient and task lighting, through spindly up-lights, to tough and powerful studio lights. Floor lamps are easy to move—some are even mounted on wheels—but for safety try to avoid having cords trailing across thorough-fares, and do not place the lamps in a position where there is a risk of causing an obstruction.

Organized living

Due to the ever-increasing cost of building
materials, and in some places, homes are getting
smaller, yet the list of goods found within them
grows ever larger. And few of us care to call a place
home until it contains what the architect
Christopher Alexander, in his book *A Pattern
Language*, calls "things from your life": items such
as family snapshots and collections that have
sentimental rather than practical value.

Organizing your home so that possessions and people can coexist in harmony is vital, for most of us know how time-consuming and exhausting it can be to live amid chaos and muddle. And as Sir Terence Conran says in his *The Essential House Book*: "Your basic approach—whether you like to leave everything out on view or to banish all your belongings to cupboards and closets—will determine the basic character of your home more surely than any palette of paint colors or soft furnishing style."

Cramming your home with cabinets is not the answer, however; and the most effective long-term solutions are arrived at by looking closely at how you use your home as a whole. Look particularly at how activity tends to be concentrated in certain areas. This might include the living room and the kitchen, a shared children's room, or a bedroom that doubles as a study. If both you and your possessions are fighting for space in these places, one solution is to try to spread the load a little. It may be possible, for example, to turn a storage room into a shared study, thereby keeping the rest of the house relatively free of homework and office clutter. Or, as is often the case in older houses, there may be circulation areas, such as landings and hallways, that can be fitted with storage or shelving.

With a little creative thinking, even areas that are usually written off as wasted space can be put to good use. In Japanese homes, the space under the floor is often fitted with shallow boxes that are accessed by lifting trap-doors in the floor. Or it may be possible to fit shallow overhead storage in a bed alcove.

Of course, organizing your home is also about being able to find things with the minimum of fuss and being able to put them away easily when you have finished with them. The first step is to get rid of those items that you no longer want or need but have simply gotten used to having around. Next, sort the remainder of your possessions according to frequency of use. Those that are used constantly, such as the frying pan in the kitchen or clothes for work, should obviously be the most accessible, while those that are used on a seasonal basis or only once in a while can be stored in more out of the

◄ *Look beyond the idiosyncratic appearance of this kitchen, and it becomes clear that a great deal of thought has gone into the selection and siting of each item of storage. Wire baskets and the like allow air to circulate, and no shelf is so deep that it would be difficult to reach items stored at the back.*

▲ *Storing items close to where they are needed is the most important thing to consider when planning any kind of storage. That is why it makes sense to hang clean clothes near where you wash and bathe. However, leaving them on show may not be such a good idea if you are less rigorous than this in your choice of colors.*

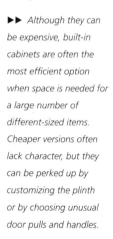

▶ *There is no reason why the inside of a cabinet shouldn't be as good to look at as the outside—and a glimpse of brilliant color whenever you open a kitchen cabinet door may be just what you need momentarily to forget about the daily grind.*

▶▶ *Although they can be expensive, built-in cabinets are often the most efficient option when space is needed for a large number of different-sized items. Cheaper versions often lack character, but they can be perked up by customizing the plinth or by choosing unusual door pulls and handles.*

such as kitchen condiments, it is better to arrange them in single rows on several narrow shelves than on a single deep shelf.

Personal taste, finances, and the size of the available area are other factors to bear in mind. In small rooms, wall-mounted cabinets or shelves can help to increase the feeling of space, as they allow the floor to be kept clear. Also, the visual impact of different styles of storage varies greatly. Imagine an alcove filled with glass shelves, then with built-in cupboards that match the surrounding walls, and finally with an ornate piece of furniture. Each of these styles is more prominent than the last and affects to a greater extent how you perceive the space around it.

A common dilemma is not knowing how much storage is necessary. Interior designers often say it is twice as much as you think. Certainly, it is always advisable to err on the generous side. If nothing else, it allows you to find room for future acquisitions. It is also a good idea to build more strength into a storage system than you need, not only to make it last longer but also to allow for changes in use at a later date.

▲ *An inexpensive solution to the problem of closet overflow is a fabric hanging wardrobe. This can be used for storing winter clothes in summer, or vice-versa, or for temporarily converting a study, for example, into a guest room. These wardrobes are available in several styles and sizes and fold up flat when not in use .*

way places. It does not take long to pack winter coats and sweaters away in an attic or out-of-the-way closet at the onset of summer, and doing so will not only make it easier to find those clothes that you do want to wear, but also keep them in better condition.

Remember, though, that some items do have specific storage requirements. Large suitcases, for example, are bulky and therefore difficult to maneuver in and out of tight spaces, while medicines and household chemicals should be kept away from children and extreme temperatures.

Now you can begin to devise solutions for individual rooms or areas. Decide which parts of the room are to be given over to storage while taking into account factors such as whether this is likely to impede movement around the room or to block your view of focal points such as windows. Large

cabinets are focal points in themselves, and if they are attractive they should be placed where they can be appreciated.

On the whole, it is better to group storage together in one part of the room, in the form of a row of built-in cabinets or shelves, perhaps, or a freestanding cabinet that is also used as a room divider, rather than scattering it. However, avoid placing it in front of electrical outlets, switches, faucets and other services.

Knowing which type of storage to buy is not easy, as the choice of styles is enormous and it is not always clear why some cost much more than others. To a certain extent you should be guided by the objects that are to be stored. A row of books weighs more than a few wooden ornaments, so the shelf supporting them should be correspondingly stronger. If you are trying to store a lot of small items,

Storage and shelving

Although storage systems come in all shapes and sizes, they can all be regarded as some form of variation on the idea of a shelf, a hook, or a box, or, of course, a combination of the three. A chest of drawers, for example, is a series of boxes placed on top of one another. Many modular storage units allow you to combine boxes, in the form of drawers and cabinets, with open shelving. A peg rail is simply a row of hooks joined together.

The inside of a unit should be tailored to suit the items that you plan to store. Good storage is governed by the "divide and rule" principle, which states that items are easier to see and much likelier to remain tidy when stored in groups that are as small as possible. Short runs of shelving, baskets on a shelf, and a wall of cabinets, each one sub-divided by adjustable partitions, are just some of the options that make this possible. Take a look inside your closets, too. There may

be space above the rail or shelf that could accommodate small storage units. Small items are usually stored in drawers, but they can also be arranged in lidded jars, hung from pegs, or sorted into files or trays. It is all a question of scale. The smaller the item, the more compact its home needs to be. The only exceptions to this rule occur when small objects are massed together for visual effect, as when a collection is displayed in a glass cabinet.

Some items need special treatment if they are to be stored efficiently. A television set, for example, can be attached to a hydraulic-lift mechanism or a shelf on gliders so that it can be pulled out and retracted as necessary.

Putting a face on storage, in the form of doors and drawers, protects the contents from dust and prying eyes, as well as making it look neater. It can also, of course, add decorative interest and character to a room. In small spaces it may be necessary to use sliding or

▲ In an open-plan apartment, it is essential to keep clutter under control, and create private areas without carving space up insensitively. Well planned storage can help to do all this and a great deal more; here, steps double as drawers, and bookcases act as a screen to section off a raised sleeping space.

folding doors, as they take up less space. Glass or wire-mesh doors will give a unit a sense of lightness, and the right handles and hinges could well turn a bland or beaten-up piece of furniture into something rather special.

Shelving

Open shelving is often regarded as the simple, inexpensive answer to every storage need, and there are plenty of times when it cannot be improved upon, especially if you want to be able to display objects, or have them instantly to hand. It can be much the best solution if you are on a tight budget, but it needs to be designed as carefully as any other form of storage.

It is also a good choice when you want your storage to be as unobtrusive as possible. Slim glass shelves or solid shelves that are

The thickness of your shelving material and the span (distance between the supports) determine its load-bearing capacity. If you plan to use your shelves to store anything heavier than lightweight ornaments or glassware, they should obviously be able to take the strain.

Making the most of storage

- High shelves should be narrow, so that you can see what is on them from below. If they are deep, use them to store light and infrequently used large items, such as spare blankets and towels.
- When storing large numbers of objects on a shelf, arrange them in rows, with taller items at the back.
- Try to store heavy items at waist height to avoid bending and stretching with them.
- Items stored at ground level with a shelf or some other obstruction above are easier to reach if they are stored in boxes on wheels or with grab handles.
- Use the insides of doors to store small items, such as saucepan lids in the kitchen and ties or scarves in a closet.
- If storage units are large or deep, consider fitting a built-in light.
- Decorate the insides of open storage units to show off the contents to their best advantage. Multicolored displays, such as books, look good against neutral backgrounds, while shiny or clear objects, such as glass, could be set against deep colors or lustrous textures.

colored to match their surroundings focus your attention on the displayed objects. A freestanding shelving unit makes a great room divider, as it helps to enclose a space while offering you glimpses of what lies beyond.

Open wall shelving can be mounted by a number of methods: fixed brackets, which are available in a wide range of styles and materials; adjustable brackets that slot into tracks screwed to the wall; and cantilever strips which hold the shelf along its entire back edge in a U-shaped channel. It is often recommended that brackets be put some way in from the ends of the shelf, to distribute the load more evenly, and that the front of the shelf should project no more than 1 inch (2.5cm) beyond the end of the bracket.

Alcove and closet shelves are almost always attached at the sides. The simplest method is to support them on wood or angled metal battens screwed in place. An adjustable system, in which the shelves rest on small pegs or studs pushed or slotted into holes made at regular intervals in each side, is fairly easy to install. Or the pegs may be hooked into a continuous metal strip, often called bookcase strip. Two supports are usually required for each side.

Whichever method you decide to use, it is essential to attach the supports with fixings that are appropriate to the construction of your wall. General-purpose plastic plugs are fine for solid walls made from brick or concrete, but cavity walls (consisting of hollow bricks or blocks) and stud partition walls (made from a wooden framework covered with gypsumboard and plaster) require special anchors or toggles.

Storage and shelving guide

▶ In this cottage, built-in cabinets and shelves insure that the space in boxed-in corners and partitions does not go to waste. Restricting their size—the top rail of the cabinets is just below head height—prevents them from ever seeming overwhelmingly tall, something that is likely in a room where you spend much of the time seated or lying down.

▲ With its exaggerated height, this tallboy almost becomes part of the architecture of the room—one can imagine it serving much the same purpose as a chimney breast or column. In the room beyond, another wooden column, this time of Shaker boxes, provides more convenient access to smaller items.

Built-in storage

Most modern houses and apartments already have a certain amount of built-in storage, ranging from broom closets to walk-in closets for clothing. However, many people find, after living in their home for a while, that they could do with more closet space, especially some that is tailored to their individual needs. Although having this installed can be expensive, you may find it well worth the price. Closets or cabinets can often be constructed in previously wasted space, such as under-stair areas. And a large room can be given architectural interest with a handsome wall of built-in cabinets and shelving.

Freestanding storage

The most traditional storage options take the form of freestanding furniture pieces, such as bookcases, chests of drawers, sideboards, and wardrobes. They are often larger and more decorative than other forms of storage and so lend themselves well to being used as focal points. However, they do waste space, and the bulky appearance of older examples can be overwhelming in smaller rooms, although they can be improved by using paint to give them a lighter feel (see pages 274–275).

Modular storage

A modular storage system can be built out of something as simple as a row of pigeonholes or lockers, or it can be a sophisticated mixture of cabinets, shelves, and drawers. Mass-produced systems can be added to over time and are often sold as ready-to-assemble units, which makes them ideal for anyone furnishing on a budget. Some are stacked on the floor like building blocks while others can be mounted on the wall. A surprisingly large number are too shallow to accommodate items such as large books, so choose a system that is suitable for your possessions.

Storage containers, boxes, and baskets

Although they are often overlooked in the search for whole-room solutions, boxes, baskets, and other containers play a vital role. They can impose order on chaotic open storage and allow you to shift possessions easily from one place to another. If they are sturdy enough they can simply be stacked on a surface to create temporary structures. However, non-transparent containers should always be labeled so that you can tell at a glance what is inside. There is nothing organized, or amusing, about unpacking several boxes to find one elusive item.

Hooks

A hook may be all you need to turn dead space into useful storage. Screwing one or two into the back of a closet door allows you to use the space to store belts and other accessories, while you can keep bicycles and cumbersome sports equipment out of the way by hanging them from the wall or ceiling high above your head. A use can be found for hooks wherever objects need to be kept to hand, yet off the floor and other surfaces. Used in quantity, in the form of a row of knobs, perhaps, or to store a variety of items on a Peg-Board, they add a touch of pattern to a scheme.

Freestanding shelving

Rough-and-ready answers to many a storage problem can be provided by freestanding shelving. At its cheapest and most basic, it consists simply of lengths of board that are stacked on top of one another, with spacing provided by bricks or boxes. If this seems a little too radical, most home improvement stores sell systems that allow you to create units from uprights and shelves with cross-braces added for stability. Look for one with a high degree of adjustability. Screw units to the wall if there are children around.

Open-wall shelving

The term open-wall shelving covers any situation where the sides of a wall-mounted shelf are open to the room. Shelves that are placed in this way can be approached from several angles, so they need to be fixed securely to their supports. Small shelves are often decorative as well as functional; the brackets or supports are attractive objects in their own right, and the shelf itself may be given an unusual profile or fashioned from a distinctive material.

Alcove shelving

Alcove shelving is extremely space efficient and it is cheap to install if it is supported on fixed battens. It is also very versatile. It can be painted so as to blend into its surroundings. Attaching a chunky trim or lipping to the front edges will give it an architectural feel. Combining alcove shelving with a low-level cabinet will turn it into a piece of built-in furniture. If you possess basic woodworking skills, this type of shelving can also be vastly improved by the simple addition of vertical dividers. These create convenient partitions and prevent wide shelves from sagging, but they should be used over the entire height of the shelving so that the weight can be transferred to the floor.

◀ *A modular system of glazed and closed cabinets provides a flexible mix of storage and display space, and can be a welcome source of pattern in a simple scheme, as here. The light-reflecting properties of glass and the right choice of color will also help to brighten a dull room.*

▶ *You know a shelving system works when it draws attention to your possessions rather than itself. Inexpensive slotted metal uprights and laminated particleboard shelves can look perfectly at home in a smart living room, as long as they are spaced at useful intervals and securely fixed to the wall.*

Display principles

Creating displays is a bit like putting on makeup. Although not strictly necessary, it can make a room look wonderful, and it is often the easiest way to create a new look. As with cosmetics, we use displays to make a dramatic visual statement—perhaps by placing a picture where it creates a focal point—and to make the most of a room's good points—such as by drawing attention to a mantelpiece arrangement above a fireplace.

In fact, it is hard to see how you might stamp your personality on a space without resorting to some kind of display, and few rooms are so perfectly conceived that there is no need for a picture or some other point of focus to break up an expanse of wall. Personal possessions provide evidence of human activity, and a room that lacks this is regarded by most people as alienating and uncomfortable.

Some of the most satisfying displays are created simply by storing useful objects efficiently, such as a wall of books on sturdy, well-spaced shelves or shiny saucepans hung on hooks above a range. However, most of us also collect "stuff" that serves no practical purpose whatsoever, which can probably also be attractively and effectively displayed.

Much of the skill in displaying objects lies in making them look as though they belong where they have been placed, rather than as though they have been left lying around. Giving them due prominence, perhaps by keeping the surrounding area clear or by picking their features out with accent lighting, subliminally reinforces this message.

Displays are seen as part of a larger whole. The size and color of a display surface, as well as any items nearby, will greatly influence how an exhibit is seen. Most of us have held a picture up to a wall only to find that it was too large or too small. You may also have seen how repainting a wall or the interior of a display cabinet can suddenly bring the objects on show to life.

The simple act of grouping similar or related objects also increases their impact. As any child knows, the most unprepossessing items can be turned into great collections so long as they are amassed with commitment and passion. As grown-ups are quick to point out, however, they are seldom seen at their best when scattered over the floor or piled up in a drawer. Each item needs to be clearly seen. A stockpile of beer cans from around the world will look much more impressive if

◄ Here, a formally arranged group of prints adds a welcome sense of order to a casually furnished and rustic hallway. Placing a mass of plants and other objects directly in front of the pictures links them visually to the rest of the room and helps to make them appear less out of place.

it is ranged over several closely spaced, narrow shelves rather than on a single, deeper surface.

Not everyone has a passion for collecting, and displays often need to be created out of rather muddled groups of objects. A set of pictures in different shapes and sizes, for example, can be lent a sense of unity if you hang them as a group on one wall. If they still look lost and out of place, you could try hanging them above a piece of low furniture. If the pictures are linked by color, it can be fun to emphasize this with matching frames, although you do run the risk of making the framing more important than the images.

Rather than lining objects up like soldiers, try forming them into groups that display strong contrasts of scale, form, and material. Curvy or spherical objects will seem even more rounded if they are mixed with a rectangular item, such as a propped-up tray or an empty frame. Try combining transparent objects, such as those made from glass or wire, with solid stone or earthenware pieces,

and natural materials with synthetic or man-made ones. It does not matter if a grouping looks a little unbalanced or strange. Better that than a "perfect" arrangement that merely looks lifeless and contrived.

There are occasions when a more three-dimensional approach is called for, as when a table or a shelving unit is used as a space divider. In such cases, it makes sense to display things that can be viewed from all sides. Leave plenty of space between objects, so that you can see through an arrangement to the other side.

In many ways, the hardest part of creating displays is knowing when to stop. The line that divides collections and clutter is a fine one. You can be fairly certain that a display has grown too large if it begins to spill over into living space by colonizing surfaces that are used for eating or working or if you find yourself placing objects where they could easily be damaged. When this happens, the time has come to rethink a display or do some serious weeding out.

◄ *In this room, convention is turned completely on its head by casually propping works of art on the floor and windowsill, while formerly commonplace items, including a collection of empty beverage bottles, are prominently displayed in ways that force us to look at them afresh.*

◄ *With their delicate construction and graphic outlines, model boats are tailor-made for displaying, especially when they are seen in a flotilla, as here. Matching the background color to the sails insures that the boats blend in with the rest of the scheme, and the most fragile examples are placed high on the wall, to keep them safe.*

WALLS

Walls almost always dominate the look of a room, so they are one of the most important aspects of decorating your home.

As we move away from the more showy and "decorated" interiors of the 1980s and into a more organic, evolved, and understated look, it is important to find an effect that suits you perfectly. If this sounds like a difficult task, bear in mind that it is also immensely liberating. Quite literally, anything goes. If you wish to combine a Mediterranean sense of color with your favorite primitive oil paintings and a collection of Chinese ceramics, you can. It is simply a question of balance.

But how do you choose a style when the choice of wallcoverings is so dazzling in its breadth and variety? Deciding on the final scheme is a source of enormous anxiety to most home decorators. How many of us have considered fantastically colorful swatches of paint, paper, and fabric for months, only in the end—out of fear, confusion, and terror of blowing our budget—to settle for off-white in a cowardly fashion? But choosing a color scheme does not have to be such an ordeal or fraught with difficulties. Color is the most wonderful tool; it literally transforms everything it touches. Whether you wish to create a sense of peace in a bedroom, or a sense of drama in a dining room, the color of the walls will have a profound effect on the finished product. Start thinking of color as your ally, rather than as a source of anxiety, and you are on your way to a wonderful decorating adventure.

Before you start, gather together lots of samples of wallpaper and paint. If possible, get into the habit of carrying around Polaroids and fabric and color swatches so that, wherever you are, you can match things up.

If you are keen to use specialist paint techniques, try them out on large sheets of paper first, in order both to perfect the technique and to get a realistic sense of the color and effect you are going to achieve. You can also assemble the paint, wallpaper, tile, and fabric swatches you have collected into color boards, just as a professional interior decorator would.

Ideally, you should pin these up in the room where you intend to use them and then live with them for as long as you can. You will be amazed to see how that terracotta can look cozy and warm in one room and yet can appear a sleazy or garish orange in another. This exercise also allows you to get a sense of how the different elements work together, and gives you some idea of the effect daylight has on color. This exercise may initially require time and patience, but it is worth the wait and the effort, as it means that you are more likely to avoid expensive mistakes and also—ultimately—to create a scheme you are happy to live with for a long time.

Old houses present particular challenges. Often, the desire to be historically correct can be overwhelming, but today the trend is against the slavish imitation of historical styles. Houses should reflect the lives, passions, and preoccupations of their owners, rather than recreating an uncomfortable museum or quaint period drama. It is a

▲ The wall treatment almost invariably dominates the whole look of a room. In this instance, a fabulous mosaic inspired by the planets and stars demonstrates that in a small space a bold scheme allows you to keep the rest of the interior furnishing details simple.

question of reaching a successful compromise between sensitivity to the quality of your surroundings and your desire for a workable, modern scheme. And remember, the colors used in old houses were often much more vivid than fading interiors, pictures, and samples of fabric now would lead us to believe.

Practically speaking, several factors determine what kind of wall treatment is right for your home: budget; decorative style; your own level of skill and/or willingness to experiment with new techniques; and finally, practicality.

Of all the materials available to you, paint is probably the most versatile. Certainly, it is ideal for the budget decorator. Its versatility and dramatic potential have endeared it to many people working within strict financial constraints.

Wallpaper is available in a myriad of styles and patterns. Whether you are after floral abundance or formal restraint, there is something for you. For those people who are hesitant about attempting paint techniques such as dragging or sponging, there are wallpapers that imitate these effects quite realistically. Papers can be combined with borders and friezes for additional dramatic effect. And if wallpapering frightens you, because you think it takes a high level of skill, developments in recent years should take away any residue of anxiety. For example, prepasted papers can be hung straight from the roll and, more to the point, repositioned instantly if you make a mistake.

There are several other options if you are feeling courageous and would like to try something a little more unusual, or something a little less conventional than paint and paper. Fabric makes a fantastic wallcovering, and wood or metal paneling on interior walls has been through something of a revival in recent years.

The key to success is to spend some time evaluating the options open to you before you start to make any major decisions. You must work out exactly what is going to look right for your space. After that, be bold, be brave, be prepared to experiment—and follow the correct techniques to get it right!

◀ *The wall treatment you choose should be in keeping with the room's other decorative and practical elements. Here, a rough plaster wall distressed in warm ocher perfectly complements the simple cabinets and collection of rustic kitchen accessories.*

▲ *A sense of harmony is created in this peaceful bathroom by using simple, blue-stained wood on walls, floors, and window. The staining, when teamed with classic white fixtures and a Matisse-inspired motif, creates a chic look rather than a rustic effect.*

Paint

Paint has often been called the decorator's best friend. Quite justifiably so, for not only is it the most versatile and the least expensive wall treatment available, it can also be used to create an enormous range of effects. Even a novice can produce some dazzling wall treatments in a relatively short period of time. It is also an enormously liberating material to work with, for even if your experiments go disastrously wrong, it is a relatively inexpensive and quick exercise to paint over them.

Whether you are inclined toward a bold modern look or a delicate, subdued scheme, you can create any effect with paint; practically anything is possible. Your best guide will undoubtedly be the room itself.

There are, of course, some things that you probably cannot change—short of a complete remodeling job. The room's proportions and the size and position of windows and architectural details are probable starting points when you are deciding how to tackle the space. If you have a small room, for example, a pale color will give you a brighter, more airy look. But equally, you might like to go in the opposite direction and use dark colors to enhance or create a cozy feeling.

However, there is little point in setting yourself an impossible task. You can work against a room's natural inclination only to a certain point—farther than that, and it proves to be a frustrating, fruitless, and expensive exercise. For instance, a dark, north-facing room can rarely be made to look bright and cheerful, whatever its proportions. Indeed, a chilly light on bright, jolly colors can even make them look harsh, dreary, and depressing. It is always best—as with other aspects of decorating—to work with what you have, enhancing and developing it. It is probably better to choose dark colors such as terracotta, mossy green, or midnight blue for a north-facing room and then enjoy the challenge of creating a rich, opulent scheme.

In a badly proportioned room, using the same color throughout, on walls, ceiling, and even the floor, will blur the confines of the space. But remember that you can also combine paint colors and finishes to great effect. So, in a small room, gloss paint will reflect the light and give a more spacious feel. And if a room seems too high for its dimensions, a dark, matte paint on the ceiling will "lower" it; alternatively, you could add a chair rail and paint the area beneath it in a darker color than the rest of the walls. If your room has low ceilings, you can create a more lofty appearance by painting the walls with vertical stripes (see pages 70–71) or by making the ceiling either matte white or a paler color than the rest of the walls. Of course, there are many different paint effects you can use to disguise the room's less attractive features; but equally, such effects can be used simply to create a dramatic effect. Trompe l'oeil effects, for instance, can also be used to create architectural interest where once there was none—and at a fraction of the cost of the real thing.

These days, we have moved away from some of the showier effects of the 1980s, when many a decorative crime was committed in the name of sponging and marbling. The look now is more subtle; the colors are more subdued; and, ultimately, final appearances are more sophisticated. If you are a decorating novice, this trend works to your advantage, for if you are working with two different shades of cream, terra-cotta, or gray, mistakes and irregularities will be less obvious than if your colors had been more strident and your overall schemes altogether less subtle. The fact that more casual interiors, featuring distressed finishes, are increasingly popular probably also works in your favor.

Not only the color(s) of paint you choose—from the enormous range available—but the kind of paint will have a huge bearing on the look you eventually achieve. Some purists would never use anything except latex flat on the walls and eggshell on the woodwork, but gloss finishes have gone through something of a revival recently. Semigloss and gloss finishes are wonderful in areas such as halls, bathrooms, and kitchens which receive a lot of wear, as scuff marks can simply be washed off. Remember not to ignore the possibilities of textured paint, either. This is no longer restricted to highly textured effects; manufacturers have recently developed a new range of paints, designed to cover minor cracks and imperfections in walls and ceilings, while appearing only slightly more textured than ordinary latex flat paint—useful and unobtrusively interesting.

Paint's possibilities are almost endless. Practically speaking, it is simply a question of finding a product that suits the surface you are decorating and creates the look you want.

◀ In a small room where solid terra-cotta walls could be rather oppressive, the decorator has used a clever, if simple, technique. The walls are painted off-white and small pieces of masking tape are stuck in a random pattern on the wall. The walls are then colorwashed and the tape peeled off to reveal white space beneath.

▲ Paint is the simplest and least expensive way of making a decorating statement. In this instance, a monochrome scheme is given an injection of humor with one wall coated in matte black paint. It's such a good idea, there is no need to restrict it to the nursery.

Directory of paint

Standard paints

The range of paints on the market presents the home decorator with a daunting array of possibilities. Although many different paints can be used for the same type of job, each will give a slightly different effect, and each has advantages and drawbacks.

Latex (water-based) paint

This kind of paint is the usual choice for painting interior walls and ceilings. It comes in several finishes ranging from flat (a matte finish) to semigloss. The terms "satin," "velvet," "eggshell," and "low luster" are often used to describe finishes lying between flat and semigloss. Some latex paints are described on the label as "gloss," but this has less sheen than an oil-based gloss. Latex paints are sometimes referred to as vinyl paints.

These paints are easy to use and fairly odorless. They can be applied quickly and dry quickly (latex flat, in 4 hours), so that two coats can be applied in one day. Latex flat can be used on new plaster (once it is dry) or on rough, porous surfaces such as interior stone or brickwork. It can also be used for paint effects; thinned to create a wash, it is a good base for stenciling.

Satin-finish latex, or latex velvet, gives a slight sheen to walls and is more durable than latex flat. It is a good base for decorative finishes.

Latex eggshell is quicker-drying (2–4 hours) than its oil-based equivalent and is a good choice for woodwork that will not be subjected to hard wear.

Latex paints can be cleaned off brushes with soap and water.

Alkyd (oil-based) paints

Although they are less easy to use than latex paints, and take longer to dry, alkyd paints offer a highly durable and washable surface. Gloss-finish alkyd is especially hardwearing—ideal for

children's rooms, hallways, kitchens, and bathrooms. It can be used on woodwork, metalwork, and walls, and can even be used on plastic without an undercoat. Alkyd gloss must be used over a proprietary undercoat, whereas non-drip and self-undercoating alkyd gloss paints do not need one. Drying time: 12–16 hours. **3**

Oil-based eggshell paint yields a softer, more attractive finish than gloss. It can be used not only on woodwork but also on furniture and interior walls and ceilings, as it provides a resilient surface and wears beautifully. It can also be used for paint effects. A low-odor version is available, which overcomes one of the disadvantages of most oil-based interior paints: the smell. The drying time for eggshell is 12–16 hours. **1**

A mid-sheen oil-based paint is also available—known sometimes as semi-sheen or satin finish. Similar to eggshell but with a less attractive finish, this paint has been adapted for faster application; some varieties need no undercoat, require only one coat, and are drip-resistant. They can be used on

woodwork and dry in about 2 hours.

Flat oil paint is a favorite with some decorators, either as a finish or thinned as a glaze. It can be obtained from some specialist paint dealers. The drying time is 6–12 hours. Cleanup for alkyd paints is with a solvent such as mineral spirits or turpentine.

Enamel

This is a high-gloss oil-based paint which is more quick-drying than other oil-based paints and gives a very durable finish. It has many uses, including woodwork, furniture, and garden equipment.

Epoxy paint

This paint gives an extremely durable gloss or semigloss finish and is used on hard, non-porous surfaces such as ceramic tiles, plastic, fiberglass, and glass. It often comes in two cans, which are mixed together just before

for creating an authentic country feel. Made from soaked, dry pigment, buttermilk, and a small quantity of fungicide to prevent mold, this kind of paint has a matte appearance. As inconsistencies in mixing show up more markedly in dark colors, it lends itself better to paler shades. **4**

Historic colors

Enjoying a huge revival, these paints—many based on colors found in houses from Colonial times—are sometimes mixed by eye using traditional materials, recipes, and techniques. They do provide a wonderful depth of color and the range of colors is surprisingly wide. Available in a variety of types and finishes: flat eggshell, gloss, exterior paint, floor paint.

Use a brush, rather than a roller or pad, for a truly authentic effect.

Metallic paints

The use of metallic paints in interiors is increasingly popular. Basic metallic paints are cheaper than gold leaf, although the finish is not as lustrous. Hammer-finish paints provide a variegated texture. Metallic paints usually require proprietary primers and thinners; they give a better finish if sprayed rather than applied with a brush, although on smaller areas they can be brushed on if preferred. **5**

Whitewash

Inexpensive matte paint with a soft, powdery finish. Also known as "soft" calcimine or distemper, it is easy to make, using a combination of calcium car-bonate powder, rabbit-skin glue (or white glue), and water. Despite its name, whitewash may be mixed with powder pigment to tint it to the color required. Experiment until you get the right consistency and color. Because whitewash cannot be cleaned, it may be short-lived; it can even be rubbed off with time. Remove before applying oil-based or latex paint. **2**

useful for covering up minor imperfections and rough surfaces. Difficult to clean—and extremely difficult to remove if you change your mind.

Undercoat

A thick, opaque paint that fills in small cracks and irregularities. Matte, slightly chalky texture. Available in oil- or water-based versions. Easy to apply, and though it comes in few colors, it can be tinted. Use on primed surfaces. Do not use on plastic or stainless steel. Not intended as a finish but sometimes used as such. In heavy-use areas likely to get scuffed, use a matte varnish to protect it. Drying time: 8–12 hours.

Special paints

Milk paints

One of the earliest domestic paints, milk paints were used widely in early American interiors and are still good

painting begins. The paint is very fast drying, which means you must work quickly to avoid leaving brushmarks.

Primer

Specially designed to seal bare surfaces and available in water- or oil based

versions, special primers should be used for wood, plaster, and metal.

Textured paint

A water-based paint that adds texture to plaster surfaces. Usually applied on walls and ceilings, it is particularly

Preparing the surface for painting

Preparing to paint

▲ Paint is truly the simplest—and cheapest—way of making a decorating statement. Here, walls in blue and orange pick out colors from the stained glass window to stunning effect and require no further adornment. These colors are further reflected in the floor and furnishings.

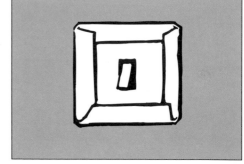

1 Protect light switches, electrical outlets, and woodwork with strips of masking tape before you start.

2 Wash down the walls with a sponge and a solution of detergent.

3 Use a squeegee mop and a solution of detergent to wash the ceiling.

4 Before painting, prepare the surface, using a wide-bladed scraper to remove flaking paint.

The quality of a paint finish is almost entirely dependent on thorough preparation. It is worth spending as much time as you can on this stage, in order to get it absolutely right.

A clean, smooth starting surface is vital to a smart finish. A good preparation will also make the application of paint easier, unless you want to achieve a "distressed" effect (see pages 62–65). Invest in good-quality equipment—buy the best you can afford because it will last longer than cheaper alternatives.

Estimating quantities

The amount of paint you will need will depend upon the kind you are intending to use and the color of the existing walls. For example, if you are painting dark green walls white, you will need more coats than if you were painting white walls dark green. If a wall has been replastered, bear in mind that new plaster will absorb more paint than old. The instructions on your can of paint will give the amount of coverage you can expect from 1 gallon (3.8 liters) if you use it undiluted. This is sometimes called the "spreading rate." It is easy to work out how many square yards (meters) you have to cover. For the ceiling area, measure the length and width of the floor and multiply one measurement by the other. Calculate each wall separately: multiply the height by the width. Then add the wall areas together.

To calculate the amount of paint you will need, take the total area you are going to paint and divide it by the figure specified as the coverage for 1 square yard (1sq m) on the can. The result of this sum will be the number of gallons (liters) of paint required.

Preparing to paint

Before starting to paint, remove as much furniture as possible. Cover the remainder with dropcloths and the floor with plastic sheeting. Protect window frames with masking

Filling cracks

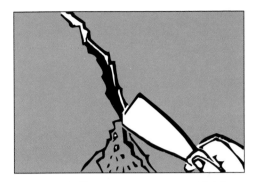

1 Use a putty knife or scraper to remove any debris from larger cracks.

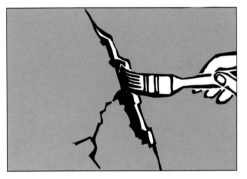

2 Remove any remaining dust with a soft-bristled paintbrush; or you could use a vacuum cleaner hose.

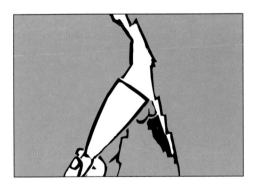

3 Fill crack with a spackling compound and a putty knife. Fill deep cracks in layers; allow each to dry for 24 hours.

4 When the filler is dry, gently smooth the crack with a sheet of sandpaper wrapped around a sanding block.

tape. Cover anything you do not wish to paint, such as a radiator, with plastic sheeting, sticking it down with masking tape. Mask areas such as a ceiling with wide tape, if you are painting the walls, and vice versa. Assemble all the equipment you will need before you start and make sure that the room is ventilated. Wear overalls, but avoid woolens as fibers might stick to the paintwork.

Preparing the surface

Before painting a wall, you need to insure that the plasterwork is in good condition; if it is not, it is essential that the old plasterwork be professionally removed and replaced before you begin. New plaster generally needs about four to five weeks to dry properly, so be sure to allow for this in your decorating schedule. It will then need a coat of latex primer-sealer before being painted. New plasterboard walls require a coat of latex primer-sealer or diluted white glue.

A previously painted wall should be thoroughly cleaned with strong detergent diluted in warm water. With walls, work from the bottom to the top, and pay particular attention to the areas around light switches where fingermarks accumulate. Wash ceilings using a clean squeegee floor mop. Rinse all surfaces with clean water. Allow to dry thoroughly before repairing minor defects in the walls. Remove flaking paint with a wide-bladed scraper. Then rub down walls with fine sandpaper to ensure a smooth finish, and dust off.

Treat any water stains or mildew with proprietary stain blocks before you start.

Filling cracks

Any cracks should be filled with spackling compound. Using a scraper, first clean out the crack, removing any loose plaster or dust. Then, with an old paintbrush and clean water, dampen the crack and the surrounding area, so that it will bond well with the filler. Overfill the crack with the compound. Large holes can be built up in layers, but you will need to allow plenty of drying time between each one. Allow the filler to dry thoroughly; finally sand it smooth and level with the surrounding wall surface.

Tools and equipment

Have all the equipment you are likely to need to hand before you start, in order to minimize the time you spend preparing the wall or other surface to be painted. It is a good idea to put together a basic decorator's kit, somewhat as you would a family first-aid kit. This means that you are always equipped to tackle modest painting jobs, and need add to it only for more specialized tasks.

- **Sandpaper:** fine and coarser grade sandpapers, including wet-or-dry sandpaper, to "key" woodwork or smooth over repaired cracks.
- **Sanding blocks:** made of wood or cork, to wrap the sandpaper around; you can also buy blocks made of aluminum oxide for sanding.
- **Lint-free rags:** to wipe up spills.
- **Turpentine or mineral spirits:** solvent for oil-based paints.
- **Masking tape:** narrow tape to protect light switches, outlets, windowpanes etc., from paint; wide tape to mask off large areas such as edges of ceilings or walls.

- **Dropcloths:** either plastic or fabric.
- **Old spoon:** handle to be used to open cans of paint.
- **Scraper:** wide-bladed, to remove patches of flaking paint.
- **Putty knife:** for filling holes and cracks.
- **Wooden stick:** to mix paint.
- **De-greaser soap or household detergent:** to clean down walls prior to painting.
- **Spackling compound or all-purpose filler:** to fill cracks or holes in walls.
- **Large decorator's sponges:** to wash down walls.
- **Clean glass jars:** to soak brushes, store small quantities of paint, and for numerous other purposes.
- **Face mask, goggles, and disposable gloves:** essential when working with solvents and other harsh decorating materials.
- **Painting platform:** for reaching high ceilings and painting in hallways.

Using brushes, rollers, and pads

▶ *Walls painted in contrasting solid blocks of color have immense visual impact. When using solid color, however, you must achieve an immaculate finish; so it is imperative that the surface preparation be thorough. Large expanses of wall without obstacles to paint around perfectly suit the use of a roller and paint tray.*

Brushes, rollers, and pads

Make sure that you have the correct equipment for both the material you are using and the surface being painted, in order to minimize the time the task will take. Never use brushes, rollers, and pads that are past their best; the end product will not reflect the amount of time you have invested.

Good brushes have a decent length of bristle; they should not be stubby. Rollers can be messier than brushes, as the paint is more likely to splatter, but they are a good choice for large areas such as walls and ceilings because they speed up the application.

Rollers produce a slightly more mottled surface than brushes. In fact, if you want a super-smooth surface, do not use a foam roller, because the air trapped in the foam will produce an "orange-peel" effect. This texture will survive subsequent paint layers.

Paint pads are similar to rollers; using a paint pad is an excellent and speedy way of covering large surfaces. Generally made from mohair bonded onto a foam backing, they are available in several sizes. There are special edging pads for precision painting, and small pads to use on moldings and muntins (also called glazing bars). Best used with water-based paint, paint pads produce a smooth finish, but they do apply less paint per coat than rollers, so you may need an extra coat for the same density of finish.

Buy enough of the appropriate paintbrushes, rollers, and paint pads for the task,

but it is probably not worth buying heavy-duty industrial equipment unless you are renovating a whole house from top to bottom. If you require any expensive or specialized tools, consider renting them instead.

First steps in painting walls

Before you start, dust the rim of the paint can with a dry brush or damp cloth to remove any dust or grit which could fall into the paint and contaminate it. Work your way around the can with the spoon handle, levering gently until the lid flips off. Stir the paint thoroughly in a figure-eight movement with a clean wooden stick.

Pour a quantity of the paint into a clean paint kettle, tray, or plastic bucket; when you are moving up and down ladders, this is easier to handle than a full can.

Using a brush

Before using a new brush, get rid of loose bristles by working it vigorously backward and forward across the palm of your hand.

To begin painting, dip the brush into the kettle until one third to half of the bristles is covered. Remove the excess by dabbing the brush against the inside of the kettle, not by scraping it against the rim of the can. Scraping it pulls the bristles out of the brush, contaminates the paint with stray bristles, and can make a mess of the outside of the can. Alternatively, tie a piece of string taut across the top of the kettle and wipe the brush against that. Do not be tempted to overload the brush, as it will be more difficult to maneuver and it will almost certainly result in drips that will show on the finished paint surface. It is also essential not to apply the paint too thickly and to leave enough drying time between coats; consult the directions.

If you are using latex paint, you need to work fast—the rapid drying time of the paint can lead to shading. Using a 4–6-inch (10–15cm) brush, work across the room in areas about 30 inches (75cm) square. Use crisscross brushstrokes to cover the area evenly and finish on a light, upward stroke. This is called "laying off." Move swiftly and methodically as you paint across the wall.

Handling the tools

1 When completing an area of painting, and before reloading a brush, finish with a light upward stroke.

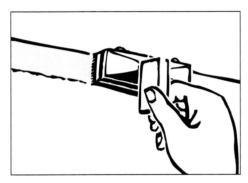

2 Use a small pad or special edging pad to go around the edges of the wall before you tackle the central area.

3 With a pad, apply the paint in overlapping crisscross strokes working on an area of 1sq yd (1sq m) at a time.

4 With a roller, apply the paint in overlapping crisscrosses followed by solid strokes.

Oil-based, or alkyd, paint requires a different approach. It dries more slowly than latex and thus allows a little more flexibility. Use a smaller, 1–2-inch (2.5–5cm) brush, held between thumb and forefinger, like a pen, and begin to make parallel vertical lines of paint across an area measuring approx. 12 square inches (30sq cm). When you have used up most of the paint on the brush, work swiftly across the vertical lines, blending them together into a solid layer of paint. Finish the area off with light, vertical strokes and move on quickly to the adjoining area.

Using a paint pad

Pour some well-mixed paint into a paint tray; you can use either a standard roller tray or one specially designed for use with pads. Load the paint by running the pad backward and forward over the ridged area of the paint tray, or over the loading roller in a paint-pad tray, to insure an even application. Work on the edges of the wall first, using a small pad or a special edging pad. Then, using a larger pad (approx. 8 inches [20cm] long is usually best), apply the paint in overlapping crisscross strokes, working on an area of 1 square yard (1sq m) at a time. If you are painting ceilings or high walls, fitting the pad to an extension pole will speed up the process.

Using a roller

Select a suitable roller cover for the wall surface and slide it onto the roller until it clicks shut. Pour some well-mixed paint into a roller tray and run the roller down the sloping part of the tray into the paint. Roll it up and down along the ridged slope to remove excess paint.

After cutting in (see pages 60–61) with a paintbrush at the edges of the room, apply the paint in side-to-side, up-and-down strokes, spreading the paint evenly over areas approx. 24 inches (60cm) wide. Lay off on a light upward stroke before reloading for the next area, taking care to blend the edges of the two areas together. If you are working on a ceiling or on high walls, you may wish to add an extension pole to the roller.

For advice on patterned rollers and use of rollers with textured paint, see pages 70–71.

Tools and equipment

- **Containers:** for paintbrushes, use metal or plastic buckets; for rollers, plastic trays.
- **Decorating brushes:** a selection of latex brushes for water-based paint and natural bristle brushes for oil-based paint.
  4–5in. (10–12.5cm) brushes for walls.
  1–2in. (2.5–5cm) brushes for details.
  2–3in. (5–7.5cm) brushes for "cutting in" around the tops of walls.
  1in. (2.5cm) brushes or angled-headed brushes for window frames.
  a selection of artist's brushes for details.
  2–4in. (5–10cm) oval-headed brushes for applying varnish.
- **Roller cage:** can hold a variety of covers.
- **Roller covers:**
  short-pile mohair for applying latex semigloss.
  medium-pile sheepskin for latex flat.
  medium-long pile for textured surfaces.
- **Extension pole:** for pads and rollers, when painting high areas such as ceilings.
- **Long reach roller:** small roller on a long handle for reaching into awkward spaces, for example behind radiators.
- **Paint pads:** often have hollow handles so they can be used with an extension pole.
- **Mahl stick:** from art stores, to steady your hand for details.
- **Stepladder or ladders:** to create a painting platform.
- **For decorative paint effects:**
  pieces of natural sponge.
  dragging brush: for dragging.
  dusting brush or specialist graining brush.
  selection of stenciling brushes.
  large stippling brush.
  blender brush: to soften brushmarks.
  fitch brushes: for spattering and stippling.
  specialist rollers, rockers, and combs.
  lint-free rags: for rag rolling.

Equipment to rent

- **Spray guns:** to cover large areas very quickly. Always wear a face mask.
- **Battery-powered paintbrushes and rollers:** the paint is pumped from an attached reservoir along a plastic tube.

Applying paint

Sequence of painting a room

Professional decorators always paint a room in a particular order. They start with the ceiling. The walls are next; then the woodwork around doors and windows; then coves and baseboard; and finally, the floor. This insures that paint spattering down from the ceiling does not ruin newly painted walls. Another tip is to clean off any paint that drips onto woodwork immediately. It is easier to remove when it is still wet.

Applying paint

Before covering the walls in swaths of color, you need to give some attention to the smaller details to insure a professional finish. It is very important to create a precise finish around doors, windows, and light fixtures, as well as obtaining a neat line between ceiling and wall, as these are junctions that you will notice every time you enter or leave the room, or open or shut a window. You need

Order of painting

1 Professional painters paint a room in a particular order. Follow this order for a professional finish.

2 Paint walls and ceilings in strips—top to bottom for walls; for ceilings, in alternating directions.

to use a technique called "cutting in." Using a small brush, 1–2 inches (2.5–5cm), pressed firmly against the wall surface so that the bristles are slightly splayed, paint a band of paint approx. 1 inch (2.5cm) wide into the internal corners, wall, and ceiling angles and above the baseboard.

You will need to make a similar band around doors and windows. You can do this in the same way or use a slightly different technique which insures a neater finish. Paint a series of small, horizontal strokes at right angles to the door or window frame. Join together with a steady, firm vertical stroke of the brush, easing the bristles of the brush tight against the wooden frame.

Paint the ceiling using a roller attached to an extension pole. Paint sections in strips, working from one side of the room to the other and back again, so that the direction of application alters with each strip. In order to give solid paint coverage, within each strip apply the paint as when using a roller on a wall: starting with overlapping crisscrosses and finishing with straight strokes. When painting walls, paint in strips from the top of the wall to the bottom, starting from the side of the wall closest to any natural light source. Having painted the walls and ceiling, you should turn your attention to the precision painting areas: the doors and window frames.

Painting plaster moldings

Next item in the sequence is any plasterwork: moldings such as crown moldings and rosettes.

Because of the porous nature of plaster, moldings are particularly susceptible to staining caused by damp, mold, mineral salts, or nicotine. You must make sure that these have been adequately dealt with, and the surface made good and primed before you start repainting. Ask at your hardware store for suitable products to tackle specific problems.

Moldings should be painted with small paintbrushes or artist's brushes, depending on their size and the amount of detail they contain. Start by using a 1-inch (2.5cm) brush to apply the base color, insuring that the bristles are gently splayed to create a neat outer edge. When this color has dried, you may wish to pick out some of the detail in a

Applying paint

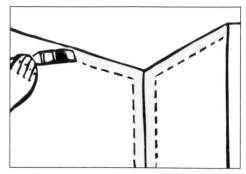

1 Before painting the wall, "cut in" around edges with a 1–2in. (2.5–5cm) brush, with bristles slightly splayed.

2 Next, begin applying paint with a roller—in crisscross strokes followed by vertical strokes.

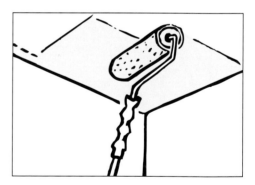

3 Paint the ceiling with a roller attached to an extension pole, working in alternating strips across the ceiling.

contrasting color using a smaller artist's brush. If you are trying to paint a straight line or particularly fine detail, steady your hand by resting it against a mahl stick.

Painting metal pipes and radiators

Before you paint pipes or radiators, make sure that heating or hot-water appliances have been turned off. Check that the metal fixtures have had time to cool down. Make sure that previously painted surfaces are free of dust by washing them down with a solution of household detergent. Key a high-gloss surface by rubbing down the paint with wet-or-dry paper. Rinse and leave it to dry completely before starting to paint.

The longest-lasting finish for metal is created by using a proprietary metal or radiator paint or enamel. On radiators, use a 2-inch (5cm) brush and apply the paint as thinly as possible, working quickly with long, light strokes. Be very careful to avoid getting paint on or near the valves, as dried paint will cause them to stick. Use a piece of cardboard to avoid flicking paint onto the wall surface when you paint the edges of the radiator.

Pipes should be painted with the same paint as the radiator with a 1-inch (2.5cm) brush, working vertically from top to bottom.

Painting tiles

Applying paint to ceramic tiles is usually a short-term solution, because no matter how careful you are with preparation and application, paint will eventually chip or peel away from the glazed surface.

However, if you have a row of ugly tiles, giving them a quick coat of paint can act as a good facelift. Prepare the tiles for painting by washing them down with household detergent and a damp cloth.

It is now possible to purchase a proprietary tile primer which may prolong the life of a coat of paint. After this primer you should use two coats of enamel paint if you want a durable, waterproof finish.

◄ *When painting details in contrasting colors, such as here on the wooden paneling and molding, precision is essential. Use low-tack masking tape to define the areas to be painted. When painting on wood, first apply a primer and then an undercoat to obtain a smooth, problem-free finish.*

Painting other areas

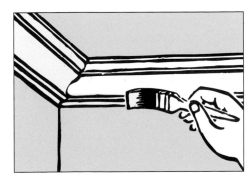

1 When painting details in contrasting colors, precision is essential. Use tape to mark off the areas to be painted.

2 Use a 1–2in. (2.5–5cm) brush to paint radiators. Work quickly, applying the paint in a thin coat.

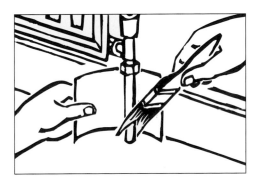

3 When painting pipes, use a piece of cardboard to avoid flicking paint onto the wall or baseboard.

Paint effects guide

▲ Oil glazes are a simple way to give walls a sophisticated sheen. However, when you are deciding on what color and how much to tint the glaze, it is worth bearing in mind that the color will become noticeable quite quickly once on the walls. Here, a preliminary coat of pale yellow eggshell has been given greater depth and texture with a gray-tinted glaze.

Before embarking on painting a whole wall with a special technique, try out your chosen effect, either on a piece of board or on an inconspicuous corner of the wall. This will give you a chance to perfect the finish you require, and an opportunity to see how the colors work together. Cover your practice area with a coat of paint, allow to dry, and only then start work on the rest of the wall.

Glazes and washes

Glazes

Transparent, oil-based glazing liquid can be bought ready-colored, but you can tint pro prietary oil glaze to match a color. For a basic tinted glaze, mix 1 part glazing liquid with 3–4 parts mineral spirits and 1tbsp. (15ml) white eggshell per 1 pint (approx. 500ml) of glazing liquid, colored with tinting colors.

A glaze must be applied over non-porous paint, such as eggshell. Depending on the composition, it may take up to two days to dry hard, which gives you plenty of time to correct and rework if you get it wrong first time. For this reason, glaze is easier to handle than a wash (see below) for an amateur.

If you are preparing your own glaze rather than using a readymade one, it is essential to mix up enough for the whole project before you start, because it is almost impossible to duplicate a color exactly later.

Using glazes

Possibly the simplest material for the amateur to master, a tinted oil glaze applied on a base coat will add a subtle layer of color, softening it and giving it greater depth.

Walls need to be carefully prepared (see pages 56–57) and then coated with one or two layers of eggshell paint. Sometimes it is possible to use latex flat and a water-thinned wash as an alternative to glaze. However, the finished effect is seldom as elegant as that produced by an oil-based finish.

You can prolong the life of the effect—whether oil- or water-based—by applying a coat of matte varnish when it is thoroughly dry. This is very important if you have painted a heavy-traffic area such as a hallway, or if it is likely to need frequent sponging.

To apply, paint the glaze onto the wall with a medium-sized natural bristle brush, covering 1 square yard (1sq m) at a time, using quick, random strokes. Soften brush-marks with a wide, short-bristled brush, and continue until the surface is evened out, creating a thin film of near-transparent color.

Washes

Washes are made from water-based paint. They provide a soft finish but they are less flexible and less easy than glazes for the beginner because they dry quickly.

Washes are best applied over a latex flat base. For effects such as rag rolling, the wash needs to comprise 1 part latex paint to 3–5 parts water. For colorwashing, it needs to be thinner: 1 part paint should be mixed with as much as 8 parts water.

Colorwashing

Colorwashing imitates the appearance of old-fashioned, calcimine- or distemper-painted walls and, as such, is particularly appropriate today, when natural interiors are popular. Although it is no longer generally available, it is relatively simple to recreate the same rough, slightly chalky look with thinned latex.

Because of the essentially uneven appearance of a colorwashed finish, it is a simple technique to master and looks particularly good on walls with a slightly irregular surface.

Because this is a very wet wash, make sure that you have covered everything that is not to be painted before you start.

Apply a coat of latex flat to the wall and allow it to dry thoroughly. Create the color-wash by thinning latex paint: 1 part paint to 4–8 parts water. Then experiment on a small area until you find a mixture that is easy to work with and which creates the soft gradations of color that you require. Using a large decorating brush, apply the wash in random, bold, crisscross strokes over an area

of approx. 1 square yard (1sq m); do not attempt to cover the whole wall. Then, take a slightly damp paintbrush and go over the wash to soften the brushmarks and wipe up any drips.

Do not worry if the walls look very messy and unattractive at this stage. Leave this coat to dry overnight, or for at least 12 hours, and it will improve with the wait.

Repeat the wash technique, again working on 1 square yard (1sq m) at a time. This time apply crisscross strokes to the areas you

missed the first time. If you are working in a heavy-use or humid area such as a hallway or bathroom, it is possible that the finished effect would benefit from a protective coat of matte polyurethane varnish.

Dry brushing

Dry brushing creates a rougher, more intensely dramatic effect than either glazing or colorwashing. First of all you need to apply a base coat of latex flat paint, and then pour some latex in your chosen top-coat color into a paint tray.

Dip a wide, hard-bristled decorating brush into the paint and scrape off the excess against the tray's ridges or on a wooden board. Then, with cross-hatching strokes (as with colorwashing), apply the top coat. It is very important for this effect that you be sure to keep the brush very dry—as the name "dry brushing" suggests—and that you apply the paint in light strokes using the tip of the brush rather than its flat surface. Allow some of the base color to show through to create a slightly misty effect.

For a greater depth of color and more intensity, repeat the process, having first allowed the paint to dry thoroughly overnight, or for at least 12 hours. And once again, you may wish to finish the effect with a coat of matte varnish.

▲ Although a simple technique to master, two-color colorwashing in the right color combination can bring elegance to a plain wall. Here, the layers of wash have deliberately been built up in some areas more than others, so that the varying degree to which the base color shows through creates a sense of texture.

▶ Dry brushing is a great technique to use with strong colors, the dramatic texture of the cross-hatched brushstrokes enhancing vibrant shades; here green and yellow zing off each other. Equally, if you find solid color boring, dry brushing can create a slightly distressed look: dry brush a lighter emulsion over a darker tone, say.

Faux finishes

▲ *Walls that imitate materials such as terra-cotta or plaster are a wonderful foil for casual interiors. Such effects look particularly good as a backdrop for wood or rich textiles. Picking out the color and, as here, the texture of the wall in the furnishings of a room brings cohesion to a scheme that may in fact contain many disparate elements.*

Once you have mastered some basic paint techniques, you may wish to try something a little more adventurous. Faux finishes allow you to imitate the effect of wood, stone, fabric, and other materials at a fraction of the cost. The key to success is to use a light touch—and to know when to stop. Never be tempted to splash on too much paint; rather, build up the effect in layers.

Draw inspiration from a wide variety of sources. Begin by looking at the real thing—marble, wood grain, and stone—then at postcards, books, paintings, even films.

Antiquing

Few people are fortunate enough to live with genuine, original old plaster walls. "Aging" a surface is a relatively simple process,

however, and fun to do, too. Dry brushing (see pages 62–63) is an effective way of re-creating the effect of an old wall, or you may wish to use layers of paint in slightly different tones. Start with the brightest shade and gradually "age" the surface with layers of wash, working with the original shade and darkening it by degrees with a little raw umber. Smear on the paint roughly with a brush or cloth, then, when it is dry, rub gently at the paint surface with some sand-paper or steel wool, revealing glimpses of the original color and even touches of plaster.

Marbleizing

There are many different kinds of marble and, consequently, many different kinds of marbleizing. Study the real thing to decide

on the kind of effect you want to recreate, and practice on a piece of paper or board before you embark on your paneling or walls.

Use a soft cloth to rub some transparent glazing liquid onto a base of two coats of eggshell. Dip a fine artist's brush into a glaze of the required color; quickly and gently flick some veins across the paint surface. Do not worry about a few breaks and blobs in the paint; this will add to the finished effect. Using the tip of a blending brush, softly stroke the veins to blur them. Dip a fine artist's brush into mineral spirits and gently go over the glazed surface, roughly follow-ing the lines of some of the veins. Soften the surface again, this time in one direction only. Finally, take a clean blending brush and go lightly over the surface, eliminating any brush-marks, and creating the desired cloudy finish.

Faux bois

Elaborate wood-graining effects that are designed to imitate rich and desirable marks and patterns—those found in burled walnut,

for instance—will take some time to perfect, but even a decorating novice can achieve good basic graining effects.

Choose a suitable base color—deep red is a good base for a mahogany effect; a pale golden cream creates realistic oak grain—and apply two coats of eggshell. Mix up the graining color by thinning some transparent glazing liquid with mineral spirits and coloring it with a little artist's oil paint: a dark purplish brown or even black creates a realistic glaze for mahogany, while a little burnt umber can suggest oak. Apply the glaze in an even, dense coat on top of the eggshell.

Take a dusting brush and drag it along the length of the surface in a light sweep. Repeat this sweeping brushstroke to blur any hard lines. With a clean blender or dusting brush, quickly and gently work across the grain.

Imitation terra-cotta

Warm "terra-cotta" walls are the perfect backdrop for today's rustic interiors, and a convincing effect is simple to achieve.

Paint the wall with a base coat of latex flat paint in a creamy gold color. Dilute terra-cotta-colored latex flat—equal parts of paint to water—and coat the wall with a wide decorating brush, brushing backward and forward over the painted surface, continuing even when the wash starts to dry.

Allow the paint to dry out completely and then take a clean decorating brush dipped in water to dampen down the surface, working on the usual 1 square yard (1sq m) at a time. Dilute some cream-colored latex: mix 1 part paint to 2 parts water. Using a 1-inch (2.5cm) decorating brush, make a rough pattern of lines across the damp area of wall.

▲ *The key to successful marbleizing is subtlety. Here soft creams and grays applied with a very light touch look as appropriate with the wooden floor as they do with the more contemporary chrome table.*

◄ *There are really no limits to the kind of effects you can achieve on your walls. These walls have been given the soft, coppery bloom of verdigris. As with all faux techniques, it is essential that you study the real thing before you start, to insure that you get the effect right.*

Using a slightly dampened natural sponge, dab at the paint surface to blur and smudge the lines. Keep gently sponging the area until you have achieved the soft, cloudy bloom of terra-cotta. Use this technique (with different colors) to imitate lead or unfinished plaster.

Verdigris

To recreate on walls the wonderful blue-green patina of weathered copper, brass, or bronze, start with a dark brown coat of latex flat. When it has dried, stipple a light covering of bright turquoise green over the entire surface, allowing a trace of the base color to show through. Repeat the process in some areas, making the turquoise deeper.

Then look at a real piece of verdigris to get an exact color match for the kind of effect you want and choose a bright shade of green. Go over parts of the turquoise green with a stippling brush. And finally, with a very light hand and an almost dry brush, stipple some of the wall once more—with faint traces of dark gold or bronze paint.

Finally apply a coat of matte varnish; you might perhaps like to mix a little white paint into it to dull the finish slightly.

Faux leather

A leather effect in deep oxblood, bottle green, or dark brown can look very smart, particularly when used to add richness to a small space. Using a small to medium-sized decorating brush, stipple the wall thickly with a paler-colored latex flat than the finished effect you are looking for. Allow to dry for at least 24 hours.

Repeat the process with a darker shade of latex flat, this time splaying and twisting the brush as you work to create texture. Allow this layer to dry, again for at least 24 hours.

Mix some artist's oil paint—one part raw umber to one part burnt sienna—into a transparent glazing liquid, and rub this over the surface of the wall with a cloth; take another soft cloth and gently but thoroughly rub off the excess glaze, allowing the texture of the latex to show through. In places, rub the surface with fine sandpaper to reveal some of the latex; finally protect the surface with a semigloss varnish.

Stripes, checks, and patterns

▲ *Paint allows you to get the effect of hand-blocked wallpaper at a fraction of the cost. This sophisticated-looking lattice was created by painting a red top coat over the undercoat to which masking tape had been applied in a crisscross pattern.*

Making stripes

Stripes and checks are a decorating trend that never goes out of fashion; they have a strik-ing, graphic quality, and a fresh, well-ordered, clean-cut appearance, whether or not their edges are sharp, making them suitable for practically any situation—in combination with areas of plain color or with each other. Extremely versatile, stripes and checks are equally varied in their effect; wide stripes will be bolder than narrower ones, or you can create a more sophisticated rhythm, follow-ing one wide with three narrow stripes, for example, and then repeating it.

Think too about the effect of color on your chosen stripes; you could create a stun-ningly dramatic study using dark paint and wide stripes, provided that you could then light it efficiently, but that combination would not work in a kitchen or dining room, where a fresher and lighter effect would be better. All you need is a little patience, a plumb line, your paint, and tools.

The quickest, simplest method of creating stripes is to paint the wall in your chosen base color and then use a roller to create stripes in a contrasting shade using a plumb bob as a guide. If you wish to create broader stripes than it is possible to paint with a roller, mark out the area to be painted with masking tape before you start, again using a plumb bob to establish a true vertical. If you like stripes but are wary of the crisp, band-box look, roughly and lightly paint in your stripes and then immediately go over the wet paint with a dry roller to create a

Making stripes

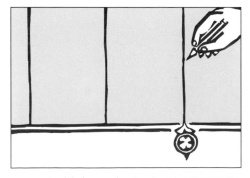

1 Use a plumb bob to mark out vertical stripes. Use a soft pencil and a very light touch.

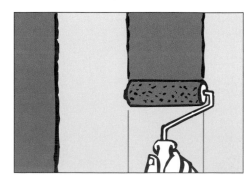

2 With the pencil marks to guide you, carefully paint the stripes with a wide roller.

slightly distressed effect. A smaller, pinstripe effect can be created by dividing a foam roller into narrow portions, using tape to keep each part of the roller separate.

You could use this stripe both vertically and horizontally, and in more than one color, to create a checkered effect.

Using patterned rollers

Patterned rollers have been used to decorate walls for several centuries. They are enjoying a popular revival because they are easy to use and create interesting effects inexpensively; you can roll one color over another or use the roller to create texture in one color. You can make your own, but specialist suppliers stock rollers and rockers for more difficult effects—from wood graining to damask.

Using textured paint

Apart from the practical aspects of textured paint—very useful for covering less than perfect surfaces—it also has a much under-rated aesthetic potential. You can buy patterned roller covers specially for textured paint, and with a little time, effort, and imagination, it is possible to achieve sophisticated, sculpted effects for relatively little cost.

▶ *Few paint effects are simpler to achieve or more dramatic in appearance than stripes. In this country-style bedroom, all four walls have been painted with wide stripes. Marked out using masking tape and a plumb bob and then roughly painted in deep red, they are bold and yet disciplined.*

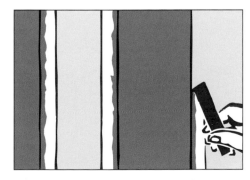

3 If you are worried about creating precise edges, use masking tape to mark off the lines.

4 To create narrow stripes, divide the roller in two with a rubber band.

5 To create checks, use the roller to go across the vertical lines in a horizontal band.

Stamping, stenciling, and gilding

▶ *Stamping is the ideal paint technique if you're short of time —or skill. A repeat design, such as this simple pattern of hearts stamped onto a colorwashed wall, gives a dramatic effect, but takes only a matter of hours to achieve.*

Stamping

Compared to other paint effects, stamping really can be, quite literally, child's play. Make your own stamps from medium to high-density foam in the same way as a child makes potato-cut stamps, drawing a design on the surface and then cutting away the excess foam with an X-Acto knife. Glue the sponge onto a piece of wood, and attach a small doorknob to the back of it to make application easier. If, however, you would rather buy a stamp, there are many outlets that stock a wide range of designs made from rubber or foam, and thus very hardwearing.

Apply the paint either with a roller or by dipping the stamp into a plate containing a small amount of paint. Give it an even coating and then set to work, taking your design across the whole wall.

Stenciling

This is one of the least expensive ways to provide a decorative finish. Use stencils to create a dramatic pictorial effect, or use a motif to create a border or allover pattern at a fraction of the cost of wallpaper. Choose from the enormous selection of pre-cut stencils available or make your own. Draw your design on an acetate sheet and cut out with a sharp knife. Attach to the wall with masking tape or removable spray adhesive.

Next, apply the color. Whether you are using a stencil brush or a spray can, the secret is a light touch. With a spray can, waft it quickly and gently over the surface, gradually building up the color in subtle layers. If using a stencil brush, rub it on a piece of paper towel until almost all the paint has been removed from the head of the brush, then stipple or swirl it over the stencil. Remove the stencil, reposition, and repeat the process.

Gilding

Few decorating projects are more satisfying than working with gold leaf. However, the expense of the material puts it far outside the pocket of most amateur decorators. There is no reason, though, why you should deprive yourself of using lustrous metallic materials in small quantities, perhaps on a motif against

Stamping

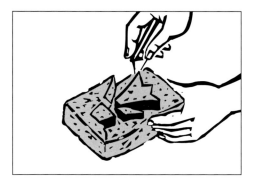

1 First draw the outline of your design on the sponge. Cut away the surrounding areas using an X-Acto knife.

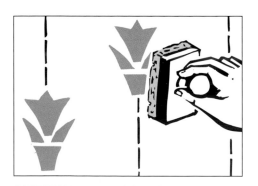

2 For large-scale patterns, chalk guidelines on the wall. Coat the sponge evenly with paint and dab on firmly.

Stenciling

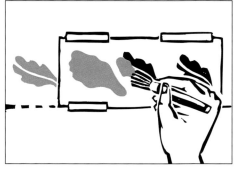

1 Remove excess paint from the brush with a paper towel before swirling or stippling it lightly over the stencil.

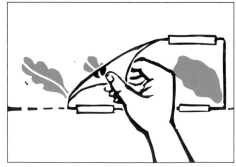

2 Gently peel off the stencil, taking care not to smudge the paint, and reposition it.

a wall painted in a deep rich color such as lacquer red, midnight blue, or forest green. Composition gold leaf, or Dutch metal, is a less expensive alternative to real gold leaf, while aluminum leaf can be made to gleam like gold with one or two coats of orange shellac. These, and the substances mentioned below, are available from specialist suppliers.

First, give the wall to be gilded a coat of flat or semigloss oil-based paint. Decide on your design or motif, and either draw it freehand on the wall or use a stencil as a guide. Paint the areas to be gilded with readymade red gesso for composition gold, or cobalt blue casein for silver or aluminum leaf. When this is dry, paint on a thin layer of gold size, following the manufacturer's directions.

When it is only slightly tacky, gently press on a sheet of leaf, leaf-side down, on the sized area. Carefully peel away the leaf's wax backing, and lay down the next sheet so that it slightly overlaps the first. Continue until you have built up your pattern. Leave for several hours to dry, and rub off the loose leaf with a soft cloth; the rest of the leaf should remain in the sized area of your motif.

Finish by varnishing the whole surface with a clear, semigloss oil-based varnish.

For those who long for glitter, it is a good idea to check out the wide range of metallic paints, powders, creams, and pens on the market. These can be put to a wide range of decorating uses, from painting a whole wall to picking out molding detail.

Gilding

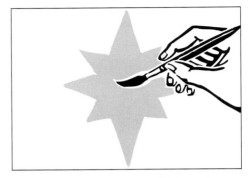

1 Paint the motif in red gesso or cobalt blue casein. When dry, paint a layer of gold size over the top.

2 When the gold size is only slightly tacky, press on the sheet, leaf-side down.

3 Carefully peel away the wax backing and apply the next sheet, overlapping the first slightly. Let dry overnight.

4 Rub off the excess leaf with a soft cloth, leaving the original motif intact.

▲ Given the costs involved, it makes sense to restrict the use of gilding to small areas. This random design of horizontal and vertical gold blocks is restrained but nonetheless extremely effective, giving interest to plain white walls and mirroring the angular patterns of the parquet flooring.

Problems with paintwork

Most flaws in paint surfaces can be avoided if you are scrupulous in your preparation and always use the correct materials. Even with the utmost care, however, some problems may occur, but these can usually be salvaged and sometimes do not entail too much extra work.

Blistering

This is caused by moisture or air trapped beneath a coat of oil-based paint. The answer is to strip off the paint, carefully fill any holes, and then repaint. With wood, it may be necessary to prime, undercoat, and then repaint.

Flaking

When the new surface reacts badly to what is underneath it, flaking occurs. Latex flat paint, for example, can flake when painted over a high-gloss finish. Unfortunately, if flaking occurs there is no alternative but to strip off the flaking surface, get back to the base, prepare it again properly, and paint the area once more.

Wrinkling

If you apply a second coat of oil-based paint, such as eggshell, before the first coat has dried thoroughly, the surface may wrinkle. Strip the paint and reapply it.

Runs and drips

Possibly the most common problem, runs and drips are caused by loading too much paint onto the brush. Let the paint dry, rub the blobs gently with fine-grade sandpaper, remove the dust created by the sandpaper, and touch up with fresh paint.

Paint faults

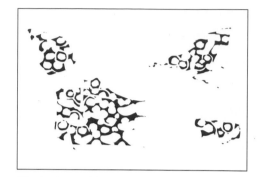

Blistering is caused by air trapped beneath a coat of paint. It has to be stripped off and the surface repainted.

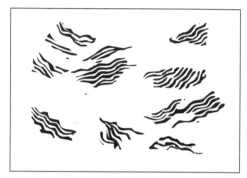

The only solution for an area that is flaking is to strip the area back to the original surface and begin again.

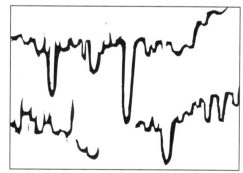

Drips can be corrected by rubbing them flat with sandpaper, cleaning off the dust, and repainting.

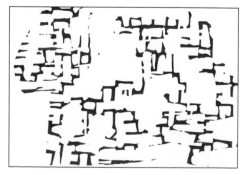

Crazing occurs when the top coat of paint reacts badly with the surface beneath. Strip off and repaint.

▲ *Strong blocks of contrasting solid color can work wonderfully if walls are in good condition and prepared thoroughly. When using strong colors, however, it is wise to create some kind of continuity. Here, the midnight blue dining room has a terra-cotta picture rail and yellow stained chairs to continue the scheme from the living room.*

Cleaning equipment

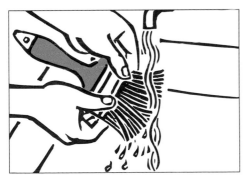

1 *Clean off excess latex paint under cold water. Then wash in a weak solution of warm water and detergent.*

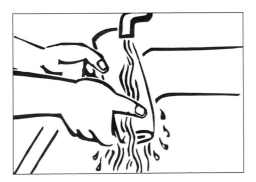

2 *Prolong the life of a roller by rinsing out latex paint under a cold running tap until the water turns clear.*

Crazing

This occurs when a layer of new paint reacts badly with a painted surface underneath, or if layers of paint have different drying times. The only option is to repaint, removing all the layers of paint and preparing the surface again from scratch.

Grit, dust, or insects in the paint

If this occurs, wait until the paint dries, then sand the area gently with fine sandpaper and wipe off the dust. If you sand lightly enough, you may not need to touch up the paint.

Stains in paintwork

Stains occur when insufficient preparation is done before latex paint is applied. Mineral salts, molds, and other residues and impurities can react badly with the water in the paint and will seep through the surface. Get back to the original surface and coat it with a proprietary primer-sealer; when that has dried, repaint.

Poor coverage

This is most likely to show when you are applying a light color over a dark base. Streaky flashes of the base color will appear under the top coat. Apply more coats of paint, until you have a solid top color.

Cleaning equipment

Cleaning your equipment after you have finished painting will significantly prolong its life. Brushes, rollers, and pads that have been used with water-based paints should be rinsed with cold water to remove excess paint, paying particular attention to the base of the bristles, and then washed in a weak solution of warm water and detergent to remove the residue.

Equipment used for oil-based paint or varnish should be cleaned with turpentine, mineral spirits, or a proprietary cleaner, making sure that it is worked well into the bristles or pile. When all the paint has been removed, all equipment should be rinsed thoroughly in warm water and shaken vigorously to remove the excess.

To keep their shape, brushes can be wrapped in clean paper towels fixed with masking tape. Hang up brushes and rollers, and place pads face-up to maintain the pile, and your equipment should last you for years.

Directory of wallpaper and vinyl

There is a massive choice of wallpapers available, in every kind of finish—from traditional patterns to imitation paint effects. Decoratively, the possibilities are endless. Practically, some papers are more suitable for some tasks than others.

Cheap papers tend to be thin and are therefore tricky to handle and consequently more difficult to hang. They are also more liable to show wear and tear. Sturdier—and therefore more expensive—papers are usually a better investment.

Most rolls come in standard sizes: 24 feet (7.4m) long and 18 inches (45cm) wide. Fabric papers are generally exorbitantly expensive—so much so that they are sometimes sold like fabric, by the yard (meter).

Most papers are treated to repel moisture to different degrees: spongeable papers can be wiped clean; washable papers can be washed with water. Vinyls, which are coated with a tough plastic, can be scrubbed clean.

Textured papers are very good for covering small cracks and other minor imperfections in the wall surface. Lending a variety to the texture of surfaces in a room is a good alternative to using a variety of colors or tones.

Woodchip

A tough, durable paper designed to cover small imperfections in wall and ceiling surfaces. It is inexpensive and is supplied in an off-white color, to be painted to match the room's color scheme. It is extremely difficult to remove once it is in place and has rather fallen out of fashion recently. If your walls are imperfect, go for a more interesting embossed paper or for a distressed paint finish for a more dramatic effect. **1**

Lining

Heavy-duty off-white paper which can be applied to plastered walls after any leveling out of the plaster

but before any painting and papering. It is used to achieve a smooth, professional finish.

Vinyl

Possibly the most widely available species of wallpaper, vinyl is now obtainable in a massive variety of designs, many with coordinating borders or friezes. A paper backing is covered with a layer of waterproof vinyl, thus making the surface extremely durable. It can be washed without any risk of spoiling the finish. Easy to hang and remove, vinyl is available with an unpasted or ready-pasted backing. If you intend to use an unpasted paper, it is advisable to use a fungicidal adhesive to prevent mold from growing underneath.

Embossed

Available in a wide selection of relief patterns, from floral designs to patterns imitating wood paneling, ready to be finished with gloss or latex paint. Its hard-wearing finish makes it popular for the area below the chair rail in hallways and for any walls with a less-than-perfect finish; once painted, its tough surface is washable.

Embossed papers have a texture that can resemble anything from tiles to wood grain. A solid paper backing is coated with pliable filler and linseed oil, and pressed into a pattern while it is soft, and when it hardens, it makes a tough, scrubbable wall-covering, particularly if coated with eggshell or a high-gloss oil-based paint, as many manufacturers recommend, especially in a heavy traffic area.

Lighter, more flexible papers are available which are also extremely durable. They are made from two layers of paper pressed together and embossed with a wide variety of relief patterns.   **2**

Hand-block-printed

These papers come in a huge variety of designs, and their quality and depth of color cannot be surpassed. They are, however, expensive to buy. To defray the costs and make a little paper go a long way, you could consider hanging them as panels edged by narrow wooden molding, or using them above or below the chair rail in combination with a less expensive paper or paint. They are bought unpasted and hanging them requires great diligence.   **4**

Machine-printed

The most widely available kind of wallpaper, machine-printed papers come in a huge variety of designs and finishes, and are less expensive than

hand-blocked paper. They can sometimes be dressed up with a coat of flat polyurethane varnish.   **5**

Foamed polyethylene

A soft, lightweight paper. Comes in a wide choice of designs and is relatively easy to hang.

Friezes and borders

Wallpaper selections now nearly always include a series of coordinating borders or friezes, which means that making a decision about detailing and finishing can be completely straightforward. However, you should feel free to create different effects, using more original combinations, and picking up on painted finishes, too. Borders and friezes are sold in rolls and are roughly 3–12 inches (7.5–30cm) wide. And although friezes are usually hung horizontally at the level of the baseboard, chair rail, or picture rail, borders can also be used to create "panels," by making squares or rectangles from them.   **3**

Planning

Pattern matching

The thought of matching patterns is perhaps one of the most daunting aspects of hanging your own wallpaper. However, as long as you buy enough paper and take some time and care with matching it up at the cutting stage, this process is relatively straightforward.

A plain paper, or one with a continuous or small, random pattern, such as vertical stripes or a tiny floral print, does not need matching. You can simply cut equal lengths straight from the roll; all you need to remember is to add 4 inches (10cm) to each length (to allow for 2-inch [5cm] overlaps at each end).

To match other, more complicated designs, lay the cut strip of paper design-side up on the pasting table, and then lay another strip beside it, matching the pattern as accurately as you can on the adjoining widths, and then make sure you add the standard 2 inches (5cm) at each end to the measured matching drop to allow for the overhang—a total of 4 inches (10cm).

Check, before you cut, that the two drops have the same number of pattern repeats, and that each has an overhang allowance. A straight-match pattern has the same part of the design running symmetrically down each side of the paper. This kind of paper is not very difficult to hang. All you need to remember is, once again, to add enough allowance at each end to line up the pattern exactly; you do not need to match adjoining strips horizontally.

On a drop-match pattern, the motifs are staggered, which means that you have to add extra in the cutting: the amount of stagger in the pattern—or length of pattern repeat—is usually indicated on the roll. You could try cutting alternate drops from different rolls, but this may prove more confusing than helpful.

Establishing a vertical

It goes without saying that hanging your first strip of paper vertically is crucial. On a practical level, it will be very difficult to reproduce exactly, time and time again, an off-vertical hanging line, and gaps and cracks between strips of paper will appear with no hope of correction. Another reason the first strip must be vertical is that most patterns are designed to hang straight and will never look

▶ *If you favor a highly coordinated look, many wallpapers now come with matching borders and fabrics. It is a good idea, however, to keep the rest of the decoration simple; here the painted floor, plain rugs, and understated window treatment provide perfect foils for a "busy" blue and white wallpaper.*

A few helpful hints

1 Paper in a logical sequence. If there is an obvious focal point, center your first piece there and work outward.

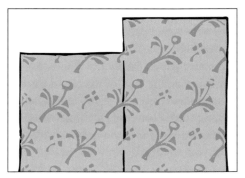

2 If there is no focal point, start on the right of the main window and work clockwise around to the door.

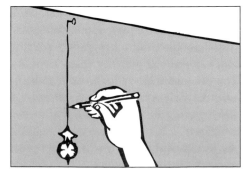

3 To match a pattern, lay a strip on the pasting table and place another beside it, lining up the pattern.

4 It is vital to establish a true vertical before you start. You can do this with a plumb bob or carpenter's level.

◄ *For those who haven't the time or the confidence to experiment with paint effects, there are now a number of wallpapers on the market that simulate different paint finishes. The subtle stripes of this wallpaper resemble the soft finish achieved by shading, and give a warm, even look to the walls in this stylish bedroom.*

right unless they do. Use a carpenter's level or plumb bob to make sure that the paper is absolutely vertical. Do not follow the line of windows or doors; they, particularly in older houses, are not always straight.

To get a true vertical, hang the plumb bob by a pin from the top of the wall and mark the line of its fall lightly with chalk or a pencil.

Obviously, it is essential to repeat this process on each wall to be papered rather than assuming anything.

Sequence of papering

There are no set rules about where to start papering; the most important thing is to work in a logical sequence around the room.

If the room has an obvious focal point, however—a fireplace in the middle of one wall, for instance—center the pattern of your first piece of wallpaper on it, and then work out from there around the room, in opposite directions, until the two ends meet at the other side, or at a convenient junction—such as a door.

If there is no obvious focal point in the room, you should start papering at the right of the main window and then work your way in a clockwise direction around the room to the door, before going back to the first drop and working counterclockwise around to the door. Remember, though, not to use the window frame as a reference for your vertical.

Tools and equipment

Tools for papering

- **Tape measure.**
- **Utility knife:** to trim wallpaper.
- **Metal ruler/straightedge.**
- **Carpenter's level:** to check true horizontals and verticals.
- **Pasting brush.**
- **Paperhanging brush:** to smooth paper into place once it is on the wall.
- **Long reach roller:** to smooth paper into place behind radiators or in awkward corners.
- **Clean household broom:** to hold up paper when applying to the ceiling.
- **Adhesives:** follow the wallpaper manufacturer's directions. If you have a problem with mold, use a fungicidal paste; you will also need vinyl adhesive if you are overlapping and pasting vinyl wallpaper.
- **Wallpaper trough:** to soak lengths of ready-pasted paper.
- **Plastic bucket:** to mix paste.
- **Pasting table:** any table is suitable, provided it is well covered and at the correct height for you to work easily.
- **Seam roller:** to smooth the paper seams once the paper is hung.
- **Wallpaper scissors.**
- **Wooden stick:** to mix paste.
- **Sponge:** to clean up.
- **Plumb bob:** to find a true vertical.

Tools for other wallcoverings

- **Small, sharp scissors and X-Acto knives:** to cut out decoupage motifs.
- **To attach fabric to walls:** staple gun, wooden battens, cardboard to strengthen seams; curtain rods or poles for shirred fabric; mounting track.

Measuring, cutting, and pasting

When you are calculating the number of rolls of wallpaper you will need, it is best to err on the side of generosity and to buy all the paper at the same time, from the same batch.

To calculate the number of rolls you need, measure the height of the walls and add 4 inches (10cm) as an overhang allowance, and the length of the paper's pattern repeat. This is the length of each "drop." Divide the length of a roll (usually 24 feet [7.4m]) by the length of your drop to find how many drops you will get from one roll (A).

Measure the distance around the room and divide that figure by the width of a roll (usually 18in. [45cm]) to find out how many drops you will need to paper the room (B).

Then divide the number of drops required to paper the room by how many drops you will get from one roll of wallpaper to calculate the number of rolls (C) you will need to complete the job (B÷A=C). Round up to the next whole roll and add a roll in case your calculations are slightly inaccurate.

Time

Hanging wallpaper is time-consuming and should not be hurried. When you are planning the job, overestimate the time needed simply as drying time—after stripping, after lining, after papering—to prevent a feeling of frustration from creeping in later, which would increase the potential for disaster.

Cutting

Remember to allow an extra 2 inches (5cm) at each end of the length of paper for trimming to fit. And always cut before you paste.

Having first established a vertical line on your wall, measure the wall from ceiling to baseboard. Unroll the wallpaper roll on the table and measure the overall length of a strip, including the overhang allowance. Mark the pasting table itself to avoid measuring each strip. Using a T-square, mark a line at a right angle to the edge of the strip at the appropriate length and cut straight along the line, using wallpaper scissors.

If you have to match the pattern, cut the first length and then turn the paper right side up to match the pattern on the adjoining length, before adding on the extra 2 inches

▲ *Highly decorative papers need not be reserved solely for the bedroom—they can also be used to great effect in other parts of the house. This wallpaper in a strong green, printed with a delicate trellis of dew drops and roses, has an old-fashioned charm, and complements the soft lavender paneled walls of the room beyond.*

Calculating the number of rolls

U.S. wallpaper

Wall Height	Distance around room (including doors and windows)												
	32ft	36ft	40ft	44ft	48ft	52ft	56ft	60ft	64ft	68ft	72ft	76ft	80ft
8 feet	8	9	10	11	12	13	14	15	16	17	18	19	20
9 feet	9	10	11	12	14	15	16	17	18	19	20	21	22
10 feet	10	11	12	14	15	16	17	19	20	21	22	23	25

Calculations based on roll measuring18 inches when trimmed x 24 feet

British wallpaper

Wall Height	Distance around room (including doors and windows)												
	9.1m	10.3m	11.6m	12.8m	14m	15.2m	16.4m	17.7m	18.9m	20.1m	21.3m	22.6m	23.9m
	30ft	34ft	38ft	42ft	46ft	50ft	54ft	58ft	62ft	66ft	70ft	74ft	78ft
2.45m (8ft)	5	5	6	7	7	8	9	9	10	10	11	12	12
2.75m (9ft)	6	6	7	7	8	9	9	10	10	11	12	12	13
3m (10ft)	6	7	8	8	9	10	10	11	12	13	13	14	15

Calculations based on roll measuring 52cm (20½in) x 10.3m (34ft)

Measuring, cutting, and pasting

1 Lay the paper on the table and measure the first length, marking the cut-off point with a pencil.

2 Use a pair of long wallpaper scissors to cut off the first strip.

3 Square up one long edge and one short edge with the sides of the table and apply the paste from the center.

4 Using a wide pasting brush, work the paste outward to the edges. Make sure the paste is applied evenly.

(5cm) at each end and then cutting across the width. Number each length on the reverse side, in order to avoid any confusion about the order you need to follow to match a pattern accurately when you come to hang the lengths. Mark an arrow on the back of each piece indicating the top if there is no obvious right way up.

Pasting

First, set up your trestle or pasting table. If possible, position the table so that you will face the light when you are pasting; this will make it easier to identify areas that lack paste —they look dull rather than shiny.

Mix the paste and lay the paper pattern-side down on the table. Keep the table clean to avoid getting paste on the right side of the paper. Distribute the paste evenly or it will bubble up. Start pasting from the center and work out to the sides, applying the paste with a wide pasting brush.

Check whether the paper requires time for the paste to soak in before it is hung. Leave the paper until it is quite supple before you hang it, but note how long this takes to keep the soaking time constant from length to length to prevent variations in stretching.

Bubbling may have been caused by too much paste. More often, it is the result of not having allowed the paper to soak for long enough; always read the manufacturer's directions and allow adequate soaking time. If you need to repair one or two bubbles in a drop, use a sharp utility knife to pierce the bubble. Smear a small amount of paste behind the opening with an artist's paintbrush and use a paperhanging brush to smooth the paper back into position. Wipe the excess paste away with a damp sponge. This is only practical for a few bubbles; if your paper has a rash of bubbles, the only remedy is to remove the drop and rehang it.

Ready-pasted and foamed vinyls

Ready-pasted vinyl is probably the best paper for an inexperienced decorator, as its tough surface means that it is less likely to tear and stretch as you work. Half-fill a wallpaper trough with water and place it next to the part of the wall where you intend to

start papering. Measure and cut the paper. Roll up the length, with the pattern facing inward, and immerse the paper fully in the trough.

Follow the manufacturer's directions on soaking time, then lift up the paper by its top edge with both hands, carefully allowing the water to drain back into the trough. Position the first length on the wall, making sure that it is straight against your vertical guideline (see pages 82–83), and then smooth it with a clean sponge rather than a brush; it helps to absorb some of the excess water.

Not only are some papers and borders ready-pasted, but they do not require soaking either. Their self-adhesive coating becomes exposed as you pull it from the roll and you can stick them directly onto the wall. Another advantage is that the adhesive takes a while to form a strong bond, so if you make a mistake in hanging, the paper can be repositioned quickly, without a problem.

Hanging ready-pasted vinyls

1 Roll one length pattern-side inward and soak in a wallpaper trough. Unroll and apply directly to the wall.

2 Position the paper so that the patterns are matched, and smooth downward with a clean sponge.

Hanging standard lengths

Hanging paper along a smooth run of wall is fairly straightforward, but make sure that you have the paper the right way up. This sounds obvious, but it is easy to make this mistake when dealing with lots of large drops.

Folding the paper

When you have pasted the entire strip, checking that there are no areas where the paste is thin or dry, take the pasted paper (see pages 84–85) and loop it into accordion folds, making the folds about 2 feet 6 inches (75cm) long. Do not crease the folds. When you get to the end of the paper, fold it back against itself so that the pasted sides are touching to insure that it does not stick to the wall as you work your way down.

If you are working with only a short length, fold the ends into the center, but be careful not to crease it as you go.

Hanging the paper

A length of wallpaper is hung from the top of the wall, brushed into place and then trimmed to finish exactly where the wall and ceiling meet. Only after completing the top do you work your way down to the bottom, brushing that into place and trimming it to fit in the same way.

Leaving a 2-inch (5cm) overlap to run up onto the ceiling, unfold the top half of the first fold of the paper and offer up the paper against the top of the wall. Make sure that the side of the paper is vertical, running exactly down the line of the plumb bob. Do not forget to check that you have an overlap.

Smooth with a brush, working from the middle of the paper outward, brushing firmly into the junction between wall and ceiling. Run the rounded edge of the wallpaper scissors along the crease to make a distinct mark.

▶ If you have never attempted wallpapering before, start with a wallpaper that has an uncomplicated pattern, such as these wide stripes. A simple design makes joining the edges a relatively easy task. Stripes, like a plain paper or one with a small, random pattern, do not need matching, so it is simple to cut lengths straight from the roll.

Peel the paper away at the top far enough to reveal the crease you have just made and cut neatly along the line of the crease with the scissors. Smooth the paper back onto the wall with the paperhanging brush; it should fit the wall neatly now. Wipe off any excess paste, and discard any offcuts too small to use elsewhere, throwing them in the trash can to keep wayward paste to a minimum.

Undo the folds one by one as you work gradually downward, and continue to brush the paper from the center out, being careful not to let the hanging paper wrinkle; if a wrinkle does appear, and if the paste is still wet, gently pull the paper away from the wall at the point where the wrinkle has occurred and carefully reposition it. On the other hand, if it is dry, cut open the wrinkle with a sharp utility knife, and proceed as you would to repair a bubble (see pages 84–85).

Do not stick the bottom in place yet. Unfold the last piece at the bottom and repeat the creasing process for the top of the wall to trim the bottom edge. Wipe away any excess paste with a sponge before it dries. Continue to hang lengths of paper along the wall until you reach the corner. Press down

Hanging the first lengths

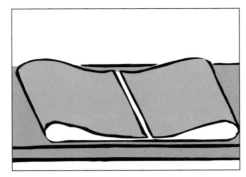

1 *Fold over the bottom end of the paper, pasted sides together.*

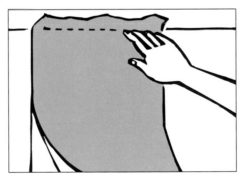

2 *For long lengths, loop the paper back and forth into uncreased accordion folds.*

3 *Place the top of the paper at the top of the wall, leaving the 2in. (5cm) allowance to run up to the ceiling.*

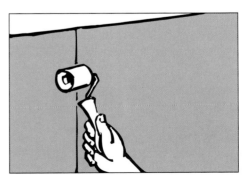

4 *Smooth the paper with a wide brush, working from the center out.*

5 *Form a crease. Peel the top of the paper away from the wall and trim it before smoothing it back on.*

6 *Carefully trim the edge of the paper with scissors to insure a clean finish.*

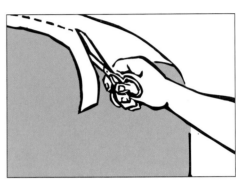

7 *Carefully wipe away any excess paste with a clean sponge before it dries.*

8 *Press down adjoining edges of the wallpaper using a seam roller.*

▲ *Few things look fresher than stripes: their uniform crispness lends them to most rooms in the house. Blue and white are perfect for this nautical-look bedroom, where they combine with a coordinating border and fresh paintwork to create a look that is pulled together, but calm and unfussy.*

the joining edges using a seam roller. If the seams of paper are pulling away from each other or the wall, the paste has not been spread to the edge of the roll. Lift the edge slightly with a knife and apply a little paste to the edge with an artist's brush. Press smooth again with a seam roller.

If you are using ready-pasted paper, it is advisable as a matter of course to run a small artist's brush loaded with some vinyl glue along the seams of paper. Smooth it into place to create a strong, clean seam. And after hanging four full strips, go back over the seams with a seam roller. Check the surface for any paste and remove it with a damp sponge. It is always easier to remove paste immediately before it has dried.

Turning corners

When you have worked your way along a wall, you will arrive at a corner. Papering around corners requires taking the paper around the corner edge and overlapping it with a new length of wallpaper, regardless of whether the corner faces in or out. Given that you will be working with two strips from the same length of paper and creating an overlap, you will inevitably lose some of a pattern repeat in this process. However, a slight loss of pattern match is not very noticeable at a corner.

Inward corners

Measure from the edge of the last full width of wallpaper to the corner at the top of the wall, then halfway down, and once more at the bottom. Add 1 inch (2.5cm) to the longest measurement for the overlap.

If you are using paper with a small pattern or vertical stripes, you should adjust the width of your overlap to the width of the pattern repeat to make it easier to match on the facing wall.

Take a cut length of paper and cut it to this width. Leaving the remainder on the table, paste this narrow strip in place using the standard method, but smoothing the cut edge around the corner. Run a seam roller along the cut edge to make sure it is firmly anchored in place against the wall.

Next take the remaining portion and paste it. Then, using a plumb bob or carpenter's level, establish the vertical on the new wall; it is vital that you do this for each new wall as corners are seldom "true," or square, and your paper will be hanging well out of true by the time you return to your starting point if you do not—a small problem after four corners can appear rather large!

Finally, taking great care to butt it up right into the corner and making sure that it is positioned vertically, hang the offcut on the internal wall, matching up the pattern if necessary.

Outward corners

Smooth the paper up to the edge using the paperhanging brush and ease it around the corner, this time without brushing it firmly into place. In this instance, you

Inward corners

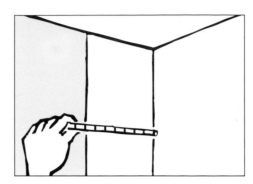

1 *Measure from the edge of the last full width of wallpaper to the corner at the top, midway, and bottom.*

2 *Add 1in. (2.5cm) to the widest measurement for the overlap and cut out. Paste and smooth around the corner.*

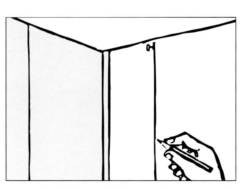

3 *Use a plumb bob to establish a vertical on the new wall at the width of the offcut.*

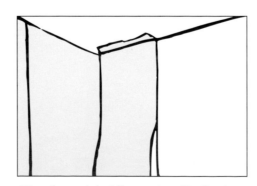

4 *Hang the remainder, taking care to position the edge very close to the corner and to match the patterns.*

Outward corners

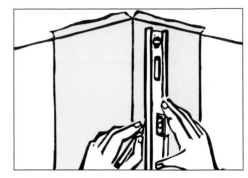

1 *Establish a vertical 1in. (2.5cm) from the corner using a carpenter's level or plumb bob. Mark line with a pencil.*

2 *Cut along the pencil line with a utility knife, using a straightedge as a guide.*

3 *Run the seam roller along the edge leading to the corner to secure the paper in place.*

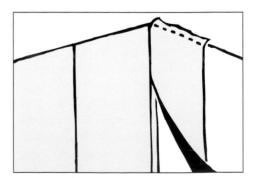

4 *Finally, hang the remainder, positioning its edge close to the corner and lining up the pattern if necessary.*

◀ *Broad stripes are a good choice for a room with sharp corners. Here a striped wallpaper accentuates the neat angles of the chimney breast, while its muted colors create an air of restrained grandeur, ideal for a formal living room.*

▼ *In a heavy-use area such as a hallway, stairway, or kitchen, it's sensible to use a wallpaper with a tougher finish, and consequently a longer life. In this case, a hard-wearing vinyl has been used below the chair rail and a standard patterned paper above.*

should rub your hand down the angle of the wall to make a firm crease along the paper. Slit the overlap allowance to allow the paper to move around the corner without buckling. Use a plumb bob or carpenter's level to establish a vertical about 1 inch (2.5cm) from the outward corner and use a straightedge or metal ruler to mark the line in pencil. Using the straight edge and a sharp utility knife, cut the paper along this line. Gently remove the cut-away portion and place it on the pasting table, pattern-side down.

Run the seam roller down the edge of the paper leading to the corner, making sure that it is firmly stuck down. Next, if the paste has dried too much, re-paste the remaining piece and then hang it, positioning its edge very close to the external corner, and taking care to match patterns if necessary. Run the seam roller along the seam to try to secure the edge of the paper.

Papering around doors and windows

Once you have mastered basic wallpaper positioning and trimming techniques, it is relatively simple to adapt the techniques so you can work successfully around doors and windows.

Doors and windows fitted flush with a wall are relatively easy to paper; the wallpaper merely has to be trimmed back to fit neatly around the architrave or casing. If the door or window is recessed, the increased number of surfaces of the recess requires more careful fitting—and before that, more careful planning. For example, it is important not to have seams falling on the outward corners of the frame, so establishing and checking the correct starting point before you hang a single strip of wallpaper is very important. All you need to do is adjust your chosen starting point by 2 inches (5cm) to the right or left as necessary. It is easier to paper the wall with the recess first, before the rest of the room.

▲ In an irregularly shaped room, wallpaper with a small, regular pattern or a narrow stripe is the best option. In this attic bedroom, the paper extends all the way up to the window in the eaves, playing down the room's awkward proportions and creating a sense of harmony.

Flush doors and window frames

When papering along a wall that includes a door or window, you should hang drops until you have one that will overlap the obstacle. Hang this length, letting it fall over the door or window frame. Cut away the excess paper to within 1½ inches (4cm) of the architrave or window casing and discard the cut-away portion. Then cut diagonally into the paper toward the corner of, and as far as, the outside of the frame or architrave and smooth the paper with a brush. Press the paper firmly against the architrave or casing, and form a crease with the rounded edge of a small pair of scissors, before peeling back the tongues of paper and trimming along the creases. Always take particular care when working on the corner as it is all too easy to tear the paper at this stage. Finally, brush the trimmed edges back into position around the frame.

Recessed windows

When papering around recessed windows, hang the first strip of paper to one side, overlapping the window.

Trim and fit at the ceiling level as you would a normal drop, and only then make a horizontal cut at the soffit (the horizontal recess above the window), and another at the windowsill, using a sharp

Fitting moldings, sills, and recesses

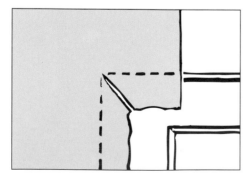

1 To fit a door or window frame, cut away excess paper, leaving a 1½ in. (4cm) overhang. Cut toward the corner.

2 Form a neat crease around the frame, then peel back the tongues of paper and trim before repositioning.

3 Steps 1–2 also apply for windowsills. Take extra care when tackling corners; it is very easy to tear the paper.

utility knife. Carefully wrap the paper around the corner into the recess. Continue to work along the top of the window as if you were papering a flat wall, but using short strips and taking the ends around, under the soffit, to the window frame. Stop when you get to the point where your next strip will be full-length, and turn your attention to beneath the window.

Now hang short lengths from under the windowsill to the baseboard, using a standard hanging technique. Having hung the same number of short strips as you did above the window, hang another full-length strip that overlaps the recess. Adopting the same procedure as before, cut the paper horizontally at the soffit and sill, and wrap it neatly around.

Fill in the unpapered spaces in the corners of the soffit with portions cut away previously, matching patterns as best you can. Cut a patch big enough to fit the space with overlap allowances on all four sides.

Crease and trim the paper according to standard practice at the window frame, and tuck in the other edges in turn: first under the short strip at the top of the window, and then rather as you would on a corner— under the wraparound on the side of the recess, and finally under the paper on the wall, on the edge that stands out from the recess. Be particularly careful when you lift the corner of the original paper, and add paste before brushing it flat again if the original paste has dried.

▲ *Papering around door frames is not as daunting as you might imagine. This regular fleur-de-lys wallpaper would have been relatively easy to line up. The pattern also helps to draw the eye away from the unusual slope of the walls and complements the handsome walnut furniture.*

Dormer windows

When working in a room with dormer windows, your first task will entail deciding which parts of the dormer should be papered—which parts are to be considered walls and which parts ceiling, and thus which sections should be papered and which painted to reflect that differentiation.

Start at a central point beneath the window itself, working out to each side. Hang short strips from the junction of the slope to the floor, creasing and trimming according to standard practice.

You may wish to leave the wedge-shaped walls projecting outward at right angles to the window painted, but if you wish to paper them, these vertical walls should be tackled next. Leave an allowance and take it around the corner; the paper on the sloping roof will butt up to the corner for a neat finish.

Finally you should tackle the sloping roof sections, taking great care to match the drops with those already in place. This may mean that the first length of paper will not be a full-width drop. Below the window, measure outward from the side of the window to the first seam. Cut to the exact width of your measurement, and your drop from top of sloping roof to floor should now align.

It will be neater to tuck the lower edge allowance on the sloping roof section under the top trimmed edge of the half-wall than to trim it, but you could also consider a border at this junction (see pages 96–97).

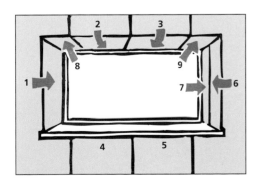

4 To fit a recessed window: start with an overlapping strip, then hang the longer drops above and below the window.

5 Fill the unpapered recesses with previously cut portions, tucking them beneath the adjoining lengths.

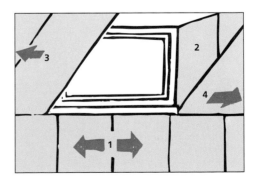

6 To fit a dormer window: start at a central point beneath the window and work outward.

Papering around obstacles

▶ *Papering around light switches can be problematic, but there are several options. You can paper around the switch, use a clear plastic switch plate that allows you to see through to the wallpaper beneath, or, as here, carefully match the paper over the plate to create a smooth, seamless look.*

▼ *There is no set technique for wallpapering around a mantel, as each will have its own unique shape and changes of angle. To achieve a neat finish rather than a scrappy, haphazard one, however, always work slowly and methodically, carefully cutting, smoothing, and trimming the wallpaper as you go.*

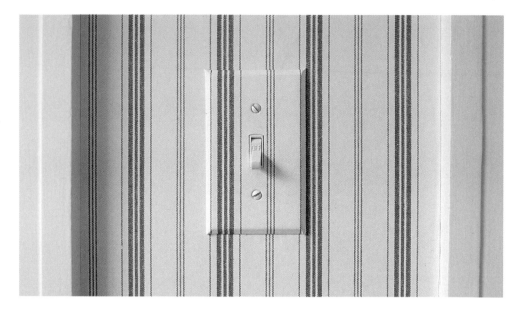

Wall switches and outlets

Before attempting to paper around sockets, switches, and any other electrical outlet, always remember to turn off the power at the main circuit breaker, and allow plenty of time for the paste to dry before you turn it back on again.

Paper over wall switches and outlets and smooth down the wall as usual. Press the paper firmly over the edges of the plate so that it creases. Cut a cross in the paper across the plate, so that each slit runs from corner to corner diagonally. Through this hole, loosen the screws that hold the plate on the wall. Then trim the flaps of paper to leave an allowance of ⅜ inch (1cm) all around. Press the paper flat behind the face plate. Tighten the screws on the plate again and switch on the electricity.

With ceiling lights, position the paper over the fixture as if you were actually going to paper it into the ceiling. Get someone else to hold the remaining length of paper against the ceiling with a broom while you cut a cross in the paper exactly where the light needs to fall and pull it through. Trim any excess paper and smooth what remains toward the light with a paperhanging brush. Make a series of small cuts in the paper and use the rounded blade of a pair of small scissors to make a well-defined crease around the light fitting. Loosen the plate and press the paper flaps neatly beneath it, then secure

Mantels, radiators, and ceiling lights

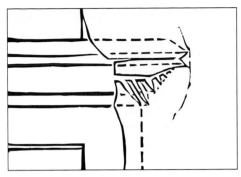

1 To paper around a mantel, work carefully downward, making new cuts to accommodate each change of angle.

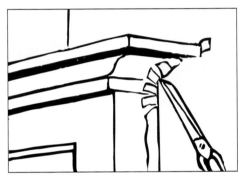

2 Smooth and trim each cut as you go. More complicated, smaller cuts may be easier to make with ordinary scissors.

3 To accommodate a radiator bracket, make a cut in the paper to the top of the radiator to form two "tongues."

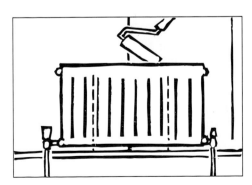

4 Push the two tongues of paper down behind the radiator using a long reach roller.

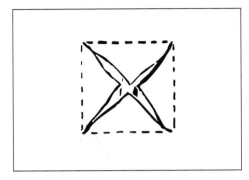

5 To paper over a switch, press the paper over the plate and crease around the edges. Cut a cross in the paper.

6 Loosen the face plate and trim the paper, leaving a ⅜in. (1cm) allowance. Tuck it behind the plate.

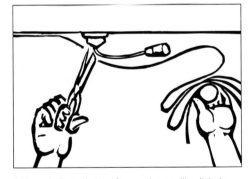

7 Use a similar technique for covering a ceiling light by cutting a cross in the paper to pull the cord through.

8 Make a neat crease around the light. Cut V-shaped nicks in the paper and tuck the flaps underneath the plate.

the plate against the ceiling. However, *do not* use this technique with any paper that includes metal in its composition.

Radiator brackets

It is awkward and disruptive to remove central-heating radiators from the wall when you want to paper a room. A better solution, although it can be rather tricky, is to paper around them. Paper the flat uninterrupted wall until you find that the next drop will have to fit behind the radiator.

Measure from the top of the baseboard to the top of the bracket of the radiator, and from the bracket to the edge of the adjoining drop of paper. Remember to add the overlap allowance to the vertical measurement and check that you are cutting from the bottom and not the top of the length of paper; then make a cut in the paper that will create two "tongues" in the lower section of your drop; they will accommodate the bracket.

Smooth the wallpaper onto the wall as usual, pushing the two tongues down behind the radiator using a radiator roller. Trim the lower edge at baseboard level as usual and smooth it down with a paper-hanging brush.

Fireplace mantels

Some mantelpieces can be quite elaborate, with lots of extra angles to cut around, but the principle is always the same: work slowly and carefully, cutting into the paper up to each change in angle, and then smoothing and trimming each flap in turn against the solid part of the fireplace, working gradually downward.

It may be, if the mantelpiece of the fireplace is very close to a corner, that you will find it easier to cut the paper carefully across—horizontally—level with the top of the mantelpiece and then to work in two halves. This means there is less risk of tearing a drop of paper, and can, if carefully done, be all but invisible.

You may also find it easier to make the smaller cuts necessary for an accurate professional finish with ordinary scissors rather than their large wallpapering relatives.

Papering ceilings and stairwells

Your primary concern when you paper a ceiling or stairwell should be safety. A platform or stepladder can be extremely dangerous when you are stretching.

It is vital to avoid stretching too far, and important to work at the correct level. This way, you will work more effectively and expend the minimum of effort, thus making a difficult and awkward job less exhausting.

When setting the height of a stepladder or platform, the ceiling should be about 3¼ inches (8cm) above your head to make the process as easy as possible.

Ceilings

Ceilings are normally painted rather than papered, but if the surface is slightly cracked, you may need to cover it with lining paper. Use a heavier grade of paper, as it is easier to work with and less likely to tear than something thinner. To create a safe work platform, ideally you should rent a couple of sturdy

scaffold boards and rest them between two stepladders or sawhorses. If the boards bend with your weight, reduce the space between the ladders.

First, mark a guideline: measure the width of the paper and subtract ⅜ inch (1cm). This gives you some leeway in case the walls are not exactly square. Mark this width on the ceiling at opposite ends. Stretch a chalk line across the ceiling, from the marks, and snap it quickly against the ceiling to create a guideline. Use the length of this guideline as your cutting length, plus 2 inches (5cm) at either end (to allow for trimming). If the ceiling is the same width throughout the room, use the first length as your template. Paste the paper and fold into a loose accordion (see pages 86–87).

Position the platform directly beneath the chalk guideline and brush the prepared ceiling with a coat of sizing ready for the first strip of paper. Hold the folded paper against

▶ A striped wallpaper makes the most of the sinuous curve of this staircase. A stylish rope border adds classical polish and obviates the need for any other detail.

Hard-to-reach areas

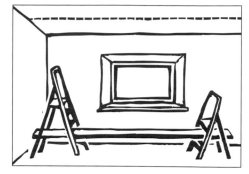

1 Scaffold boards, suspended between stepladders, make a sturdy base for ceiling work.

2 Following a chalk guideline, press, then brush, the folded paper onto the ceiling, fold by fold.

3 When papering a stairwell, position the longest drop first, then work outward to each side.

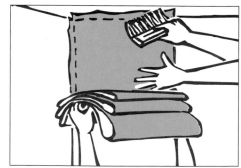

4 Enlist a helper to hold up the folds while you brush the paper against the wall.

the ceiling with your left hand or a clean broom and press the first section of paper against the ceiling with your right hand, aligning it with the guideline. Smooth the paper against the ceiling with a paper-hanging brush, remembering to let the allowance overhang against both the end and the side walls. Release another fold of paper from the broom and work along the guide-line, brushing the paper from the center out, until you reach the other end of the room. Run the rounded tip of a pair of scissors around the junction of the wall and ceiling to make a firm crease. Pull the overhang away from the wall and trim the allowance with wallpaper scissors. If you are using heavy-grade paper, it may not crease easily, so you might have to mark the seam lightly with a pencil before peeling back and cutting.

Smooth the paper back to fit neatly against the ceiling before applying a coat of size to the adjoining piece of ceiling to prepare it for the next length of paper. Butt the next roll of paper against the first; run a seam roller over the seam to secure it. And continue, using the same method, across the rest of the ceiling. For papering over electrical sockets, see pages 92–93.

Stairwells

Stairwells are even more complicated to paper than ceilings and again require a scaf-fold tower or other sturdy support. You can rent a scaffold tower or you can use a series of long ladders, stepladders, and scaffold boards. Lean a ladder against the head wall and set up a stepladder on the landing; place the boards between them to create your plat-form. You can make sure that everything is completely stable by nailing battens to stair treads to stop ladders from slipping and by tying the boards to the ladder steps with rope.

You should start papering with the longest drop. Measure it carefully, and remember to allow for the slope of the stairs; you must measure your drop to below the lowest part of the baseboard and then add the usual trim-ming allowance. Paste it generously so that it does not dry out as you work, fold the length into an accordion as for ceiling paper, and start at the top of the wall. Because of its

▲ *Here, a soft blue harlequin-patterned wallpaper has been used on the walls, archway, and hallway beyond so that the space flows from one area to another. This can be very important in narrow or awkward spaces, where careless combinations of patterns and colors can result in a visually disjointed effect.*

length and weight, you will need to enlist a helper to hold the lower half of the paper while you position the top half; if you allow it to hang unsupported, it will stretch.

Archways

Hold a drop of (unpasted) paper to the wall, allowing 2 inches (5cm) at the top, and make a crease along the line of the arch's curve. Cut the excess paper in a neat curve, following the line of the crease, but at a distance of approx. 2 inches (5cm) from it. Mark the position of the edge of the paper so that you can then measure and cut more drops of paper like this for the remainder of the arch. Only then should you paste and hang the paper.

Trim the paper around the curve to approx. 1 inch (2.5cm), and then cut small V-shaped nicks into the allowance at regular intervals so that this turnover lies flat when smoothed flat onto the underside of the arch.

Paper the wall on the opposite side of the arch in the same way, endeavoring to match the pattern with that on the adjacent wall through the arch.

Then measure the thickness of the wall and carefully cut a strip of paper to this width, with the standard 2 inches (5cm) added to each end. Paste it from the bottom upward, and repeat the process up the other side of the arch so that the two strips meet at the top center. Finally smooth the strip around the curve, overlapping the "tabs" and creating a smooth finish.

Measuring the stair angle

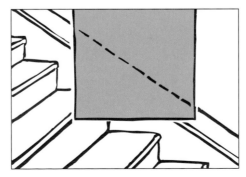

When calculating the drops in a stairwell, measure down to the lowest part of the baseboard.

Papering archways

Trim, nick, and then fold the paper over to fit the curve of the arch. Use two finishing strips to cover the tabs.

Putting up friezes and borders

▲ *In a room with little or no intrinsic architectural interest, borders and friezes can be used as an admirable substitute. In this child's room, a candy-striped paper in mint green and white combined with a lively border printed with barnyard animals creates a clean yet lively look at minimal cost.*

Borders that require ordinary wallpaper paste will not stick onto vinyl wallpapers, so use self-adhesive borders for vinyls and special overlap adhesive to apply ordinary ones.

Applying friezes

To use a frieze to create the effect of a coving or chair rail, first measure the perimeter of the room at the relevant height where you wish to apply the frieze.

Use a carpenter's level, straightedge, and pencil to draw a straight horizontal line to mark where you wish to apply the bottom edge of the frieze. Lay the frieze pattern-side down in the middle of the pasting table and apply the paste, making sure that glue reaches right up to the edges. Fold into a loose accordion and apply it to the wall, making sure the bottom edge lines up with your guideline. Smooth into place with a brush.

Mitering and joining borders

Use a carpenter's level and pencil to mark the shape of the panel. Cut each piece of border paper approx. 4 inches (10cm) longer than the exterior dimensions of the panel. Apply paste to the strips of border and then apply them to the wall, making sure that they run accurately along the guidelines with a 2-inch (5cm) allowance at each end, to overlap with the adjoining strip at the corner.

Looking at the overlapping strips as a frame, take your straightedge and position it diagonally on one corner—running from and to the points of intersection—on the outside

Plain-painted or papered walls can be transformed with the addition of a border or frieze, and most manufacturers now produce selections that complement their wallpaper. Borders are usually used to frame a feature in the room, such as a door or window, or to create a feature by forming panels on the wall or ceiling, whereas friezes generally come as a precut decorative feature which can be hung at ceiling or picture-rail height.

Applying paper friezes and borders

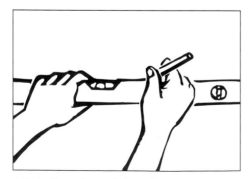

1 Mark a line to denote the base of the frieze using a carpenter's level, straightedge, and pencil.

2 Accordion-fold the frieze and apply it, using the pencil mark as a guide. Smooth into place with a brush.

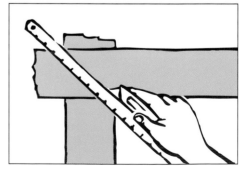

3 To create neat, mitered borders, overlap the two strips and mark a diagonal across.

Fixing a plaster cove

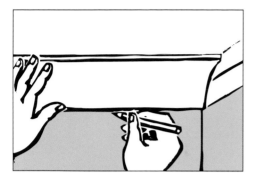

1 Dry-fix the lengths with masonry nails, marking their position with a pencil. Cut extra pieces to fill the gaps.

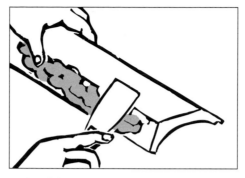

2 When all the pieces have been cut to fit, coat the back edges of the cove with adhesive and press in place.

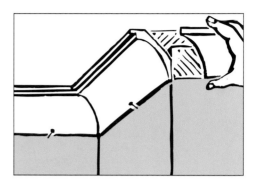

3 Hammer the masonry nails back in to support the cove while the adhesive dries.

and inside edges. Slice diagonally through both layers of paper with a knife to create a mitered corner. Peel off the overlapping border strips and remove the pieces. Smooth the seam back together with a brush to create a neat miter.

Authentic period detailing

Using embossed panels

Traditionally, these papers were used in panels beneath the chair rail, particularly in hallways or stairwells—sometimes to hide rising damp. Because of the patterned relief surface of these papers, they are ideal for covering cracked walls or for creating a tough surface. Prepare the walls for wallpapering, and cross-line with lining paper (see pages 80–81).

Embossed panels for below the chair rail are bought precut with straight, matching edges so there is no wastage or matching of patterns. Be careful when you are carrying the panels; bending them will crack the surface. Before you apply any adhesive, check that panels from different batches are the same length. Soak the panels in warm water before coating the backs with the recommended adhesive. Pay particular attention to the edges. Align the top edge of the panel with the chair rail and smooth down with a soft cloth. Never use a seam roller to smooth the seams; this will flatten the pattern.

Do not try to turn panels of embossed papers around internal or external corners unless they are rounded, because the paper will probably crack. Cut the wallcovering to finish at the corner and butt up the lengths.

Crown moldings and coves

Crown moldings and coves are mounted at the junction between the walls and the ceiling. A crown molding is a projecting ornamental molding while a cove is a plain molding with a concave profile. Both are manufactured as long lengths that can be cut to size. If you mount a small crown molding or cove and it looks rather insignificant, you can make it look more impressive by adding a narrow strip of molding along the ceiling edge and painting it to match.

Walls and ceiling must be dry and free of dust before starting work. Then anchor the full lengths, supporting them on masonry nails top and bottom and marking their position with a pencil. You will have to cut lengths to fit the remaining gaps; use a fine-toothed saw. Allow extra for mitered joints at external corners (the exact measurements will be indicated in the directions). Use the templates supplied to cut the miters.

Lightly sand any rough edges, and then, having removed the nail supports, scratch or sand the areas of the wall and ceiling to be covered. Mix enough adhesive to use in 45 minutes—the length of time it remains effective—and spread the top and bottom edges of the molding with a putty knife or trowel.

Press the lengths of molding firmly in place between the guidelines. Remove excess adhesive with a putty knife and use it to fill in the joints and miters. It's a good idea to put the masonry nails back in at this stage to support the molding while the adhesive dries; they can be removed later.

If you are using a heavy molding, drive nails through the top edge into the ceiling at each end. Punch them below the surface and cover them with adhesive. Smooth all joints with a damp paintbrush.

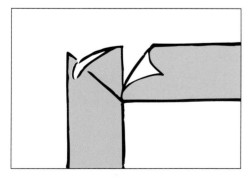

4 Cut across the diagonal through both layers. Peel back the border strips and remove the cut-away pieces.

Applying embossed panels

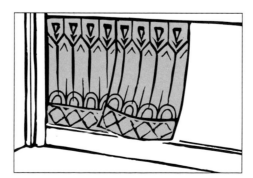

Pre-cut with straight-matching edges, decorative panels can be lined side by side following a horizontal guideline.

Creating your own papers

▶ *With a little imagination you can create some stunning effects at minimal cost. Here, the fish motifs from a roll of wallpaper have been cut out and stuck on a plain, curved wall to create a bold and lively frieze of fish swimming around. Photocopies, old prints, and book illustrations could also be used this way.*

There is such a huge variety of papers and borders on the market that it would be very easy to forget that you can also make your own, tailoring them perfectly to suit your desired scheme and creating an effect that is unique to you. Many of these home-made decorating solutions are extremely inexpensive to create, but will not short-change you on style.

As a clever but effective budget solution, nothing is smarter—or cheaper—than basic brown packing paper. Buy it in a large roll from an office stationery outlet; it comes in rolls 20–36 inches (50–90cm) wide. Apply it to the walls as you would any wallpaper (see pages 86–87). You need to buy a heavy-weight paper; otherwise the wallpaper paste may well soak through the surface, making the paper difficult to handle.

One way of making one roll of wallpaper go a very long way is by working in decoupage. The rebirth in popularity of decoupage as a craft has led to an adaptation of the technique for use on walls, so you can now dress up plain walls with borders and motifs cut from a floral or pictorial roll.

Alternatively, you could create your own motifs. Look out for strong images that would be suitable for your scheme and photocopy them in black and white or color; enlarge or reduce them so that they are exactly the right size; and arrange them on the wall—scatter them at random or place them in a regular pattern. Initially, it is best to do this with an adhesive that allows for repositioning, such as spray adhesive. But when you are happy with the design, stick the images on with wallpaper

paste. You may also wish to finish off the effect and protect it with a coat of matte polyurethane varnish.

Using the same technique, you could create a Georgian-style print room. Black and white copies of prints, complete with all the attendant bow and ribbon motifs, are now widely available, but you could recreate your own with some inexpensive old prints and photocopied motifs. This finish looks particularly good against strong colors such as golden yellow, terra-cotta, or sharp green.

Walls papered with antique maps or nautical charts are equally striking. Use standard wallpaper paste and paper the entire wall in brightly colored maps, or use them in panels framed with a piece of molding, or even lengths of rope to create a nautical theme.

◄ Maps can be used to stunning effect as wall coverings, as shown in this unusual study. Antique maps and nautical charts make striking and original wallpaper and can be hung in panels or simply papered straight onto the wall with wallpaper paste.

Using fabric on walls

▶ *A quilt in a handsome red and gold stripe makes a striking wallcovering, adding texture and color to a traditional interior. Its draft-excluding and soundproofing qualities make it practical, too.*

Although less usual than paint or paper, there are several advantages to using fabric on walls and ceilings. Like paper, it can cover up minor imperfections in the wall, but also acts as a good heat and sound insulator. With care, fabric can stay fresh far longer than paint or paper. Most fabric finishes can be treated to make them dirt-resistant; later they can be spot-cleaned or vacuumed.

Applying fabric directly to the wall

Many fabrics can be applied directly to the wall, but check before you start that they are stain and mildew-resistant. Look for those with a firm, taut weave that are of medium weight. Felt is a classic choice and comes in a wide variety of strong colors.

The biggest difference between hanging wallpaper and hanging fabric is that with the latter you should apply the adhesive to the wall rather than to the fabric.

Cut the fabric to the required length (plus a trimming allowance), and roll it inward on a broom handle for easier handling. Unroll the length onto the wet pasted wall, against a plumbed vertical line, and run a dry paint roller over the surface. To make a seam, overlap adjoining lengths and then cut through both layers with a sharp knife against a straightedge. Having removed the cut pieces, smooth back the edges into place.

It is a good idea to conceal the edges of the fabric, which otherwise could ravel, with braid or a similar trim. This can be expensive and difficult to remove, so dry-hang several varieties around the walls to make sure you like the effect before you invest.

Some fabrics such as silk, burlap, suede, corduroy, and grass cloth are available already backed onto paper to make them easier to hang; in this case, the fabric should be treated as wallpaper, so the adhesive is applied to the backing rather than the wall.

Hanging fabric on battens, mounting track, and stretch wires

If you are hesitant about pasting fabric directly onto the walls, there are several alternatives. The first of these is to attach the fabric to the walls with a staple gun. The staples can be covered with braid. This is very much a "quick fix," suitable for rented houses or short-term solutions. You will get a more professional and elegant finish if you stretch the fabric between wooden battens. Mount the battens along the top and bottom of the wall and attach upright battens along the wall at 6-foot (2m) intervals. You may also want to add extra battens in places where you know you will want to hang pictures, or mirrors, so you have something behind the fabric into which to drive picture hooks.

For a good, slightly upholstered finish—enhancing the fabric's sound- and heat-insulating properties, too—you can interline the fabric with batting.

Joining two lengths of fabric and attaching them to a wall sounds complicated but is actually straightforward. It is a technique that is crucial for a professional finish, a variation of which (using only one piece of fabric) is used as the real starting point. Two strips of fabric are placed right sides together over a batten, and a back-tacking strip laid over the top. All the thicknesses are then stapled with a staple gun, and the top layer of fabric brought away from the wall and wrapped over the seam, revealing its right side.

Start by sewing together enough lengths of fabric—right sides together—to cover one wall, allowing for trimming allowances top and bottom, and matching any pattern carefully. Then taking up one vertical edge of your fabric, place it right side down under a back-tacking strip in the corner down the right-hand side of the wall to be covered, as if it would cover the adjacent wall wrong side out. Secure the fabric to the battens by stapling through all the layers.

Take the fabric and wrap it back over the back-tacking strip so that the right side of the fabric is in front of you across the wall. Staple it in place temporarily top and bottom.

Working from the center upward and downward, and gradually outward, and smoothing firmly as you proceed, staple the fabric firmly in place. Leave a margin all around, then remove the temporary staples and finish off by trimming all edges and covering them with braid. Use quick-drying, non-staining wallpaper adhesive.

If this sounds complex, consider using mounting track to attach the fabric to the walls. This will allow you to attach the taut

Applying fabric to walls

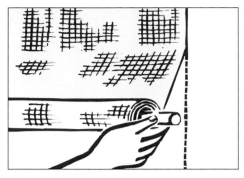

1 Roll the fabric right side inward around a pole. Unroll onto the pasted wall, following a vertical guideline.

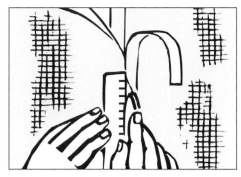

2 For a neat seam, overlap two pieces of fabric and cut through both layers along a straightedge. Remove offcuts.

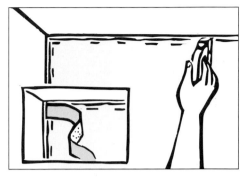

3 Alternatively, secure the fabric in place with a staple gun. Conceal the staples by edging the walls with braid.

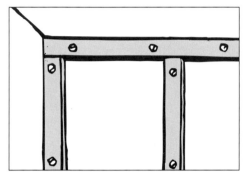

4 For a professional finish, mount battens along the walls at top and bottom and vertically at 6-foot (2m) intervals.

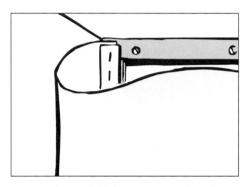

5 Have ready enough fabric to cover one wall. Staple one vertical edge right side down under a back-tacking strip.

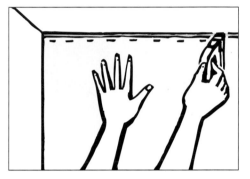

6 Working from the center up and down, staple the fabric across the wall. Trim the edges with braid.

fabric neatly without resorting to battens and staples. It comprises long plastic strips with "jaws" to hide the rough edges, and adhesive plastic strips to hold the fabric taut.

Another method is to hang the material on the walls from poles or wires. This is a good alternative if you live in a rented place; it does not mark the walls and you can take the fabric with you when you leave.

Lightweight fabrics such as sheers and pat-terned gauze can be hemmed and shirred onto poles or wires attached just below the ceiling and above the baseboard. You should allow approximately three times the wall's width in fabric to create a rich effect. It can be drawn back over the window or door, or another wire or pole can be mounted immediately above them and the fabric shirred over that.

Heavier fabric such as linen or wool can be suspended from rods or poles and left to hang freely at the bottom. It can be drawn back over windows or doors, if desired, by using fabric or cord ties.

◄ *Using fabric on walls allows you a great deal of versatility; it is simple to customize it so that it is perfect for your scheme. Here, inexpensive muslin is stretched between battens and then stenciled with a bold gold design.*

Tiles, panels, and rails

The selection of tiles available today is, quite simply,
dazzling. But before you decide on finish, color, or
design, you need to consider your surface. Dainty mosaics
may look wonderful, but they are unsuitable for the
heavy-wear backsplash area in the kitchen, where a more
robust tile would be better. Pretty handpainted tiles would
look just right in a bathroom but wholly inappropriate
inside the back door, where a strong surface that can be
wiped down easily would be more practical.

Decoratively, tiles allow you to create many different effects, whether your style is coolly Neoclassical or decidedly modern. And having the choice of the best effects is not restricted to those with the biggest purses. You could spend a fortune on handpainted, handmade imported tiles, but equally, you could simply buy just a handful of expensive tiles and use them cleverly to transform a row of more ordinary ones. Or you could arrange inexpensive tiles in an interesting way or use contrasting colors to create striking bands across a wall.

Pictorial panels, relief, mosaic, mirror, or glass tiles can all be used in a room of little architectural interest to create dramatic focal points that will draw the eye away from the room's more mundane features. Tiles can also be used to emphasize or exaggerate the dimensions of a room. A strong horizontal band of color, for example, creates an optical illusion of space—so you might want to think about adding a contrasting border tile when you are tiling a small bathroom. By the same token, an oppressively low ceiling can be made to appear higher by creating vertical stripes of color on the walls.

Tiling is not a mysterious skill; it simply requires a careful and methodical approach. Indeed, it is a relatively easily mastered technique. Walls are seldom straight, blank surfaces; they contain windows, alcoves, or doors, and these need to be taken into account before you even start tiling or major difficulties will arise.

For your first project, it is probably a good idea to tackle something modest such as a backsplash for a sink. This will allow you to perfect your technique and gain some confidence on a small area before embarking on a whole wall.

▲ *A delightful combination of textures and materials has been used in this fantasy bathroom. Although the room is small, glass and light combine to provide an additional dimension, while the imaginative use of layered wood for paneling adds a back-to-nature feel.*

◄ *Tiles are so durable and versatile, it is a shame to restrict them to bathrooms and hallways. Here, a wall of tiles in various shades of blue makes an unusual backdrop for a soft suede sofa. Glass and tiles seem to have an affinity—as proved by the way the glass coffee table beautifully reflects the tiles in its surface.*

◄ *The gentle sheen of brushed metal creates a surprisingly sensuous wallcovering and coordinates wonderfully with the textures in the rest of the room.*

Directory of wall tiles

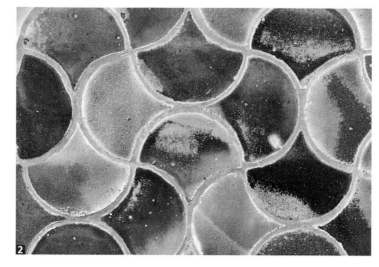

Shapes and sizes

Square and rectangular

Available in a variety of sizes, from tiny mosaic chips to large 12 x 12 inch (30 x 30cm) tiles. They are generally just over ⅙ inch (4mm) thick. Square ceramic tiles are the most common type, but for variety in a run of basic tiles, arrange them in a diamond or brick-wall design, or mix with the same type in a contrasting color. Tiles usually have square or beveled edges; some-times they are glazed on one or two edges so that you do not have to use edge trim. **1**

Other shapes

Unusually shaped, hexagonal, and octagonal tiles can be used to great dramatic effect either by themselves or in combination with square or rectangular tiles. As with any unusual tile design, plot the effect you want to achieve on graph paper before you start on the wall to avoid errors that will be difficult to correct. **2**

Border tiles

There is now a vast range of border tiles on the market; some are patterned, others solid-colored or with a glazed relief design. These can be used to give a striking and professional finish to runs of plain tiles, or a dramatic band between two large expanses of plain flat tiles.

Textured and smooth

You have to consider more than merely the color and pattern of tiles when you are planning your scheme. The texture and finish of the tiles plays a consider-able part in the general look of the room. The warmth of rustic terra-cotta goes very well with unbleached muslin, wooden floors, and coarse woolen throws. If you prefer a more streamlined effect, glitzy glass tiles can add some sparkle to stark modern schemes.

Glazed/unglazed ceramic

Glazed tiles have a glossy, waterproof surface; unglazed tiles must be sealed for protection. Acrylic varnish gives a durable surface, but wax, though more time-consuming and requiring more elbow grease, gives an infinitely more subtle and beautiful finish.

Vitreous glass

Glass tiles or blocks are a great way of breaking up a space without blocking out light or creating a closed-in, cramped atmosphere in the room. **3**

wall if you want to create a perfect, undistorted reflection; otherwise the effect will be ruined.

Metallic

A less expensive alternative to metal cladding on walls, these shiny tiles can look extremely smart, creating a similar kind of reflective effect.

Mosaic

These can be stunning, whether covering a whole expanse of wall or interspersed with plain tiles, perhaps as a border. The mosaic tiles are supplied stuck to a square of mesh, which is applied directly to the adhesive, thus eliminating the need to position many small tiles individually.

Although the tiles are occasionally available in a pattern, they are usually supplied in 12 x 12 inch (30 x 30cm) uniformly colored squares.

Relief pattern

Ceramic tiles with a raised pattern beneath the glaze provide variety in tone and texture in a long run of tiles. Relief patterns are popular for border tiles and are molded to resemble crown moldings for a professional finish.

Pictorial and patterned

Panels of pictorial or patterned tiles can create a stunning focal point on an expanse of wall and need not be expensive if you combine them with a run of coordinating plain tiles. **4**

Terra-cotta

The warm, natural, and earthy tones of glazed or unglazed terra-cotta combine wonderfully with the natural, informal elements of today's interiors. Unglazed terra-cotta tiles will need sealing with wax or polyurethane varnish to make them stain- and water-resistant. **5**

Mirror

These tiles and sheets can transform a cramped space or an awkwardly shaped room, creating a new sense of spaciousness. They come with a self-adhesive backing, which makes them particularly easy to install. However, you should bear in mind that you will need a completely flat

First steps to tiling

The quality of a tiled finish is wholly dependent on good preparation. It is vital to be meticulous with the preparation of the wall and the setting out, because by the time you get to the end of the wall, what may have started out as a small error can have grown into a real catastrophe. Once the tiles start to go out of true, there is really no alternative but to take them off and start again.

Calculating quantities of tiles

Working out the number of tiles you will need is quite a straightforward exercise. Assuming you are using square tiles, divide the width of the wall by the width of the tile. This will give you the number of tiles you will need for each row. Then, divide the height of the tile into the total height of the area. This tells you how many tiles will fit down the row. Now multiply the number of

► Small mosaic tiles allow you to create surprisingly subtle and intricate patterns. They are also very good for creating startling geometric designs in bands of contrasting color, as in this chic modern bathroom.

tiles across by the number of tiles down to reach the total number of tiles required. To this figure add a further 5 to 10 percent to allow for breakages. Buy all the tiles you are going to need at the same time, as you would for wallpaper, as there can be slight variations in tone and finish between different batches.

If you are using unusual shapes or handmade tiles, or will be fixing them in an unusual way, you will need to make yourself a tiling gauge to allow you to estimate quantities accurately. Indeed, this is an invaluable tool whatever the kind of tile you are using.

Making a tiling gauge

A tiling gauge is simple to make and will make your life easier when it comes to deciding on the horizontal and vertical positioning of tiles. It also allows you to know at a glance how many tiles will fit between two points

and insures that you center tiles accurately over bathtubs or along windows. Make a tiling gauge from a 4-foot (1.2m) length of 2 x 1-inch (50 x 25mm) wooden batten. On a flat surface, lay out the tiles as you will arrange them on the wall, allowing space between the tiles for tile spacers, which will eventually be filled with grout. Use a pen to mark clearly on the batten the widths of the tiles and the tile spacer/grouting space.

Preparing surfaces

Careful preparation is the key to successful tiling. You need a smooth, clean, grease- and dust-free surface on which to start. Any imperfections in the wall and skimping at this stage will be magnified once you have fixed a glossy ceramic tile on the top or attempted any kind of geometric design.

When tiling on bare plaster, prepare it carefully as you would for painting (see pages 56–57), making sure that there is no mold or damp. If the wall is in very bad condition you may need to consider skimming it with a new layer of plaster. If you are tiling over new plaster, make sure it is absolutely dry and has been sealed with a proprietary primer sealer. If you are tiling over a particleboard or plywood surface, seal it with a dilute solution of white glue first.

Keying paintwork

It is very simple to prepare a painted wall, whether it is coated with a water- or oil-based paint. All you need to do is to key, or roughen, the surface of the paint with some coarse sandpaper. Wrap it around a sanding block and it will be easier to hold and use. Keying allows the adhesive to penetrate the surface of the wall, so that the tiles stick to the wall rather than the painted surface.

When you have finished sanding, use a scraper to get rid of any flaking paint and a damp cloth or sponge to remove any dust from the surface. Allow the wall to dry thoroughly before moving to the next stage.

Removing wallpapers

You cannot tile over wallpaper, as it is not stable enough. It is necessary to remove all the layers of old wallcovering so that the tile

Tools and equipment

- **Sandpaper:** a coarse grade, to key (roughen) walls.
- **Wet-or-dry paper:** to rub down an existing tiled surface.
- **Carpenter's level:** to establish true horizontals and verticals.
- **Try square:** to indicate exact right angles.
- **Chalk line:** to mark straight line.
- **Tiling gauge:** to measure long runs of tiles.
- **Length of batten:** to support rows of tiles when they are first fixed to a wall.
- **Fiber-tip pen or china marker:** to mark the tiles.
- **Tile scorer:** most basic tool used for cutting tiles.
- **Score-and-snap tool:** to cut tiles. Easier and more accurate to use than a tile scorer.
- **Score-and-snap pliers:** to cut tiles.
- **Tile nippers:** to cut irregular shapes in tiles.
- **Tile file:** to smooth rough edges.
- **Tile saw (hacksaw fitted with a carbide blade):** to cut curves in tiles.
- **Suitable tile adhesive:** to fix tiles to wall. Various types are designed for different surfaces or purposes.
- **Wall trowel:** to apply adhesive to walls.
- **Notched spreader:** to spread adhesive.
- **Plastic spacers:** to space tiles evenly; some tiles have spacers attached.
- **Suitable grout:** to fill spaces between tiles and make surface waterproof.
- **Wooden dowel:** to smooth and shape surface of grout.
- **Decorating sponge:** to clean down tiles and remove excess grout.
- **Cloth:** to polish surface of tiles when tiling is complete.
- **Silicone sealant and gun:** to fill gaps between tiles and bathroom fixtures, to create a waterproof seal.

Equipment to rent
- Electric disk cutter.
- Diamond-tipped cutters.

◄ *Tiles are supremely practical and durable, as they are heat and splash resistant, but they can also make a great contribution to the decorative scheme. Here, Mediterranean blue tiles behind the range and on the floor make a decorative splash and insure that this kitchen looks stylish rather than merely functional.*

adhesive can form a strong bond with the wall surface. For instructions on stripping wallpaper, see pages 80–81. After stripping, make good the wall (see pages 56–57).

Rubbing down old tiles
It is possible—although not recommended—to tile over existing tiles if the surface is sound and smooth. Before applying your new tiles, roughen the glazed surface with wet-or-dry paper in order to provide a key for the adhesive. Then use a slightly damp cloth or sponge to remove any dust from the surface. If you prefer to remove the original layer of tiles, first protect your eyes with plastic goggles and then remove the old tiles using a brick chisel or cold chisel and 4-pound hammer.

Once the tiles are removed, you will need to render or replaster the wall before applying the new tiles, so this will increase the scope of your job enormously.

Tiling plan and preparation

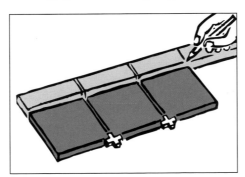

1 Use a ballpoint pen to mark the widths of the tiles and the spacers on the batten to make a tiling gauge.

2 Wearing protective goggles to avoid eye injury, remove the old tiles using a chisel and hammer.

Planning

▲ *Hundreds and hundreds of tiny tiles look very effective and professional, but it can be extremely tedious matching them up into even rows. Some brands of tiny tiles are available already plastered onto larger squares to make the task less arduous. In any case, the end result is a very pleasing effect.*

Before mounting tiles on the wall, it is important to plan where all the tiles—both whole and cut tiles—will fall. You can do this using your tiling gauge. If you are planning an elaborate design, work it out on graph paper before attempting to transfer it to the wall.

Setting out tiles

This is the most important stage in tiling, as accuracy here is essential to the overall look of the finished job. First, plan exactly where the whole tiles will be positioned, and where cut tiles will be the least noticeable. This is a relatively easy task on a blank wall: find the center of the wall and work out the whole tiles from that point outward. Most walls, however, contain some kind of obstacle such as a window or door. If this is the case, decide on the room's natural center point— that is, the point to which your eye is naturally drawn—and start tiling from there. But before you lay your first tile, use your tiling gauge (see page 108–109) to insure that you are not going to have ugly slivers of tile in obvious places. In most cases you will be tiling to the baseboard or floor, and it is unlikely that either of these will be level. It is essential to establish a true horizontal and tile from that to make sure that each row is level. This is called marking out.

Marking out

Using a batten and carpenter's level, draw a horizontal line along the wall to be tiled, about three-quarters of a tile's depth above the

Support battens

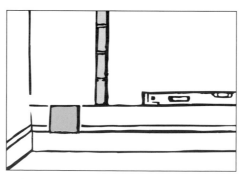

1 Plot a horizontal line no deeper than three-quarters of the depth of the tile. Measure out the tiles with the gauge.

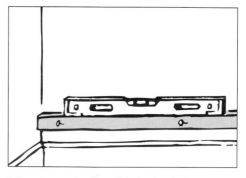

2 To make sure the tiling will be level, nail a horizontal batten to the wall. Check with the carpenter's level.

floor or baseboard. Make sure that at no point is the line more than a tile's depth above the finishing level—floor or baseboard. If it is, redraw the line lower down, or you will have to work with slivers of tile.

The tiles will need some support while the adhesive dries. Mount a line of battens on the wall with masonry nails, aligning the top of the battens with the penciled horizontal guideline. Do not nail battens too securely or removing them will be difficult.

Using your tiling gauge, establish where the outer edge of the last whole tile on a wall will be. Mark the wall by snapping a chalk line against it, and fix a vertical batten to the wall, again aligning the inside edge with the penciled guideline to mark the edge. Check that the battens form an exact horizontal and vertical before you start tiling.

Setting out tiles

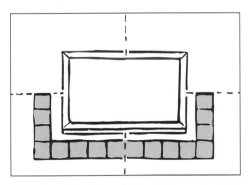

To avoid unworkable slivers of tile, the first row should be three-quarters of a tile's depth away from the edge.

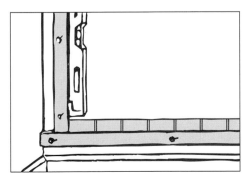

3 Attach a vertical batten to the wall. Check it is square with the horizontal batten using the carpenter's level.

▲ *Choosing the right size of tile enables both the curves and straight lines of a room to be emphasized. Tiles are often the first choice for bathroom and shower areas because, once grouted into position, they provide a perfectly waterproof surface that is very easily cleaned; but architects love them because of the design possibilities.*

Tiling with whole tiles

Once you have carefully established the horizontal and vertical with your battens and are confident that everything is true, you can start tiling.

Bonding tiles

Use the tile adhesive recommended by the manufacturer for the type of tile you have chosen, and spread it out 1 square yard (1 sq m) at a time with a wall trowel, making sure that it is no more than ⅛ inch (3mm) thick. Start in the corner where the horizontal and vertical battens meet.

Next, take a notched spreader, usually supplied with the adhesive, and distribute the adhesive evenly over the area, but leaving regular ridges. The grooves will create suction when you put the tiles on the wall, thus helping to secure them. If you are using a sealing strip, press this into the adhesive first. If you experience trouble getting it to stay in place, secure it temporarily with a couple of nails.

Press the first tile firmly onto the adhesive, resting it squarely on the support battens. Put a spacer (if required) against the corner of the tile and position the next tile. Continue to build up horizontal rows in this way, stopping occasionally to check your work by using a carpenter's level to insure that the tiles are aligned. Wipe any blobs of adhesive from the tiles with a damp cloth.

Having completed the rows of whole tiles, you will need to fill the gaps on the outside edges. To establish where to cut the tiles, hold a tile against the last full tile, glazed side to the wall, so its outer edge butts up against the adjacent wall. Mark the back of the loose tile with a fiber-tip pen or china marker at the points at which it meets the tile. Deducting the allowance for the grout that has been made by the tile spacer, use a steel ruler to draw straight across the back of the tile.

▶ *Mediterranean tiles in a geometric pattern add color but are also a supremely practical decorative option. In a heavy-wear area, such as below the chair rail in this hallway, the tiles are impervious to bumps, scuff marks, and splashes, while providing a colorful point of interest.*

Bonding tiles

1 Use the notched spreader to spread the tile adhesive evenly across the wall, leaving ridges.

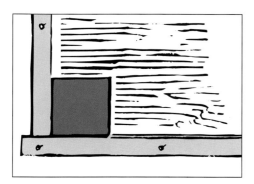

2 Position the first tile firmly into the adhesive, resting it squarely on the support battens. Continue adding tiles.

3 Check tiled rows for both horizontal and vertical alignment using the carpenter's level.

4 Hold a tile against the last full tile to find where to cut the final partial-size tile so that it fits the wall.

▲ Plain tiles in a combination of colors can be used to great decorative effect all over your home. In this case, plain tiles are perfect for this bathroom's understated style, and the combination of two colors with white takes the purely functional edge off the room.

Turning corners

▶ Tiles can fulfill a variety of functions, as in this bathroom. The stone tile creates a waterproof surface for the shower, while the mosaic tile has a more decorative function, suggesting a chair rail. The glass blocks provide essential privacy, while also allowing in the light.

it is best to apply the adhesive directly to the back of the tile with a small, notched spreader. This prevents excess adhesive from getting onto the rest of the tile.

Internal
At internal corners, you need to lap one set of cut tiles over another. Work out which edge will be less noticeable when overlapped before you start.

External
When tiling at external corners, you will need to put up an extra batten. This batten should be positioned down the corner, but projecting from one of the walls so that when you apply the last tiles on the adjacent wall, they butt up to the batten. (In effect you are creating an internal corner with the batten.) Then remove the batten and apply the tiles to the adjacent wall so that they butt up closely to the first tiles, with one glazed edge

Firmly score the loose tile with a tile scorer or the wheel cutter of your score-and-snap pliers. Use the pliers to break the tile along the scored line, or snap it against the straight edge of a table or workbench. If you are using a tile-cutting jig, it will have a marking gauge which you can set to the width of the gap before cutting. Do not be tempted, however, to cut all your tiles at once, without measuring gap by gap first, because walls are seldom square and you will waste tiles.

When you need to cut around a more difficult or intricate shape, you should use nippers and bite away a little piece at a time.

Before you stick the cut tile in place, hold it against the gap to check that it fits. If it does, lay it on a flat surface and smooth the cut edge with a tile file. It will probably be necessary to spread the back of the tile with adhesive before fixing it, to insure that it sticks firmly.

Turning corners
Many spaces will require you to tile around corners and across edges. A professional finish here will require a neat and steady hand. Again, when dealing with small pieces of tile,

Cutting tiles

1 Make a score mark across the tile using a tile scorer or the wheel cutter of the score-and-snap tool.

2 Once the tile has been scored it can be snapped apart using the snapping device of the score-and-snap tool.

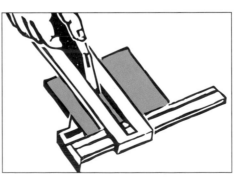

3 On a tile cutting jig there is marking gauge that you set to the width of the gap before cutting.

4 For cutting around intricate shapes it is best to use nippers, biting away a little bit of tile at a time.

Turning corners

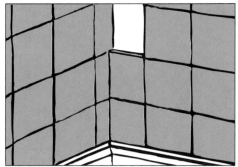

1 For an internal corner, the smaller tiling space should be at the back so that it is less visible.

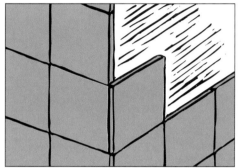

2 For external corners the full-sized tiles on the outside edge should be at right angles to each other.

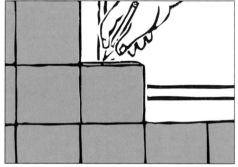

3 For recessed windows place a full tile to the edge and mark the angle that will need to be cut out.

▲ *No one ever said that tiles had to be square. You can use them as creatively as any other decorative material, as in this bathroom decorated in citrus-colored tiles. Abstract mosaic patterns are combined wonderfully here with straight runs of tile.*

of the latter tile visible. You may wish to use an edging strip to finish off external corners neatly. If so, you must remember to attach the strip to the corner first, before attaching the tiles. They should be stuck to each side of the corner simultaneously so that they will be exactly aligned.

Recessed windows

If you are tiling a recessed window but cannot work out how to achieve a neat finish, you should apply and combine the principles you have used for measuring last tiles and for internal and external corners. Tile in rows to within a tile's range of the corner of the windowsill and mark the angle that will need to be cut out. Next tile the sill section, bringing the front edge of the closest line of tiles out to butt up flush with the face of the tiled wall—treating it as if it were an external corner. Finally, tile the walls of the recess, treating the junction of the sill and the wall as an internal corner.

4 When tiling the sill, bring the edge of the closest line of tiles out to butt up flush with the face of the tiled wall.

Tiling around obstacles

Rooms such as bathrooms and kitchens often contain obstacles that are difficult or impossible to move and you must therefore tile around them. Pipes offer a particular challenge for the novice tiler. Make a paper template of the curve you are cutting around and then transfer the pattern to the tile with a fiber-tip pen or China Marker.

To cut around a large curve, such as a waste pipe or basin, cut the paper to the size of the tile. Make a series of parallel cuts in the paper ½ inch (1.2cm) apart, and then press the paper against the curve of the obstacle. Fold back the paper cuts to mark the line. Draw a line along the series of folds to form a clean curve, and cut along the line. Place the template on the tile, glazed side up. Mark the curve on the tile and carefully score along the line with a firm, even stroke.

Place the tile in a vise and cut along the curve using a tile saw. Smooth the edge with a tile file and smear extra adhesive across the back of the tile before applying to the wall.

For smaller pipes, hold the tile next to the pipe and mark the pipe's exact position on the top and side of the tile. Draw intersecting lines on the tile. Where the lines meet, draw a small circle slightly larger than the diameter of the pipe. Cut the tile in two along the vertical line; score the curve and cut away the tile in the center of the circle using tile nippers. Glue the two pieces of tile on either side of the pipe. To fit tiles around a light switch, hold the tile up against the fixture and mark the position for the

▲ *Tiling large areas in one color is an extremely effective method of creating a feeling of spaciousness. In this case, beige tiles, relieved with gray details, are coordinated with chrome fixtures and accessories to create a chic yet functional bathroom which makes the most of its natural light.*

Obstacles

1 Make cuts in a tile-sized piece of paper. Press it around the obstacle and fold back flaps. Cut along the fold line.

2 Using the template, mark the curve on the tile. Place the tile in a vise and then cut out the shape with a tile saw.

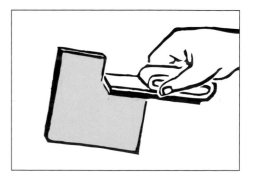

3 Release the tile from the vise and gently smooth down the cut edges using a tile file.

Finishing off

horizontal and vertical cuts with a fiber-tip pen or china marker. Place in a clamp, and cut down each line with a tile saw. Dab extra adhesive onto the back before securing it.

Finishing off

Many tiles come with a coordinating range of edging tiles. You may wish to incorporate one of these, or to use wooden molding or plastic trim strips. Wooden moldings are attached to the wall at the end of the job; plastic strips need to be attached at the beginning, before the tiles. A strip of cove base, applied where the bathtub meets the wall, makes a neat, waterproof seal.

Fill in the gaps between the tiles with grout. Allow the adhesive to dry out completely before even thinking about doing this. Follow the manufacturer's directions as to the drying time; it is usually at least 12 hours and can be as much as 24 hours. Grout can be bought as powder or premixed. Apply with a plastic scraper. Use a mildew-resistant grout and sealant (see below) in areas such as bathrooms and kitchens, where the tiling is likely to come into contact with moisture.

Remember to use mildew-resistant grout for areas around bathtubs and showers and epoxy grout for work surfaces to keep them germ-free. New stain-resistant grouts are also available; less likely to pick up dirt, they will thus maintain a fresher appearance for longer.

Force the grout in between the tile joints with the spreader held at right angles to the tile, moving it backward and forward as you

go. If you scrape off any excess grout quickly, it can be reused. Before the grout dries, take a damp cloth and wipe off excess. Use a piece of wooden dowel to smooth the grout lines into a slightly concave groove, or wipe over the grout to create a flat finish. When the grout has dried out completely, use a clean, lint-free cloth to polish the tiles.

For authenticity, if you are restoring a Victorian interior, you should follow the style of wafer-thin grouting between tiles.

To finish off the gap between a tiled area and another surface, such as a bathtub or shower tray, use a silicone rubber sealant or caulking. Apply sealant directly onto the joint, cutting the tube's nozzle to match the joint size. Squeeze onto the joint as you would ice a cake, in a smooth, continuous line, with the tube held at a 45-degree angle to the joint. Use your finger or the back of a wet teaspoon to smooth the sealant into the joint. Wipe away excess with a damp sponge.

Faults and cures

Uneven tiles

Usually caused by not setting the support battens against the walls correctly before you begin. This is either a disaster, in which case all you can do is remove the tiles and begin again, or you can decide to live with it.

Cracked tiles

If one tile in a row becomes cracked, remove it carefully with a chisel, working from the center outward and taking care not to damage the adjacent tiles. Scrape out as much of the adhesive as you can, and use a hose vacuum cleaner to remove the dust and debris. Spread adhesive on the back of the replacement tile, and press it firmly into the gap. Wipe off excess adhesive with a damp sponge, then allow to dry and re-grout.

Discolored grout

Depending on your time and inclination, and the extent of the discoloring, you can either try bleaching the grout or rake out the existing grout with a screwdriver and apply fresh. Another possibility is to paint the grout with a proprietary grout paint.

1 Force the grout between the joints of the tiles with the spreader held at right angles to the tiles.

2 Before the grout dries, use a damp cloth to wipe any smears of excess grout from the surface of the tiles.

3 Use a piece of wooden dowel, or similar, to smooth the grout lines into a neat, slightly concave groove.

4 Apply sealant to the joint in a smooth, continuous line, cutting the nozzle to match the size of the joint.

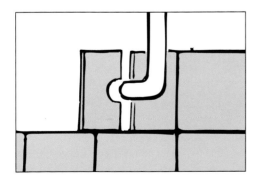

4 To cut out around pipes cut the tile in two along the vertical line. Score the curve and cut away the surplus.

Wood paneling

▶ *Wood paneling your walls can be an inexpensive but smart option, particularly if you choose softwood, which can then be given a coat of paint to create an attractive, durable surface. It is also the ideal method of disguising walls that are less than perfect.*

Wood paneling can provide a durable and attractive wall surface that is very appropriate for today's texture-rich interiors. You can choose from a vast number of grains and colors, and inexpensive softwoods can be transformed with a coat of paint, varnish, or wood stain—either a natural shade or one of the brighter colors available.

An added bonus is that wood is perhaps the best disguise for less-than-perfect walls and is an excellent heat and sound insulator.

When ordering wood, avoid unsightly joints by purchasing lengths that are long enough to reach from floor to ceiling, or from side to side if you are paneling horizontally.

You will also need to allow time for the wood to acclimatize before you start to work with it. Lay the boards flat on the floor for a couple of weeks in situ, so they can get used to the temperature and humidity in your house; move them around every few days to encourage the drying-out process. If you

neglect to do this now, the wood may shrink when it is on the wall and you will be left with ugly gaps between the planks.

Types of wood

The most usual woods used for paneling are softwoods, such as pine; they are inexpensive and take paint or stain treatments well, but if money is no object, talk to your lumberyard about available hardwoods. These can provide a much richer effect, and they actually improve in appearance as they get older. Some of the more popular hardwoods used for paneling are maple, walnut, redwood, and cedar. Cedar has a delicious scent which deters moths, so it is often used to line closets and drawers, too.

Remember to try to find wood from ecologically farmed plantations or hunt for old boards in salvage yards to avoid depleting rainforests.

Attaching the boards

To attach the boards to the wall, you will need to create a framework of 1 x 2-inch (2.5 x 5cm) battens fixed to the wall about 16 inches (40cm) apart. These are called furring strips. If you are attaching the boards vertically, the battens need to run horizontally; for horizontal paneling, attach the battens vertically. You need to add another support strip at ceiling level; but if you are adding a new baseboard, leave the existing

one in place beneath the paneling to act as a support. Fix the furring strips to the wall with masonry nails, or screws and plastic shields, and use your carpenter's level to check that they really are square.

When you are buying the wood, look for boards that are tongued and grooved. This means that the edges are designed simply to slot neatly together when you come to put them on the wall. Alternatively, you could choose something that is a little more decorative; panel moldings come in a variety of styles and can be used to create a more sophisticated look.

Boards are usually sold in 4-inch (10cm) widths, but you should estimate on twelve boards to cover a space 40 inches (1m) wide, to allow for overlapping and planing. You can also buy paneling kits, but they are more expensive because they are simpler to fit and come complete with baseboard. When you attach the paneling, it is important to leave a

small gap to allow the air to circulate freely behind it: as little as ⅜ inch (1cm) will do. This will prevent the paneling from warping, and the gap is so small it will not be noticeable when you have finished.

With the framework screwed to the wall, place your first board with its grooved edge in the corner. Nail through its face into the furring strips, checking with a plumb bob that the strip is straight. Tap subsequent boards in place with a hammer and a scrap of wood and fix at regular intervals (spaced according to the weight of the wood) either with nails as above, if to be hidden, or with panel pins as below. Before securing the penultimate board, overlap the last board and cut it to width. Spring the two boards in place together.

It is a good idea to seal wood finishes with wax or with matte polyurethane varnish when you have finished, to prevent staining, particularly in bathrooms and kitchens.

Attaching wood paneling

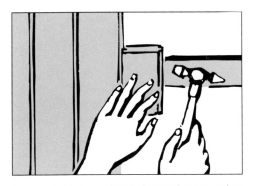

1 Tongued-and-grooved boards slot together as you place them on the wall. Knock them gently so that they abut.

2 Tack finishing nails diagonally through the paneling onto the furring strip at regular intervals.

3 At a junction with a plain wall, cut the last board to fit, snap the last two in place and face nail the last board.

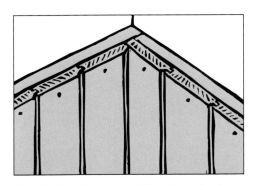

4 Butt-join internal corners and either plane a chamfer on the inside edge or finish with a length of molding.

5 At external corners plane off tongue to butt square. Finish with chair rail and moldings, if desired.

6 Pack out and remount flush electrical outlets, frame with furring strips, and cut notches in boards to fit.

Detailing for walls

▶ *Rough wooden tongue-and-groove paneling creates an old-fashioned feel in this bathroom. The slightly thicker than usual picture rail attractively finishes the top of the wooden planks and serves a practical purpose by hanging the bathroom mirror; the alternative would be to drive in nails and damage the wood.*

Chair rails, picture rails, and baseboards

When fitting a chair rail or picture rail, begin by deciding on the height at which it is to be fixed. Chair rails are usually placed about one-third of the way up the wall, or 40 inches (1m) from the floor. Or you can use the height of the chairs in the room as a guide. Picture rails should be fitted at a comfortable distance from both the chair rail and the ceiling, but nearer the latter, and their position should enable you to hang pictures where they can be seen from a seated position. This is unlikely to be less than 6 feet (1.8m) from the floor.

Once you are satisfied with the proposed height of the molding, draw a horizontal guideline with a pencil around the room using a carpenter's level, or snap a chalk line against each wall of the room in turn.

Fitting new baseboards may well reveal that the floor is not completely level, but most irregularities can be hidden by lifting the board slightly and covering the resulting gap with carpet and underlay, or by nailing a thin or quarter-circle beading along the bottom of the baseboard, to touch the floor.

Once the moldings have been cut to length, drill and countersink screw holes at roughly 2-foot (60cm) intervals. Hold the molding in position along the guideline, and mark the locations of the holes on the walls.

Set aside the molding, drill into the wall with a masonry bit, and insert plastic expansion shields that will take 1¾-inch (45mm)

Fixing chair and picture rails

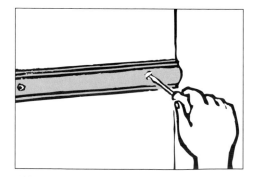

1 Mark position of screws on first cut length; drill holes and countersinks; secure rail to wall along guideline.

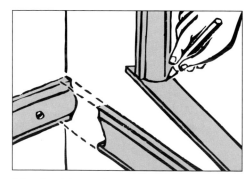

2 For a butt join at an internal corner, scribe rail's profile on back of second length, cut with coping saw and fit.

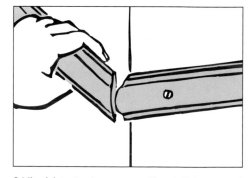

3 Miter joints at outer corners, cutting at 45 degrees, and the ends of any joined vertical or horizontal sections, too.

countersunk screws. In modern houses, or where the layout of an old house has been changed, the walls are probably made from a stud framework and either gypsum wallboard or plaster backed by gypsum, fiberboard, or metal lath backing. In this case, you will have to screw into the timber framing, as above, locating this by tapping along the wall and noting where it sounds less hollow; or you will have to use toggle bolts. It is also possible to buy moldings in kit form with special clips that allow you to slot the rail into place.

Where two lengths of molding meet at an internal angle, make a butt joint by drawing the profile of the molding onto the back of the length that will go on the second wall, at the end that is to be fitted into the corner. Cut carefully along the line with a coping saw, then fit the cut end tightly against the face of the rail on the first wall.

At external corners, use a 45-degree miter box to cut an angled joint between the two lengths. If the molding will not fit into the box, mark the cutting line on the face, and continue this along the edge at a 45-degree angle. You can do this accurately by using a combination square, or by drawing a square on the edge where one corner joins up with the line on the face, and making a diagonal cutting line from this point to the opposite corner. Follow both cutting lines as you saw through. Mitered cuts should also be made when joining two straight lengths of molding. Any small gaps in joints can usually be hidden with wood filler.

Sheet metal cladding

One of the most stylish trends of recent years is the use of metal on walls. The trend originated in cafés and restaurants but has since moved into the domestic interior. Metal is a chic and durable finish, but it is usually costly and requires heavy maintenance to keep it looking good: most finishes dull easily and show every fingerprint and scuff mark, so they need frequent buffing with a soft cloth to preserve the smart finish.

Depending on the effect you want to create, consider copper, zinc, aluminum, or the even more expensive stainless steel. If you think that a whole metal wall will exceed your budget limitations, consider using it in a more limited capacity—in panels or below the chair rail.

Metal comes in sheets or tiles and should be screwed directly into the plaster, or onto wooden panels. It is a specialized finish and an expensive material, so you may be well advised to seek professional help rather than embarking on the task yourself.

▶ *Polished metal sheets can provide a sophisticated look when combined with more traditional materials. This type of room design needs commitment, both stylistically and financially, as it is expensive to achieve and requires a considerable amount of time dedicated to keeping it looking good— every fingermark will show.*

FLOORS

▲ *Cool concrete painted a royal blue picks up on the fresh tone of the chairs in the kitchen and contrasts with the warm tones of the pale wood in the foreground. The neat demarcation between the two different materials allows the worker in the office in the foreground to separate work from the comforts of the living area beyond.*

Most decent-quality floor coverings are expensive, although the cheaper-quality carpets and vinyls are among the most economical floor coverings currently available. If you are restricted to a tight budget, consider renovating the existing floor (see pages 126–147). The result could look much better than a cheap carpet would and is one of the most potentially rewarding, if challenging, of flooring options.

Houses and some apartments built before the 1960s will probably have floors constructed from pine boards, or even oak or parquet. Bald carpets and scruffy vinyl or linoleum may be past salvation, but try lifting a corner to see what is underneath (see pages 126–127). People frequently cover up a very good wood floor with a carpet, and what you find could be the basis of a whole new and exciting range of possibilities.

Newer houses and apartments and older dwellings that have been extensively modernized may have floors constructed from particleboard or concrete. Although these materials lack the charm of old floorboards, they can be brightened up considerably with paint (see pages 138–145). Even concrete

Floors and floor coverings are not indestructible, and there comes a day when something has to be done about the threadbare carpet, the shabby vinyl, or the dirty, cracked floorboards. Even if the flooring is still in fairly good condition, it may be that you have grown tired of it, or, if you have moved into a new dwelling, that you do not share the former occupant's taste. Yet other factors may be involved in the decision to change a floor covering. Perhaps a dusty carpet that causes uncontrollable sneezing is harboring a population of house-dust mites, and a non-fabric floor covering would be less allergenic. Maybe a wood floor is looking scratched or the color is not quite right for a new decorative scheme. Although it may seem that the only solution is to rip it all up and start again, this is not the only course of action open to you—nor is it necessarily desirable.

The first step when considering a new floor is to examine the options available and to decide whether they are affordable.

▲ *This room has the original oak floorboards often found in much older houses. This type of floor naturally tends to age gracefully and looks good, in any environment, when simply waxed and polished; here the floorboards perfectly complement an informal arrangement of pale furnishings that gives an uncluttered impression.*

can be painted to imitate a more expensive material such as limestone flooring, and, of course, it will have the solidity associated with the real thing.

Indeed, there are very few existing floors that cannot be improved by one of the wide range of decorative treatments now available. For instance, floors that really seem past all hope but which are structurally sound can have plywood shapes attached to them which are then painted or stained, perhaps in imitation of flagstones or marble tiles (see pages 144– 145). Such a treatment can transform a rough old floor for very little outlay and will look far more sophisticated than cheap carpet.

Bare wood or concrete is not to everyone's taste; nor is either appropriate to every situation. Fortunately, it is a relatively easy matter to change their appearance completely by adding a new layer of floor covering. Flooring materials are diverse, and within each group there are variations and styles to suit every taste and requirement. All can be quick and easy to install. Hard tiles and stone provide hardwearing flooring suitable for any place that receives a lot of foot traffic or where water is present (see pages 158–161). Flexible flooring such as vinyl or linoleum, in sheet or tile form, offers softer, waterproof options suitable for kitchens and utility areas, and, if cushioned, is especially kind to the feet (see pages 166–169). Even new wood floors can be laid without much effort or skill (see pages 176–179). And for total underfoot luxury there is today a huge range of carpets and natural floor coverings—unsurpassed for variety and price range (see pages 182–185).

Varied as they are, all these exciting floor coverings usually require a sound, level floor upon which to rest in order to insure that they look good and wear well. Before laying any new flooring you should check the existing floor for any faults and repair or prepare as appropriate for the new flooring material (see pages 152–155).

With so many flooring options on offer, there is nothing to stop anyone from having beautiful floors, no matter what the size of their pocket. Free up your imagination and you will achieve surprisingly dramatic effects.

▲ Natural floor coverings have become very popular recently due to the wide choice available and their relatively low cost; they also look good in almost any setting. The strong texture of the rush matting here lends relief to the flat features of this room, and the neutral color works well with the vivid color scheme.

◄ Tiles are one of the most versatile flooring materials, being both almost indestructible and waterproof. The handmade ceramic tiles in this shower room give it a more countrified look, the hand-painted tiles on the floor and tiles cut into pyramids on the baseboards adding visual interest to an otherwise tiny and plain space.

Decorating existing floors

Although an existing floor may appear beyond
redemption, you do not necessarily have to cover it up
with a new and expensive flooring material. As long as
the floor is structurally sound, it can be either restored to
its former glory or brightened up with a whole range of
inspiring decorative improvements. If the floor is covered
with an old flooring material, it is worthwhile peeling this
back some way, and in at least two different places,
checking the condition of the floor underneath.

Floorboards may look worn and dirty, but it is surprising how good they can look when they have been sanded (see pages 134–135) and varnished. For renovation, though, they do need to be in reasonable condition; any damaged boards should be replaced and gaps filled (see pages 132–133). If the color of the boards is not quite suitable for the room's decoration, they can be painted or treated in any number of ways. A painted design can look breathtaking and will always be a talking point for visitors.

Cracks and pits in concrete floors can be repaired fairly easily (page 152–153) and then painted with a plain color or any type of pattern imaginable. Alternatively, a concrete floor can be covered with a pattern of plywood squares which can be cunningly painted to imitate flagstones or a marble-tiled floor (pages 144–145).

One of the few floor surfaces that cannot be easily changed with paint is tiles; the paint will chip off in the hard wear such a floor is likely to receive, especially in the places where tiles are usually laid, such as in kitchens and bathrooms. Unwanted floor tiles must either be physically removed or covered with another floor covering, such as might be used for concrete. Another surface that does not accept paint is vinyl, because the paint reacts with the plastic and peels off.

Having made the decision to renovate an existing floor rather than to cover it up, you must next decide how the finished floor is to look, for this will determine what preparation the floor will need.

Varnished floors

One of the most popular ways of improving an existing floor, and one that can be done quickly and easily, is to machine-sand old floorboards and varnish them for protection (see pages 134–135, 146–147). The result can look particularly attractive if the boards are hardwood, such as oak or ash. It is more likely, however, that an existing floor will be constructed of pine or fir boards. These cheap softwoods were used extensively for flooring up to the 1960s, after which even cheaper materials manufactured from reclaimed wood became standard.

▲ *Sanded old floorboards are an economical and practical choice of flooring, considering how many older homes were built with perfectly serviceable wooden floors. This floor has simply been sanded and given several coats of gloss varnish for a rich, deep shine; bright light pouring through the windows bounces off it.*

One difficulty with old pine floors is that the wood darkens over the years, tending to become a fiery ginger color. And as the protective varnish coat yellows with age, it exacerbates the hotness of this color, which tends to clash with many colors commonly used in decorating. Cool blues and greens are perhaps the only colors that sit comfortably with sanded pine floorboards. Thankfully, however, it is an easy matter to alter the color of pine boards to something more sympathetic to contemporary taste.

Stained floors

Stains (see pages 136–137) modify the color of floorboards without affecting the appearance of the wood's natural grain. Because they always darken the wood, use stains only in situations where this is not a problem. Dark-stained boards are a good backdrop for

▲ *Painted concrete is amazingly practical and hardwearing; this bathroom has been painted with an abstract design that not only looks good but also is waterproof, cheap to implement, and easily cleaned. The major investment to consider for a floor like this is your own time and patience—and creative skills.*

◄ *Paint is one of the most versatile and inexpensive ways of transforming an old floor. This concrete floor has been given a new lease on life with this colorful and bold pattern; an otherwise drab material has become the main focal point of the room. The design of the pattern may be varied to suit the size and function of the site.*

richly colored rugs and carpets, although it is important to select a neutral color rather than a strong one such as mahogany, which would clash with a rug that is predominantly red, for instance. Formal rooms—living rooms, dining rooms, and libraries—look more sophisticated and imposing with darker floors. As richer and darker colors tend to be used to decorate these rooms, which are often used at night with soft lighting, evoking a more intimate feel, darker floors are a more discreet choice. Of course, a darker floor can also work successfully in a very light room, either for dramatic effect or as a backdrop for darker rugs. And dark colors tend to appear less oppressive the lower down they are used in the room; a dark oak floor can work well with pale walls and furnishings.

Bleached floors

Wood darkens with age; sometimes this can turn the wood very dark, or an unattractive color, where a lighter color is more desirable for a more vital and contemporary look. Lightening the wood while retaining its "woody" appearance can be difficult,

since applying transparent color will always darken it. Chemical bleaching is one solution to the problem.

Light floors are ideal for informal settings, such as kitchens and eating areas, or in any situation that calls for a fresh and airy atmosphere. Most furnishings will work well with light-colored floors, as the floor fades against the predominant colors to provide a delicate backdrop. Darker pieces of furniture are accentuated against a light floor, useful for drawing attention to a particularly fine item.

Limed floors

Hardwood floors such as oak or ash can be lightened by using the traditional technique of liming (see pages 136–137). Also known as pickling, liming lightens a whole area generally, but specifically lightens the actual grain of the wood, resulting in a very graphic look. Liming is a labor-intensive business, but the results are stunning. Staining the wood black, or indeed any other color, beforehand creates an even more exciting look by combining light and dark tones in a natural, free-form way that virtually becomes the focal point of a room.

▲ Wood takes paint very well, and either transparent color, which allows the grain of the wood to show through, or opaque paint can be used. This wooden floor has been painted with a very loose checkerboard pattern embellished with naive motifs to complement the kilims on the bed—helping to create a tribal style.

▶ A wooden floor has been painted here with the same neutral, pale tones as the walls and ceiling. This approach tends to accentuate the colors of the features and furniture in the room, as the floor becomes part of an all-enveloping, unobtrusive backdrop, punctuated only by the strong lines of the beams and boards.

Painted floors

Floors that are in poor condition or that are made from very plain materials such as concrete or particleboard can be transformed with conventional paint which will cover any number of blemishes and provide an evenly colored surface. The floor can be painted any color imaginable, from white for an ultra-light look to black for the ultimate light-absorbing surface. Neutral grays and beiges are perfect for non-controversial and flattering backgrounds to almost anything.

If a solid color seems a little dull, patterns —anything from simple squares to a painted imitation of an intricate Persian carpet—can be incorporated into a floor. Floors can be stenciled with any type of design (see pages 140–141) or covered with checkerboard squares (see pages 142–143). Even natural-stone looks can be created to transform concrete or particleboard into a marble or flagstone floor (see pages 144–145).

Painting a floor is quick and cheap, and easily changed if it is not quite right or becomes boring. Matching the floor color to a fabric sample can be effective too, and nowadays, for a modest fee, some paint manufacturers offer a spectrophotometer service which exactly matches a paint color with a supplied fabric sample.

Sealing

Once a surface has been sanded or stained it needs to be protected against general wear and tear with one of several wood finishes, such as varnish, lacquer, or polyurethane (see pages 146–147); how heavy-duty the protection needs to be will depend more on the situation of the floor, than on any inherent quality of the raw material.

◀ *If they are still sound, pine floorboards, typically found in Victorian houses, are full of decorative potential. They have been transformed here by a subtle painted border that echoes the color of the stairs, while the rest of the floor has been left plain and simply sealed—a straightforward but effectively decorative treatment.*

Directory of decorative finishes

Wood floors can be finished in a number of ways. They can be left *au naturel* or they can be colored with stain or paint. In addition, dark wood can be lightened to counteract the effects of aging or to highlight the grain. And unless a wood floor has been finished with a floor paint or liming wax, it will have to be protected with varnish, lacquer, or polyurethane.

Opaque color

Opaque color is what most people think of as "ordinary paint," which is used for painting walls and ceilings. It is ideal for painting unattractive flooring particleboard and is also useful for poor floorboards that have been repaired with lots of wood filler. Two to three coats will create a pure, unbroken color that will completely disguise any flaws. Opaque paint is available in an almost infinite range of ready-mixed colors as well as in many finishes and types. It is perfect for very pale colors or if a plain look is desired, but darker tones are strong and dominating, which may look heavy if the color is not chosen with care. Most types of opaque paint can be used on floors, but they will usually need the additional protection of a clear sealer. Oil-based eggshell and gloss paints used in light-traffic areas such as bedrooms may not require additional protection—nor proper floor paint. But water-based paints are the most user-friendly; they have no harmful fumes, and brushes are easier to wash out.   **1**

Stained floors

Wood stains or dyes are concentrated colors designed to penetrate the wood and effect a dramatic color change without affecting the appearance of the wood's surface. They are normally associated with types of wood, the idea being that the application of the stain will transform an ordinary pine floor

into something rather more exotic. The reality is that the color of the wood influences the final color: the lighter the stain, the greater will be the effect of the original color of the wood. Stains are also available in quite bright colors, and colors of the same brand can be intermixed. Water-, spirit-, or oil-based stains are all so fast drying that it can be difficult to obtain an even finish. Stains always need protecting with a varnish or lacquer.

Varnish stain is an alternative product that stains and protects the wood in one application, although it is unlikely to be sufficiently tough for areas of heavy wear.   **2**

Transparent color

Transparent color is used to modify the color of an existing surface, retaining its texture and character rather than obliterating it. It has a much gentler quality than opaque paint, enabling the use of vivid or dark hues without the result looking heavy and solid. Complex and interesting colors can be built up in several coats for a rich and glowing look that is unobtainable with opaque paints. To make up transparent color, mix artist's color

into a transparent medium such as a water- or oil-based varnish to create almost any color imaginable. The color can be used over the whole floor area or to create a design, an easier task with transparent color than opaque color, as only one coat is required. If woody colors are used the effect will resemble inlay or marquetry. The only possible disadvantage of using transparent color is that the floor will always end up darker.   **3**

Semi-transparent color

Also known as semi-opaque color, this is useful for situations where the aim is to preserve the grain of a wood floor, yet also lighten the color of the floor. It is a mixture of transparent and opaque color, usually made up by mixing white paint with a clear varnish. The white pigment in the paint partially covers the existing wood but not to such a degree that the grain of the wood is lost. The pigment has a lightening effect, and color can be added to change the color of the wood slightly. The final result can look a little milky, depending on how much white is added, but the wood is still very visible.   **4**

Liming wax

Liming wax is another product available for lightening wood. It is a white-pigmented wax that is simply rubbed into the grain and buffed with a cloth. Less messy to use than liming paste, it cannot be varnished, as no varnish or paint product will adhere to wax. It is essential, then, to rewax the floor once the treatment wears off.

Clear floor sealers

Varnish and lacquer seal plain wood floors with a protective finish. Different sealers change the color and character of the wood to different degrees, and some also change color with age. Polyurethane, available in flat, satin, or gloss finishes, is the most commonly used sealer. Both traditional oil-based and acrylic sealers are suitable. They are widely available and easy to apply, whereas hardwearing lacquers usually require more care and entail more work. As a rule solvent-based products bring out the natural color of the wood better, giving it a richness and depth unmatched by water-based varieties; of the two, however, solvent-based sealers are the less user-friendly.

Bleached floors

Chemical bleaches are useful for lightening wood that has darkened with age, without affecting the appearance of the grain. The chemicals are applied to the bare wood and left to react and lighten the surface. When the wood reaches the desired color, the chemicals are neutralized and the floor can be varnished.

Another way to lighten the color of wood is to rub a little white paint into the grain, although this must be done sparingly to prevent the grain from being obliterated.

Limed floors

Liming (also called pickling) is a wood treatment that fills the grain of oak and ash, lightens the surface, and gives the texture a very graphic appearance. Oak is particularly improved by liming. Traditionally, real lime was used, but it is caustic and damages the skin; more benign alternatives are now available, which have the same effect. They are applied and rubbed off when dry, leaving the grain white. To introduce brighter colors, stain the wood before liming it. But always protect the lime finish with a sealer.

Repairing and preparing floorboards

▶ *These old floorboards are typical of what you are likely to find under an old carpet. Although the boards can sometimes look worryingly uneven and worn, modern sanding machines cut quickly through the wood to provide a smooth and level surface—ready for painting and sealing.*

Estimating quantities

There is nothing more irritating than running out of something halfway through a job and having to stop work to buy extra supplies. Before you start a renovation or decorating job, take time to assess accurately how much of which materials you will need. It is always worth buying a little extra to compensate for mistakes and wastage. Remember to check too on whether you have the correct tools and enough nails.

Replacement floorboards

Although floorboards are usually ¾ inch (18mm) thick, check the thickness as well as the width of your boards before ordering replacements and specify these dimensions as the planed dimensions to the dealer. When you are calculating the length of the boards, bear in mind that each replacement board must run from joist to joist; the nails holding the boards down indicate the position of the joists. If a large quantity of wood is needed, remember that new boards come in a specific length, and scraps may be too short for practical use. Over-order by about 10 percent to be safe.

Sandpaper for sanding machine

Estimating how much sandpaper you will need to sand a room is not critical, since the stores that rent sanding machinery will usually supply it on a sale-or-return basis. You will need more of the coarsest grade than of the finer grades; five sheets of grit 24, and two each of grit 40, grit 80 and grit 100 should be enough to sand 36 square yards (30sq m) of pine floorboards in reasonable condition.

Paint and stain

It is difficult to be precise about paint requirements, but you will require about ½ gallon (2 liters) for each base coat for a 36 square yard (30sq m) floor.

It is difficult to estimate how much wood stain would be needed to cover the same area, as much depends on the type of stain and the porosity of the wood. As a rough guide, however, ¼ gallon (1 liter) should cover about 12–24 square yards (10–20sq m).

Clear floor sealer

To seal a 36 square yard (30sq m) floor area you will need about ½ gallon (2 liters) of clear oil- or water-based sealer per coat. Floor lacquer does not spread quite as far: ¾ gallon (3 liters) will be required per coat.

Preparing a wood floor for painting or sealing

Any floor that is going to look good needs to have any defects corrected at an early stage. Damage must be repaired before a floor can be sanded or painted. Old floorboards can sometimes crack along their length, and any damaged boards will have to be replaced. Floorboards can also shrink with age, leaving unsightly gaps. The best and easiest way to deal with gaps between floorboards is to try to live with them; they are part of the charm of an old floor, and on a painted floor the eye tends to focus on the lines of a design rather than on the gaps. But this is not always practical, and you will probably have to fill them.

Before sealing, the floor will probably need sanding, a process that removes the very top of the wood to leave a fresh, clean, ready-to-finish surface. It is not always necessary to sand a floor before painting it, however. A good dirt-removing scrub may suffice, but where old wax or paint needs to be removed, mineral spirits, paint stripper, and lots of work will be required.

Lifting and replacing floorboards

Lifting square-edged boards is comparatively easy. Use a brick chisel to lever up the board at its end, taking care not to damage the adjacent board. Once it is clear of the surface, support it in this position with a piece of wood and lever the board up with the brick chisel where it is nailed to the joist. Do not try to lift the board up from the end, as it will almost certainly break in half. Repeat this procedure until the damaged area has been lifted; moving to the middle of the nearest joist, support the board and scribe a line across the board—using a try square to make sure the cut is square. Cut the board with a crosscut saw (see pages 154–155), taking care not to damage adjacent boards. Measure a new board and cut it to fit the removed section. Nail it in place with finishing nails.

Repairing wooden floors

1 Lift a damaged board by using a brick chisel as a lever, and then support it with a scrap of wood.

Replacing a tongued-and-grooved board is more difficult, as all the boards interlock. You will have to cut the tongue off the board to be lifted before levering it up. The easiest way to do this is to cut along the edge of the board using a circular saw (see pages 154–155); to avoid cutting through pipes and cables, set the blade to cut at a depth of ¾ inch (18mm). You can use a sharp chisel and mallet to start the cut and then continue with a handsaw, returning to the chisel when you reach a joist; but it is much more awkward. Either way, fill the hole with a square-edged board.

Filling gaps

Small gaps can be filled with papier-mâché. Larger gaps that reach from joist to joist should be disguised with a wooden fillet. Measure the gap, cut a corresponding width off the edge of a spare board, and glue it in position with carpenter's glue.

If the whole floor is full of gaps, it will probably be easier and more satisfactory to lift all the boards, push them tightly together, and re-secure them. Number the boards as you lift them so that you replace them in the same order. You will end up with a large gap: fill it with a new board or part of one.

Dealing with nail heads

Remove any old staples and carpet tacks and hammer down any proud nail heads. If you are machine-sanding the floor, you do not have to punch them below the surface, but to save on sanding pads it is sensible.

▲ It is worth noting that sanding and sealing stairs is a particularly time-consuming and awkward task. Sometimes it is not only easier to leave old floors in their natural state, it is also more authentic. This staircase is made from old pine that helps to evoke a sense of rustic simplicity that is wholly in keeping with the decoration of the rest of the house.

2 Working along the middle line of the next joist, cut out the damaged part of the board with a crosscut saw.

3 Fill a gap with a fillet cut from a spare board and glued in position. Tap it flush with a small piece of wood.

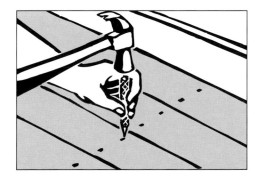

4 Hammer down all nail heads and tacks that are sticking up from the surface, punching them down if necessary.

Sanding and cleaning floorboards

▲ Old pine floorboards here have simply been sanded and sealed. The color of this type of wood can vary from quite pale to a dark orange: the lighter the shade of the floor, the easier it is to find rugs and other furnishings that work well with the plain unstained wood. The combination here results in an understated and clean look—with a touch of comfort.

Sanding a floor is usually done using two machines: a larger one to sand the main area of the floor and a smaller one, a disk sander, for finishing around the edges. The machines are very noisy and produce a lot of dust, so wear ear and eye protectors, and a dust mask.

Fix a sheet of coarse sandpaper around the drum of the larger machine; fit it as tightly as possible to reduce the likelihood of its tearing during use. Start the machine with the drum raised above the floor. Begin moving the machine forward and gently lower the drum so that it comes into contact with the floor before the full weight of the machine is lowered down onto the boards. Raise the drum off the floor gently at the end of a cut. This action will prevent the machine from grinding grooves into the

floor. Very uneven or badly cupped boards can be leveled more quickly if sanded diagonally first. Once the boards are level, sand along the boards to remove sanding marks from the diagonal cut; this is a bit like mowing the lawn, just going patiently back and forth. Change the sanding paper from time to time, as it will wear and its efficacy will diminish, and empty the dust bag when it is a third full in order to prevent the machine from throwing out dust.

When the floor is level fit the same grade of paper onto the disk sander. It is worth noting that this machine tugs away from you, which can be tiring for the back.

Once you have done the edges, use the next finest grade of paper on the large machine. It is usually only necessary to make

Using sanders

1 Tilt the drum off the floor before starting the machine and before each stroke or you will gouge the floorboards.

2 Start by running the machine in diagonal sweeps across the boards with as little overlap as possible.

3 Then run the machine along the length of the boards; the process may need to be repeated two or three times.

4 Use a disk sander along the baseboard, echoing the range of sandpapers used for the main area.

three or four passes before moving on to the next finest grade. Alternate with the disk sander using the finer grades of paper in the same way. Finish corners and other inaccessible areas with an orbital sander or by hand. On previously varnished floors, it may be easier to soften the old varnish in the corners with paint stripper before finishing by hand.

Vacuum up the dust, and also take some time to suck up dirt from the gaps between the boards; otherwise your paintbrush will pick up the debris during staining, painting, or sealing and spoil the finish.

Preparation for painting

Sanding a floor is necessary only for floors in poor condition, or if you intend to use a stain or clear finish on the wood. For painting, it is possible to scrub the floor clean with water and detergent and lots of elbow grease! The advantage of preparing a floor in this way is that more of the character of the old floor is retained; a few marks, gently bowed boards, and uneven grain add charm to the finished look which is more in keeping with older houses.

If a floor has previously been waxed, the wax must always be removed, even if the floor is to be sanded, because the machine may melt the wax and force it farther into the floor. Using steel wool soaked in mineral spirits, go over the floor two or three times to make sure no traces of wax remain; finish with a clean rag.

Old paint can be removed chemically or by means of heat. Take care not to scorch the wood if you are using heat to strip off the paint. Sand off any residue by hand.

If the floor is to be finished with opaque color, you can fill any holes and dents with a wood filler because this will not show once the floor is painted. Fill the holes, and then sand smooth with sandpaper.

▶ *An oak floor is naturally darker and is generally specially laid for decorative effect rather than simply being part of the basic structure of the building. If a pine floor is still too pale, after you have sanded it and filled any gaps, it can be stained a warmer, more sympathetic shade, which will make the room less stark.*

Bleaching, liming, and staining

Coloring wood grain

Bleaching, liming, and staining are decorative treatments that can be applied to wood to alter its coloring without losing the unique quality of the grain. Indeed, on the contrary, bleaching and liming emphasize the wood-grain, creating striking effects.

Bleaching

The bleached, grayish floors found in old Scandinavian houses create a subtle, sophisticated background which is perfect for virtually any type of decor and color. Although these floors have been scrubbed over the years to the point where the soft part of the wood is worn away, leaving the raised and harder central grain, a similar light and airy feel can be achieved on old boards without quite so much time and effort. It can be done either by bleaching the wood or simply by rubbing white paint into it.

There are a number of chemical wood bleaches available, based on either strong acids or alkalis. Always follow the manufacturer's directions when using them, and ventilate your working environment. Wear protective clothing, rubber gloves, and a mask. For further product information request a data sheet from the supplier.

Rubbing white paint into the wood—be it water- or oil-based—is a much simpler operation. Use a rag to rub the paint in, and wipe off any excess with a clean, dry cloth, finishing in the direction of the grain. Or you can make up a colorwash with a 1:3 ratio of white latex to water. Tint this wash with raw umber and ivory black acrylic color to make a warm gray, and then add raw sienna to warm the color further. Test the color on a board in a discreet corner, allowing it to dry before making any final judgments. If it is too opaque, add more water and adjust the colors to suit.

Both these treatments look best when finished with a flat sealer.

Liming

Limed (or pickled) oak has its origins in the mists of time when oak was a common building material. Coating the oak with lime, a powerful caustic material, prevented attack

▲ *Liming a hardwood, such as the ash of this staircase, will transform the natural warm tone of the wood to a cooler gray color and will particularly highlight the grain. Thorough preparation of the wood is essential to enable the liming medium to sit in the grain and achieve this distinctive and elegant look.*

by wood-boring bugs such as woodworm. It was soon noticed that this treatment created an attractive finish in its own right. Today, benign alternatives to lime are used.

The wood must be sanded back first to its bare state. Then dampen the wood with a cloth, and use a fine wire brush to "rake out" the grain. Do this by moving the brush gently over the surface in the direction of the grain. The idea is to remove the soft, porous woody material that naturally fills the grain without scratching the surface of the wood. Clean the debris off with a damp cloth. Then apply a proprietary liming paste, or a runny paste made from titanium dioxide (available from art shops) and water, and brush over the

whole surface, finishing off by brushing across the grain. Allow the paste to dry. Gently rub off the dried paste using medium-grade steel wool. It should come off the surface but stay in the grain. Gently clean off any powder on the surface with a barely damp sponge. Allow to dry, and then varnish.

Staining

Stains, available in an extensive range of wood shades and brighter colors, effectively alter the color of wood to tone in with any decorating scheme—without altering its woody appearance. Either use a commercial stain or create your own by adding artist's color to a clear sealer that has been diluted

Liming

1 Having dampened the wood, move a wire brush gently over the surface to "rake out" the grain.

2 Brush over the whole surface with the liming paste, working with and against the grain, and finally across it.

3 Rub the dried paste gently with steel wool to remove it from the surface, but leave it in the grain.

4 Take a slightly damp sponge and clean off any remaining powder from the surface before sealing.

▲ *Certain woods, such as pine, cannot be limed, because of the characteristics of their grain. Instead, a pine floor such as this can be given the pale quality of limed wood by a process of bleaching, which actually lightens the wood itself. This look particularly suits the airy atmosphere of a room like this, filled with light and furnished in soft tones.*

by one third with its appropriate thinner. If you want a very dramatic color change, though, it is probably easier to use a commercial stain. Colors can be mixed to modify the final shade to suit a particular room. Complex and interesting effects can be created by applying different colors in layers. For example, mahogany stain can sometimes look an artificial purple-red but applying a walnut color over the mahogany will turn it into a rich, warm glow; such a color could never be achieved by just mixing the two colors together. Try out the colors first on a scrap piece of wood to make sure that they are right for a particular room; and bear in mind that the same stain can look quite different on different types of wood.

The best way to apply stain is by wiping it on with a rag, working along one board at a time. This will leave a thin color, so you must build up to the final color by applying coat after coat until you are happy with the effect. Stains must be protected with a sealer, which will bring out the color of the wood for a deep, glowing effect. If you are using a varnish stain, treat it like varnish and apply it with a brush rather than a rag.

Staining

1 When applying stain to a floor with a rag, work along one board at a time, building up thin layers of color.

2 Apply varnish stain with a brush, but work back across your floor moving along one board at a time as before.

Painting floors

▶ This concrete floor has been painted a primrose yellow before being stenciled all over with a geometric repeat pattern. Although the design looks quite complex, it is in fact very simple. The advantage of this type of design is that it has no borders to accommodate, making the whole job much easier—from planning to finished floor.

flooring, the only really limiting factor on utilizing the full potential of floors with paint is that of time.

Because the choice of designs is so immense, another problem is knowing where to start, what to do. The key to a successful painted floor is to "keep it simple." A room with the minimum of plain, simple wooden furniture and neutral fabric colors could have a blaze of deep color and intricate pattern on the floor as a stunning focal point, but it would be rare. Most rooms have some mixed colors in the form of fabric and furnishings; others are positively cluttered due to small-space city living. For a floor that is to act as a quiet backdrop to the rest of the room, choose neutral tones; introduce one color, or perhaps at the most two, that match some other color in the room. Shades of the same color look very effective together.

A neutral floor can be transformed by the addition of a simple colored line acting as a border. For example, the floor could be a soft semi-transparent series of cool cream squares divided by mid-oak parquet blocks. The same colors could be used in the border, delineated by two Gustavian green lines; these would "lift" the whole design and give the border greater definition.

Painted floors offer the home decorator tremendous scope for choosing colors, either to match exactly or to complement other furnishings in the room. The range of commercial colors available is huge, and there is an increasing number of so-called historical paint ranges on the market which offer particularly sympathetic and easy-to-live-with hues. In addition, colors can be hand-mixed to offer limitless possibilities. Transparent colors enable you to use quite clear and bright hues that are colorful yet gentle on the eye; a vivid blue that is applied as a diluted wash, for instance, has all the quality of light reflected off water.

Any number of design options provide virtually limitless scope for further improving and manipulating a floor space with paint, allowing for the exercise of personal creative ability. Since paint is such a cheap option compared to all the other types of

▲ Instead of using an allover design, you can leave the floor basically plain and just add a border around the edge. Old boards have been left here in their natural state, and a simple border, which picks up the color of the door frame and floorcloth, has been added, not only offering decorative interest but also helping to unify several elements in the room.

Floor areas that have furniture and rugs on them can be broken up by being painted with simple squares, or perhaps given a faux-parquet look for greater visual interest. There are opportunities for simple trompe l'oeil: by setting out painted paving slabs as though they were stepped, for example, thus causing new guests to tread with the same care over the floor as children playing hopscotch. Furniture that is arranged to form a central focal area can be enlivened by the addition of a design that fits within that area—large stars or circles enclosing a geometric design, say, or an exotic and colorful carpet.

Large and empty hallways offer unclut-tered scope for a central design or a more elaborate repeat pattern. Awkward rooms with too many projecting corners can be tidied up by running a border in a straight line in front of these obstacles. Borders look better if they are of a generous width, and squares should not be too small and fussy unless you are trying to re-create the look of handpainted tiles.

Inspiration for designs can be found in books, but frequently the room itself provides its own clue: a simple border on a cast-iron fireplace can be adapted; an interesting crown molding design can be mirrored in the floor below; or a motif might be taken from a rug. Perhaps a design seen in a museum or on an expensive item in a store can be simplified for the floor. Or you could choose a theme such as the seasons as a starting point. Ideas can be related to a particular style: for example, folk art imagery would offer con-siderable scope. Some people have even taken their company logo and used that, or taken ideas related to a particular hobby such as seashell collecting.

If you want to try floor painting, there are many paint techniques from which to choose; those discussed here are a good start-ing point. Stenciling allows for easily applied repeat patterns or varied arrangements using cut-outs (see pages 140–141). Painting a floor as a checkerboard is dramatic, to say the least (see pages 142–143). And creating fake stone and marble effects on floors provides rustic or sophisticated flooring at a fraction of the cost of the real thing (see pages 144–145).

▲ This floor has been painted to imitate loosely the style of a rug that fills the whole floor space; smaller versions that sit in the center of a room work equally well. Various motifs have been stenciled on vivid bands of color so that the floor becomes an integral part of an exuberant and richly decorated room—with highly painted walls and furniture.

Stenciling

▲ *It is much quicker to execute a complex design with a stencil, and for one like this, it is easier to use a separate stencil for each color. Aerosol spray paint has been used for this design—quick, but the fumes are unpleasant. Remember, it is not possible to stencil an unbroken line: you will need bridging struts like those at the edge of the central panel here.*

Stencil designs

There is a comprehensive range of ready-to-use stencil designs on the market—an ever-expanding range—or you can cut your own. Most designs require little bridging struts to hold the stencil together; if desired, you can paint in the area covered by the struts after the design has been applied. You can mix and match elements from different designs; transfer them into a sketchbook first to see how they will look. It is often useful to do a scale drawing of a design at a comfortable size, then enlarge it on a photocopier to the desired size.

Registration

The purpose of registration is to insure that the stencil is always placed where it is meant to be and that the second color is applied in the correct position relative to the first. Draw guidelines in pencil on the floor first. For a border, mark a line the required distance from the baseboard around the room, and place the stencil against it as you proceed. An allover pattern will require a grid to keep the stencils correctly spaced.

Registration can be aided by penciling little marks on the floor corresponding to the exact location of the stencil for each color; make sure that all the stencils are the same size. Cutting a stencil so a repeat border has at least one and a half repeats will help with registration. Or trace the first design over the second stencil and match it up at the edges of the painted stencil. Viewing windows cut in the cardboard may help.

Cutting the stencil

Stencils need to be waterproof and robust. Oiled cardboard, the traditional material, has the advantage of economy but transferring a design onto it involves an extra stage using tracing paper. Acetate, a thin clear plastic, is more expensive than cardboard and is not really suitable for intricate designs as it tends to curl up. It is very flexible, though, which means that it bends willingly into awkward corners, unlike cardboard. Because acetate is transparent, it is easy to make sure that the second stencil has been placed exactly over the first part of a design. And transferring the

Essentially, a stencil is a template for effectively and quickly transferring a design, even a complex and elaborate one, onto a surface. For each additional color of the design you must either use a separate stencil or, if you are reusing one stencil for the whole design, mask off a different section each time. Almost any style can be created with stencils.

Borders can vary from delicate natural affairs, with leaves and flowers spilling out onto the main part of the floor, to severely delineated geometric patterns that powerfully define the whole shape of a room.

Stencils are also useful for decorating the main area of a floor. Loose flowing designs can almost blend into each other to provide an overall pattern that is not too overbearing. You can use stencils on top of checkerboard squares. They can even be used to create an intricate checkerboard design or one that incorporates curves and circles. Very small squares or a mosaic type of design can also be painted onto a floor in this way.

Specialist stores sell a variety of dedicated stencil paints, but you can easily use your own colors. Acrylic paints are probably the most convenient, as they are easy to apply and dry quickly, thereby minimizing the risk of smudging; oil colors, on the other hand, can take days to dry. If the colors are too concentrated, dilute them very slightly with the appropriate artist's medium, but be careful not to make it runny. Remember to mix enough color at the beginning to complete the job. Standard house decorating paint is too thick and sticky for stenciling.

Cutting and using a stencil

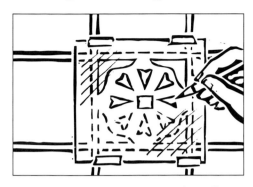

1 Tape your tracing paper in position over the motif you intend to use as a stencil, and carefully copy the outline.

2 Turn the tracing over and tape it to a piece of oiled cardboard. Scribble over the outline to transfer it.

3 With a sharp utility knife, cut out the design and registration marks, remembering to leave bridges.

4 Tape the stencil in position, using registration marks; apply the paint slowly, building up the required intensity.

5 When the paint is dry, check that the design is complete, then carefully peel back and lift off the stencil.

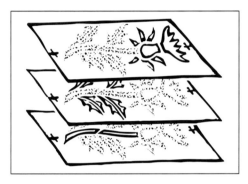

6 For a multicolored motif, cut separate stencils for each color, with dotted guidance lines on each.

7 When repositioning a repeat border design, place the stencil in part over the previously painted section.

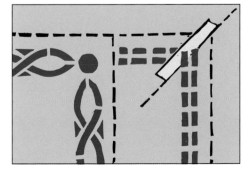

8 At corners, patterns can be either adapted, or mitered by masking off the approaching patterns at 45 degrees.

design onto the acetate is simplicity itself: just tape the acetate to the design and trace the outlines using a fine fiber-tip pen. A thicker, semi-transparent polyester film is now also more widely available: rigid and long-lasting, and facilitating easy registration, this is an attractive option to consider.

A sharp utility knife is the best tool for cutting out a stencil. Cut it out on either a sheet of glass or a cutting board, taking care not to tear the acetate. Cardboard is easier and more satisfying to cut; try to cut it with a beveled edge toward you. To cut fluently is best, so try to avoid cutting curves in a series of jerks. Stay in a comfortable position and move the stencil as you cut. Cut right into corners, and remember registration marks.

Applying the design

Stick the stencil down with masking tape at the corners so that it cannot move, or spray the back with spray adhesive, which enables the stencil to be peeled up and repositioned several times. Make sure that the adhesive is removed from the floor with an appropriate solvent before varnishing.

Use a minimal amount of paint. Dip the tip of the brush into the color, and work it into the brush on some newspaper or a plate. The brush should appear dry. Stipple the color over the stencil or brush with a swirling motion so that the color gradually builds up in intensity. Resist the temptation to apply the paint heavily, as it invariably seeps under the edge of the stencil. Once the first color is dry, remove the stencil, then apply a second and further stencils in the same way, using your registration marks as a guide.

Turning corners

Unless they are very linear, border designs do not go around corners, so you will need a separate stencil, such as a circle, for the corner. The main pattern finishes just short of the corner, and the new stencil is used to fill the space. If the border pattern is to be continuous, lay low-tack masking tape at 45 degrees across the path of the stencil. Work up to and just onto the tape. When the paint is dry, reposition the tape on the other side of the angle and stencil the other side.

Painting checkerboard squares

Simple squares help break up large spaces and provide the opportunity to introduce two colors in a floor, or two shades of the same color. And once a simple grid is established the basic alternating squares can be embellished: interspersed stripes could be painted in a variety of arrangements or a stencil design could be added to each square.

With painted squares it is, of course, possible to choose the exact size of the square to suit the scale of the space to be filled. It is easiest to choose a size of square that divides exactly into the floor's area. With a little calculation the squares can be sized to coincide exactly with three walls of any room. In the unlikely event of a perfectly square room, the squares would then fit the fourth wall as well. If you have a number of alcoves, it may be easier—and look better—to paint a central area as a checkerboard and leave a border, in one of the two colors, to stretch to the edges of the room.

Simple squares look more interesting if they are arranged on the diagonal, and this is easy to lay out. Begin by setting out the basic grid by following the procedure for setting out tiles (page 156–157). Mark the basic center point of the floor, adjusting it if necessary, and establish a diagonal line as described. You can work back from this basic central diagonal to mark out the whole room with all the squares on the diagonal. A chalk line is useful for establishing the grid but do go over it with pencil, as the chalk will rub off as you walk back and forth over the floor. A soft pencil (2B) gives darker, more definite lines which help to give the squares sharp edges—useful if your hand tends to wobble as you paint the edges of the squares.

Applying the paint

Painting the squares is simplicity itself. A 1-inch (2.5cm) brush is the most versatile tool unless the squares are very large, in which case use a 2-inch (5cm) brush. Thinned transparent—rather than opaque—color is the easiest to use. Start by the wall farthest from the door and work back toward it, painting every alternate square. Start by outlining your square—some people use the brush sideways to achieve a straight edge.

▲ This hallway has been painted with a simple checkerboard design. The squares have been painted in the same colors as the rest of the woodwork in the room to provide a simple and effective unified scheme, and the baseboard acts as a border for the floor. To reproduce this, paint the whole floor white and then paint the darker color on as the squares.

Checkerboard squares

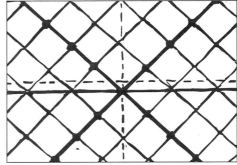

1 *Find and adjust the center point of your floor as necessary, and mark out all the squares on the diagonal.*

2 *Using one color, paint every alternate square. Outline the square, then fill in the corners with an artist's brush.*

3 *Block in the center of the outlined square. Then fill in the remaining squares with the second color.*

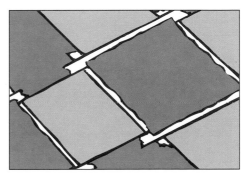

4 *Masking off the squares for a top color over a lighter base will result in neater lines between the squares.*

▲ *This kitchen has been painted in the style of classical tiling. The alternating squares are painted in a slightly darker shade to differentiate between them (in the absence of grout). The border has been painted in a bold green, along with most of the key squares—though occasionally one is red, for fun and additional interest.*

Then use an artist's brush to color in the apex of each corner. Finish by blocking in the center of each square. When all the first color is finished and dry, repeat the process for the alternating squares in the second color. If you are using opaque color, it will be necessary to prime and undercoat the floor first, then to paint the whole floor with the lighter of the two checkerboard colors, and finally to paint on the darker color as alternating squares. If the first coat of the second color does not cover satisfactorily in one coat, you will have to go over the paint again when it has dried. For sharper edges (or if your hand is very unsteady), mask out the outline of every alternate square with low-tack masking tape, and brush color over the edges.

Wood stain colors can be used on bare wood for a quick result. Score along the pencil lines with a utility knife. Paint wood stain as close to the line as you can. The stain will bleed into the wood, like ink spilled onto blotting paper, but will stop neatly on the scored line preventing further color spread. When the color is fully dry, protect the floor with a clear sealer.

Painting faux-stone effects

Real marble and stone floors are beyond the means of most people but can be imitated easily and cheaply using paint. Stone-effect techniques look very convincing, as they are rarely examined close to; being on such a large scale, the eye takes in an impression rather than focusing on detail. Use painted stone effects where the genuine material would be used. For example, a hallway can be given a palatial air by painting alternating black-and-white faux-marble squares or colored-marble panels over the whole floor. For floors in poor condition, or if you find the texture of cement or particleboard unforgiving, a covering layer of plywood will provide a more sympathetic surface.

The paint techniques used here rely on glazing liquid, a transparent medium that is designed to have color added to it to create texture for decorative effects such as rag

▲ *Real stone flagstones and plywood squares painted to resemble stone are effectively juxtaposed in this hallway. The original floorboards beyond the stone were in poor condition; now the gaps between the "stones" have been grouted for maximum effect, and the whole scheme pulls together very happily—with no ugly junctions.*

Creating a faux-marble effect

1 Lay plywood squares as flagstones. Leave gaps for grout between the squares to strengthen the illusion.

2 Apply the base coat and leave it to dry. Paint on the glaze, and use a rag to break up and mottle the surface.

3 With a fine artist's brush, draw the veins onto the wet glaze, keeping the movement in one overall direction.

4 Soften the veins with a soft brush in the direction of the veins, then backward, and then with the grain again.

rolling and stippling. Slow-drying, and normally diluted with mineral spirits before use, it is applied over an eggshell base paint. As it has a marked tendency to yellow, take care when using it for pale colors. The addition of a little white undercoat helps to minimize the yellowing. Glazing liquid has to be given a coat of varnish for protection.

Installing plywood "stones"

Plywood is generally sold as 4 x 8 feet (1.22 x 2.44m) sheets, but you can ask your lumberyard to saw these up for you into smaller, more appropriately sized squares— say, 2 x 2 feet (61 x 61cm)—to create a checkerboard or flagstone effect. Provided the floor is reasonably level, ¼-inch (6mm) plywood is thick enough.

Allow the boards to acclimatize for 48 hours in the room before laying them, and then lay the plywood following the guidelines for laying tiles (see pages 174–175). If you leave a gap between the squares, you can fill it with a flexible grout or colored filler reinforced with polyvinyl acetate adhesive (white glue) to add to the illusion. Fix the plywood onto concrete using panel adhesive or onto wood surfaces using small finishing nails. Prime and paint the plywood, and finish with two coats of white eggshell, an ideal base for subsequent paint finishes.

Faux marble

For a simple and discreet finish, marbleize the floor using one base color, perhaps with a darker shade for veining. For a darker and more dramatic looking marble, use a dark base color and light veining. For alternating checkerboard squares or inlaid panels choose two contrasting base colors, either very dark and light squares or a neutral background color combined with a brighter, more vivid hue.

Find some examples of real marble and copy the colors and the style. Due to the large areas involved, marbleizing on floors is best kept simple; you are trying to create an impression of the real material rather than a slavish copy. The secret is to get the veining right; once you develop the feel for veining you are almost there.

Oil-based paints make marbleizing easier. Start by mixing up the base coat as a glaze with 50 percent glazing liquid and 50 percent mineral spirits to the consistency of single cream. For pale gray marble add some white artist's oil paint or undercoat, and mix in thoroughly. Mix in a little ivory black; this is a very powerful color, so add only a little at a time. If the color seems like a thin black rather than a creamy gray, add more white until the balance is right. Check the color on the floor; samples can easily be cleaned off with a little mineral spirits.

Paint the base color over an area about 2 feet (60cm) square or, ideally, a whole "paving stone" at a time. Break up the glazed surface with a rag so that it becomes mottled. Use artist's oil paints as veining color, squeezed onto a plate and diluted with a little mineral spirits to provide a more workable consistency. A very fine artist's brush is ideal for veining. Draw the veins onto the wet glaze; marble has an overall direction and the veins are angular rather than rounded. Veins never stop abruptly; they either gradually fade into the rock or join other veins. Do not overdo the veining. The last thing you want is something that looks like a road map. Dab off any excess paint from the veins with a rag. So that they become blurry at the edges, soften and blend the veins using a hog's-hair softener, a very fine-bristled brush available from home decorating stores, or a less expensive decorator's dusting brush. Soften in the direction of the veins first, then lightly against the veins to spread them a little. Finish off by softening with the veins. Allow the paint to dry thoroughly before applying varnish.

Faux limestone

A warm, creamy limestone is the essence of restrained good taste yet can be imitated with paint for a fraction of the cost of the real thing. A floor painted as stone is an imposing yet quiet backdrop that harmonizes well with almost any decorating scheme.

Mix up the base coat as a glaze with 50 percent glazing liquid and 50 percent mineral spirits to the consistency of single cream, using raw sienna and plenty of white undercoat as the coloring, and then add a little raw umber to "dirty" the color. The objective is to mix a pale yet warm cream. Paint the base color over an area about 2 feet (60cm) square or, ideally, a whole "paving stone" at a time. Stipple the surface to break the color up into millions of tiny flecks. Use a stippling brush or improvise with a 2-inch (5cm) brush. Allow the paint to dry.

The second application consists of a light and a dark version of the same color, to give the "stone" the appearance of age and wear. Use a well-thinned glazing liquid or a diluted clear oil-based sealer. Mix some raw umber and a little black to create a dirty color that takes the edge off the cream. Make up two shades of the same color, one dark and one pale, for a variable effect. Paint random patches of the two colors together, and stipple as you did for the first color. Use a greater proportion of the darker color where the floor is subjected to greater wear, near a door, for example, for authenticity.

Creating a faux-stone effect

1 Paint on the glaze, and then stipple the surface to break up the color into flecks. Leave this coat to dry.

2 Brush on lighter and darker versions of the same color in random patches, and then stipple them as before.

Laying new flooring

Because flooring materials are so varied, laying a new
floor may involve anything from a few hours of easy work
—involving a few basic tools and common sense—to a
major upheaval requiring specialized knowledge and
equipment, and a serious commitment in terms of time
and energy. Prior to embarking on a project yourself, take
time to examine what is really the appropriate solution,
and ponder the practical and aesthetic ramifications of
your choice before making a final decision.

The first step is to establish what the existing floor is constructed of. Peel back coverings such as carpet or vinyl to see what is underneath. It is worth checking in more than one place, as it is not unknown to have a cement floor and a suspended wood floor in the same room. Look carefully, because things are not always as they seem. Plain floorboards, for instance, although usually indicative of a suspended wood floor, could also be wood-strip flooring laid over concrete or particleboard.

Next, you have to establish what type of flooring can be laid over the existing floor. Most materials can be laid over all types of floor, but in some cases adequately preparing the subfloor can involve additional costs. Most types of flooring can be laid quickly and easily, although some jobs are more complicated than others. It is generally more disruptive, for instance, to lay hard floors (see pages 158–165), than flexible (see pages 166–175) or wood (see pages 176–181) floors. Be prepared for some mess and inconvenience.

Once you know what sort of flooring you are dealing with, you can then decide what type of floor covering you prefer and whether it is going to be practical for the situation. Jute flooring looks sophisticated in the right setting, for instance, but is not suitable for a bathroom where water is splashed around. Disappointment will set in quickly when the jute starts to turn black and rot, and deep frustration will soon follow when it is discovered that there is no satisfactory way of cleaning it.

The next stage is to assess the affordability of your preferred material. Measure the room and estimate how much is needed of the product in question (see pages 154–155).

Shop around to find out all the costs involved. Some materials span a wide price range. For example, carpet can be one of the cheapest or one of the most expensive floor coverings—depending upon quality and type. Some flooring materials are so expensive that it may be worth paying a little extra to have it laid by a professional to make sure that the end result justifies the overall cost. Other materials are cheap to buy but expensive to have laid, and, provided you feel sufficiently confident and have the spare time, these are well worth laying yourself. There is also the satisfaction to be derived from working through for oneself from the first glimmer of an idea to the completion.

Fitting might be included in the price, although "free installation" is rarely what it claims to be. See what the ancillary costs are, such as underlay and carpet-tack strips or special tile adhesive needed for a problem floor. The savings made by installing the floor yourself may enable you to buy a more expensive material. Check also to see if costly tools are needed to do the job and whether these can be rented (see pages 154–155). Read the relevant sections in this chapter to decide whether you feel sufficiently confident to install the flooring yourself.

Having established which is the most suitable floor covering, check on availability and delivery times. Most products can be delivered in a week but sometimes a special order is required and delivery can take something like six weeks. Now is the time to obtain the fixing materials and any special tools needed for the job. Either buy them or, for an expensive tool, reserve one for rental.

A few days before the due delivery date, remove the old floor covering and repair or prepare the existing subfloor. Concrete, particleboard, or floorboards may need some attention—dips and bumps to be leveled or cracks to be filled—before new flooring can safely be laid on them (see pages 152–153).

It may be necessary to acclimatize the new material to its new environment for a day or two before laying it, in order to insure a successful job (see pages 144–145, 152–153). Before tiling a floor you will need to mark out guidelines against

◀ *Laying wood-strip flooring is one of the easiest D.I.Y. flooring tasks. It is also one of the most versatile, in that it can be laid over most types of subfloor. The finished floor provides a very practical and easy-to-clean surface, which is particularly important in a dining room like this, where it is likely that food and drink will be spilled.*

▲ *Laying flagstones is the most difficult and disruptive flooring project it is possible to undertake, but the floor will last forever once it is finished. These polished limestone flags might seem like an unusual choice for a bedroom, but in fact work well with the clean lines and warm tones of the built-in furniture.*

which to work. Although the principles are the same for any type of tile, the starting points are adjusted according to whether the room is square, rectangular, or irregular (see pages 156–157).

Concrete floors

Concrete might seem an ugly and unforgiving material, but, in fact, it provides a perfect base for all types of floor covering, as long as it is smooth and level. Carpets (see pages 186–187) and wood flooring (see pages 180–181) are easily laid over concrete. It is also an ideal base for tiles (see pages 162–165) and is really the only material with the structural integrity required for laying heavy materials like flagstones and brick (see pages 160–161), which makes it highly versatile.

Particleboard and plywood floors

These floors are constructed in the same way as traditional suspended wood floors except that boards of particleboard or plywood are used, instead of floorboards, to cover the joists. In recent years, they have been commonly installed in housing because of the increasing cost of traditional materials and because man-made boards are easy to lay and very stable. They are also found in older houses where rotten boards have been replaced. Both particleboard and plywood are perfect as subfloor surfaces for most types of floor covering because they are very smooth and level. Take care when laying very heavy materials over any type of suspended wood floor, however, as the joists might need to be reinforced to take the extra weight.

▲ Concrete floors are commonly found in newer houses and apartment blocks and can be covered with most flooring materials. Floors as smooth and level as the one illustrated here can be easily painted—a stylish and economical finish for what is often considered an ugly and difficult raw material.

▶ Newer and renovated properties often have particleboard and plywood laid over joists, and this can either make a good base for other materials or be painted easily. At the bottom of the stairs here, plywood has been laid as large squares and painted black, so that it is almost indistinguishable from polished slate.

▲ *Provided that the boards are waterproofed first, wooden decking can be used to define the space occupied by a freestanding bathtub, and is both a practical and a smart design solution. Thin tiles have been carefully laid over well-prepared old floorboards on the rest of the floor, creating an interesting variety of texture in a monochrome room.*

Suspended wood floors

Although pine floorboards are one of the most attractive types of flooring in their own right, they need greater preparation than some other materials before certain types of floor covering can be laid over them. Wood-strip flooring (see pages 180–181) can be laid directly over floorboards if they are reasonably level. Before laying carpet (see pages 186–187) or flexible floor coverings (see pages 166–169), however, a hardboard base needs to be installed (see pages 152–153).

Tiles can be laid directly onto boards as long as they are level and reasonably rigid and you use a flexible adhesive; otherwise you can lay ½-inch (12mm) plywood sheets over the floorboards to provide the necessary rigidity. Special underlays and flexible tile adhesives that eliminate the need for laying plywood are now available; consult your tile retailer. Many stones and slates are available in a thinner tile format which can be laid over wood floors, but thick traditional flagstones should always be laid on a solid base.

Preparing surfaces

Before you lay any new floor covering, you will need to check that the floor is in good enough condition to receive it. Generally, most flooring requires a smooth, even surface that is free from cracks, dips, and bumps. Some may require a new intermediate surface to be installed over the existing sub-floor. It is worth estimating for this before you start; not only could this hidden cost be an unpleasant shock if revealed as a necessity halfway through the job, but it could actually have an effect on the type of floor covering you can afford to choose.

Concrete floors

Laying any type of flooring on concrete requires a smooth and level surface—with the possible exception of materials that are bedded on mortar or thick-bed adhesives. Concrete floors are normally finished with a sand-and-cement screed laid over the coarse cement base, and they should incorporate a vapor barrier.

Check the level of any dampness present using a moisture meter. If the levels are higher than those specified by the manufacturer for the type of floor covering to be laid, a vapor barrier must be added before you begin work. This can take the form of either a polyethelene sheet or a bitumen waterproofer which would be brushed onto the concrete base.

Special precautions may have to be taken if the floor incorporates underfloor central heating. Tile adhesives may require the use of special additives; in the case of a wood floor allow plenty of room for expansion.

Filling cracks
Cracks in concrete floors are a common problem and are easily repaired with mortar. First rake out and widen the cracks with a brick chisel and hammer, then dampen the area to be repaired with water.

Mix sand and cement in a 3:1 ratio with water to form a workable mixture and press the mortar into the cracks using a trowel. Smooth the surface level, and allow the repair a few days to dry before you start to lay the new floor covering.

▲ This concrete floor has been sanded and polished to provide a tough and practical surface that seems perfectly appropriate in this modern interior. Obviously, a floor in as good a condition as this would need no further preparation were it to be hidden under some sort of covering—whether for practical or aesthetic reasons.

Preparing concrete floors

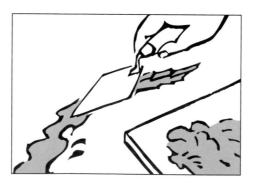

1 Using a trowel, fill the dampened crack with mortar. Smooth level, and leave for a few days to dry thoroughly.

2 Self-leveling compound is applied as a runny paste to a dampened floor. Leave it to find its own level and dry.

Sealing the surface

Concrete floors that are very dusty with the top layer flaking off as a powder should be treated with a concrete sealer or with a general-purpose polyvinyl acetate builder's sealer, diluted with water according to the manufacturer's directions.

Leveling with compound

Rectify unevenness in concrete floors caused by lots of cracks and shallow depressions less than ⅛ inch (3mm) deep with a self-leveling compound, obtainable from hardware stores. Dampen the floor with water before starting work. Mix the compound with water to form a runny paste. Starting at the corner farthest from the door, trowel the mixture onto the floor to a depth of ⅛ inch (3mm) using a float. Leave the compound to find its own level and harden off; the floor covering can be laid the following day.

Wood floors

Replacing particleboard and plywood boards

There is very little that can go wrong with particleboard and plywood floors: damp or leaks, however, can cause particleboard to disintegrate and plywood to swell. If you find that damage has occurred, simply lever up the damaged board and replace it with a new piece cut to the same size as the original.

If you are aware that noise is likely to be a problem in the room below you, lay a sound-deadening material between the existing surface and the new one when you are laying wood-strip or flexible flooring.

Pine floorboards

Boards that have become very cupped with age or that have large gaps between them will ruin virtually all types of new floor covering. Carpets and vinyl will wear on the ridges, ceramic tiles will crack, and wood-strip floors will creak and lurch continually unless action is taken. Individual damaged boards can be replaced (see pages 132–133), but an uneven floor should be entirely covered with a layer of hardboard or, if it is in really poor condition, thin plywood, which is more rigid.

Laying hardboard and plywood boards

The same technique can be employed for both hardboard and plywood although there are slight differences in the way they are fixed. Both types of board are normally sold as 4 x 8 feet (1.22 x 2.44m) sheets but are easier to handle and to lay if they are cut smaller. Ask your dealer to cut them in half so that you end up with 4-foot (1.22m) squares. Allow the boards to acclimatize for 48 hours in the designated room before laying them. Hardboard can be dampened with water to allow it to settle more evenly.

In a regularly shaped room, start laying the sheets against the longest, straightest wall and work toward the opposite wall. In an irregularly shaped room, begin in the center and work outward; find the center as you would before tiling a floor (see pages 156–157).

Lay the boards so that the middle of each new sheet adjoins the bottom of the join between the two previously laid sheets, rather like a brick wall. Use small nails, no more than ¾ inch (18mm) long, at 6-inch (15cm) intervals, to secure plywood boards. If laying ½-inch (12mm) plywood for hard tiles, screw the boards down at 12-inch (30cm) intervals.

Hardboard should be laid with the rough side facing upward. Nail it to the floorboards from the center outward in a radial pattern so it does not buckle. Space the nails at 6-inch (15cm) intervals but 4 inches (10cm) apart at the edges of the sheets. This is less critical for plywood, which is much more rigid. Determine where to cut the edging boards by placing them (upside down and with one edge against the baseboard) over the last of the laid boards. Using a pencil, mark where the edges of the bottom boards touch the top ones. Cut the boards at these points, using a saw, and secure them in position the right way up. This technique works only if the edge of the board against the baseboard is cut square. If you are using a scrap as an edging piece, make sure that the uncut, square end of the scrap is against the baseboard. Use a profile gauge (see pages 154–155) to transfer the profile of an architrave onto the board so that it can be cut to fit, and stop the boards against the doorstop.

Laying hardboard

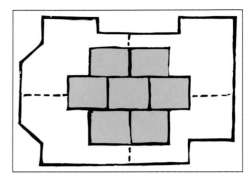

1 In an irregularly shaped room, establish your center point and work outward, laying the boards like bricks.

2 Secure the boards with short nails, working in a radial pattern, and with more nails going in at the edges.

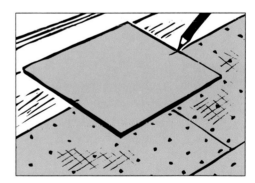

3 Simply turn a board upside down and mark an overlap in order to cut board to fit exactly at the room's edge.

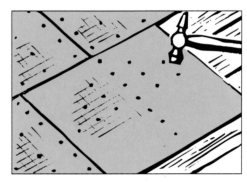

4 Use a profile gauge to produce an accurate pattern to cut when it comes to door frames and the like.

Estimating and equipment

▲ *It is wise not to over-order expensive materials like the ash flooring here, so draw a scale plan of the room, taking particular care to be accurate if this room is an irregular shape with obstructions such as kitchen cabinets—and curved-edge stairs—to work into the calculation. It is equally frustrating to underestimate, which can lead to poor color matches.*

Ordering the right amount of materials is vital to make sure that there is enough to finish the job neatly. This is particularly important with flexible sheet materials, in order to avoid having to make unnecessary ugly seams and because of the risk of color variations between different batches of material. While over-ordering is simply a waste of money, it is nonetheless essential to order slightly more than you calculate you will need, to compensate for the inevitable wastage that arises when you are working around obstacles, and for mistakes and breakages. It is unlikely, for example, that you will be able to find a place for all the half-tiles left over when you tile the border of a room. Obviously, it is crucial to estimate as accurately as possible to minimize wastage, and to estimate accurately you must measure accurately. Take your time; double-check measurements and sums; and you will probably save both time and money.

Measuring up

It is always worth taking an accurate plan of your room to your retailer, who will know the best way to save material—particularly in awkwardly shaped rooms. However, rooms with square or rectangular walls without any interruptions along them are easy to measure. And to calculate the area, simply establish the width and depth of the room and multiply one figure by the other; this is the number of square yards (meters) to be covered. Most rooms have various obstacles, however: built-in closets, chimney breasts, and alcoves. In order to include these in your estimate, first measure the width and depth of the unobstructed rectangle forming the room's central part, and calculate that area. Then measure the width and depth of every recess and add these together to calculate the total area occupied by these recesses. Finally, add this figure to the first figure to calculate the actual

Tools and equipment

General tools

In addition to everyday tools, some more specialized implements will be required for preparing surfaces and laying floor coverings. The more general of these are described below, but task-specific tools will be explained in the relevant sections of this chapter.

- **Straightedge:** length of metal used to make sure that edges or lines are straight. Also useful for checking that tiles are laid level and for joining up points with a straight line.
- **Chalkline:** length of string that pulls out from a unit rather like a retractable tape measure except that it coats the line with a colored chalk. Used for marking out straight lines on a large scale. The string is stretched taut between two points and plucked against the surface leaving a line of chalk.
- **4-pound hammer:** heavy hammer used when brute force is needed. An ideal partner for the brick chisel.
- **Brick chisel:** large, blunt, flat-bladed metal chisel useful for tasks as diverse as levering up floorboards, breaking heavy tiles and stone in two, and laying carpet.
- **Try square:** used to mark a line at 90 degrees to an edge and for marking the line of a right-angled corner.
- **Trimming knife:** bulky handle holding sharp blade that can be changed when it becomes blunt. Used for cutting flexible materials, such as cork or vinyl, and carpet.
- **Utility knife:** smaller and sharper than a trimming knife. Particularly useful for cutting stencils.
- **Trowel:** used for repairs to concrete floors: for mixing small quantities of cement, filling cracks, and final smoothing of the repair.
- **Float:** smoothing tool used for screeding. Use a metal plasterer's float for spreading self-leveling compound.
- **Profile gauge:** a series of metal pins that pass through a holder. The gauge is pressed against any intricate areas and the pins are displaced in the shape of the profile. Useful for measuring the profile of architraves when cutting flexible flooring materials.

area of floor space to be covered—in square yards (meters). In a trapezoid shaped-room, there is really no alternative but to draw a plan to scale on graph paper.

Flexible flooring

For flexible sheet materials you need to order enough material to fit between the two widest dimensions of the room, as the excess is simply trimmed away from any obstructions to avoid making unnecessary seams. Large areas of trimmed material can often be used elsewhere, but try to tuck seams away in an unobtrusive corner. Seams should run at 90 degrees to a window, as they are less visible in that position. Sheet materials are available in various widths, so make sure that the sum of the widths is the same as or greater than the width of the room. The total length of material required is the number of widths required, allowing for pattern-matching and wastage, multiplied by the length of the room.

Tiles

Calculate how many of your tiles are required per square yard (meter) and multiply that by the number of square yards (meters) in the room. Remember that you will have to cut tiles to fit at the edges. Estimate the number of extra tiles you will need by allowing enough to tile one additional strip along half the walls, and then add a few more in case of breakages. With larger or more expensive tiles it may be worth calculating if partial tiles can be used. Your final figure will have to be rounded up—tiles are supplied in boxes —so you will probably have tiles left over.

Wood-strip flooring

Calculate how many strips of the desired planking are needed to fit the width of the room. Multiply the number of strips by the length of the room to calculate the total length required. Allow a little extra for cutting, as there are bound to be a few short lengths that will be unusable. Pre-finished flooring is sold by the box, so your final figure will have to be rounded up to the nearest number of complete boxes.

▲ *When calculating how many tiles to order, allow for the fact that you will probably be cutting a lot of tiles at the walls and along any diagonal edges. Generally, some of the cut-away portions can be used elsewhere, which minimizes wastage—at the right-hand end of the diagonal strip here, for example—but this should not be relied upon.*

Tools and equipment

For wood floors

- **Crosscut saw:** long saw for general-purpose wood-cutting across the grain, normally used for cutting floorboards to length.
- **Ripsaw:** long saw with large, widely spaced teeth for cutting wood along the grain, most often necessary when the last board in a floor is too wide.
- **Backsaw:** small handsaw with a reinforced back, to prevent the blade from flexing, and very fine teeth for intricate work.
- **Floor saw:** saw with a curved cutting edge to enable a floorboard to be cut without damaging the boards on either side.
- **Coping saw:** thin blade supported by a large metal frame for cutting curves in wood, normally used if a floorboard needs shaping to fit around an obstacle.
- **Chisel:** tool with a very sharp blade, available in various widths. Useful for cutting where a saw cannot be used. Used in conjunction with a wooden mallet or a hammer.
- **Circular saw:** circular-bladed power saw, useful for cutting wood in all directions.
- **Electric jigsaw:** a small, powered blade supported at one end. Primarily designed for cutting curves in wood, metal, and plastic.

Hard flooring

As their survival in the oldest buildings testifies, the most enduring and practical of flooring materials are natural stone and tiles. Stone, marble, and slate were once the only hardwearing flooring materials available, and could be found on the ground floors of cottages and cowsheds alike, wood being reserved for the gentler life on the upper levels once these were introduced. Tiles have been used since ancient times for the same reasons, but additionally they offer greater decorative possibilities.

▲ *As their shape and texture vividly illustrate, these ancient flagstones have almost certainly been in place for generations. Expensive to lay new today, flagstone is the sort of material we associate with unspoilt country cottages, although it would once have been commonplace, in a wider range of houses.*

Indeed, our knowledge of the Roman Empire is derived in part from the patterns and scenes depicted on the mosaic floors of the period, often the only remains of a building and its contents.

Today we have an ever-increasing choice of hard-flooring materials with which to decorate our homes (see pages 160–161). Exotic multicolored slates and marbles are brought from all over the world, as are dozens of styles of beautiful and vividly colored ceramic tiles. Even simple terra-cotta, always a popular choice, is now available in many different shades, shapes, and sizes (see pages 160–161); the handmade tiles in subtly varying colors are the best.

The way in which a seemingly straight-forward material is manufactured or prepared makes an enormous difference to the atmosphere that it helps to create. The textured surface of cleft slate flagstones, for instance, is naturally at home in a simple country room that has been decorated in a traditional style; however the same material can equally be the perfect partner to, say, chrome and modern fittings if used in a contemporary bathroom, but first cut into regular squares and honed smooth.

Fairly expensive and very durable, tiles and stone floors are a long-term investment, and care should be given to the choices to be made. Hard floors are the preferred choice of those who live in warmer climates for practical reasons, as indoors they create a cool refuge from the hot sun, both physically and psychologically. In many countries nearly all interior floors are tiled, with rugs being used to provide decorative relief and to help engender a sense of warmth and luxury.

For those who inhabit the cooler regions of the northern hemisphere, warmth is at a premium. In the kitchen and bathroom, however, where tough practicality is just as important, tiles and stone are still ideal. They are both waterproof and virtually indestruc-tible, although dropping china or glass onto tiles or stone will result in a breakage.

Hallways, too, are a perfect environment for hard materials; stone's austere luxury will cause visitors to pause just briefly enough to reflect upon the initial impression it creates. In rooms that combine function with relaxation, such as a kitchen with a dining or seating area, two different mat-erials can be used to demarcate the spaces. Tiles can be used for the kitchen floor, for instance, and wood for the living area. The wood is gentle and welcoming, the tiles provide practicality, and the two materials work well together.

Tone and color are also important criteria. Brightly colored tiles can be used as a dominant feature, or neutral ones as a back-drop for brighter walls, fabrics, or rugs: a cool slate floor simply decorated with a Persian rug in warm reds and blues is an especially rich combination.

Tiles are the perfect material for incor-porating borders. Most manufacturers produce a range of complementary border tiles, but it is possible to use any tiles as such, provid-ing they fit together. For those with patience, mosaic offers interesting design potential, although it is probably wiser to use it in smaller rooms, and to stick to designs that do not use too many colors. Always use tiles made especially for floors, such as terra-cotta floor tiles; they are thicker than wall tiles which, being thin, might break.

◀ *Hard flooring is an ever-popular choice for transitional areas like hallways, because it is so practical. Slate tiles here have been laid on the diagonal, which always lends a certain elegance; and the alternation of light and dark tiles—despite being of the same material—is charmingly decorative in its subtlety.*

▲ *Brightly colored and patterned encaustic tiles provide a visual splash at the right-hand end of the bathroom and contrast strongly with the plain tiles used under the bathtub and to the left. Interestingly, the pattern painted on the bottom half of the door has been copied from one of the tiles in the patchwork arrangement on the floor.*

Directory of hard floorings

Out of all the exciting hard-flooring materials on offer, the most commonly used in the modern home are tiles. Due to a range of manufacturing processes, floor tiles offer a wide choice of practical hardwearing products, suitable for most domestic situations. Ranging from natural earthy shades to bright and vibrant colors, they can also be chosen to complement any decor. Terra-cotta, the simplest and one of the oldest types, remains a time-honored favorite for kitchens. Quarry tiles, which are at once economical and hardwearing, are also enduringly popular. Ceramic floor tiles, available in many colors and styles, are perhaps the most versatile. And mosaic, used for centuries to decorate floors, is the perfect material for re-creating a design, although simple, colored borders set against a plain background are the easiest designs with which to work.

In addition, floor bricks can be used to create regular patterns, and stone, whether it be natural or reconstructed, can provide just the right touch for some interiors. Slate, for instance, is a very practical material and comparatively easy to lay because it is so thin; some sheets are hardly thicker than a ceramic tile. Finally, while metal flooring may not be a viable option for most people, it is the ideal material if the ultimate in industrial chic is required.

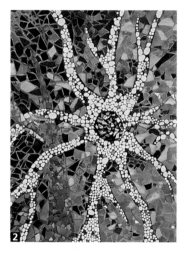

Terra-cotta tiles

Unglazed and softer than other types of tile, terra-cotta is made from extruded or hand-formed clay. It is available in a number of shapes and sizes, from small hexagons to large squares. The colors range from dusky ochers to oranges through to reds. Part of the charm of terra-cotta is precisely this color variation, within each tile and from tile to tile, as well as the textural variations of the surface. These porous tiles must be finished with linseed oil and waxed for protection.

Quarry tiles

Quarry tiles are made from extruded or hand-formed clay which is fired at higher temperatures than terra-cotta to vitrify it, a process that gives the tiles their durability and makes them very hardwearing and waterproof. The color range is a little limited; buffs, reds, and browns are the dominant tones, although white and black tiles have been produced. The tiles usually have a dull satin finish. Variously sized square or rectangular quarry tiles are available—and some "key squares" too (see pages 164–165). **1**

Ceramic tiles

Ceramic floor tiles are made from a dust-pressed clay that is fired at high temperatures. Fully vitrified ceramic tiles are the most waterproof of all tiles, making them suitable for the wettest areas—such as bathrooms. Ceramic floor tiles are not glazed; glazed tiles are normally too slippery, unless the glaze has a roughened surface. They may have decorative patterns or little studs on the surface for textural variation and slip resistance. Oxides, added during the manufacturing process, give these tiles the widest range of colors of any unglazed tile—including plain white. Ceramic tiles are thinner than quarry or terra-cotta tiles, and their uniform thickness enables trouble-free installation. They can, however, be polished for a more glamorous look.

Mosaic tiles

Mosaic tiles are tiny, and are cut from glass, colored ceramic, terra-cotta, stone, or marble and fixed to a backing sheet for speedy installation. Their appearance varies according to both the material and whether it has been machine- or hand-cut. **2**

Encaustic tiles

Encaustic tiles are either plain-colored or have a decorative pattern applied to their surface which has a soft, matte quality with colors that blend into each other. A design is painted onto a mold using natural oxides, and then a plain tile is pressed into the design to transfer the design onto the tile's surface. **4**

Brick

The bricks that are used for decorative floors are much the same as terra-cotta tiles. They are, however, thicker, and they do require a solid base. Because of their small, regular size, bricks are perfect for creating patterns: herringbone is traditional but something more individual works equally well.

Limestone

A sedimentary rock formed from coral and shell deposits at the bottom of warm seas, limestone has a considerably varied character that ranges from

4

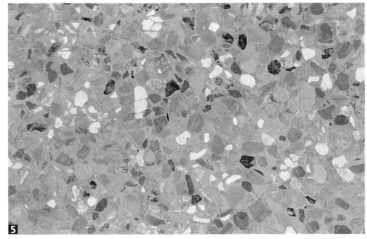

5

Marble

Metamorphosed limestone, marble is characterized by the colored mineral veins that run through it. It is extremely diverse: for example, Carrara marble is a soft gray interspersed with a blurry, indistinct black veining that is quietly elegant, whereas Brochella marbles are vivid reds and blacks, with colorful swirling veins, perfect for proclaiming wealth and power.

Terrazzo

This is a material manufactured from marble chips bound together with a cement-based adhesive. It is made into slabs or tiles and polished to a high sheen. The color is dependent on the type of marble used. Different colors can be incorporated into one slab to create patterned borders and centers that simply fit together to complete a repeating or symmetrical design. Traditionally found around the Mediterranean, terrazzo is an extremely hardwearing material often used in commercial environments.   **5**

Quartzite

One of the hardest natural stone flooring materials, quartzite comes in a wide range of plain and variegated colors from soft grays to warmer buffs, as well as much darker colors such as somber greens and near-black. Quartzite has a cleft, slip-resistant surface, which—together with its durability—makes it a popular choice for commercial applications.

Metal flooring

The ubiquitous aluminum treadplate is found everywhere nowadays: from the backs of trucks to warehouses. It is available in 4 x 8 feet (1.22 x 2.44m) sheets and is easy to lay over an existing floor, either as large sheets or cut into tiles. Aluminum treadplate is slip-resistant and non-corrosive. The gleaming surface perfectly complements a contemporary interior.

almost white and fine-grained, through a coarser texture with embedded fossils, to very dark greens and blues. It can be finished in a variety of ways, from a rough to a highly polished surface. Since it is very porous and stains easily, it should always be sealed. Antique limestone is sourced from a number of historical sites, but these cannot last forever. New limestone is more regular and

lacks the distressed quality of well-worn limestone—although some manufacturers have tried to recreate examples with an aged look.

Slate

A metamorphic rock formed from mudstones and shales, slate splits neatly into thin sheets. Cleft slate has a naturalistic, rough, and uneven appearance. Typically it is cut into squares or

chopped, which gives the edges a complementary rougher look. Slate is usually blue-gray with a silvery quality, although there are some extraordinary colors available too, ranging from pale parchment with warm buff highlights, to dark reds and rusts. Because slate is so varied, it can be used successfully anywhere that calls for a hardwearing and practical surface.

Sandstone

Sandstone is a sedimentary stone, formed from the grains of igneous rocks. It can be found in colors that range from a soft cream to ocher and warm brick red. Because it is hardwearing, it has come to be associated with flagstones. It is particularly useful in situations where slip resistance is important—in shower rooms, for instance—although it may be too rough for some feet. Its gritty surface can make it difficult to clean too, which also makes it less than ideal for kitchens.   **3**

Laying ceramic tiles

▲ *Machine-made ceramic tiles always look smarter if tile spacers are used when the tiles are set into the adhesive, to make sure that joints are evenly spaced and neat. This type of tile is easy to cut cleanly, which is a useful characteristic if a lot of cuts need to be made—around obstructions, for example, or if the tiles are laid on the diagonal.*

Modern ceramic floor tiles are regularly shaped and quite thin, making them easier to cut than other types of tile. If you are laying tiles on a wood floor, prime the floor first with either a general builder's polyvinyl acetate adhesive (white glue) or a special tile primer for wood floors. If the floor is at all uneven or insufficiently rigid, first cover it with plywood or weather-proof particleboard (see pages 152–153).

Laying the tiles

Begin by setting out and drawing up a grid of "boxes" across the floor (see pages 156–157). Mix up the tile adhesive according to the manufacturer's directions, adding any special additives for greater flexibility if you are covering a wood floor. Tile adhesive will stay soft for only about 20 minutes, so do not mix up more than you will realistically be able to use in the time available.

Lay your first tile in the corner farthest from the door. In order to position this tile accurately, dry-lay a line of tiles from the center point to the far wall along the center line, and then draw a line at right angles to the center line along the far edge of the last whole tile. Dry-lay tiles along the new line, and in the same way as before, draw a line on the far side of your last whole tile at right angles to your guideline. Providing this line is parallel to the center line, the last tile you

dry-laid is your "first tile." Spread the adhesive only over an area of about 1 square yard (meter) at a time. Using the side of a notched spreader or trowel, apply the adhesive to the correct depth, normally about ⅛ inch (3mm). Depending on the adhesive being used, it may be necessary to spread the back of the tile with adhesive as well. Press the tile into position with a slight twisting motion; it is important to bed the tile into the adhesive without any air gaps. For neat and even joints, usually ¼–½ inch (6–12mm), use plastic spacers between the tiles. Continue laying the tiles in the first marked square, checking that the tiles are even with a level and straight-edge. You need to work fast, as you have a very limited amount of time to reposition any tiles that are incorrectly laid. If any adhesive gets on the surface of a tile, clean it off immediately with a damp cloth; make sure too that the joints are adhesive-free.

When the first grid box has been laid, apply adhesive to the second and continue laying tiles along the far wall. Then complete the second row of squares and continue laying the tiles in rows of boxes, working back toward the door. Allow the tile

▲ *Wide joints look particularly effective when used between small tiles. They are also helpful if the tiles are not all the same size: different-sized gaps are less noticeable than different-sized tiles. Two widths of joints have been used here deliberately, adding to the charm of this arrangement of handmade and painted tiles.*

Laying ceramic tiles

adhesive to dry thoroughly before walking on the tiles. Conventional adhesives usually need at least 24 hours, although fast-setting adhesives can take only a few hours.

It will probably be necessary to cut tiles around the edges of the room to fit; if you lay the tiles on the diagonal, you will need to cut at least one in every two tiles. Ceramic tiles can be cut using a tile-cutting jig.

To determine where to cut a border tile, place a whole tile over the last laid whole tile. To allow for the grout, place a tile on its side between this tile and the wall and place another tile up against it. Mark the middle tile with a soft pencil where the tile above it ends. Place the tile in the jig, and cut along the marked line. Spread the back of the cut tile with adhesive, and press it into position. Continue until all the border tiles have been laid, leaving the corners until last.

Where a tile has to go around an architrave, use a tile nipper to chip away the edge of a tile. For pipes, the tile will have to be cut in half and a semicircle nipped out of each half to take the pipe; or cut a notch into one edge. When laying the two halves, leave only a thin joint between them so that the cut is less noticeable when grouted.

Grouting the tiles

When all the tiles have been laid and the adhesive is dry, fill the tile joints with a tile grout suitable for floors. Conventional grout is a powder mixed with water according to the manufacturer's directions. It is available in colors ranging from off-white to dark gray. For tiles laid over wood floors, remember to mix in a flexible additive.

For food-preparation areas, an epoxy grout is a good idea, because it is extremely hard and easily cleaned. Epoxy grout consists of two components that are mixed together, and then a powder filler is added to bulk it out. Always follow the manufacturer's directions. Pour the grout onto the surface, and spread it into the joints with the aid of a sponge, working on small areas at a time. After 15 minutes, clean any excess grout off the surface with a damp cloth. Once the grout has hardened sufficiently, polish the tiles with a clean, dry cloth.

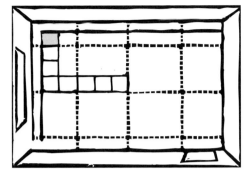

1 Lay your first tile in the farthest corner: dry-lay two lines of tiles from the center to find the correct position.

2 Spread adhesive over a manageable area, and press the tiles into position; use plastic spacers for even joints.

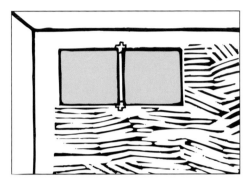

3 Working fast, continue to lay tiles to complete the first marked square, checking frequently that they are level.

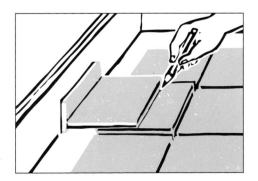

4 Cut border tiles accurately using the simple method described, remembering to allow for grout at the edge.

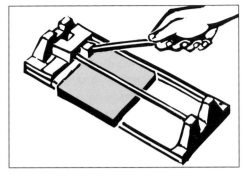

5 To cut all the border tiles effortlessly and efficiently, place the marked tile in a jig and press the lever to cut.

6 The cut border tiles will need to be spread with adhesive before being pressed into position.

7 When the adhesive is dry, pour grout onto the surface. Spread it into the joints a small area at a time.

8 Any excess grout should be cleaned from the surface with a damp cloth, before it is polished.

Resilient flooring

Probably used in more environments than any other type
of floor covering, resilient materials are the unsung heroes
of the flooring world. Consisting of just a thin layer, a
fraction of an inch thick, they add color and texture to
any floor, transforming it at a stroke. Their tough
practicality, economy, and easy maintenance assure their
presence in all kinds of location, from the kitchen
to the factory floor, and they are ubiquitous in
hospitals, airports, and schools.

Although resilient floorings are usually laid in the more demanding areas of the home—the kitchen and bathroom—flexible materials can be used in any room and would be a particularly sensible choice for a hallway. In practice, these materials should never wear out in a domestic situation.

Linoleum, the forerunner of more modern materials such as vinyl, was once all that many people could afford to lay over their floorboards by way of increasing their practicality while at the same time enhancing their appearance. In its most usual manifestation, a dreary shade of brown, it was used in many public buildings. Linoleum virtually disappeared as domestic flooring with the introduction of the more versatile vinyl flooring, but having only recently shed its traditionally dowdy image, it is currently undergoing a real renaissance. It has brightened up considerably and now offers a dazzling array of bright and lively colors that look bang up to date.

Due to its ready availability and particularly extensive potential for decoration, vinyl has been the flooring material of choice for many years. It is possible to add far more color and design to the surface of vinyl than to linoleum, and consequently it is made in a wide range of patterned, flecked, and marbled hues, as well as imitations of expensive natural flooring materials. In some cases it is hard to tell vinyl from the real thing. Indeed, it can be even more expensive than the real thing, such as stone. The vinyl version is often chosen because of its low maintenance and because it is warmer and softer than its natural counterparts.

Rubber, another material that has recently increased in popularity as a domestic floor covering, is extremely durable. It recovers from minor surface nicks and resists burns, so it continues to look good for longer than other flexible flooring products. The raised and studded non-slip surface of rubber makes it an appealing material.

Cork has, in the past, been a very popular natural product, although in recent years it has gone slightly out of favor. In the right setting, however, it can still prove extremely practical. Available in a small range of brown and tan shades, it is an attractive choice, and worth considering for any budget-conscious scheme aiming for a natural effect.

Resilient flooring materials are available in either sheet or tile form and are so thin that they never cause problems at thresholds. Because sheet floorings can be tricky to install, it may be worth having an expensive material laid professionally. A large sheet is heavy and awkward and can be difficult to maneuver in a room. And just one small slip of the knife can spoil what would otherwise be a perfect finish. Linoleum also contracts and expands unpredictably, which can make it difficult to fit. Vinyl is easier to lay than other sheet materials (see pages 170–173).

Tiles are among the easiest resilient materials for the amateur to lay at home (see pages 174–175). They are also easier to use creatively than the sheet equivalent: installing borders or key squares, for example, is a comparatively straightforward matter (see pages 174–175). Vinyl and linoleum can both be cut and inlaid with different-colored pieces of the same type of material. With linoleum this can be done either when the floor is laid or later, when you want to brighten it up, when you can inlay shapes. Some vinyl manufacturers provide a comprehensive range of designs for inlaying, either off the shelf or to special commission.

It is possible to create complex borders and designs for vinyl and linoleum using sophisticated cutting technology, but intricate designs require professional installation by highly skilled practitioners.

◄◄ *Modern linoleum not only is supremely practical but is now available in an excellent range of contemporary colors. It can be inlaid to create very intricate designs: indeed, an extravagant abstract inlaid design in watery blues and grays is the main point of visual interest in this plain white-paneled bathroom.*

◄ *Cork is a very practical material; its natural golden color will warm any room—both decoratively and physically. The raw material usually appears on the market as tiles; these can be made of granulated cork, or arranged as simple patterns within a tile format, as is illustrated in this kitchen.*

Laying sheet vinyl

▲ *It is preferable to lay sheet vinyl in one piece, not only because a single piece is less prone to damage than strips, but also because it looks neater. Seams would spoil the clean lines of this room. It is surprising and interesting to note how well this modern gray vinyl sits with old wooden paneling and antique chairs.*

Ideally, sheet vinyl should be laid in one piece so as to minimize the number of seams. These not only look unattractive but also attract dirt and moisture, which can cause problems in the future. Most sheet vinyls are available in widths of up to 13 feet (4m), so only quite wide rooms should require a seam. It is much easier to lay vinyl in an empty room, before kitchen cabinets, for example, or bathroom fixtures are installed; the fewer the obstructions requiring tricky cutting, the more likely it is that the end result will have a professional look and be fully waterproof. If you need to remove the vinyl at a later date, just cut around the cabinets or fixtures placed over it with a utility knife.

All sheet vinyl should be unwrapped loosely and left in the room in which it is to be laid for at least 24 hours before laying. This will give the material time to settle and acclimatize to the atmosphere before you start making cuts.

Fitting the vinyl

Cut the sheet of vinyl to size, allowing 2 inches (5cm) extra on all edges. This can be done in a room larger than the one it will be fitted in; if there is not a large enough room available cut the vinyl outside, making sure that it is kept clean. For vinyl that has to be fitted as two strips, unroll it and trim the ends only. It may be necessary to cut more off one end than the other to make sure that any pattern matches from one strip to the next.

Choose the longest and straightest wall to work from. Bring the sheet into the room and unroll it diagonally. Then shuffle the material around so it is square to the long wall with a 1-inch (2.5cm) gap between the edge of the vinyl and the long wall. The material should curve up the baseboards or walls on the other sides of the room. Check that the vinyl is square to the wall by measuring from the wall to the pattern at both ends of the room, and adjust if required, and then push a soft broom over the vinyl to insure that it is flat on the floor and that there are no air bubbles trapped underneath.

Scribing a line

To cut the vinyl to fit the long wall precisely, use a small block of wood pressed against the wall and overlapping the vinyl to scribe a line first. Slide the block along the wall from one end to the other, at the same time holding a marker pen against it with the tip pressing on the vinyl. The line should exactly follow the contours of the wall. Cut the vinyl along the marked line using a sharp utility knife. If you are feeling confident, you can simply run the knife along with the block of wood (instead of the pen) to cut the vinyl directly. Push the cut edge against the wall; it should fit perfectly.

Cutting corners

To enable the vinyl to lie flat, make relief cuts at the corners. At external corners press the vinyl against the base of the baseboard, and

Laying sheet vinyl

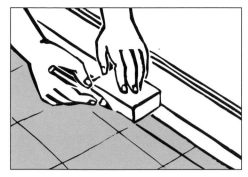

1 Using a block, scribe a line along the edge of the vinyl with a marker pen, following the contours of the wall.

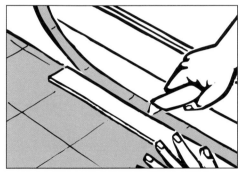

2 Cut the first edge of the vinyl to fit exactly by cutting along this marked line with a sharp utility knife.

3 At external corners, press the vinyl into the bottom of the baseboard, and make a series of relief cuts.

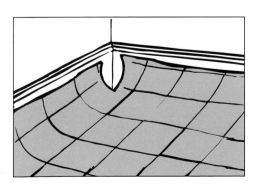

4 At internal corners, cut the corner off the vinyl as described at the measured point to let the vinyl lie flat.

5 Using a paint scraper, push the vinyl right into the base of the wall; create a series of flaps to aid neat trimming.

6 Alternatively, if you are confident, push the vinyl with a metal ruler and cut along its edge in one stroke.

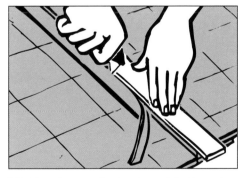

7 Cut through two overlapping pieces of vinyl to create an invisible seam, preferably along the line of a pattern.

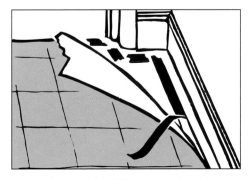

8 Secure the trimmed vinyl sheet at strategic points using special vinyl-to-floor double-faced tape.

cut up from that point to the edge of the vinyl so that the material lies flat. At internal corners cut off a triangle from the corner of the vinyl so that when the vinyl is folded up, the two flaps of excess material do not overlap. Do this by folding the vinyl back toward the center of the room by about 2 inches (5cm), and measure from the corner to the fold. Measure from the fold toward the corner point of the vinyl by the same amount as the first measurement. Cut the corner off the vinyl at the measured point; the vinyl should now lie flat against the wall with neat flaps of excess material along the walls. Trim these by first pressing the vinyl into the bottom of the baseboard at intervals of 6 inches (15cm). Use a stiff paint scraper to push the material into the angle between the baseboard and the wall. Cut along the fold and remove the piece. Repeat this process until you are left with a series of flaps. Pull the material away from the wall and place a straightedge along the base of the flaps, then trim them off so the vinyl fits neatly against the wall. If you are confident with the knife, cut along the edge of the vinyl in one stroke; use a metal straightedge when you would otherwise use a paint scraper, and cut.

Cutting seams

Where a seam is necessary, lay the second piece of vinyl over the first so that the pattern matches up. Lay a metal straightedge over the two pieces of vinyl where the seam is to be. Try to place the seam on the line of any pattern, as the seam will be less noticeable there. Cut along the straightedge through both pieces of vinyl; the edges should fit perfectly together.

Fixing and gluing

Sheet vinyl sold for domestic use is usually the cushioned type, which is used without an adhesive, although you will find some gluing is necessary in certain areas; near doorways; around heavy objects that might be moved, dragging the vinyl with them; and on any seams. Use a special vinyl-to-floor double-faced tape or an acrylic vinyl floor adhesive to secure the floor covering, and follow the manufacturer's directions.

Laying linoleum and cork tiles

► In a narrow hallway, work toward the edges of the floor from a center line running down the entire length of the hall. Plan well and adjust the center line as necessary before you start. Butt the tiles closely together and trim at the edges. The use of a threshold strip at the door prevents the tiles from being kicked up and damaged.

Laying resilient floor tiles is an easy and straightforward job. The tiles are simply butted together without any need to grout or fill joints. They are easily cut to shape and are much more manageable than their sheet equivalents. Tiles are also more versatile than sheets, as they can be used decoratively: by incorporating a border, for example, or creating a focal point in the center of a room.

With linoleum tiles it is possible to inlay a simple design. A checkerboard pattern using two colors, for instance, can be enlivened by insetting key squares at the center of four big squares. Ready-cut designs can be purchased for laying, or you can cut and lay your own key squares.

Before starting the work, prepare the floor as described on pages 152–153. It is particularly important for the floor to be absolutely level, for even the smallest bumps or hollows

will be visible on the finished floor and will spoil the effect. For the best result, use a latex smoothing compound.

If you are not using self-adhesive tiles, your retailer will advise you as to an appropriate adhesive. Unsealed cork tiles should be finished with a sealer as for floorboards (see pages 146–147).

Laying the tiles

Set out the floor as described on pages 156–157, although you should not really need to mark out a grid to cover the whole floor; being machine-cut, resilient tiles should—provided you follow the main guidelines—butt up against each other and remain square right up to the edges of the room. Begin in the center and work toward the walls.

Use the correct adhesive for the materials. As a general rule, a water-based acrylic adhesive, which is free from unpleasant

solvent fumes, is quite suitable. Spread the adhesive with a notched spreader of the size recommended by the manufacturer, covering only the area that you can comfortably tile before the adhesive dries. Roll the adhesive smooth with a paint roller wetted with adhesive to minimize the risk of the adhesive pushing up under the tiles and showing through as ridges.

Self-adhesive tiles are much easier and less messy to lay. All you have to do is peel off the protective backing paper and place the tile in exactly the right position, then press it down firmly.

Place the first tile on the intersection of the two main guidelines and press it down from the center outward to expel any air that might be trapped beneath which could cause bubbling. Butt the next tile firmly against it and press it down. Clean off any adhesive from the surface with a clean rag. Tile one side of the room, laying the tiles in a pyramid pattern and working toward the wall. If the tiles that follow the main guidelines are correctly positioned, all the subsequent tiles

▲ Particularly convenient to lay are the cork tiles that come with a self-adhesive backing, but no cork tile is difficult. Remember that unsealed tiles should always be varnished, and that prefinished tiles benefit from a coat of varnish if they are being laid in an area where they need regular mopping—kitchens or dining areas.

should fall into place precisely; with factory-cut tiles there are always two edges to work from, insuring that the tiles are laid square.

Fitting border tiles

When all the main tiles have been laid, start laying the border or edging tiles. Place a tile exactly over the last whole tile in a row. Lay another tile on top that so its edge butts up against the baseboard. Mark a line along the opposite edge on the loose tile underneath. Cut this latter tile along the marked line using a sharp knife and a straightedge; the trimmed-off piece should fit neatly into the border. Repeat the procedure for each of the rest of the border tiles. Any obstacles can be dealt with in the same way that they would be if you were laying sheet vinyl (see pages 172–173).

Laying key squares

Key squares not only add interest to a bland floor, they can be used to make a simple checkerboard pattern more sophisticated, and to introduce a new color into a flooring scheme with relative ease. If pre-designed, ready-cut materials are not available locally, you can cut your own key squares.

You can use the same technique to cut out other shapes, such as stars, but remember that cutting out complicated shapes is a highly skilled operation and that it is all too easy to end up with gaps around the inlaid pieces. Before cutting up a floor, practice on some scrap pieces first or stick to simpler shapes.

Mark out the square on stencil cardboard; cut out the shape. Divide the square into four equal triangles with a penciled cross. Place the stencil over the intersection of four tiles, making sure it is correctly positioned with the lines of your penciled cross aligning exactly with the lines between the tiles. Using a fine pencil, trace the outline of the key square onto the tiles. Then cut out the outlined square using a sharp knife; cut along the lines as carefully as possible, and gouge out all the linoleum within the square. Use the same stencil to mark out a square on the linoleum you intend to inlay. Carefully cut out this square and glue it firmly in place in the appropriate position on the floor.

Laying soft flooring tiles

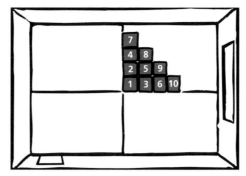

1 Having established and adjusted your center lines, start to lay your tiles from the middle and work outward.

2 Spread the adhesive with a notched spreader; the glue must not be so ridged as to affect the surface of the tiles.

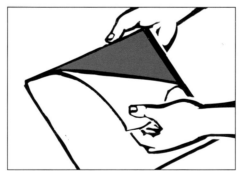

3 Alternatively use adhesive-backed tiles; they are less messy to lay. Peel off the backing and press in place.

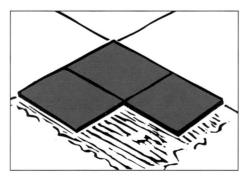

4 Position the first tile at the two guidelines' intersection and work outward, smoothing out any trapped air.

5 To cut a border tile, lay one tile on the last whole tile, another against the wall, and mark the loose tile.

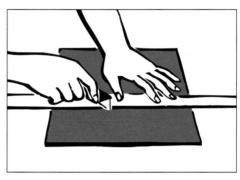

6 Cut along the marked line; the piece you trim off should fit neatly into the space at the border.

7 To position a key square, place the stencil on the intersection of four tiles and trace the outline in pencil.

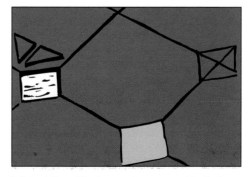

8 Cut out the outlined corners to accommodate the key square; spread glue on its back and press in place.

Decorative wood flooring

Wood has long been used for flooring, as it is so readily
available, besides being an easily worked and practical
material. Diverse, beautiful, and with a natural complexity
and depth unmatched by most other flooring, it is a
material with infinite appeal. Its practical, easily cleaned,
and durable surface always feels warm and welcoming.
The distinct elegance and luxury of new decorative wood
flooring probably makes it the only flooring material that
will look right in virtually any room in the home.

However, it is perhaps unwise, for practical considerations, to install wood floors in very wet environments; a bathroom that is continually soaked would not be an ideal place for a wood floor.

New sanded and sealed wood, without any gaps between the boards, is particularly suited to a modern and minimalist interior, which relies on simple, clean shapes and the use of natural materials for maximum impact. But wood also suits any style of contemporary room. A more traditional, country room, on the other hand, might look better with old, wide boards that have moved and twisted over the years, leaving gaps and some imperfections. Yet such is the never-fading appeal of wood that this type of floor could equally suit a more up-to-date scheme. And wood always ages gracefully, in most cases darkening and gaining character as the decades pass.

Each type of wood has its own distinctive color and grain, ranging from pale ash to the near black of ebony, although this is too rare today to be used for flooring. In between are a multitude of warm browns, reds, and rich beiges. Furthermore, wood can be stained for additional color variations. The grain can be almost plain, with a few small flecks, or have wild, swirling patterns with great diversity in the coloring. The degree of patterning is dependent upon the type of wood but varies considerably within species. The plainer, knot-free examples tend to be more expensive than types with a busy grain and some imperfections.

The color range of wood is such that it will live happily with most other types of furnishing. The hues are generally muted and neutral. Plain wood is usually sufficiently interesting to be left as it is, although it provides the perfect backdrop for loose-laid rugs when a little extra splash of color and warmth is desired.

Fortunately, wood is one of the easier flooring materials to install. Traditionally, wood planks are laid over timber joists, but these days floating floors are widely used. All that is required to create a brand-new floor in a matter of hours is for pre-finished boards to be fitted together over an existing subfloor.

Manufactured wood floors are nearly always made from a hardwood, even if the real wood element is only a thin veneer. The lighter-colored hardwoods are traditional wood types such as ash, maple, and beech. Beech and maple have a particularly unobtrusive grain, ideal for rooms where a light and plain-looking floor is wanted, which would not add any textural detailing to a room. Oak is a darker hardwood with a particularly interesting grain, and it is widely used for flooring. Other darker woods such as walnut are sometimes used for floors, too, as are more exotic species such as mahogany and teak, which are a rich golden-red color. Take care when choosing wood types; tropical hardwoods are likely to have come from non-sustainable primary forest.

All woods can be stained to change their color. The lighter woods such as beech are frequently stained or have a semi-opaque lacquer applied, to lighten their color even further. If you want a rich and warm tropical wood, a stained American variety can actually make a very satisfactory alternative. Quality can vary; the more expensive grades are sold knot-free and uniform in color while the cheaper qualities can vary considerably in color from board to board. All the hardwoods are sufficiently tough for domestic use, although some, such as maple, are much harder than others. The laminated products can be even harder than solid boards because the middle layer is designed to cushion shock. New pine, however, is very soft and can be dented easily.

◀ *Modern wood-strip floors have a clean simplicity that suits contemporary taste particularly well; the pale and neutral tones of the floor here show off the furniture without any unnecessary distraction. Available in a wide variety of colors and textures, wood floors are stylish and practical and will complement almost any room.*

▲ *This room is perhaps typical of modern informal living. The floor is light-colored with a discreet grain that provides an easily cleaned, non-allergenic surface that is warm and inviting at the same time. A simple rug provides extra color and comfort, while the rest of the furniture sits easily in the scene.*

Directory of decorative wood flooring

Manufactured decorative wood floors of all types can be supplied either unfinished or pre-finished. Unfinished floors are plain, bare wood, so that the floor is installed before it is sanded and lacquered. Although the wood is initially cheaper to purchase, the finishing costs must be added on when you are deciding what you can afford. Because installation is much quicker and less disruptive, pre-finished floors are very popular. An acrylic lacquer is frequently used; this can be a fraction of an inch (several millimeters) thick and may have a subtly textured surface for greater slip resistance. Some pre-finished floors have wear guarantees lasting as long as 25 years, although 5 to 10 years is more usual.

Solid wood

A solid wood floor consists of planks of wood laid across joists or over an existing subfloor. Traditionally, the boards would have been quite wide and straight-edged but most modern solid wood flooring is tongued and grooved. Tongued-and-grooved boards eliminate drafts from under the floor and make any shrinkage and movement of the planks less noticeable. The main advantage of a solid floor is that it can be re-sanded several times, making it an excellent long-term proposition.

Load-bearing wood flooring should be at least ¾ inch (20mm) thick, although wood being fitted over an existing subfloor can be as thin as ⅜ inch (10mm). The boards used for flooring come in a wide range of sizes, all the way from narrow strips of 2¼ inches (6cm) to 7-inch (18cm) planks. Planking of random widths can be installed to create an Early American look. Wide planks are sometimes supplied already fitted with wooden pegs, which imitate the functional wooden pegs originally used to lay such floors. One advantage of using narrow wood strips is that shrinkage is less notice-

able because the gaps are smaller, and any warping of the boards is less pronounced. The boards can be either finished or unfinished. **1**

Unit block flooring

This flooring comes as tongued-and-grooved solid wood blocks, normally about ¾ inch (20mm) thick, which are manufactured in a variety of styles. These include herringbone, brickwork (formed of staggered planks), and a basketweave pattern of short strips placed at 90-degree angles. More elaborate parquet designs (see below) are also available.

The units are installed on an existing subfloor using a special adhesive; better varieties have a slatted base which permits them to be adjusted to fit irregularities in the subfloor. The blocks come in several thicknesses, ranging from ½ to ¾ inch (12–20mm), and normally measure between 6 and

20 inches (15–50cm) square. The resulting floor is highly durable and easy to care for. **4**

Laminated wood floors

This is man-made board constructed of several layers. The top layer is a veneer of decorative hardwood, but the layers beneath are usually plywood or sometimes cork. The great advantage of a laminated-board floor is that it is relatively cheap to produce because the hardwood layer can be as thin as ¹⁄₁₆ inch (1mm), although it is normally more substantial than this. Another advantage is its potentially greater directional stability, because the laminated construction minimizes the movement of the boards once they have been installed. Laminated-board floors are available in thicknesses ranging from ¼ to ¾ inch (6–20mm). The heavier grades can be sanded down several times for an extra-smooth finish.

This type of floor is generally prefinished with a hardwearing layer of lacquer. The finished effect is similar to a solid floor although each "board" is often two or three times wider than the laid floor would suggest in order to facilitate speedier installation. Some laminated floorings are so sophisticated that it is debatable whether they are wood floors at all; there is one product available as ⅛-inch (3mm) strips that are

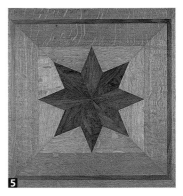

glued down rather like vinyl tiles, the real "wood" element of the floor being an extremely thin sliver of the product.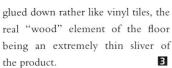

Parquet

Originally found only in aristocratic houses and palaces, these intricately patterned floors were laid by highly skilled craftsmen using hand-cut blocks and strips of wood. Their illustrious

origins are evident in the names of some of the patterns, such as "parquet de Versailles" and "Marie Antoinette." It is still possible—though extremely expensive—to have parquet floors laid piece by piece by a specialist craftsman. And if you want a floor using different kinds of wood and intricate motifs, such as stars, this would obviously be a job for a professional. The reasonably priced option is to buy parquet flooring as unit blocks. These come in many different patterns and in different kinds of wood, including oak and walnut, and will give an air of true elegance to your home.   **5**

Wood mosaic panels

Wood mosaic is a very economical type of flooring. The small wooden blocks are either fixed to a backing material that holds the whole pattern together or can have a paper fixing on their face which is removed after fitting.

The blocks are arranged in various simple patterns: basketweave pattern is one of the most popular. To fit wood mosaic, you glue the panels to a sub-floor, normally in the same way as resilient tiles (see pages 174–175), although some are available with a self-adhesive backing. In addition, some types of mosaic panels are tongued and grooved so that the tiles slot together without the risk of high spots (one panel sitting proud of others) developing. Mosaic panels are supplied either pre-finished or sanded ready for subsequent varnishing.   **2**

Laying wood-strip flooring

The easiest of all wood flooring to lay is a floating floor where boards are fixed together but not attached to the subfloor underneath. The boards can be either solid or constructed of laminated layers and are available in various thicknesses. The thicker boards last longer but do obviously raise the level of the floor more noticeably.

The subfloor needs to be reasonably level, although it does not have to be perfect. The new flooring can be laid over existing floor coverings, even on a fitted carpet if it has a firm, close pile. Indeed, laying a floating floor over an old carpet in an upstairs room will increase the sound insulation between that floor and the room below. Equally, you can lay an underlay of some sound-insulating material such as cork—or a special foam. Concrete floors must be dry. If there is dampness coming up through the floor, it may be necessary to install a vapor barrier (see pages 152–153).

Most wooden floors require a ¼-inch (6mm) expansion gap around the edge, but check with your flooring retailer. Ideally, the gap is covered by the baseboard but if it proves too disruptive to remove the baseboard before laying the floor, the gap can be covered subsequently with wooden beading, or it can be filled with a cork strip. The boards should be laid parallel to the longest walls, so if the room is square, it is your choice which way you lay the boards.

Normally, the boards of the first row are laid full width and the boards of the last row

▲ *The direction of the planking here draws the eye down the corridor into the room beyond. This not only looks better but is easier to install too. Floors such as this wood-strip floor can be laid on almost any surface, provided it is smooth and level. For a neat finish lay the floor first and then fit items such as kitchen cabinets and baseboards.*

are sawed down their length to fit. It is worth measuring the room before you start in order to calculate how wide this last strip will be, because if there is room only for a thin strip, the floor will look more balanced if you saw the first boards down the middle before you start, making both the first and last strips cut strips of a similar width.

Laying the floor

Start laying the boards against the longest and straightest wall. Place ¼-inch (6mm) wooden spacers against the wall for the expansion gap and lay the first board against them, with the grooved edge facing the wall. Apply a little wood glue to the tongue on the end of this first board. Slot the next board against the

---

Laying wood-strip flooring

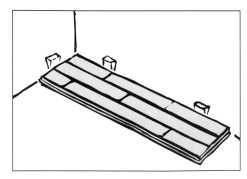

1 Lay the first board against wooden spacers, with a little glue on the end and the grooved edge facing the wall.

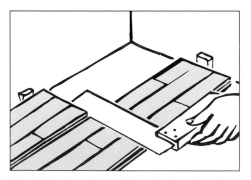

2 Turn the last board around, place it against the wall with a spacer, mark it in line with the laid board; cut.

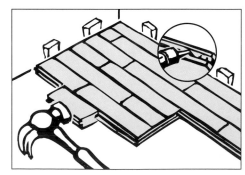

3 Use a hammer and a scrap of wood gently to tap the glued second row of boards home securely.

Laying wood-mosaic panels

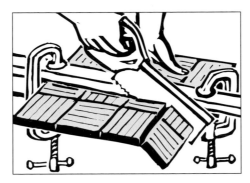

1 *Adjust your center point so that as many border tiles as possible can be trimmed in whole blocks.*

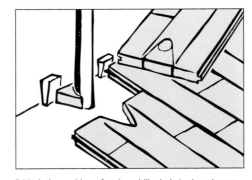

2 *If you have to cut through the middle of a block, clamp the panel in place on a workbench and use a backsaw.*

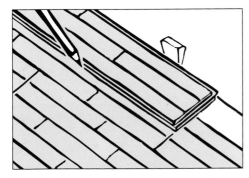

3 *To fit neatly around a pipe, separate two blocks from the backing, cut two semicircles and reposition snugly.*

end of the first board and continue until you reach the last board along this row. To cut this board to fit, turn it around and place it against the wall, allowing for the expansion gap, with the tongue end facing the tongue end of the board already laid. Using a try square, mark the board to be cut in line with the edge of the laid board. Cut the board with a backsaw, glue the tongue on the end, and slot the cut board into position with the cut end facing the wall. Position wedges at both ends to prevent the boards from moving.

To prevent the joint lines from creating lines across the room, which would spoil the floor's appearance, lay the boards in a staggered pattern—like bricks in a wall. Use the remainder of your first sawed board as the first board of your second row, with the cut end facing the wall. Apply a 4-inch (10cm) line of carpenter's glue at 24-inch (60cm) intervals into the groove, and push the board

firmly into position. Using a hammer and softwood block or a scrap slotted into place, gently tap the board home. Wipe off any glue from the surface of the wood with a damp cloth. Continue working across the floor until you reach the penultimate row.

Position the first board of this row without any adhesive and then lay the last board on top so that it butts up against the wall, allowing for the expansion gap. Run a pencil along the edge of the top board to mark the board beneath it. Remove the board and saw carefully down its length along the pencil line. Next glue the uncut board in place and finally the cut board—to complete the floor. Knock wedges into position to hold the floor tightly together until the glue has set.

To fit the boards around a radiator pipe, mark the board where the pipe will go and drill a hole (allowing room for expansion). Cut a V-shaped slot from the edge of the

board to the hole. Lay the board and glue the cut-away piece back into place. The easiest way of fitting boards around an architrave is to place a scrap against the architrave and cut away the base of the architrave. The board can be slid underneath the architrave for a neat finish. Alternatively, use a profile gauge (see pages 154–155) and cut the board so that it fits the profile of the architrave.

Laying wood-mosaic panels

Wood-mosaic panels are easy to install. The technique employed is similar to that used for laying resilient tiles (see pages 174–175). You need to use an adhesive specially formulated for wood-mosaic panels, unless you decide to lay self-adhesive panels, in which case you simply need to peel off the backing.

Because the tiles are harder to cut than resilient tiles, try to adjust your center lines so that at least some of the tiles around the edge can be trimmed in whole blocks—by merely cutting the backing between individual blocks. Where cutting through the wooden blocks is unavoidable, you will have to clamp the panel between a workbench and a wooden batten to immobilize the blocks and then use a backsaw.

At a doorway, cut the bottom off the architraves as described for wood-strip flooring; or use a profile gauge and cut out the profile using a coping saw. The panels can be made to fit neatly around pipes by separating them from their backing at the point where the pipe is to go and then cutting two semicircles out of the blocks. Once fitted, these are held in place by the adhesive backing.

4 *With the last board on top of an unglued penultimate board, mark the latter's edge on the board beneath; cut.*

5 *Mark the position of a pipe; drill a hole in the relevant position; cut a V from there; fix both cut piece and board.*

Soft floor coverings

In cool climates carpet is favored for its warmth and is used widely for any room that requires bright color and pattern, combined with a luxurious quality. Once carpeting was reserved for the well-to-do, but today the invention of synthetic materials, coupled with steadily rising standards of living in the industrialized countries, has brought carpet within the reach of most people. Ironically, nowadays, carpet can be one of the least expensive flooring materials available.

Good-quality carpet is costly and specially dyed, and woven wool carpet remains one of the most expensive of floor coverings. Most wool carpets contain a proportion of nylon to increase their durability; cheaper carpets are generally made with a higher percentage of synthetic materials and are more loosely woven than traditionally made wool carpets. High-quality carpets, though, can also be made from synthetic materials.

Carpet is, in fact, very hardwearing and is suitable for most environments, including those that have to endure very heavy foot traffic; it is widely used in commercial premises. It is less suitable, however, where there are likely to be spillages, such as kitchens and bathrooms. If carpet is used in a demanding environment, it will need more expensive, specialized care than would a hard floor.

Because carpet is such a forgiving material, the tendency in some countries has been to lay it in almost every room, but unless a house is very cold, the sense of warmth afforded by carpet may not be the key factor, and in recent years other materials, particularly wood, have gained in popularity. The increase in allergies to dust mites, which carpet harbors by the million, has also caused more people to turn to alternative flooring materials. For some rooms, however, carpet will always be a sensible and popular choice of flooring. Indeed, nothing can beat a fully carpeted bedroom in winter, as one's feet sink into the soft pile, warm and softly reassuring; even noise deadened to a soft hush. Inner sanctums—living rooms, studies—unlikely to be tainted by mud benefit too from that special sense of luxury.

Carpet is available in a huge range of colors and types. Darker colors are more suitable for areas, such as hallways, where dirt is likely to be brought in from outside, and you can choose from a vast range of neutral colors for a simple backdrop to a decorating scheme. Or you may choose to make the carpet itself the focus. Borders, repeat patterns, and central motifs are all easily incorporated into a carpet design. Stair carpet is available with attractive borders which can add restrained interest to an otherwise plain flight of stairs.

◄◄ *The cool austerity of bare brick is considerably softened by the warm, deep pile of a wool carpet. This carpet has been made on a traditional narrow loom and has alternating strips of patterned and plain carpet with the same background color, the strips indicating that this is an English Axminster or Wilton carpet.*

◄ *Natural floor coverings have become very popular recently. This living room is enlivened by the robust texture of rush matting, which looks perfectly at home with all the different elements in the room. Note how this floor covering is not wall-to-wall but stops just short of the walls, the edge being finished with braid.*

Carpet is not the only type of soft flooring. Natural floor coverings are increasingly popular, because they can provide a room with an elegant and sophisticated backdrop and are excellent for showing off colorful rugs. They are derived from plant fibers woven together to form a mat.

The fibers of natural floor coverings are often left undyed, so they take their color from the plant from which they are made. They may be bleached to offer a lighter, more neutral look.

Although some plant fibers will not take dye, others can be dyed very successfully; sometimes an interwoven colored weft gives the material a subtle hint of color without impairing the natural, undyed look.

Part of the appeal of natural floor coverings is their very definite texture. Some are quite soft and can be woven into fine patterns; others seem rough and hairy. These are used to create textured and robust patterns.

Natural floor coverings are economical to buy but, apart from sisal, they do not always wear well, and they can be difficult to clean. It is worth buying matting that has been treated with a stain inhibitor, although latex backing makes day-to-day care easier and the matting can be laid like rubber-backed carpet. There is a new range of floor coverings in which fibers such as sisal are blended with wool. These combine the practical advantages and softness of carpet with the character and look of natural floor coverings.

Laying carpet

Carpet is made from wool and/or a variety of synthetic materials —rayon, polypropylene, or nylon—all with different properties which are used according to the carpet's function; the fibers can be mixed to combine their various advantages. Synthetic materials are cheaper than wool, and synthetic carpets can be very hardwearing, although their appearance may be less attractive. They also melt if a cigarette end is dropped on them. Wool is a natural, environmentally friendly product; it wears well and has an excellent appearance and superior insulation properties. Pure wool carpets are rare now. Most wool carpets contain some man-made fibers for increased durability—usually 80 percent wool: 20 percent nylon.

Carpet is normally manufactured in 12-foot (3.7m) widths and is known as "broadloom," to distinguish it from the narrow strips in which it was formerly made (dictated by the size of the loom). It is still possible to buy narrow widths of carpeting for stairs. In fact, the edges of tufted broadloom (the most common variety) are ragged and must be trimmed, so that the usable width is slightly less than 12 feet (3.7m). A seam at some point is thus often necessary.

The pile of carpet is either looped or straight. Looped carpet is usually woven from one long length of yarn that loops in and out of the backing material, while straight pile is made either by cutting the tops off the loops or by inserting short lengths of material into the backing so that the two ends stick up. Pile varies in length. Short-pile carpets resist flattening more readily. They tend to look good for longer, although this does depend on the pile density and material. Long-pile carpets feel more luxurious, although shag carpet has gone out of fashion. One way of making the pile more resilient to flattening is to twist a wool yarn tightly while heating it, somewhat like crimping hair, before weaving: twist carpet appears more textured than a smooth, velvet pile and is a good choice for areas, like stairs, that have to endure heavy traffic.

Woven-backed carpet

Traditionally, woven carpet has a jute or burlap backing but sometimes it is woven polypropylene. Woven-backed carpets are laid over a rubber or felt padding which helps to even out irregularities in the subfloor and also makes the carpet feel softer and more substantial. Rubber feels softer underfoot, but felt is more resilient and thus a good choice for an uneven floor or a carpet that needs to include a seam. A combination padding, then, combines the qualities of both.

Laying woven-backed carpet is a tricky task for the amateur; it is, however, a very quick operation for a skilled person and comparatively inexpensive. It is probably not, therefore, worth laying such a carpet

Laying carpet

1 Fix underlay and tape to floor. Butt carpet against first wall, trim, and secure—removing backing from tape.

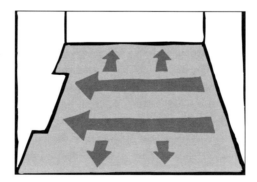

2 Walk carpet from the taped edge to opposite wall, fit, and secure. Work to remaining two edges; secure.

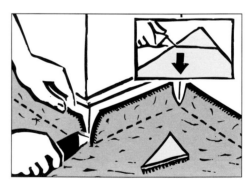

3 Make release cuts at external corners and trim diagonally at internal corners to make sure carpet lies flat.

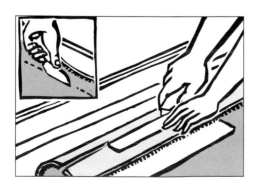

4 To trim, press into bottom of baseboard with brick chisel, turn back, and cut on a board, along metal edge.

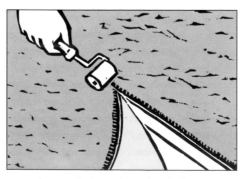

5 To make seam, bed one edge on length of carpet tape, butt up the next piece, and bond with seam roller.

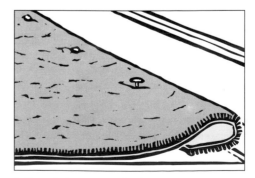

6 Alternatively, cut carpet slightly oversize, turn under and staple or tack through the double thickness to fix.

yourself, particularly because if it is not properly laid, unstretched woven-backed carpet will ruck up and wear quickly.

Rubber-backed carpet

This is less expensive than woven-backed carpet; it has a rubber backing bonded to the carpet, which renders a separate padding unnecessary. Felt paper is laid over the floor instead to stop the rubber from sticking to the surface when the carpet is subsequently replaced. The main advantage of rubber-backed carpet is that it does not have to be stretched over tack strips to fit. Having simply cut it to size, rather like laying sheet material (see pages 170–173), you can just tape it into position. Or you can turn the edges under and tack it down.

Lay the paper underlay and apply double-faced tape down the longest, straightest wall. Keep the tape's backing paper in place, butt the carpet up to the wall, and trim it if necessary. Remove the backing paper from the tape and stick down this edge of the carpet. Stretch the carpet across the room to the opposite wall, fitting carefully at corners with release cuts, as necessary. Walk the carpet flat and trim this opposite edge to fit, before securing on a strip of double-faced carpet tape as before. Finally, walk and stretch the carpet flat to the other sides of the room, and trim and secure these edges with tape.

Use a brick chisel to press the carpet into the bottom of the baseboard, and score a line along this junction. Turn back the carpet and cut along this line against a metal straight-edge on a board. To make a seam, bed one edge onto a length of carpet tape, and then butt up the first edge of the second strip. Press down the edges firmly with a seam roller. If you prefer, tacks or staples can be used to fix the carpet edges. Having cut the carpet oversize, turn under excess and tack through the double thickness of carpet.

Laying carpet tiles

1 Mark the direction of the pile, place tile face down over the gap, and mark the overlap by making slight nicks.

2 Cut tile, as marked, with a sharp knife on a board. Border tiles should be secured with double-faced tape.

Carpet tiles

These are easy to install. The rules for fitting them are the same as those for linoleum or cork tiles (see pages 174–175) except that carpet tiles should not be glued permanently in place. Use a special pressure-sensitive adhesive, which will fix the tile and yet still allow it to be easily pulled up and repositioned. Alternatively, in areas where the tiles are likely to move and under heavy furniture, fix tiles using double-faced carpet tape. Make sure the pile all lies in the same direction by following the arrows marked on the back of the tile or running your hand through the pile to see which way it lies. Border tiles are easily cut to size. Place the tile upside-down over the gap between the wall and the last laid tile, with the tile against the wall. Make two nicks on the tile, one on each edge, adjacent to the edge of the tile underneath. On a cutting board, using a utility knife and metal straightedge, cut the tile between the two nicks. Reposition the cut piece at the wall; it should fit the gap exactly.

▲ The rather stark look of this bedroom, created by the monochrome color scheme and skeletal, twisted metal furniture, is softened by the addition of a thick, highly textured carpet with a woven diamond pattern. An expanse of snow-white carpet can create quite a dramatic effect, but bear in mind that such carpets rarely look spotless for long.

Laying natural floor coverings

▶ *Sisal is versatile; it can be woven robustly, as here, or with a fine texture. This basketweave sisal matting is installed in a way similar to wall-to-wall carpet using tack strips so that it fits neatly against the walls and does not ruck up when the chair is moved. But natural floor coverings are glued rather than stretched into position.*

When you buy a natural floor covering—as opposed to a conventional carpet—you may have to pay quite a bit extra for installation and underlay. The labor cost can be much higher than for carpet-laying because carpet intallers tend to dislike laying natural floor coverings. Because the underlays can also be fairly expensive, laying your own natural floor covering can make a significant saving.

Before embarking on such a project, however, bear in mind that some aspects are tricky. For example, some materials can be difficult to cut to size. They have to be glued to the underlay, which is stuck to the subfloor, and then tack strips are installed to help hold the floor covering in place and minimize any shrinkage. It is possible to lay natural floor coverings without an underlay, but the end result will not be as comfortable

to walk on and any slight irregularities in the subfloor will quickly manifest themselves as wear ridges.

Plan the laying arrangement before beginning work. Natural floor coverings come in broad widths, like carpet, so that they can be installed without a seam in most rooms. Remember to allow 3 inches (7.5cm) on each edge for trimming. A seam, if one is necessary, should run along the longer dimension of the room. In some cases it may be convenient to piece the strip used for the extra width. Thus you would order a piece only half the length required, then cut this lengthwise and join the two strips end to end. This would be much more economical than buying the full length.

Natural floor coverings require no complicated sewing of seams. The edges are

simply butted together, although using an extra adhesive bond is recommended on the joints. Lay the floor covering with the pattern of the weave running in the same direction. Unroll the floor covering in the room in which it is to be laid at least 48 hours before installing to allow it to acclimatize.

Laying the underlay

Begin by nailing or gluing the tack strips in position ¼ inch (6mm) away from the baseboard with the spikes pointing toward the walls. Use a pressure-sensitive adhesive to secure the underlay to the subfloor. This type of adhesive does not go solid to form a permanent bond, but stays slightly tacky so the floor covering can be lifted at a later date without damage to the subfloor. Apply the adhesive with a notched trowel or paint roller according to the manufacturer's directions. Allow the adhesive to dry to clear, as specified by the manufacturer—depending on conditions, about 40 minutes. Unroll the padding over the adhesive with the rubber side down and trim it to fit against the spikes; each length of padding must butt up against the one already laid. Go over the floor with a carpet sweeper or a long-handled soft broom, pressing down firmly to obtain a good bond. The natural floor covering can be laid over the underlay immediately.

Laying the floor covering

Cut the material roughly to size, allowing an extra 3 inches (7.5cm) on all edges for trimming. If the room is wider than the floor covering, start at the wall farthest from the door and lay the material loosely in place on the floor. Mark the edge of the floor covering with a pencil or chalkline as a rough guide for the application of the adhesive. Roll the floor covering back on itself and away from the wall, without moving the whole piece, and exposing half the floor area. Use a suitable notched spreader and apply the correct amount of permanent carpet adhesive to the underlay. Some of the rough-backed floor coverings, such as coir, will require the use of a coarse spreader which applies a greater quantity of adhesive in order to ensure a strong bond. Your retailer will

Laying matting

advise you. Carefully roll the floor covering back over the wet adhesive and go over the glued area with a carpet sweeper to press the material into place. Now roll the unglued half of the floor covering back on itself and repeat the process on the other side. If a second strip of material is required, apply the adhesive only to within 8 inches (20cm) of the marked line. The second strip should be cut to length allowing the same extra 3 inches (7.5cm) for trimming, as described above. Then lap the second piece over the first by 3 inches (7.5cm) and cut the excess from the wall, again allowing a margin for trimming. If a third strip is needed, the trimming will be necessary only on the final length.

The second strip can be glued into place as described for the first length, starting from the seam. Remember to leave an 8-inch (20cm) strip at the seam without glue. Finally, glue the half-strip adjacent to the wall.

Trim the excess from the walls with a sharp knife, taking great care not to cut your-self with the knife or snag your hands on the tack strip spikes, which are very sharp. Fold the material against the baseboard and cut it along the base—against a scrap of wood to protect the baseboard—making sure that you allow enough material to tuck into the gap between the tack strip and the wall.

Trim the seam or seams using a straight-edge and knife. Cut through both of the overlapping strips at the same time, for a perfect finish. Place a piece of hardboard or plywood under the floor covering to prevent the knife from slicing into the underlay. Cut edges do not need binding because the floor covering is backed, which prevents raveling. Fold back the edges of the seams and apply adhesive to the underlay, then press the edges firmly down. Go over the whole floor again with the carpet sweeper or broom, or a roller, to make sure that the floor covering is firmly bedded into the adhesive. Finally, use a brick chisel to press the material home at the edges for a neat finish. In a doorway install a special tack strip designed for thresholds. Secure the strip in position adjacent to the doorstop, mark the position of the center line on the floor covering, and trim. Press it in place under the bar with a brick chisel.

1 Secure tack strips close to baseboard, spikes toward the wall; if using nails, use cardboard to protect baseboard.

2 Apply adhesive with notched trowel up to the strips to fix the underlay to the subfloor; let dry to clear.

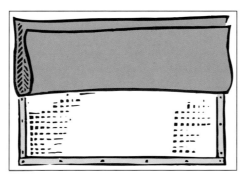

3 Lay the underlay rubber-side down, and trim to fit against tack strips; press firmly for good bond.

4 Roll back material on itself, apply adhesive on exposed half, roll back matting, and press. Repeat with other half.

5 Taking care to avoid spikes, trim excess with sharp knife at bottom of baseboard against a protective board.

6 For a seam, overlap two strips on a board, and cut through both layers. Fold back, glue, and press into place.

7 Use a brick chisel to tuck the trimmed floor covering snugly into the tack strips at the edges for a neat finish.

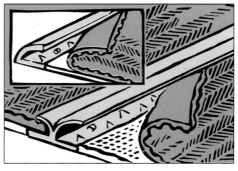

8 Cut threshold strip with a hacksaw, nail in place, trim floor covering to fit, and press home with a chisel.

Area rugs and carpets

The weaving of carpets and rugs is an ancient tradition
embraced by virtually every society in the world at some
time, whether small independent groups of nomadic tribes
or a large collective society. Rugs and carpets are made for a
far greater diversity of reasons than any other type of floor
covering. Rugs afford warmth and a degree of comfort for
people inhabiting colder climates and mountainous regions
and also make an important aesthetic contribution to any
environment, regardless of its geographical location.

Most carpets and rugs are constructed from one of two types of weave. Tapestry or flatweave rugs have no pile. The weft is woven over and under the warp threads and pulled tight. Cut-pile rugs, on the other hand, have a softer and more luxurious surface and are made by knotting individual strands of yarn into the warp. In tufted carpets, the number of knots over a given measurement determines the fineness of the weave. Carpets with a high number of knots per square inch (sq cm) can incorporate intricate curved or floral designs and will also feel softer to the touch, while those with a lower density of knots per square inch are generally characterized by geometric designs.

Traditionally carpets were dyed with natural dyes derived mainly from local plants, but today both chemical and vegetable dyes, or a combination of both, are employed. Natural dyes are considered superior because they give softer and more attractive colors which age gracefully, although it is possible to find exceptional chemically dyed rugs that have the same qualities.

Most countries have their own distinctive design traditions. Carpets from the East usually follow a design style and colorings peculiar to the tribe or region of origin of the carpet. Designs in the West tend, instead, to reflect the style of a particular period. Architects and designers have often tried to design rugs and carpets alongside their more usual occupations; William Morris, C.F.A. Voysey, and Charles Rennie Mackintosh, among many others, all produced a wealth of rug designs. Today rugs can be very modern and free-form in style; many are, in effect, artworks for walking on.

Because a large carpet is inevitably a major focal point, it is better to purchase a fine rug first and decorate a room around it than the other way around. Carpets look best when placed over a neutral background; both wood and natural floor coverings such as sisal make a perfect backdrop, and stone can also look very sophisticated. Rugs can be used to provide a simple focal point or relief in a large floor area or to provide a greater sense of warmth and softness on an otherwise hard and unrelenting flooring material.

Buying carpet and rugs

The purchase of a carpet is something that should be approached with great care. Beware of spending a huge sum on a carpet, because the carpet trade is like the second-hand car market: some carpet dealers can only be described as of somewhat dubious character. It can be extremely hard to tell if you are buying a genuine antique or a modern copy; equally, it can be difficult to distinguish between natural and chemical dyes, and the former would nearly always add to a carpet's desirability—and price! It is better to go to a reputable dealer who will give you a fair deal. It is also probably more sensible to buy a carpet from a reputable source on home territory than when on vacation; it may well be possible to secure a bargain when traveling, but equally you might end up with something that could be purchased more cheaply and easily at home.

Backings and fixings

Although it is possible to put a rug straight onto the floor, it will last longer and will not move around if it is placed on an underlay, or padding. This is important on wood floors, as rugs are potentially dangerous if not held in place. The underlay used with wall-to-wall carpet can be used, but corrugated types should be avoided for thinner carpets, especially flatweave rugs like kilims, because you will see the corrugations through the carpet. Special rug underlays, coated with a slightly tacky adhesive (which does not damage the carpet) are recommended; these will prevent the carpet from moving around. While giving added protection from general wear and tear, particularly if the carpet is lying on a hard surface, underlay will have the added benefit of giving the carpet a softer feel. Thinner underlay can be used with rugs placed on wall-to-wall carpet.

◄ *Wall-to-wall carpets are not everyone's preference, but while bare floorboards are wonderful in summer, they can look cold and stark during the winter months. This is when rugs, the most adaptable of all floor coverings, come into their own. This thick, hard-wearing rug with a checkerboard weave would help to ward off winter chills.*

▲ *A quirky interior, with more than a touch of the surreal, called for an unusual floor covering. This white rug decorated with parallel lines of black dots has a trompe l'oeil twist: the two dots in the center have been cut out and replaced with plastic veneer to give the illusion of wooden flooring beneath.*

Directory of rugs and carpets

Flatweave carpets and rugs

Kilims

Kilims are flatweave rugs made from wool. The term usually applies to rugs that come from an area stretching from Eastern Europe through Turkey and Iran to as far east as Afghanistan. For many years considered the poor relations of hand-knotted carpets, kilims became popular in the 1960s when the bold, bright colors and simple geometric designs appealed strongly to the hippie culture of the time.

Kilims can be woven much more quickly than a pile carpet—important to nomadic peoples who were constantly moving on. Designs are much simpler and more geometric than those of the knotted carpet because of the limitations of the type of construction. Kilims frequently contain a series of slits, which occur when one color of yarn adjoins another along a warp thread. Designs incorporating a series of long vertical lines are thus avoided, as the length of the resulting slits would weaken the kilim. Usually created using horizontal and diagonal lines with very short verticals, designs vary according to origin: Anatolian kilims are very colorful with particularly abstract geometric patterns, whereas traditional eastern Bulgarian kilims have a predominant black background characterized by floral motifs rendered in pinks, beiges and gentle yellows. **1**

Dhurries

The dhurrie is the traditional flatweave rug of India. Dhurries are made from cotton rather than wool, which gives them a slightly harder quality than a kilim. Because the dyes are taken up differently by the yarn, they tend to be less brilliantly colored than their wool cousins. Traditionally there were three types of dhurrie: the bed dhurrie was

placed under a mattress; the prayer dhurrie was divided into a series of prayer niches; and the room dhurrie was intended for use in rooms. This latter type was the largest and could be enormous. The finest dhurries were woven in Indian prisons between 1880 and 1920—an enlightened policy designed to relieve the monotony of prison life. Sometimes carpet designs were copied from imported Persian or Afghan carpets by prison warders or their wives, or new designs were drawn. Because of the influence of colonialism, traditional folk design tends to be watered down. Mosques or Hindu shrines appear frequently, although they tend to be geometric due to the construction of the dhurrie. Today, dhurries are manufactured in factories for the Western market and are characterized by insipid pastel colors and sparse designs.

Needlepoint

Needlepoint is the sewing of a yarn, usually wool, using different stitches, but chiefly tent stitch, into a canvas mesh backing. During the eighteenth

century needlework carpets enjoyed some popularity. Copies of traditional designs are made today in needlepoint, as very few of the originals survive, along with designs associated with other types of carpet, in the style of the French Aubusson, for example. The origins of this particularly elegant and sophisticated style were tapestry-woven carpets made almost exclusively for French royalty and aristocracy, which as a consequence makes the original Aubusson carpets rare and very valuable.

Needlepoint is also used in the recreation of other eighteenth- and nineteenth-century European designs and for creating original work as well, although many of the rugs are likely actually to be made in places such as China, where labor costs are low. **2**

Pile carpets and rugs

Gabbeh

The gabbeh is a rug woven by the tribes of southern Iran. They are unlike more traditional Oriental carpets, because they are woven for

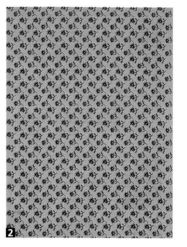

personal use in a much freer and more spontaneous style, their designs often taken from the weaver's immediate surroundings. Animals, birds and people, and simple shapes such as diamonds or the Tree of Life also feature, the motifs often being used more sparingly than on traditional carpets, with larger areas of solid color. Largely made in factories now to satisfy Western demand, gabbehs are made from either natural or dyed wool, left unclipped and shaggy.

Floral carpets

A "floral" carpet is a carpet that makes use of curvilinear design, as opposed to rather more geometric representations and patterns. This can be achieved only by the use of a very high

density of knots per square inch (sq cm), which produces highly complex and fine designs. Carpets of this type, such as the "Persian" carpet, are manufactured in organized workshops from designs produced on paper by a professional designer. The design is then woven into a carpet by a weaver who has little to do with the design process. Carpets made in this environment used to be produced almost exclusively for sale and export, often for the Western market. They are characterized by highly sophisticated and intricate designs of a very delicate nature, often using dark and rich colors.

Geometric carpets

Geometric carpets are produced principally by tribal peoples, either nomadic or living in villages. The designer is also the weaver, and the carpet design is made up as it is woven, although unlike the gabbeh mentioned above, the design uses traditional patterns and motifs. Each of these carpets is unique and is made for the use of the particular tribe. Some will be made for sale, and this is becoming increasingly common today

as these smaller groups enter the global economy. Tribal carpets originate from a huge area stretching from Turkey through Iran to Afghanistan. Each region or tribe has its own distinctive designs and color range, although some motifs are universal and are also utilized in floral carpets.

The reason for this type of design is cultural and is in some part due to the difficult conditions under which the rugs are made. Tribal rugs are less formal and looser in style than floral carpets. More folk art than classical art, this type of rug is more suited to contemporary interiors than the manufactured carpets; consequently they are much in demand.

Contemporary carpets

These are modern carpets produced by artists and designers—art for the floor. They are produced for their own sake as purely decorative pieces, unlike some of the more traditional types of carpet. Designs vary widely according to the style of the individual designer, and can be entirely free-form and expressive, or more representational, either with or without borders.

Some of these rugs are woven in the traditional carpet-producing areas of the East using hand-knotted wool and vegetable dyes, like the more traditional carpets of these regions. There are very few hand-woven carpets produced commercially in the West today, as labor costs are so high. This type of carpet may well be made in China or India, or in other parts of the East, and indeed, most patterned rugs (whether designed or solid-color) originate from these areas.   **4**

Fabric rugs

Rag rugs

The early American settlers living in remote areas produced many of their own goods, rugs being one such item. Because of the scarcity of manufactured goods, including cloth, the colonists were very good at recycling materials. They made rugs from strips of cloth obtained from clothes that had reached the end of their useful life and wove these into rugs of several different types. Rag rugs were the most common type of rug and were made from narrow strips of cloth that are woven on a loom, rather like a flatweave rug. The rug can be made from a fabric of one color or other colors can be incorporated.

Rugs of this type have a simple nubby appearance and are an inexpensive and effective way of covering up a bare floor. Today, rag rugs are easily found, but are likely to be made in Third World countries such as India.   **3**

Braided rugs

Three or more strips of cloth are braided together to form long braids, which are then formed into a coil and laced together. This type of rug is started in the middle and worked outward, with more braided lengths added to the outside of the rug until the desired size is reached. The rug was often circular or oval.

The color of the rug is dependent upon the color of the cloth used in making the braid, and the overall color is controlled by varying the fabric used in each subsequent braid; in this way a pattern can be built up. Today this type of rug is often machine-made, although it is possible to make one at home.

Hooked rugs

Hooked rugs are pile rugs made by pulling a strip of fabric (or sometimes yarn) through a backing material using a hook. The pile is made from a series of fabric loops that can be varied in height to create either a firm, close pile or a longer, more shaggy look. The pile lengths can be varied on the same rug to create a more sculptured appearance. The loops can be clipped in the same way as for a plush carpet to create a soft, more velvety feel. Quite complex designs can be achieved using this technique, depending on the density of the loops and the number of colors used.

Representational rugs, abstract patterns, or copies of Oriental designs can be tried. Hooked rugs can look more sophisticated and less folksy than the other types of rugs made from recycled materials, but this will obviously be dependent on the design used.   **5**

Floorcloths

Floorcloths are an alternative to conventional carpets and rugs. They are really the fore-runners of linoleum, which, in turn, was displaced by vinyl. Floorcloths were popular in the eighteenth century, as they could be painted to imitate expensive pile carpets. Sailcloth was the material generally used; it was given many coats of linseed oil to create a very heavy and durable surface. Floorcloths could be left plain or painted with a design. They were used in corridors and hallways, indeed any area of heavy wear that would have quickly ruined a carpet or rug, and in servants' quarters, where a real carpet would have been considered extravagant. The great advantage of a floorcloth is that it can be painted with any imaginable design at minimal cost. Moreover, it is a surprisingly hardwearing "carpet," which makes it an excellent choice for a hallway runner. And it can be made to fit any particular room's shape.

Making a floorcloth

Preparation

A floorcloth is really a blank canvas onto which any design can be painted, somewhat as an artist paints a picture, except that the floorcloth requires a protective coat of varnish once the design has been completed. Artist's canvas can be used, but it is probably better to visit a theatrical scenery supplier and buy the canvas from them; or use cotton duck, a satisfactory, inexpensive alternative.

You can make a very large floorcloth, for it is possible to buy cotton canvas up to about 10½ yards (9.5m) wide, although some of the cheaper alternatives may be a little narrower. You will need to buy a piece of canvas slightly larger than you expect the finished floorcloth to be, because the canvas will shrink by about 7.5 percent once it has been primed. You will also need to allow 1 inch (2.5cm) extra all around to fold under as a hem, to make a neat edge.

It will be necessary to find a space larger than the floorcloth in which to work comfortably. Begin by ironing out any creases in the canvas with a conventional steam iron. The canvas should be stretched before priming, otherwise there is a risk of its

▲ *A floorcloth makes a stylish and original alternative to a carpet or rug. The turquoise blue used here was probably specially mixed to offset the warm ocher used on the walls. Laying the cloth over gray colorwashed boards shows off both the colors and the design to maximum effect. In fact, the floorcloth forms the focal point of the room.*

rucking up unpredictably once it has been painted. A frame like an artist's stretcher can be made to the required size using 2 x 1-inch (5 x 2.5cm) battens and the canvas fixed to that; otherwise pin the canvas along the edge to an existing smooth and level floor using plenty of thumbtacks, though these will leave small holes. The canvas should be sized before painting; traditionally, artists use an animal hide glue which is purchased in granular form. A quicker and easier alternative is to brush the canvas with a white glue and then let it dry. Now prime the canvas with

two coats of ordinary acrylic wood primer/undercoat, allowing two hours between coats; it is a good idea to give the underside of the canvas a coat too, as this will give the floorcloth greater rigidity. The canvas will shrink so that it becomes very taut. Only at this stage can the thumbtacks be removed, or the canvas be taken off its stretcher. Use a yardstick and pencil to mark out the size and shape of the finished floor-cloth and also mark a second line about 1 inch (2.5cm) away from the first line toward the edge of the floorcloth. Cut away any excess material beyond this line. Use a sharp utility knife and a long metal ruler, and score along the first line—very gently, just to break the weave of the fabric—and cut diagonally across each corner on the marked line. Apply a fabric adhesive or white glue up to the marked edge and fold it on the scored line to give a neat, finished edge. The floorcloth is now ready for painting.

Painting the floorcloth

Almost any design can be painted on a floorcloth; as usual, the only limiting factors are the skill and patience of the painter. Indeed, there is no reason why a full-scale painting cannot be created on the floorcloth; it is, after all, a blank canvas. It is probably better to stick to conventional rug designs used on floors or to copy a picture of a real rug that you particularly like but cannot afford to buy. Simple checkerboard or grid-type patterns can be painted, somewhat as they would be on a wooden floor: decide on the width of the border and mark it out using a pencil and ruler; then mark out the squares on the center of the floorcloth. If the floorcloth has one predominant background color, paint the entire piece with that color first before marking out the design. Floorcloths should be easier to paint than real floors, as they are usually smaller and more manageable; the smallest floorcloths can even be painted on a table. More complex designs will need to be carefully planned and drawn on the canvas, while complex borders or repeat motifs may be more easily painted using a stencil (see pages 140–141). As with painted floors, the paints themselves do not take any wear so you can use either artist's oils or acrylics, both for tinting large amounts of white paint and for painting in fine detail. You can use either oil- or water-based paints, either as opaque color or, for a softer, more washed-out look, semi-transparent tones.

Finishing

Once the paint has dried, the floorcloth must be varnished. Use an acrylic varnish or an oil-based polyurethane, but remember that the latter will yellow with time. It is better to avoid floor lacquers, as these are very hardwearing but rather brittle and may crack. The floorcloth should have at least three coats of varnish—or more, if it is going to be subjected to especially heavy wear.

Once the varnish has dried, the floorcloth can be placed in its chosen location. If this is a hard surface (wood or tiles), it is best to stick the floorcloth down with a few squares of double-faced carpet tape to minimize skidding and to prevent the edges of the floorcloth from being continually rucked up, which will eventually cause the edges to curl and the paint to crack. Or try attaching an underlay as you might for a rug; this will not only prevent slippage but also give the floorcloth a more luxurious, padded feel.

▲ *Floorcloths make particularly effective runners, though they can be made to fit any space. The plain yellow floorcloth warms the walls in this hallway, while the one in the foreground is embellished by a simple and effective design that picks up on the wall color for a delicate balance, making it the epitome of discreet classical style.*

Making a floorcloth

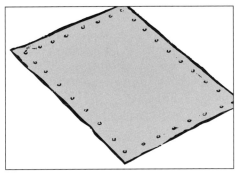

1 Having ironed the canvas to get rid of any creases, secure it flat with thumbtacks along the edges—or on a stretcher.

2 Size the canvas as described, brushing on the glue and leaving it to dry; then prime it with undercoat.

3 Cut away any excess canvas outside the scored line on the sized, shrunk canvas, leaving a turn-under allowance.

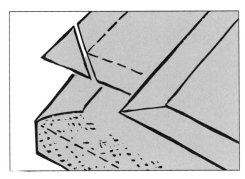

4 Cut across the corners of the hem diagonally; turn under the glued, trimmed edge to make a neat finish.

WINDOWS
& DOORS

One of the wonderful things about windows and doors is that they are architectural. Good windows have structure and form that relate to the history of your home, its date, and its style. They genuinely have that often misrepresented quality, "character." Your windows may be things of beauty: elegant multi-paned Georgian-style sashes; Victorian, with an interesting pattern of muntins; or rolled-steel casements typical of 1920s houses and apartment buildings.

Even an ordinary plate-glass double-hung window, a dormer window, or a handsome pair of modern wood-framed French doors can have proportions and an honesty of appearance that make them a pleasure to look at. Large plain windows in a contemporary building with a modernist or industrial look are equally attractive in a different way. Windows should be decorated in a decisive style that is sympathetic to, though not necessarily imitative of, their particular period and setting.

Doors, too, come in innumerable shapes, sizes, and styles. Flush doors (a relatively modern invention) are flat on both sides. Paneled doors have recessed sections, often

▲ A modern flush door is painted a strong dusky blue, the same color as the bedroom walls. The cylindrical steel knob reinforces the clean simple lines of this former workshop in London's Spitalfields neighborhood. The radiator, painted to contrast with its background, becomes a feature, rather than being disguised.

edged with molding: two or six panels if Georgian, or Colonial, four if Victorian or Victorian-inspired, three if early twentieth century. On old farmhouses one often finds simple plank doors, some of them with exposed hinges.

In spite of their significance and tremendous potential, windows and doors are often treated as the poor relations in a decorative scheme. Walls and floors are usually planned first, followed by the furnishings, while the windows and doors are thoughtlessly painted white or cream, or perhaps stained brown and varnished, and expected to merge into the background. This is not to say that in many circumstances white, cream, or brown is not exactly the right color. The point is that whatever color and treatment you decide upon for your doors and windows, the choice should be a positive one, not a case of "Oh well, white will do!"

Color, even strong, vibrant color, can look wonderful on the wood- or metalwork of doors and windows. It draws attention to them so that they make a greater contribution to the whole look of a room, perhaps reducing the need for elaboration elsewhere.

The original doors in your home are more likely than the windows to have been altered over the years in response to changing fashions in interior decoration. Paneled doors may have been covered on each side with a sheet of hardboard, which can be removed and the door restored. If your doors are not consistent with the period of the house, or just do not look right for some other reason, you can simply change them.

Inappropriate flush doors can be replaced by paneled doors of the right size and period. These can be found in salvage yards, bought new from do-it-yourself stores, or made for you by a carpenter. Or you can make flush doors look like paneled doors, at a fraction of the cost of replacing them, by adding moldings corresponding to the size and position of real panels.

Like doors, windows come in a variety of styles which reflect their history and sometimes their geographic location. A traditional double-hung window has two sashes, one above the other, one or both of which

slide up and down. In some modern windows the sashes slide horizontally. The frames of sash windows are often subdivided with muntins, which generally adds to their interest and charm.

Another common window type is the casement, which swings open from one side. It is usually part of a series of similar-sized windows, the casements on some of which may not actually open. Like double-hung windows, casements may be subdivided by muntins. Houses built in Tudor-style often have casements in which lead strips form small diamond or rectangular shapes. In some modern-style houses, a casement may be part of a metal window unit that includes a couple of non-opening casements below a transom (a window that swings open but is hinged at the top).

Other interesting window types include two that let light in through a roof. The dormer is a vertical window that projects

◄◄ In the charming inner hallway of an English country house, sage-green paint unifies several doors of different styles: one is a ledged and braced door with strap hinge, one four-paneled, and the other a half-glass door.

◄ Six-over-six double-hung windows, painted plain white and uncluttered by draperies or blinds, make a strong contribution to the cool, airy atmosphere and pared-down look of this living room in a French country house.

from the slope of the roof and usually has its own roof; a skylight is usually overhead, following the line of the roof. The porthole is, as you would expect, a round window.

The picture window is ubiquitous in modern houses and high-rise apartment buildings. Though lacking in architectural interest, it may serve as a framework for a dramatic expanse of draperies.

Most windows are dressed in some way, either with curtains or draperies or with shades or blinds. Although draw draperies are enduringly popular, they have in recent years been partially supplanted by other window treatments. Louvered shutters are among the most attractive possibilities; available in a variety of natural and colored finishes, they have great architectural quality, and their folding panels and adjustable slats permit innumerable variations in lighting a room. The once-despised Venetian blind is making a comeback.

▲ Two pairs of dramatic arched, glass double doors allow light and (when open) fresh air to flood into a living room in Umbria, in Italy. Outside, a simple iron balustrade across each window contributes to the modern look and prevents the possibility of anyone falling out.

Some eighteenth-century houses have solid wooden interior shutters. In some cases these have been later nailed into the window recesses and are waiting to be rediscovered. If you have a Colonial-period house with recessed windows but no shutters, you might consider hiring a carpenter to make some.

There is, of course, no requirement for you to cover your windows at all. Shutters, draperies, shades or anything else are used for a number of reasons, such as privacy, draft exclusion, and visual appearance. But if a window has none of these requirements, and especially if it is well proportioned or looks out on a striking view of countryside or rooftops, leave it bare. This will be particularly effective in a room with a fresh, clear-cut, simple look.

Not all windows are positioned in external walls or the roof, nor are they always see-through. A window in an internal wall

▲ Typically, double-hung windows in an eighteenth-century house would have had hinged interior shutters that folded back neatly during the day. When closed at night they excluded drafts and lent a degree of security. Nowadays, shutters can be made by a carpenter to fit almost any window—at a price.

▶ A simple, blue-framed dormer window, adorned only by a plain white roller shade, looks out over a tiled roof and into the greenery of trees. Dormer windows project through sloping roofs so that rooms in the eaves might receive adequate light, a little extra space, and some non-sloping headroom.

gives "borrowed" light to the room beyond. A glass door does the same job; it might have been originally designed as such, or it could be a traditional paneled door with some or all of its panels replaced with glass.

Plain clear glass is usually the obvious choice for most windows because it lets in the most daylight (which is, after all, the point of a window). But there may be windows in your home—on the stairs or overlooking a less-than-beautiful view, for example—where this need not be the primary consideration. A window that looks out into a dingy courtyard or other depressing sight, for instance, could be replaced with tough glass blocks that hide the view while letting in plenty of light. (It is possible to have an interior, or even exterior, wall built using these blocks, which are usually associated with industrial buildings of the early twentieth century, to allow daylight into a room.)

▲ *Light floods through this renovated warehouse in Anvers, France, thanks to an expanse of metal-framed interior window that even has its own opening casements. Double doors are left bare on one side, painted white on the inside only. External windows are veiled with unbleached linen.*

Another possibility is to replace the clear glass of the window with a type that you cannot see though.

Rooms such as bathrooms and powder rooms call for glass that provides privacy, such as patterned glass. This could be embossed, in which a raised pattern has been stamped onto the glass, or etched with a flat pattern. Etched glass is now manufactured in a variety of fairly traditional allover designs. A plainer alternative is frosted glass. Where a window is in two sections, one above the other, as in a subdivided casement or a sash, you can install frosted glass in the bottom half only for privacy and still get maximum light through the top. You can quite easily make "frosted" glass to your own design using self-adhesive plastic (see pages 222–223).

Yet another approach would be to commission an artist to design and make patterned glass which would be unique to your home. Or you could create your own design—perhaps incorporating your initials or something else with special meaning for you—and have it sandblasted onto a pane of glass by a glazier.

Colored panes and window shelves are two other assets you could use in planning the decoration of your windows. They can be used to create a degree of privacy or to mask a view, as well as for their intrinsic decorative qualities. You can either replace the existing panes with colored glass or paint color onto it (see pages 222–223).

Window shelves—strips of toughened or laminated glass—are fixed like shelves across a window in the depth of the recess. Colored glass objects look radiant exhibited there; or you could display a collection of items connected with the use of the room—shells and toy boats in the bathroom, perhaps, or antique cooking equipment in the kitchen.

Decorative finishes for window frames and doors

The technical advances made by big industrial paint companies, combined with the recent upsurge of interest in historical colors, traditional finishes, and "old-fashioned" and organic varnishes, stains, and paints, has created a huge choice of materials with which to finish doors and windows in any decorative scheme.

An increasing number of specialist companies, most of which offer a mail-order service to customers, have nurtured the renewed interest in paints and interesting finishes from the past, as well as the enthusiasm for organic products and natural finishes. Many small manufacturers are proud of their particular products, which include items such as biodegradable varnish and milk paints.

Before making a choice about the type of finish and color you want for your doors or windows, it is well worth undertaking some research to find out more about the range of available products. The first step is to visit a well-stocked hardware or do-it-yourself store, where you can read information on the paint cans and pick up manufacturers' information and color cards. Also ask specialist suppliers for their product literature.

An option for stripped woodwork in good condition is to leave it bare or treat it with a protective varnish or sealant, or to nourish it with oil or wax (see pages 218–219), so that the natural beauty of the grain contributes a decorative element. If the color of the wood is unsatisfactory in any way, it can be modified with the application of a wood stain (see pages 218–219). This can be a conventional "wood" color or a more brightly tinted shade to complement any overall color scheme. Many stains are widely available in the usual D.I.Y. and decorating stores, but some specialist companies make stains that can be diluted as much as you want to produce a washed-out look on wood.

Paint is the most wonderful stuff, and it can be used in a number of ways to draw windows and doors into a decorative scheme. In addition to conventional painting techniques, special treatments can be applied to create different effects (see pages 210–211), including a distressed finish, in which previous coats of paint are allowed to show through worn-away areas, chips, and scratches in the top coat.

Among so-called "new" colors are many vibrant shades inspired by eighteenth- and nineteenth-century house decoration. These colors look magnificent on woodwork, emphasizing the architectural qualities of doors and windows. They are equally impressive whether the tone of walls and other features is pale, in which case they stand out, or strong, in which case colors on the woodwork add richness and variety to the overall look.

Some unusual modern paints which have caught the imagination of interior decorators can be used to create striking effects. Metallic-colored spray paint, for example, was designed for retouching car paintwork, but it can be applied in allover swirls on a suitably primed door or with a stencil to create a pattern on doors or on fabrics for window treatments. Paints designed for use on metal include all-in-one rust inhibitor, metal primer, and top coat. They are easy to use and practical for metal windows and doors.

The choice of paint may have changed, but many of the old techniques for applying it have not. Whichever method you use, the aim is to have a smooth surface without blemishes at the end of the process. You could slap your paint on without any thought for technique, and as long as you work quickly and apply the correct thickness, the result will probably be perfectly satisfactory to the untrained eye. But the great attraction of techniques tested by use over a long time is that they work, and last (see pages 210–215). It is worth following them if you are serious about decorating, because they are more likely than not to give good results with a minimum of fuss and mess.

Getting set up for decorating doors and windows involves little financial outlay. Compared to other decorating materials, paints, stains, oils, and varnishes are inexpensive, though the cheapest is not necessarily the best value; cheap paint contains extenders that fill up the can on the shelf in the store but reduce its covering power at home. You do not need any special clothing (except for safety gear if you are using chemical strippers), just old, comfortable things that you don't mind getting splashed. The most expensive items are likely to be electrical equipment, such as a heat gun for stripping old varnish or paint, and a set of good-quality brushes. Consider these as investments, to last you for many years.

▲ *A pair of Spanish-style wooden doors has a flower motif carved into each panel, and paintwork that is so distressed that it remains in only a few mottled patches. Doors bought from junk yards sometimes still have attractive layers of old paint.*

◄ *In this house belonging to a textile designer, the color scheme uses old-fashioned paints in sumptuous colors from the English National Trust range: dead flat (matte) oil on the doors and woodwork and "estate emulsion" (a water-based paint that has a chalky rather than a rubbery finish) on the walls.*

Preparing surfaces for decorative finishes

▲ *The doors and windows of this room have been painted with hard-wearing high-gloss oil-based paint. The better the surface preparation before painting, the smoother and longer-lasting the finished surface will be. In this case, the quality of finish is very important, as imperfections would be highlighted by the bold color.*

How much preparation doors and windows require before they can be painted, stained, or varnished will depend on whether they have been previously finished. What needs to be done to previously finished wood- or metalwork is dictated by the condition of the finish and what you want to cover it with.

The putty on window frames must be sound before the outsides are painted. Check the putty's condition before you paint, and replace any that is dry, cracked, or missing.

Discolored patches in stripped woodwork can be bleached, as can large areas of wood that are an unsatisfactory color, in preparation for a finish. Use special wood bleach, available from decorator's suppliers.

Preparing new wood
New wood requires relatively little preparation before paint, stain, or varnish is applied. It must be clean and dust-free, however, since any debris will spoil the finish. Rough areas should be sanded and the dust wiped off.

Before new wood can be painted, the knots must be sealed with stain-blocking sealer to prevent them from seeping resin, which can

stain the paint even after it has dried. It is a good idea to remove some of the resin before sealing the knots. To do this, apply heat using a heat gun to encourage them to bleed, then wipe away the resin with a cloth soaked in mineral spirits. Apply the sealer with a small brush and wipe the surface clean with denatured alcohol. Two coats are ideal (it is extremely quick to apply as it dries very fast), but one coat will suffice.

Preparing previously finished wood for painting or varnishing
If the existing finish is painted and in good condition, and door panel moldings, architraves, or muntins have clear edges and are not clogged with paint or varnish, wash the surface thoroughly with de-greaser or liquid sander (see pages 206–207). Rinse well and dry. If you are not using liquid sander, lightly sand the surface with sandpaper or wet-or-dry paper wrapped around a cork block to create a key forthe new paint to grip, and to soften the edges of any chips in the finish prior to touching them up with primer/ undercoat. Bad chips may need filling and re-sanding. Always fill after the first coat of primer or primer/undercoat has been applied, as this helps the filler to grip.

If the existing finish is oiled or waxed, the wood will need thorough washing down before painting (see pages 206–207).

Paint or varnish in poor condition will have to be completely stripped and the woodwork freshly primed and painted. Dry, flaky paint can be brushed off with a wire brush or dislodged with a scraper. The surface must then be sanded, with extra attention being paid to any stubborn patches of old paint. For large areas use an electric orbital sanding machine.

Thick, gungy paint that is clogging moldings can be removed using a heat gun or by applying a paint stripper.

Heat gun: If you use a heat gun, keep it moving along the wood to avoid scorching;

Preparing painted surfaces

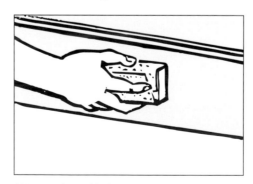

1 Use a sandpaper block to smooth surfaces and provide a key for painting. Work along the grain of the wood.

2 If the paint is hard to shift, or if large areas must be removed, an electrical orbital sander may be helpful.

scrape off the melted paint immediately. Use a shavehook on any moldings. Take care not to let hot paint fall on you. It may be advisable to wear cotton gloves for protection. Catch the scraped paint in a metal container such as an old cake pan and throw it away later, wrapped in old newspaper, in a garbage can, to prevent the possibility of fire indoors. When stripping muntins, add an attachment to the heat gun, with a rounded flat plate to one side, to protect the glass from the heat and the danger of cracking it.

Chemical paint strippers: Liquid and paste chemical paint strippers used in conjunction with scrapers and shavehooks are available for removing both oil- and water-based paint. On windows and doors use either a paste or a non-drip liquid or gel stripper. Other liquid strippers will, of course, run off vertical surfaces. Brush on the liquid and wait until the paint softens. Paste stripper is especially good for moldings. Apply a thick layer and leave it for several hours. Once the stripper has had time to work, scrape and peel off the old paint and then wash down the surface. It is advisable to follow the manufacturer's directions for application, removal, disposal of waste, and, above all, safety to yourself. Paint strippers are necessarily corrosive, so protect yourself with goggles, gloves, and long-sleeved and long-legged workwear when using them, and keep the work area well ventilated. You may also need to wear a mask, especially in less-well ventilated spaces.

◄ *Rubbing back old paintwork creates an attractive distressed finish you may decide you don't want to paint over. Sanding has created uneven, rough patches of color on this door and table, giving them a convincing look of age that complements the colorwashed walls.*

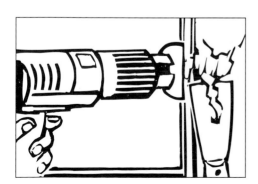

3 *A heat gun softens paint so that it can be scraped off. A heat deflector allows the gun to be used near glass.*

4 *Liquid stripper also softens paint. Brush it on, wait for it to work, scrape off the paint, and wash the surface.*

5 *A paste stripper is especially good for moldings. Leave for several hours before peeling off, then wash down.*

Wood veneer and shellac-polished wood should never be cleaned in this way. Instead, use a specialist wood cleaner or, if the grime is superficial, wipe with a cloth dipped in a warm solution of water and white vinegar, well wrung out so that it is barely wet. Wipe dry immediately.

Preparing new metal

Before painting new metal make sure that it is completely dry and free from rust and grease. Rusty patches must be cleaned and cured with rust inhibitor before metal primer or paint is applied, unless you are using an all-in-one rust-preventive paint.

▲ *The stripped pine windows and paneling beneath them in this city bedroom help to create a clean, uncluttered feel. Their pale finish is emphasized by the milky whiteness of the limed floor, and is enhanced by the unbleached muslin draperies. Together, they provide a neutral background for the antique chair and bed.*

▶ *Rusty metalwork requires a fair amount of preparation before it can be painted: scrubbing down, cleaning, treating with rust killer and metal filler, and sanding. A little effort, however, pays dividends, and a smooth paint finish on a well-prepared surface can make once dilapidated metal frames look flawless.*

Preparing previously finished wood for staining

Because stain cannot penetrate paint, wood that has been painted must be completely stripped before stain can be applied; any overlooked patches of paint will give a blotchy and unsatisfactory result. Use a paint stripper in liquid or paste form. To remove any stubborn patches of paint that may remain after the initial stripping, scrub along the grain using steel wool dipped in mineral spirits or alternatively you can apply more chemical stripper.

Preparing previously finished wood for oiling or waxing

Before re-oiling, re-waxing, or painting woodwork that has previously been oiled or waxed, clean it thoroughly to remove all the old waxy/oily deposits. Scrub the surface (not a veneered or shellac-polished surface) with steel wool dipped in mineral spirits, following the wood grain, then wipe down with a clean rag or paper towels. You may have to repeat this action several times. Finally, wash and dry the woodwork ready for treatment.

Preparing previously finished metal

If paintwork on metal window frames is in good condition, it can be repainted with relatively little in the way of preparation. Just wash it with de-greaser or a solution of soda crystals, rinse and dry. Then sand the paint lightly, with fine sandpaper wrapped around a cork block, in order to create a key for the new coat of paint. Before starting to paint, thoroughly clean off any dust.

If the paintwork is in poor condition, however, it will require considerably more work before it can be repainted. Be sure to protect your eyes with goggles before

brushing off all the loose material—rust as well as paint—using a sturdy wire brush. Next, scrub the metal with a solution of de-greaser or soda crystals, and rinse. Wipe down the entire surface with mineral spirits on a clean rag to remove any remaining grease. When it is thoroughly dry, paint rust killer onto bare or rusty patches, making sure that it thoroughly permeates boltheads, hinge areas, and joints. When this has dried, fill holes and depressions in the framework with

metal filler. Allow this to dry, then sand all over to create a smooth, even surface for painting. If priming the surface first, use a primer formulated specifically for metal, containing rust inhibitor.

Alternatively, strip off the old paint completely using a chemical paint stripper suitable for metal, and steel wool. A heat gun is of no use when stripping paint off metal, as the heat is absorbed by the metal, and the result is to bake the paint on.

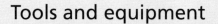

Tools and equipment

The preparation of doors and windows for a new finish requires relatively little in the way of specialist tools and equipment. In addition to the items described below, you will need a screwdriver for removing all hardware from the door or window.

- **Stain-blocking sealer:** an oily sealant made from shellac and denatured alcohol which is painted onto the knots in new wood, especially pine, to prevent them from weeping resin (see pages 204–205), which can stain a paint finish.
- **De-greaser or soda crystals:** washing existing paintwork with de-greaser or old-fashioned soda crystals dissolved in hot water is a marvelous way of removing dirt and grease, and even decades of caked-on grime.
- **Liquid sander:** a solution for cleaning surfaces before applying a new finish. It is particularly useful for cleaning and smoothing intricate moldings and corners.
- **Sandpaper or wet-or-dry paper:** essential at every stage of preparation to feather the edges of cracked or flaked paint or varnish; to create a key, or tooth, on existing finishes ready for the next one; to smooth and level dried filler after application; and between new coats of paint for a really glossy result.
- **Wire brush:** extremely useful for removing flaky paint and rust from metalwork.
- **Heat gun:** the cleanest, neatest and, some say, the safest way to strip paint is using a heat gun. Shaped somewhat like a hairdryer, this machine melts paint, even layers deep, which can then be scraped off with a scraper or shavehook. Some have integral scrapers

and heat deflectors that allow paint to be stripped near glass. When it is fitted with an attachment shaped to channel the heat away from the panes, it is an ideal tool for stripping paint from muntins. Never pass your hand in front of a heat gun to test how hot it is, as it will almost certainly burn.

- **Shavehook:** a triangular tool for scraping narrow surfaces. The type with curved edges is designed to be used on the curved profiles of moldings and muntins.
- **Chemical paint stripper:** powerful paint strippers can be used for removing paint. Special strippers are available for stripping paint off metal windows. Use these with steel wool. Whatever type of chemical paint stripper you use, whether a paste or a liquid, always protect eyes and hands. Cover arms and legs, however warm the weather, and carefully follow the manufacturer's directions for safe storage and disposal of chemicals.
- **Rust killer:** preparations can be painted onto metal windows and doors where rust has pitted the metal. Clean the areas to be treated of all rust, and paint on the solution. Fill the crevices with metal filler to create a smooth surface before painting.
- **Filler:** often necessary when renovating wood or metal to repair damaged surfaces. It is normally applied after the priming stage. Use the right kind of filler for the material you are working on. If mixing a filler up yourself, rather than using a ready-mixed type, be sure to add thinner in exactly the correct proportions, as directed by the manufacturer.

Preparing to paint

▲ *Narrow double doors are useful for dividing two connecting rooms that are often used together, as they look more welcoming and create less of a barrier when open than a single, full-sized door. Here, a paneled effect is suggested with roughly applied white paint.*

To work out how much finish you need to buy, measure the surface area of your windows or doors to get a rough idea of the area that needs to be covered, and check the estimated coverage details on the cans. Check, too, whether the finish requires any treatment: for example, some paints are sold in a slightly concentrated form and need to be thinned with turpentine or other thinner before application.

Most are applied with brushes, although some, such as stains, can be put on with a cloth. It is worth having a few improvised tools on hand in addition to the necessary decorating tools. An old spoon, for instance, is useful for lifting paint-can lids, especially ones that have been resealed for a few days.

Equipment choices for different paint effects

Always buy the best brushes you can afford. There are brushes specifically designed for different kinds of paint. Check that each brush is well made, with no loose parts and with a solid pad of flexible, springy bristles. You need a selection of paintbrushes for different jobs. Another point to remember is always to use a brush of the appropriate size: one that is too big will not get the job done any more quickly. For painting windows and doors you will need a 1-inch (2.5cm) decorating brush for moldings, a similarly sized angle sash brush for muntins, a 2-inch (5cm) brush for flat areas on paneled doors, and a 3-inch (7.5cm) one for flush doors. Look after your brushes properly, and they will last for many years.

For creating decorative effects with a glaze, brushes in different sizes will be useful. They are used dry. A dragging brush or other long-bristled brush, for example, is invaluable when dragging, and a wallpaper-paste brush can be used to soften the lines. Combs are used for patterning glaze. These can be bought, made of steel or rubber, but can be improvised from cardboard. Cut the teeth even, or, for a freer effect, cut less symmetrical teeth. Rubber rockers for patterning a wood grain are like curved rubber stamps and are, quite literally, rocked over and through tinted glaze to produce *faux bois* finishes.

Lining brushes, available from good art supply stores, are useful investments for obtaining a stable flow of paint over a long distance and are especially suitable for painting faux panels. Sword-liner brushes have bristles that taper away to a point, and these brushes are used for such effects as marbling, lining, and detailed work.

Paintbrushes must be dry and clean before you begin a job. If a brush is new, work it against your hand to encourage the loosest bristles to drop out. More loose bristles can be removed by dipping the brush in water and then painting this onto newspaper or a rough surface such as an outside wall. Next, wash the brush throroughly in warm soapy water, rinse well and squeeze out most of the water. To speed drying, spin the brush between your hands then suspend it with its bristles hanging downward.

Most decorating brushes have a hole drilled through the wide part of the handle, large enough to take narrow-gauge doweling. (If any of your brushes lack this hole, drill one in it.) Cut sections of doweling long enough to sit on top of a jar and to extend each side, so you can store the brushes suspended from the doweling with their bristles hanging downward when not in use (see pages 224–225).

Cleanliness

Cleanliness is important when applying any finish. When wet or tacky, the surface acts like a magnet to dust and dirt, which will spoil the final finish into which you have put so much effort. So even if you think your doors and windows are already clean, wipe them down again with either a clean rag that is barely damp or a tack cloth before beginning decorating. Remove dust from the crevices of moldings on doors and windows after sanding filler or paint. A vacuum cleaner with a brush attachment is useful for this.

To prevent dust and pieces of dried finish, especially paint, from dropping into the can when you open it, clean the can before removing the lid, brushing loose bits out of the rim. If debris does fall in, or if paint has formed lumps, strain the contents of the can through a piece of fine cotton muslin

▲ *Wide double doors look majestic when closed and create a generous, welcoming space when open. These examples have been painted in two colors, gray on the frame and mustard on the panels, both drawn from the curlicue pattern painted on the walls.*

stretched over another clean container. Always remove the skin on paint, however thin; do not be tempted to work it into the paint in the hope that it will disappear.

Cloths and neat rags without trailing threads are useful for wiping up spills and drips, but they must be clean to avoid transferring dirt onto fresh paintwork. Tack cloths, for wiping surfaces clean, can be bought from D.I.Y. or decorating stores.

Protecting yourself and your furnishings

Lay protective sheeting everywhere, even where you think splashes will never reach. Fine plastic sheeting is impermeable but can

be slippery and cannot be satisfactorily repaired if torn. Decorator's drop cloths, used by professionals, are available in sheets of various sizes and weights.

It goes without saying that you should wear old clothes; they are going to get splashed with paint. Do not wear wool, as wet paint will pick up the fibers. To protect your hands during decorating work, you can use special protective handcream, available from decorator's suppliers. This gets into creases and cuticles and is as effective a barrier as wearing gloves, but with none of the disadvantages. You simply wash it off when you have finished painting, leaving cuticles and creases clear and clean.

Using paint

▶ *There is no paint so shiny and hard-wearing as good-quality alkyd gloss, also called enamel. The deep-blue gloss used in this country-style kitchen-cum-dining room is practical as well as decorative; it can be wiped down and will withstand the onslaughts of dirt and steam.*

Paint on woodwork

Both oil- and water-based paint—alkyd and latex—can be used on woodwork. Traditionally, bare wood is prepared for top coats of paint with both primer and undercoat. Primer seals the wood and smoothes any slight blemishes. Undercoat, which can be colored, gives a solid ground for the subsequent coat(s). All-in-one primer/undercoat is popular. The acrylic form dries quickly and can be painted over with oil-based paints as well as water-based ones.

Paint on metal

Metal requires special primer, filler, paint, thinner, and cleaner. It is best to use products from the same brand to make sure that they are compatible. The more specialized paints do not need undercoat, and have rust-proofing qualities. They also need only one coat for complete coverage.

Applying paint

Most paints need to be stirred thoroughly with a clean implement before use. A wooden stick is ideal. However, do not stir non-drip paint, or it will lose its non-drip qualities. If you do so in error, cover and leave the paint for several hours to stabilize.

Working with a heavy can of paint can be difficult and dangerous. Decant a proportion of the paint into a smaller paint kettle, or a clean metal or plastic container with a handle.

Loading the brush

Dip the lower end of the bristles in the paint. A length of string stretched across the top of a paint kettle is useful for removing the excess. You need enough paint to work with, but not so much that it will dribble or form ridges as it dries. Read the directions on the can for any additional advice about the particular paint you are using.

Paint choices

Alkyd (oil-based) gloss: Tough, hard-wearing and shiny, oil-based gloss paint is best applied in several thin coats (a minimum of two) rather than one thick one. Drying time is 12–16 hours, although it may take several weeks, depending on the weather, for the paint to harden completely.

Alkyd (oil-based) semigloss: Oil-based semigloss paint has a smooth, silky finish which is not as shiny as full gloss paint. It is made by most industrial manufacturers but is given different names according to the brand. Drying time is 12–16 hours.

Alkyd (oil-based) eggshell: Oil-based eggshell paint has a smooth, hard-wearing surface and a slight sheen. This paint gives a more elegant finish than gloss. Drying time is 12–16 hours.

Flat oil: Also known as dead flat oil, it has a chalky, totally matte finish. Until recently it was considered to be exclusively a professional paint. Now more readily available from specialist paint companies, rather than from regular D.I.Y. or decorating stores, it is well suited to the wood-work of doors and windows. Drying time is 6–12 hours.

Water-based (acrylic) gloss: Although not as brilliant as oil-based gloss, acrylic or water-based gloss paint has other advantages. It does not have a strong smell, it dries quickly, and it gives a good shine. It can be painted on more thickly than oil-based gloss, but needs immediate working out as it dries rapidly. It is easy to wash off hands and brushes with water and soap.

Whatever type of paint you choose to use, the way you load your brush and apply the paint can make all the difference to the finished paintwork. Avoid painting doors and windows during hot and humid weather, as the paint will not dry properly and there is a likelihood of moisture becoming trapped between coats to cause problems later on (see pages 224–225).

Applying paint

1 Dip the lower third of the bristles in the paint, and wipe off excess on string stretched tightly across the container.

2 Paint three downward strokes, parallel but not touching, in the same direction as the grain of the wood.

3 Without reloading the brush, work over the strokes to spread the paint, at right angles to the original direction.

4 Finish by lightly "laying off" in the original direction, to remove any brush marks and leave a smooth surface.

First brushstrokes

Start painting at the top. On flat areas, first apply three downward strokes of paint, parallel with each other but not touching, and painting along the grain. Without reloading, work over these downward strokes crosswise to spread the paint, until it forms a solid block of color.

Finish by "laying off" in the original downward direction, with the grain of the wood, gliding your brush lightly over the surface. The point of laying off is to remove any marks made by the bristles of the brush, leaving a smooth surface. Reload and paint more sections in the same way, blending the paint over adjoining sections.

Special paint effects

Special paint effects can be applied to the woodwork of doors and windows to bring extra interest to otherwise plain paintwork. Effects such as dragging, combing, and woodgraining are achieved using a choice of tools, from decorating brushes to special rubber rockers, in order to pattern another layer of paint over a base coat of oil paint.

Apply a base coat and leave it to dry. Tint transparent glazing liquid, mixing 1 part glaze to 3 parts mineral spirits. Add 1 part white alkyd semigloss per 20 parts of glaze; and add artist's oil paint to add color. Mix up enough for all the woodwork you want to cover. While the glaze is still wet, lightly drag a wide decorating brush over the surface.

Dragging involves just that: dragging a decorating brush such as a bristle grainer through the top layer of tinted glaze so that the patterning of the brushstrokes remains visible when dry. Combing, with a special wide-toothed comb, is particularly effective, if a substantial proportion of the tinted top coat is combed away, allowing a contrasting undercoat to show through.

Woodgraining may be done using a special rubber rocker patterned with a woodgrain effect or, for a more impressionistic effect, using a lining brush to pull thin distressed lines over the base coat in a pattern similar to the veining of marbleizing. The technique for using the rocker is first to rock and then to drag it gently through the glaze.

Dragging

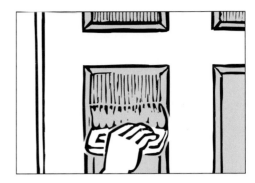

1 Apply glaze over the base coat, then drag a decorating brush through it to leave a brushstroke pattern.

2 Follow the direction of the grain roughly, or the effect may be too mechanical.

▲ *A top, colored glaze wash can be dragged, as here, or treated using a range of other techniques—including combing and woodgraining—to create subtle paint effects. The soft color combination of blue over cream on this cabinet door makes a clear visual link between the woodwork and the marble backsplash behind.*

Painting windows

Painting a window is a finicky job that should not be rushed, yet it needs to be done in one session to avoid ugly ridges in the paintwork. Start early in the day, and leave the window open so that the paint will be dry enough to close the window at night; do not attempt to paint in windy weather, as dust will blow onto the wet paint and spoil it. Immediately before starting work, remove handles and catches, and clean the panes thoroughly so that dust or dirt cannot transfer onto the wet paint.

Applying the paint

If you are using an oil-based paint, remember to build up the paint in layers, beginning with a wood primer, progressing to an undercoat and then finishing off with one or two layers of top coat. Use a 1-inch (2.5cm) brush for flat areas and an angle sash brush, which has an angled tip for painting moldings and muntins, of the same size. Apply the paint downward, along the grain if painting wood. Without reloading the brush, lightly work over this, making sure that paint (but not too much) gets into all the grooves of any moldings. Finally, glide the brush down again, making sure that the paint on all the surfaces is smooth and even.

Protecting glass

To protect window panes from paint, either use a paint shield or stick masking tape on the glass close to the glazing bars or frame. Whichever method you use, let your paint

Painting around glass

A paint shield is invaluable when painting window frames, to avoid getting paint on the glass.

▲ *A dramatic use of color draws the eye. vibrant blue on the wall and emerald green on the window. Despite having been built up in layers, the paint around the window has become worn with age; but, far from offending the eye, this softens the brash green and adds to the window's charm.*

Painting sequences: casement and double-hung windows

To paint a casement window, follow the numbers, painting the opening windows first.

To paint a double-hung window, first reverse the position of the sashes, then follow the numbers.

the inner sash and the vertical bars of the inner sash. Finish with the top runners and behind the cords, the frame, and the sill.

Casement windows

Hold the window open with a piece of wire wound around a nail tapped into the bottom of the opening casement. First paint the muntins, next the upper and lower rails, then the hinge stile and this window edge. Follow with the outer stile, and finally the frame and sill.

Shutters

Louvered shutters should be spray-painted by a professional. If you have solid interior shutters, treat them as if they were a paneled door, taking care to wedge a whole shutter open before you start work. Leave the window itself open to help the paint dry.

overlap onto the glass by about 1/16 inch (1mm) to seal the join between glass and frame and protect it from damp.

A paint shield is a piece of shaped metal or plastic with a fine edge along one side. While you paint, hold the fine edge against the glass, almost touching the muntin or side of the window. Wipe it frequently to prevent it from causing smears.

An alternative is to stick masking or decorator's tape around the edge of the glass close to the frame. Wide decorator's tape, which is half self-adhesive and half plain paper, is easier to remove when painting is complete. Peel away the tape before the paint has dried, or it may take some paint with it.

Double-hung windows

Begin by reversing the window positions so that the bottom sash is pushed up and the top sash is pulled down. Paint the meeting rail and the vertical bars of the outer sash as far as is possible. Next, paint the area beneath the inner sash and the runners. Following this, paint the lower cross-rail and the underside of the inner sash. Leave to dry. Reverse the window positions and start by painting the upper cross-rail of the outer sash, and then the remainder of the vertical bars of the outer sash. Now paint the upper cross-rail of

▲ This roomy Colonial interior boasts an abundance of louvered shutters. They are ideal here, behind the desk, where their versatility can be exploited to advantage. One half of the shutters can be closed to shade the eyes while air and sunshine can still stream in above or below to refresh and inspire the mind.

Painting doors

Like windows, doors should be painted in one session to avoid ridges in the paintwork. Remember that, as with all decorating, you will be able to see your handiwork more clearly in natural light than in artificial light. Cover the floor underneath a door and wedge it open firmly so it won't wobble as you paint. Before getting down to work, remove knobs, handles, catches, keyhole escutcheons, fingerplates, and any other hardware. Have an old screwdriver handy for cleaning out the groove of hinge screws after painting them.

Paint the edges of a door outward, toward the corners, to prevent paint being drawn off by the corners of the wood and running down in dribbles. On panel doors use a 2-inch (5cm) brush for stretchers and a 1-inch (2.5cm) brush for moldings. For a flush door a 3-inch (7.5cm) brush is suitable.

Furniture

Metal hardware should be cleaned (see pages 226–227) and coated with an appropriate paint; always make sure that moving parts and screw holes are not clogged.

Wooden doorknobs, especially cabinet knobs, can be painted to match a color scheme. Use a hard-wearing paint such as enamel, and apply several thin coats. Consider a final coat or coats of marine varnish to help protect them from wear and tear.

Paneled doors

Always working with the grain, first paint the moldings around each panel, then the panels themselves. Next paint the center stiles and the cross-rails including those above and below the panels. Now paint the stiles down each side of the door, then the edges, and finally the door casing (jamb and doorstop, and architrave) if these were not painted at the same time as the baseboard. When you paint the outside edges of the architrave use a paint shield (see pages 212–213) to prevent paint from getting on the wall.

An old-fashioned technique for painting paneled doors is to use slightly different tones of the same color on different parts of the door. By painting the panels the darkest shade, the frame the lightest, and the moldings a shade in between, one can make the architectural features of the door more noticeable. The door looks like a three-dimensional object rather than a two-dimensional one.

Flush doors

The best way to paint the large flat expanse of a flush door is to divide it mentally into six or eight equal parts, two across and three or four down, rather like the sections in a candy bar. Start by painting the top left section, then the top right, then the next left, then next right, and so on down to the bottom of the door. Paint each in turn, blending the wet edges together as you work down the door. Paint the edges, jamb, and architrave as for paneled doors.

Flush doors can offer greater and more varied opportunities than paneled doors for extravagant painting styles. Their flat sides

▲ Paneled doors provide the opportunity for having fun with color. Here light and dark blue paints have been used to make a striking entrance to the room. In times past, the panels were painted in slightly different tones of the same color to provide a subtle sense of depth.

Painting sequences: paneled and flush doors

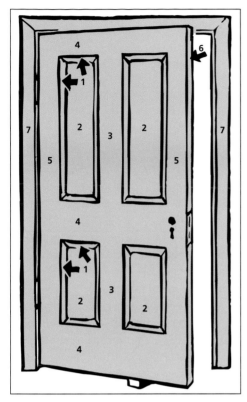

For a paneled door, start with the moldings around the panels, and then follow the sequence of numbers.

▲ The frame of a metal glass-paneled door is painted black, drawing attention to the geometry of the glass. The squareness of the panels contrasts pleasingly with the generous curve of the red-painted wall in front of it. Glass blocks above this wall serve to create an internal window as well as echoing the panels of the door.

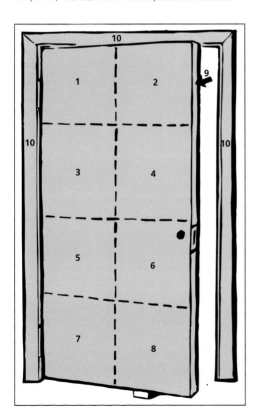

Work down a flush door from the top in imaginary sections, blending wet edges together before they dry.

lend themselves to allover designs such as the eye-bending geometric patterns found in the work of pop artist Bridget Riley or the blown-up cartoons of Roy Lichtenstein. Some of the most famous examples of door painting can be seen at Charleston Farmhouse in Sussex, England, where the artists Vanessa Bell (Virginia Woolf's sister) and Duncan Grant used every surface, including the doors, as a canvas. You can find inspiration for making your own designs or pictures almost anywhere.

Glass doors

Glass doors can be painted following the sequence recommended for paneled doors, starting with the area around each pane of glass. If the door is multi-paned or entirely glass except for the frame, treat it like a large casement window instead. Protect the panes from splashes with tape or a paint shield (see pages 212–213).

Protecting the floor

Use a paint shield or a piece of cardboard under the door frame to prevent the brush from picking up dust from the floor and to protect the floor from paint. This applies when painting baseboards too.

Protecting the floor

Besides keeping paint off the floor, cardboard under a door or baseboard stops dust from spoiling the finish.

More ideas for painting doors

Two-color doors

Use two different colors, but make sure that none of the wrong color is visible when the door is closed.

▲ *Brilliantly colored high-gloss paint has been used here; flame in the hallway area and bright Matisse blue woodwork inside the room. Although with the door open the effect is busy, vibrant, and full of contrasts, when the door is closed no blue will be visible from the landing.*

Different colors on either side of a door

It often happens that a door needs to be painted in different colors on each side, corresponding to the decoration of the rooms or areas it links. It does not matter which side you paint first, but it is important that every part of the surface you see on one side of the door should match.

For the purpose of description, imagine that the door opens from a passage into a room. On the opening side, paint the architrave, the frame up to and including the edge of the doorstop, the leading edge of the door, and the door face in one color. On the other side, where the door faces the passage, using the second color, paint the architrave and frame up to and over the doorstop, the hinged edge of the door, and its other face.

Faux panel effect for flush doors

To lift the flatness of a flush door, painting faux panels creates an effective three-dimensional illusion. First measure your door. Determine the number and size of the panels you want, and the dimensions of the faux rails and stiles. Measure and draw in the panels in pencil directly on the surface. Mix up two shades of the chosen door color, one lighter than the other, and then apply the darker shade to each of the panels. When dry, paint the rest of the door in the lighter color, beginning with the center stiles, progressing to the rails, and finally painting the outer stiles. When completely dry, you can paint in the shading at the sides of the panels to give the panels depth. You will need another, darker version of the original

Painting fake panels on a flush door

1 Measure and draw panels with a pencil before painting them in a slightly darker shade of your chosen color.

2 When the panels have dried, paint what remains in a lighter shade, in the usual order (see pages 214–215).

3 When the door is dry, paint the "moldings" with a fine brush, using a ruler; make sure the corners are mitered.

4 Taking note of the natural light source, use a lighter shade on two sides to reinforce the illusion.

◀ *Several faux panels have been incorporated here to create a simple, triumphant and humorous trompe-l'oeil door—complete with cat flap, mail slot, and bolts. The reliance on lines without shading in the paneling, and the strong, joyful colors used, complete the effect, proving that stylish interiors can also be witty.*

color and a paler version too. Establish in which direction your light source (real or imaginary) will hit the door. The tops of the panels and the sides closest to the light should be lined in the darker tone; the bottoms and farther sides in the lighter tone. The thicker the lines you draw, the deeper your panel will appear to be. It is not advisable to make them too thick. You must judge this to suit the proportions of the panels you have created and choose the width of your brush accordingly. A fine brush is recommended. Use a wooden or plastic ruler with a beveled top. Turn the bevel against the door so that it stands proud of the surface. Line the ruler up with the edge of the panel, rest the ferrule of the brush on the inside edge, and drag the brush gently along it. You will need to miter each corner, so be sure to let the paint dry before attempting this in the corner where the two tones meet. If you do not feel you have a steady enough hand to use a ruler, you can create the lines by applying strips of low-tack masking tape and painting between these instead.

Finishes for woodwork

Doors and windows that are made of wood do not have to be painted to look good or to complement a decorative scheme. They can be left bare, completely stripped of old paint, varnish, or any other finish, to allow the beauty of the grain to be admired. The two possible disadvantages of leaving wood unfinished are that it is not protected from dirt such as greasy fingermarks and that the stripping process may have left the wood dry and even slightly rough. The wood of old doors that have been industrially stripped in hot chemicals is likely to be in the worst condition; cold chemicals do not do nearly so much damage but are more expensive. Sanding will help and may even cure a roughened surface. In addition, there are a number of finishes that can enhance or seal bare wood to protect it from dirt. Before choosing a particular type of finish, do some research to make sure the finish will achieve the results you want.

Before applying any colored finish, practice on a piece of wood of the same type until you get the right effect. Where more than one material needs to be applied in succession, use products from the same brand to avoid incompatibility and later problems. Always follow the manufacturer's directions.

Staining

There are many different types of stains, all of which you wipe onto the woodwork with a wad of cloth, except for moldings, on which, for greater accuracy, it is better to use a brush. Quick-drying stains can be tricky to apply evenly, so try the color first on a scrap of wood. If staining a door, lay it flat before you start, so that the color does not run. Wood must be clean and completely free of other finishes before application.

Water-based stains give the brightest and best colors. D.I.Y. shops tend to favor shades of brown, which reflect natural wood colors. Oil- and spirit-based stains are also available. Household dyes in many colors are widely available, and today, various types of colored stains can be bought from specialist paint suppliers. Some sell pigments or concentrates with which you can mix up your own color; some stains are concentrated and can be

thinned to the shade you want, giving anything from an intense color to a washed-out effect. You can also make your own stain by seriously watering down latex flat paint so that the grain will show through when it is brushed onto the wood. A stain does not give wood protection from wear, so consider adding a varnish or sealer; seal either the whole door or window, or only the areas around handles where fingers may eventually make dirty patches.

Varnishing

To protect bare or stained wood from becoming marked, you can paint it with a varnish or sealer. Varnish is available in a clear form, colored in shades of brown, or tinted with more interesting colors. Some types have three alternative finishes: gloss, satin, and matte.

Oil-based varnish that is billed as "clear" generally has a yellowish tinge that will become more yellow with age or in direct sunlight. Acrylic (water-based) varnish is clear and does not yellow with age. In steamy rooms, oil-based varnish is better. For extremely hardwearing qualities, look for varnish containing Teflon. It should be noted that colored varnishes are very difficult to remove, should you ever want a change.

Varnish is simply brushed on. For a really smooth finish, rub down with sandpaper between coats.

Oiling

Bare wood doors can be nourished and given a soft, mellow glow with specialist oil or even stale olive oil. All oils will darken the wood to some degree. Linseed oil mixed equally with button polish will give a slight sheen. Some finishing oils are waterproof. Rub oil into the bare wood using a soft cloth. Except for some special finishing oils, oil does not protect against dirt and spillages.

Waxing

Wax is not waterproof and may pick up grime unless the wood is first treated with a sealant. Color can be added to clear wax such as beeswax by melting the wax gently with artist's oil color. This should be allowed to

▲ Varnish, whether clear or tinted, will allow the grain of the wood beneath to show through. Where the color of the walls is bold, doors in good condition often look their best left unpainted. The door, floors, and ledge on this landing have simply been varnished, so that their light-colored wood becomes a major, brightening feature.

cool before application. Alternatively, you could use a colored shoe polish.

When polished up, wax gives a glossier finish than oil, but, like oil, it allows the grain of the wood to show through. Wax does not protect against dirt and spillages.

Bleaching

Wood can be lightened to produce a soft, sun-bleached effect, like that of driftwood. Use specialized wood bleach available from good decorator's suppliers.

Liming

Especially suitable for oak and other woods with a distinctive grain pattern, this milky finish (also known as pickling) lightens and

adds interest to natural wood. Liming wax is available from some specialist paint and wood product suppliers. The wax comes with clear directions, but the process basically involves opening the grain of the wood by scrubbing along it with a wire brush, cleaning, working in the liming wax, wiping off the excess, and polishing the dried wax. The wood must be clean and completely free of other finishes before the wax is applied.

Staining the wood between cleaning and liming will make the liming more noticeable. You can also obtain an effect similar to liming by repeatedly painting bare wood with coats of watered-down white or lightly colored latex flat paint, then wiping it off. This finish will need sealing with varnish.

▶ *If you feel that carrying out the liming process properly sounds too lengthy, or too complicated, try the cheat's method: a similar effect can be achieved quite easily by painting bare wood with several coats of watered-down latex flat paint, wiping off the excess each time, and then sealing with a coat of varnish.*

Using paper, fabric, and metal

In addition to the more conventional ways of painting or finishing doors described earlier (see pages 214–219), there are several exciting treatments that can be applied to them. With a little imagination and a bit of flair, any door can be transformed into a work of art by being decorated with painted patterns or large pictures.

Doors can also be covered with materials as diverse as different types of paper, fabric, or even sheet metal.

Papering doors

If you do not feel up to devising an allover design yourself, you can cover a flush door with virtually any kind of paper and varnish over it. The door and paper both need to be clean, and the type of adhesive used should be appropriate for the job.

To create a bright and jolly, even kitsch, look, inexpensive paper items such as the covers of fashion or interior design magazines and bright-colored packaging of food products—especially those from other parts of the world—can be used. The latter would be particularly appropriate in a kitchen.

For a more sophisticated look, you could use black and white or delicately colored paper such as old sheet music, pages from out-of-date road atlases or maps, newspapers (which will yellow), old prints bought from a street market, photocopies of prints in a book, or even old letters.

Textile cover-up

Another approach is to face the door with a single piece of fabric such as green baize, colored felt, or imitation leather, using decorative brass-headed upholstery pins. Obviously the material needs to suit the overall decor of the room.

The material can be cut to the exact size of the door and glued on all over with an adhesive appropriate for the fabric. It must be smoothed out to insure that it is bubble-free, and the edges must be turned back, if necessary, and securely glued down. Alternatively, the material can be slightly padded and secured with tacks. This gives a more generous, sophisticated look and is easier to remove when you want a change.

▲ *Metal foil has been applied to the surface of the door to provide an unusual and extremely eyecatching focal point in this silver-themed room. Applying metal foil to wood is a straightforward—if time-consuming—job, but the results are worth the effort. Finish with a layer of clear glaze to prevent damage to the foil's surface .*

▲ *Large, square, black metal studs appear at intervals around the raised parts of a pair of handsome paneled doors—and in the corners. Although the studs have been used sparingly, their effect is impressive, and the overall look of the doors is reminiscent of those found in a medieval castle. Heavy knobs provide the finishing touch.*

A padded door

First remove the door handle and then paint the edges of the door an inch or two (3–5cm) around the edges of the front of the side you are covering. Choose a color that tones in with the facing material. Cut a piece of padding slightly smaller than the size of the door. This padding could be a piece of thick felt or a piece of leftover carpet under-lay. Attach this to the door using tacks or a staple gun (available from hardware stores to suit various sizes of staple).

Before attaching the facing material over the padding, mark the door at regular inter-vals around the edge where the tacks are to go. Cut the fabric slightly larger than the door. Turn back the edges so that you have a panel of fabric the same size as the door. Press these edges, if appropriate for the fabric, and then glue or sew them down. At the same time, cut off the bulk of the material at the corners and fold back, first along one edge and then the other, to miter them.

Decorative tacks for attaching this fabric panel can be bought from suppliers of uphol-stery equipment in a variety of designs and sizes, including the traditional brass-colored domed-top type. Or, instead, simply attach the fabric to the door with a staple gun, then hide the staples by gluing a braid or edging over them.

Attach the fabric to the door, making sure the material is hanging straight. Insert a tack (or staple) through the center top of the material into the middle of the top of the door. Make sure that the tension is just right—not too tight and not slack—and position the second tack through the center of the bottom of the material into the middle of the bottom of the door.

Finish attaching the fabric along the top, the bottom, and lastly the sides, always checking tension and making sure (using the weave if there is one) that it is straight. Place a tack in each corner for a neat finish. Other tacks can be placed on the door face in lines to make a pattern or a panel effect.

Cut a small hole through the layers of fabric for the spindle of the door handle or doorknob. Put the door handle or knob back in place.

Sheet metal

For a really dramatic, industrial-style finish, face a door with sheet metal such as zinc or stainless steel. This is not a difficult job, but it requires care, and the end result can be stunning. Begin by measuring the door precisely. Then find a steel retailer who will supply you with a single panel of metal and cut it to size. From the wide choice available, choose a metal and finish you like, bearing in mind that a lightweight flush door may be able to support only a thin sheet of metal. The optimum thickness is just under 1 mm.

When the piece is to be cut, specify that the corners must be cut exactly square, and the sheet must be without scratches or blemishes. Handle pieces with extreme care as the burred edges can cut; smooth the edges with heavy-duty wet-or-dry paper.

You can attach the metal to the door using a wide range of finishes and sizes of fasteners, including escutcheon pins, drive pins, round-head screws, pop rivets and even tin tacks. The choice of fastening is entirely personal, as the finishes are equally effective. Pop rivets give a pleasing industrial look and are applied with a pop riveter, which is available from hardware and D.I.Y. stores.

Whichever fastener you select, begin by drilling a small hole through the metal and into the wood, using a drill bit of the same diameter as your fastener or slightly smaller (experiment on a scrap of wood). If you are hanging a new door, you can attach the metal before hanging it, to make working along the bottom edge easier. Otherwise, attach the metal at the top first, so it hangs down while you fasten the rest. Use an adhesive suitable for gluing metal to wood, or double-faced tape, to insure that the edges of the metal sheet stick to the door. Attach the metal with fasteners applied in your chosen pattern, perhaps by using various sizes or types for a more elaborate effect.

To make a hole for the doorknob, first drill a small hole in the metal, to act as a guide, then a larger hole with a ½ inch (12mm) drill bit. If you are in any doubt about your ability to do this correctly, there is always the option of getting a professional to fit it for you.

Metal sheeting and rivets can of course be used to transform the doors of cabinets or closets anywhere in the house, but it is not necessary to use real metal. Metallic paint is effective too. Car paints are available from car goods suppliers in a range of colors as well as the silvery gray associated with real aluminum or steel.

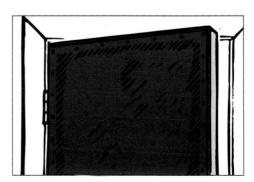

◀ *Rich red leather has been used to cover the outside of these impressive doors, made even more stunning by arranging rows of brass studs in various rectangular forms to create a paneled-door effect. Upholstery tacks or studs could be used to achieve a similar effect.*

Making a padded door

1 Cut a piece of padding slightly smaller than the size of the door, and attach its edges with a staple gun or tacks.

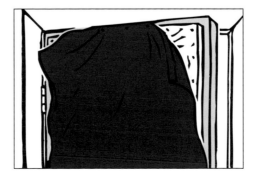

2 Cut the fabric slightly larger than the door and turn the edges over. Start attaching it at the center top.

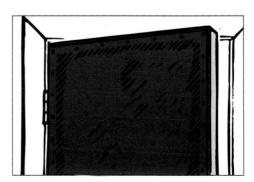

3 Finish attaching the fabric at the top, then the bottom, followed by the sides, fastening it at regular intervals.

Cleaning up and problems with paintwork

Tools and equipment should be cleaned and put away before the finish dries on them. Close a can by placing a piece of wood across the top of the lid and tapping it with a hammer. Throw away dirty rags in a garbage can, preferably a metal one, after chemicals have evaporated. Clean metal tools such as shavehooks with water or mineral spirits and put them away.

Cleaning and storing brushes

If you take the time to care correctly for your brushes, you will greatly extend their life. Wash brushes used for water-based paint or wood stains in water. For brushes used for oil painting, wash in mineral spirits to loosen the paint, then wash in warm soapy water; proprietary brush cleaner is expensive but worthwhile if you have invested in the best brushes. Rinse cleaned brushes thoroughly, then work them against a clean rag to get most of the water off.

For overnight storage, suspend brushes with oil-based paint on them in water, with the brushes clear of the bottom, by a wire through a drilled hole in the handle. For shorter-term storage, wrap in foil or plastic wrap to keep them wet.

For long-term storage, when brushes are clean, shake any excess water off the brush and place a rubber band around the bristles to help it to keep its shape as it dries. Rest it on its side. When completely dry, wrap brushes in paper and store in a dry place.

Cleaning up paint spills and splashes

Paint on glass is quite easy to remove: let it dry and then scrape it off. Dry paint on the floor is more difficult. On wood, scrape it off carefully as for glass, taking care not to scratch the surface. It may be necessary to sand a paint blob very carefully, trying not to damage the surrounding wood and, if necessary, touching up the floor with scratch cover or other wood treatment.

Paint on a carpet is extremely difficult to remove. If the paint is only lightly on the surface of a carpet with a pile, it may be possible to snip away the top of the fibers when the paint is dry. If it has soaked into the

▲ *Gloss paint can look stunning. These paneled walls and wooden door have been given a glossy sheen in a warm shade of cream which reflects the incoming sunlight. However, if undercoat or primer is incorrectly applied, a top coat of gloss can end up looking dull. If this happens, wait for the paint to dry, sand and clean it, then reapply the gloss.*

carpet, you can try removing it with a strong dry-cleaning fluid, but this may spread the color. If the stain cannot be removed, it will be necessary to cut out and replace a small square of carpet.

If you get paint on a recently painted wood surface, lightly sand the surface and touch up with the appropriate color. In certain situations, if a blob of oil paint has splashed onto a water-based paint, for example, it may be necessary to prime the patch before repainting.

Paint problems

Blistering

This will occur if moisture has been trapped between the layers of paint. To correct, strip off the offending layers (this is not difficult if the blistering is extensive, as much of it will simply peel off) and reapply the paint. Blistering may also occur if the wrong type of paint has been applied—for example, a water-based paint over a layer of oil-based paint—so check that your paints are compatible.

Wrinkling or sagging

If you apply paint too heavily, it will begin to sag. To resolve this, wait until the paint is dry, sand sufficiently heavily for a smooth surface, and reapply the top coat. Alternatively, strip off all the top coats entirely and reapply the paint less heavily.

Dribbles

This is a consequence of too much paint on the brush. If you notice a dribble or "run" as you are painting, work across it with your brush before the final laying off (see pages 210–211). If the dribble has begun to dry, leave it until it is completely dry, then sand it down and touch up as necessary.

Undercoat showing through

This could happen for a number of reasons. Either the wrong color of undercoat has been used (too dark for a pale top coat or too pale for a dark top coat) or the top coat has been applied too sparingly. You may even have forgotten to add a second top coat. To rectify, paint on another layer or two of top coat.

Storing brushes used for oil painting

For long-term storage, wash brushes first in mineral spirits to loosen the paint, then in warm soapy water.

For overnight storage, suspend unwashed brushes in jars filled with water, or wrap in paper or plastic wrap.

▲ *A beautifully smooth paint finish in vivid yellow draws the eye toward this window frame and the garden beyond. Few of us have so steady a hand that we can paint a window frame without leaving splashes on the panes. Fortunately, paint is easily removed from glass; simply wait for the paint to dry, then carefully scrape it off.*

Foreign bodies stuck in the paint

Wet paint will trap anything that touches it, such as clothing fibers, dust specks, or small insects. Experts usually recommend leaving the paint until it is dry, then sanding and touching up with paint. But if the paint is wet and the foreign body is just one item (a fly or paintbrush bristle, for example, rather than a cloud of dust) you might feel confident enough to have a try at removing it in one neat swipe with a clean rag.

Crazing

This will appear if one layer of paint has been applied before a previous one was completely dry, or if the paints are not compatible. Unfortunately the only way to correct crazing is to strip off the paint completely and reapply.

Paint will not dry

This occurs for several reasons. Either the paint was not stirred properly before application, the surface was not clean, or the weather is too hot and humid. Try opening the windows for a few days, if possible. If this does not work, you will have to strip off the paint and reapply, this time making sure the surface is absolutely clean.

Gloss looks dull

This is caused if the primer and/or undercoat was improperly applied (or omitted) or is not completely dry. Alternatively, the top coat could have been applied during frosty or exceptionally cold weather. You will have to wait for the paint to dry completely, then sand lightly, clean the surface thoroughly, and apply another top coat during normal weather conditions.

Brush marks show

This will occur if cheap brushes, which are more likely to leave brushmarks in paintwork than better-quality ones, were used and/or the paint was applied too thickly and not laid off properly (see pages 210–211). To address this problem, sand, wash, and dry thoroughly, then reapply the top coat using a good-quality brush, and taking special care with your technique.

Directory of window and door hardware

Doors and windows are equipped with various fittings to help facilitate their movement and security. These pieces of door hardware may be unobtrusive or more decorative and in a style to suit the period of your home. Except for some doorknobs and handles, they are usually made out of metal, including iron, brass, and chrome.

Additional paraphernalia can be fitted to doors to perform various functions, including providing security with bolts and locks. A front door might also be fitted with a spy hole, a knocker, a mail slot, and house numbers, with a bell nearby on the outside wall. These items can be handsome or elaborate antiques, reproductions, or interesting modern designs, or anything in between, so long as they are appropriate to the door in scale and design.

Doors

Knobs

Doorknobs are twisted to operate the opening mechanism, except for those on cabinets which are designed to be pulled. Traditionally, they are made of iron, brass, glass, china, plastic, or wood, and are sometimes finished in other materials such as copper or chrome. Some eighteenth- and nineteenth-century examples are elaborately decorated and mounted on interestingly shaped back plates. Contemporary designs range in shape and type from sleek steel to colored resin "'shells." Old knobs can be bought from industrial stripping workshops, secondhand markets, and junk or antique shops. **1**

Handles

Because of the pressure exerted on them, handles are generally made in fairly robust materials such as iron, brass, or plastic. Their design ranges widely.

Rim locks

A rim lock contains the opening mechanism of a door in a metal box which is fitted to the door's surface. The box may be plain and painted black or it may be more decorative. Brass rim latches and locks are available in imitation of antique ones that were fitted to the doors of important rooms in the eighteenth and nineteenth centuries. Rim latches have an appealingly unpretentious appearance especially suited to old houses but do not appear to have caught the imagination of contemporary door hardware designers.

Because they can be prised or kicked off a door, rim latches are less secure than mortise latches (below) and therefore not generally acceptable for exterior doors; however they are useful on an interior door that is too thin for a mortise look. **3**

Mortise latches and locks

A mortise latch or lock is fitted into the thickness of the door and is thus hidden from view. Insurance companies generally specify the type of mortise lock acceptable to them for exterior door security. **2**

Thumb latches

A thumb latch is the type of fastening mechanism that is appropriate on farmhouse-type batten doors. You grip a vertical handle while pressing down on a protruding iron (or wood, if the latch is wooden) plate just above it. This raises the latch which lifts the bolt (known as the "beam") to open or secure the door. All the mechanics of the fastening are on the surface of the door, which gives the thumb latch a special charm and interest.

Escutcheons

These are the small plates, sometimes with a swinging flap for draft exclusion, that surround keyholes. Door handle back plates often incorporate an escutcheon.

Finger plates

These are narrow rectangular panels placed vertically above and sometimes below a doorknob. They are designed to protect much-used doors from greasy fingermarks. Antique ones are made of the same variety of nonporous materials as doorknobs; modern ones are just as likely to be made of plastic, resin, or a metal such

the frame, the action also cuts out drafts. Sash fasteners come in a variety of designs, most commonly traditional styles made either from iron, which you oil or paint, or lacquered brass, which you do not.

Casement fasteners

Casements require two fittings, a fastener at the side and a stay along the bottom which not only helps to keep the window closed but also allows it to be left open without flapping. Perhaps the prettiest design widely available is the rat-tail, which ends in a spiral shape.

Metal casements sometimes have a cockspur fastener; in this type, the part that turns onto the window has two or more teeth, allowing the window to be fastened open just a fraction for ventilation.

Espagnolette

This is the long bolt that fastens a pair of French doors. A handle, fitted on one of the doors, turns the bolt, which shoots up and down into the window frame.   **5**

Restoring hardware

Door and window hardware can be cleaned then restored with household metal polish, paint stripper, or old-fashioned recipes.

First wash the item thoroughly with soap and water or a solution of soda crystals, to enable you to establish its condition. Then clean it up: old lacquer can be removed with acetone; soak iron hardware in kerosene, then scrub with steel wool to remove rust; wash chrome with a solution of dishwashing liquid and a small dash of ammonia; de-tarnish brass by rubbing it with half a lemon sprinkled with salt. Finally, polish the item with a product appropriate to the material in which it is finished. If you like a bright finish and do not like polishing, add clear acrylic lacquer.

as stainless steel. Few people today bother with finger plates, because modern paints have excellent wash-down qualities, but they do serve a purpose, especially for a bare wood door, and add smartness. You can decorate a clear glass or plastic finger plate by painting it on the back before attaching it to the door.

Hinges

Hinges are barely noticeable, except for the elongated "strap" hinges used on old ledged and braced doors. Often shaped and decorative, these are usually painted black, in contrast to the color of the door. The recessed hinges

used on a paneled or flush door are usually either brass, in which case they should not be painted, or iron, which can be painted. It is advisable to remove paint from the screw heads so that they can be unscrewed easily at a later date if necessary.   **4**

Portière

This is an ingenious piece of hardware, seen in some European houses, which helps to exclude drafts. Consisting of a hinged metal curtain pole attached to the wall at one end and the door at the other, it hangs a drapery across the inside of the door and opens with it.

Windows

Sash fasteners

These secure the two parts of a double-hung window, pushing them apart vertically and together horizontally. By pushing the sashes firmly into

▲ *A length of muslin, tie-dyed in vibrant colors and knotted at each end, is looped over a simple wooden pole. This sill-length curtain is dramatic and will veil a dull view, but won't give draft exclusion or much privacy. The window's exuberant cut-out frame adds to its impact.*

window seat, will dictate the latter, as anything longer will not fall straight. Below-sill-length curtains are more effective at keeping out drafts, as the entire window is covered. They also look more generous than curtains that just touch the sill.

Shorter curtains that barely graze the sill are a practical option in a kitchen or bathroom, although a blind would perhaps be a better and more economical choice.

Budgeting

Whatever your style preference, your budget is also a significant factor. It will naturally influence your choice of fabric, which varies widely in cost, as well as the amount of material you can afford to buy. Even on a limited budget, extra-long, extra-full draperies are not out of the question, for they can be made of inexpensive fabric and can be left unlined. Or consider other styles of curtain or drapery and combinations with

▲ *An ingenious curtain made from pieces of Chinese paper, each decorated with a sheet of gold leaf and glued to a string of natural hemp pulled down with a weight. The paper is hung in carefully staggered rows so that the pieces do not touch and the light between them makes a zigzag pattern.*

Floor-length draperies are also the best option for draft exclusion, especially if they drape luxuriously on the floor.

Long draperies and curtains use the largest quantity of fabric and are therefore more expensive to make than shorter draperies, but you do get a great deal more effect for your effort. Another important factor in their favor is that, if you are a beginner and are worried about getting your

hems straight, even as much as an inch or so (a few centimeters) out will not show with draperies that flow onto the floor.

Sill length

Short curtains and draperies look more informal than long ones and suit small windows as well as those that are square or wider than they are tall. They fall either a little below the sill or just to it; a prominent sill, or a shades, which can achieve a similar effect using less fabric—for example pull-up curtains or a shade beneath a valance.

It is possible to buy readymade curtains and draperies, and you may be lucky enough to find exactly what you want all ready to hang. But if you have a particular effect or fabric in mind, you will either have to make the window treatment yourself or have it made for you. The latter option is likely to be expensive (though you might have a friend or relative who is skilled in this type of work.) If you have draperies custom-made, you might save a little money by choosing a less expensive fabric. Look in the classified ads in the back of home decorating magazines; you can often find bargains offered by fabric wholesalers.

Making curtains and draperies

Making curtains or draperies yourself (see pages 240–253) will obviously save money, but consider carefully whether you have the sewing skills, patience, and time for this job. If all that is required is a pair or two of simple curtains, making them yourself may be a good idea—and will give you valuable experience that can later be applied to more ambitious projects. However, full-length lined draperies are a big job—the sheer bulk of the fabric can be daunting.

Headings for window treatments

An important decision is the choice of heading for draperies. This plays a major role in setting the style. For curtains, a simple casing is often all that is required. For draperies, the choices are almost limitless. French pleats and a concealed rod are unbeatable if you want a classic look suitable for both traditional and modern interiors. But if your ceilings are high, or if you want to make more of a feature of the draperies, you may wish to add a valance or a cornice.

Fabric

The choice of fabric suitable for draperies and curtains is so huge it can seem baffling (see pages 236–239). Take the general style of the room as your starting point and establish which type of window treatment is most appropriate: flimsy fabric for creating floaty effects or for layering; solid-colored fabric, pale or richly colored, perhaps with a velvety pile or an interesting weave; refreshing checks or stripes; printed graphic motifs; traditional fabric like floral chintz, tartan, printed linen, or *toile de Jouy*; pictorial fabric; ethnic-style fabric like crewelwork, kilim print, or Indian hand-blocked cotton; rich silk or damask.

Practical considerations are often involved in the choice of a fabric. Silk fades and rots in sunlight; washable cotton is useful in a kitchen or bathroom. Scale is another factor: a large window can take a huge print which would look entirely out of proportion on a small window; and conversely a small print might look insignificant on a large window.

Trimming

Trimmings can make all the difference to curtains and draperies but they must be used with great care (see pages 238–239). A constrasting braid or ribbon set back from the edge of a plain curtain or shade gives it weight and definition. A substantial fringe along the bottom of a pull-up curtain or balloon shade can transform it, making it look serious and luxurious.

Lining

The final but important consideration when making draperies is whether or not to line them (see pages 248–253). Lightweight, unlined draperies are the simplest to make, whereas lined draperies keep out light and drafts better and look more substantial. If you want to give your draperies an opulent look, add an interlining. This extra layer not only adds a touch of Old World elegance but also serves a practical purpose, insulating rooms against winter cold. Detachable linings are versatile as they can be taken off for laundering, or removed in summer to give the curtains a lighter effect.

◄ *Flowing elegantly onto the floor, these unlined draperies have an integral valance and are tied to a slender wooden pole. Because the draperies are made from preshrunk muslin, and the valances, edging, and ties from preshrunk linen-cotton blends, these draperies can be machine-washed without problem.*

Directory of drapery hardware

There is an astonishing variety of rods, poles, and other accessories to help you achieve exactly the kind of window treatment you have in mind.

Traverse rods

For draperies that are intended to draw back and forth, a traverse rod is essential. This kind of drapery rod is fitted with cords, which operate two master slides, to which the leading edge of each drapery panel is attached. The movement of the master slide draws the drapery panel across the window.

It is possible to buy electric traverse rods. A small motor at the end of the rod draws the draperies, activated at the touch of a button.

Although traverse rods come with directions, it is a good idea to have them installed by a professional, unless you have an aptitude for dealing with mechanical objects. Most draperies are fairly heavy, and it is most important that the rod be fixed securely to the wall and that the system of cords and sliders function smoothly.

Conventional traverse rods

This type of rod is intended to be concealed by the top of the draperies when the draperies are closed. It is usually made of white-painted metal. Flat rods are adjustable to suit different widths of window treatment. They may be two-way draw (for two drapery panels) or one-way draw (for a single panel); two one-way draws could, for example, be used at a corner picture window, one drawing a single panel to the right and the other drawing a panel to the left. There are double traverse rods, to be used with two layers of draw draperies (normally an opaque pair over sheers) and combinations of traverse and curtain rod, where simple glass curtains are used under draw draperies. Special traverse rods designed to fit around bay and bow windows are also available.

A conventional traverse rod is suitable where there is little wall space between the top of a window and the ceiling. The drapery heading can fit just below the ceiling, giving the impression of being suspended from it.

If the draperies are reasonably lightweight, the two cords controlling them can hang loose. For heavy draperies, a cord extension pulley is required. This is fixed to the baseboard or floor and holds a continuous cord, which operates the draperies, keeping them under an even tension.   ■4

Decorative traverse rods

This type of rod works on the same principle as a conventional traverse rod; the difference is that it is intended to be seen. Decorative rods come in a great range of styles, including "brass" and "wood" poles imitating the traditional simple pole with rings, and are embellished with finials. The rings are only partial rings, being attached to the cord and slider system.

Poles and rods

For hanging stationary draperies and curtains there are many kinds of rods, both decorative and purely functional.

Wood and metal poles

These are the traditional method of hanging draperies. Although unsuitable for draw draperies—because pulling the draperies by hand will eventually damage the fabric—they can be used where draperies are intended to remain stationary most or all of the time. The poles are normally intended to be seen and are decorated with finials. They have the advantage that they can be stained or painted to harmonize with any color scheme. Natural wood suits many interiors. Plain black, gray, or white is discreet, whereas a gold-painted pole would make a splendid foil for rich brocade.

Metal poles are generally made of brass, iron, or steel. Iron and steel are often painted black, but they could equally well be painted another color.

Matching rings are used to hang the draperies from wooden or metal poles, but a handmade cased or looped heading could be used instead.   ■1 ■3

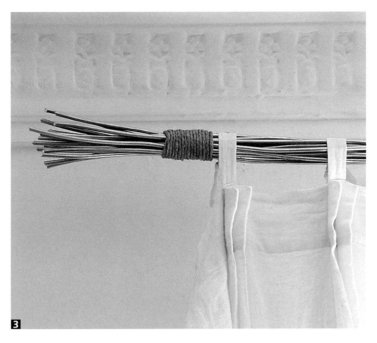

3

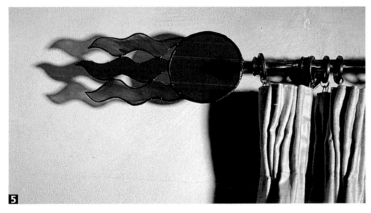

5

rings should fit the pole, but not too tightly or the draperies will be difficult to draw. A ring at each end of the pole secures the outer edge of each drapery panel.   **2**

Clip-on rings

These small rings are suitable for lightweight curtains and are often seen on café curtains, where they clip onto the center of each pleat.

Sew-on rings

These are most commonly available in brass (or brass-finished metal) and plastic. They are suitable only for lightweight curtains, and are more often used on the backs of Roman and balloon shades.

Finials

A finial is usually fitted onto each end of a decorative rod. They finish the rod with a flourish and need to be in proportion to it. A fussy little finial on the end of a stout pole, for instance, would look silly. There is a wide choice of finials, including balls, spear heads, arrow ends, curlicues, rams' heads, pineapples, and many more, in a range of materials and finishes.   **5**

Weights

These can be sewn into the hem of a drapery to give it added weight and help it hang well. They come in two forms: disks and tape. If a disk is not sewn into position, this kind of weight will gradually move along the bottom of the drapery. Leadweight tape consists of a narrow tube of fabric with small cylindrical weights which is placed in the bottom of the hem.

Eyelets

These are useful for making neat holes in a curtain heading, through which a ring or hook can be inserted. They are most often used on shower curtains, but can also be used to create an informal style of curtain.

Simple drapery rods

For curtains and draperies that seldom need to be opened, such as sheers, an alternative to a traverse rod is a drapery rod that has sliders but comes without cords. The drapery rod is invisible when the draperies are closed, and the draperies are moved back and forth by hand.

Round curtain rods

A variety of slim round rods is available for hanging different types of curtains. One of these is designed mainly for café curtains and, because it is generally on view, is often given a decorative brass finish. If the curtain needs to be hung inside the window

frame or in the recess, you can get a rod with a spring-tension socket, which holds the rod in place, without brackets and screws.

Flat curtain rods

These metal rods, which are normally painted white, project out from the wall and can be adjusted to different widths of curtain. The curtains are headed with a casing, also known as a rod pocket, which slips over the rod. A recent variation on the flat rod is the "Continental" rod, which is made in widths ranging from 2½ to 4 inches (6.5–10cm). The wide casing gathered over the rod gives extra interest to the top of the curtains.

Accessories

Hooks

The type of hook required depends on the type of rod used and partly on the heading of the drapery. With some heading tape the pleats are formed by the hooks themselves. Called "pleater hooks," these have four prongs, which slip into four adjacent pockets in the tape, producing three folds on the right side of the drapery. Single-prong hooks are used to anchor the draperies at the leading and outside edges.

Different hooks are used for cord-type drapery tapes. These slip into small pockets or loops in the tape and through the sliders on the traverse rod.

The range of single hooks available includes styles that are sewn into the heading and ones with points that slip into the heading. Some of the hooks are designed for pleats that finish below the rod, while others are for pleats that conceal the rod.

Drapery rings

Large rings are used with metal and wooden poles. If you buy a kit, the brackets and rings will be included; otherwise buy the rings separately. The

Mounting poles and rods

Although a traverse rod should, ideally, be fitted by an expert, there are some curtain and drapery rods that anyone with basic carpentry skills can fit. Flat curtain rods are quite easy to attach to a wall, as are the round rods used for café curtains and those used for casement window curtains. The simpler types of drapery rod can also be fixed by the do-it-yourself enthusiast.

Mounting poles

Poles are designed to be face-fixed to a wall with support brackets, one at each end and possibly an additional central bracket. Some rods can be end-fixed by slotting them into side wall fixings.

A bracket prevents the rings from moving any farther along the pole, so the position of the end brackets (and indeed the length of the pole) depends on the fullness of the drapery and how far back from the window you want the drapery to pull. A frequent mistake is to place the brackets too close to the window. As a guide, fix brackets at least 6 inches (15cm) out from the window frame on each side, and allow about 4 inches (10cm) between the bracket and the finial. The outer ring sits between the bracket and the finial to hold the drapery in place when closed.

The pole should be installed parallel to the top of the window, unless this is wildly out of true with the line of the ceiling, in which case you can position the pole strictly level, using a carpenter's level, or somewhere in between level and parallel to the window, whichever looks better. The pole should be high enough above the window for the drapery to cut out light at the top, but not so high that there is a great expanse of wall between it and the top of the window.

If you would like the curtain to hang farther into the room than the brackets allow —perhaps to clear a deep windowsill or to fall in front of a shade—mount each bracket on a wooden block. The blocks can be finished in the same way as the wall, with paint or paper. Since the brackets (or brackets and blocks) will be bearing considerable weight, make sure that they are securely mounted on the wall with long screws.

▲ Simple cotton draperies are hung with iron rings sewn directly to the top of the drapery. The rings are then strung on a narrow iron pole with decorative curled finials. Because the pole is narrow and the draperies long and therefore quite heavy, the pole is given added support by a central bracket.

▶ Pretty, short gingham draperies are ideal for the kitchen of a farmhouse. They are hung from a standard traverse rod which is concealed by a covered board. The board has been decorated with the same fabric as that of the draperies, and extends down behind the ruffle but in front of the rod.

Mounting rods

Fitting lightweight rods is easy, as the ends can be slotted into small metal brackets with integral sockets, either recessed or face-fixed. Telescopic rods are also available; they have a spring that enables them to expand to fit the window. Doweling, being less rigid than a standard curtain rod, needs to be well supported in the middle to prevent it from sagging. A small decorative hook of the type onto which you loop a tieback will do the job. Generally speaking, the thicker the pole, the farther it can go without a central support, but even a full-sized pole may need one if it is required to carry heavy draperies.

Mounting a simple drapery rod

The height at which a rod is fixed depends on the look you want and whether there is to be a valance. It can be attached either to the wall or to the ceiling.

A rod is attached to the wall by brackets which can be either of fixed size or extendable to the required length. Supplied with kits or bought separately, extendable brackets are useful if you want the drapery to stand clear of a shade or glass curtains that

1 *Rods are held by matching brackets, screwed into the wall. Use plastic anchors if fixing onto a masonry wall.*

2 *To mount a rod, draw a horizontal line with a carpenter's level to show the position for the brackets.*

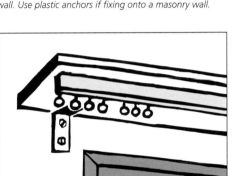

3 *Valance shelves are supported by right-angled brackets screwed to the underside, behind the rod.*

4 *To conceal the rod, make a small cornice board and cover it with the same fabric as the draperies.*

will hang behind it. They can be screwed directly to the wall or to a wooden batten mounted on the wall, which will spread the load. Special brackets also allow more than one rod for a layered effect.

The rod should be fitted at least 2 inches (5cm) above the window and 6–16 inches (15–40cm) beyond either side of the window. First screw the brackets to the wall, making sure they are level and spaced at regular intervals. Use a hacksaw to cut a plastic or a metal rod to the exact measurement you require. Clip the rod to the brackets, and then secure it to the wall according to the manufacturer's directions.

When the window has a valance or a similar covering, the rod can be attached either to the wall or to the base of the valance shelf. Its position should be far enough back from the front edge of the shelf to allow room for the thickness of the pleated drapery fabric, but not so far back that the rod is visible when looking up at the valance.

The rod can also be hidden when the draperies are drawn open by use of a cornice board. This is a narrow piece of wood, covered with the drapery material and attached with hook-and-loop tape, tacks, or glue around the edge of a valance shelf.

Returns

To exclude light and drafts properly, draperies are normally made with a return. This is a permanently fixed section of the drapery that blocks out the gap between the end of the rod and the wall. If the rod is attached to the wall by short brackets, very little light and few drafts will get through, and so a return may not be necessary. If the brackets are longer, make a fixing for the end of the drapery with a screw eye. If there is no valance shelf, either attach a block of wood to the wall for this purpose or use a special return kit. This includes an arm which goes at a right angle to the end of the rod and into which the drapery is hooked.

Tartar, the Scottish plaid beloved of Queen Victoria, who decorated whole rooms with it, has a sober, masculine feel. The colors are mostly rich and resonant, though some are rather drab and disappointing. **1**

Graphic print fabrics

Sometimes sharply defined, sometimes loose and painterly, but generally fresh and uncluttered, images such as stars, heraldic motifs, circles, triangles, and letters of the alphabet are favored motifs for this sort of fabric. Colors vary from pale and subtle to knock-out brilliant. Many are manufactured in several colorways, so that the draperies in one color, say, can be combined with a valance in another— the pattern being the unifying force.

Picture-print fabrics

These have picture images scattered across them, and the best are wonderfully fresh and attractive. Because of their content, such as circus performers, boats, animals, cups and saucers, fruit and vegetables, classical motifs or playing cards, some are better used in one type of room than another. Some designed for children's rooms are particularly delightful. **2**

Ethnic fabrics

These can add variety and interest to almost any style of interior, not only those with an ethnic feel. Indian crewelwork, woolen chain stitch worked on a cotton background, usually depicts birds and leaves in light shades of blues, greens, and pinks. Kilim print is strongly colored printed cotton with bold and distinctive geometric patterns drawn from kilims, woven cotton and wool rugs made in central Asia. Hand-blocked Indian cotton can be fragile, so it needs to be handled with care.

Rich fabrics

These gorgeous fabrics are useful for creating a grand or sumptuous interior and an aura of luxury. Pure silk is the most lustrous of fabrics but varies greatly in type, quality and price. It is available in a dazzling choice of colors, some with warp and weft of different hues, for an iridescent effect, **4**

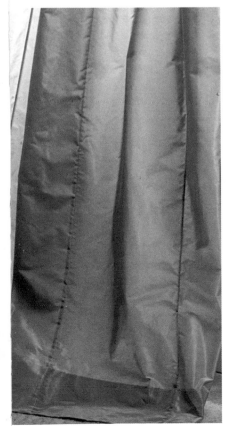

Interlinings

The custom of interlining draperies is just beginning to catch on in the United States. In European countries, it has long been in favor—no doubt originally for providing more comfort in cold rooms. In England draperies are generally lined with a thick woven fabric called "bump." You may be able to order this from a specialist fabric supplier. An alternative is table felt, which is more readily available. Thin batting is another possibility. Or you could use any soft material, such as flannelette. The effect will not be so luxurious as that produced by bump or table felt, but it will give some added body to the draperies.

Trimmings

Interesting trimmings can transform a handsome curtain or drapery into something really special. A ribbon, ⅝ inch (1.5cm) or more wide, adds interest and definition if you choose a contrasting color and set it back from the edges of the fabric. Braid is a looped and woven trimming available in a multitude of colors and designs, some of which are wonders of textile engineering and fiercely expensive. Some base fringe, sewn along the leading edges of a pair of simple muslin or sheer curtains, will completely transform them. Other kinds of fringe, too, come in endless variations of color and design. One of the best uses of fringe is at the bottom of a balloon shade or pull-up curtain (see pages 266–267). When the shade is pulled up, the fringe looks pretty against the light; when the shade is let down, it gives weight and definition to the bottom edge. A valance or shade with a shaped lower edge can be made to look positively exotic if tassels are attached to each downward point. Alternatively, you can sew or string beads along the edge of a sheer curtain for added weight, detail, and a delicate touch of color. **3**

some overprinted with a pattern, some woven into checks or other patterns. Although it is not hardy enough for shades and it rots in sunlight, it should not necessarily be excluded from window treatment, but it must be used with care and forethought. **4**

Damask can be made from silk, cotton, or man-made fibers. It has a woven, two-tone pattern, usually of intertwined leaves and/or flowers. Really grand damask comes with appliqué and/or embroidery added to the surface. Like damask, brocade has a woven pattern but in more than the one color.

Velvet, the most luxurious of fabrics, has a pile which must always lie in the same direction, otherwise the color will look different. Available in a wide range of colors and patterns, it is incomparably sumptuous and invaluable for creating an atmosphere of comfort and elegance. The thickness of its pile makes it unsuitable for making into shades. Plush has a pile like velvet, but it is longer and less closely woven. It was particularly popular in the nineteenth century for tablecloths and as draperies in a multi-layered window treatment.

Lining fabrics

Drapery lining is available in a range of colors to match or contrast with different fabrics. Although some are certified fade-proof, the safest choice is always cream or white. There is also a choice of qualities, the best having a certain amount of body that will survive cleaning.

Blackout, a special fabric for excluding light, is available in various weights, the heaviest of which can be difficult to work with. Thermal lining, known as milium, is coated on one side with aluminum and gives excellent thermal protection without adding bulk to curtains in the way that an interlining does.

Cutting, matching, and joining fabric

▲ *A simple yellow and white striped cotton has been cleverly transformed by dividing the curtains into bands with the stripes going alternately down and across. The bands of fabric are separated by a narrow black stripe. For added visual interest, a checked Roman shade hangs behind each pair of curtains.*

Cutting fabric

Iron the fabric to make it easier to measure. Cut this to the individual lengths you require, making sure that both top and bottom raw edges are cut straight—at 90 degrees to the selvages. With loosely woven fabric and linens, a weft (crosswise) thread can be drawn out, enabling you to cut along the line left by it in the fabric. For other fabrics you will need to use a right-angled triangle.

Solid-colored fabric

Measure out your lengths, marking each cutting line with pins at each side on the selvage. If necessary, use a yardstick to align the two marks, and, using tailor's chalk, draw a line to cut across the fabric. As you cut each length, mark the top of the fabric with a safety pin. Fold each length neatly or roll it onto a cardboard tube to prevent it getting creased or crumpled. If you are making two panels, then you will need to divide the number of widths in half at this point (e.g. 4 widths = 2 panels of 2 widths each; 3 widths = 2 panels of 1½ widths each). The total width of fabric you need rarely coincides with an exact number of fabric widths. If the discrepancy is small, it may be preferable to absorb some extra width by taking it up in the heading. Certainly for unlined, fine fabric, distributing excess fabric in the spacing of the folds as it hangs is less of a problem than for a heavy fabric with a pleated heading.

If you do need to remove excess fabric, trim a width at the outside edge of each panel, never at the inside or leading edge. If a width of fabric is being split into two to make up the total width, add the part width to the outside or edge in the same way.

Patterned fabric

Before you start work, check for faults and misprinting. The fabric should be cut following the grain. If the pattern is not square to the selvage or is printed off the grain, consider returning it to the store or adjust your cutting to follow the pattern.

Try to arrange a patterned fabric so that the bottom of the panel falls at the end of a repeat. Mark a line across the fabric along the base of the first pattern repeat, then mark a second line for the hem allowance—6½ inches (16cm) below for lined curtains, 4 inches (10cm) for unlined. Cut on this second line. For full-length draperies that are to hang from a decorative rod, using a hand-made heading of slight fullness, you might prefer to have the complete repeat at the top. In this case, you will need to measure your lengths from the top of the fabric downward. Draw your first line across the fabric at the top of the pattern repeat, then a second line 1½ inches (4cm) above that for the heading allowance. Cut on the second line.

It is important that the pattern matches across the widths and across both curtains if there are two. Line up the first cut length against the uncut fabric, matching the pattern exactly before cutting a second length.

Joining widths

Solid-colored fabric

To join the drops, pin right sides together along the edge. Baste along each seam then stitch, ⅝ inch (1.5cm) in from the edge, from the bottom. Press flat. For unlined draperies, you can make a flat fell seam. Having pressed the seam flat, trim back one seam allowance to half its original width. Fold the other one over to cover it, then fold under this edge of the seam allowance to enclose the raw edges. Top stitch through all the layers. This will show on the front of the drapery.

Patterned fabric

To join patterned fabric, fold under and press a ⅝-inch (1.5cm) seam allowance down the side that is to be joined of one length of fabric. With right sides facing upward, place this over the unfolded seam allowance of the second piece, matching the pattern horizontally and pinning it in place. This should be basted using ladder stitch. With a knotted thread starting under the fold, stitch up through the fabric and across the seamline and down through the bottom piece and back up through the fold. Repeat to form horizontal "ladder" stitches across the seamline. To machine stitch the seam, place the right sides of the fabric together and stitch in the usual way.

Cutting, matching, and joining fabric

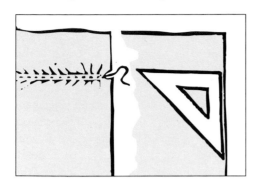

1 *To get a straight, right-angled raw edge, pull out a weft thread, if possible, or place a triangle on the selvage.*

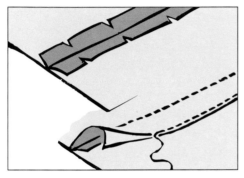

2 *Either press seams open or trim back one side, fold over the other to enclose the raw edges, and topstitch.*

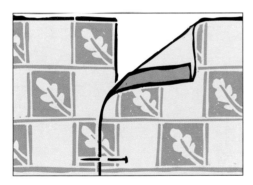

3 *To join patterned fabric, fold under one seam allowance, place it over the other, matching the pattern, and pin.*

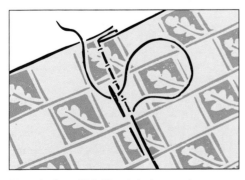

4 *Baste in place with ladder stitch, then turn the top piece back and machine stitch along the seamline.*

▲ *In this elegant window treatment, fixed linen curtains have a cased heading made from the same bold stripe as the shade behind, and the linen has been carefully matched to insure the pattern works perfectly across the seams. The curtains' static heading allows them to drape beautifully, and the decorative pole and finials complete the effect.*

Headings

The way that the top of the drapery is gathered or folded into a pattern of pleats is referred to as the "curtain heading." The type of heading affects how the fabric falls when the curtains are closed as well as the amount of fabric required to make them.

For heavy interlined draperies, the heading is best made by hand, with the pleats and hooks sewn in individually. This is a job for a professional or someone with experience of making draperies. The usual way for amateurs and beginners to arrange the top of draperies (simply lined or unlined) is to use ready-made heading tape.

Heading tapes vary in depth and stiffness, according to the style. In the most familiar type of heading tape, four-pronged "pleater" hooks are inserted into pockets in the tape, forming elegant French pleats. An alternative is the kind of tape in which cords are used to pull up the heading and drapery; they also contain pockets for simple hooks that are used for hanging draperies.

Heading tape is sold by the yard. The length required is a little more than the total fabric width required for each panel.

Types of heading tape
Different multiples of fabric are suggested for the tapes listed below. The range of multiples for some tapes allows a choice between the minimum amount of fabric required to make the heading look respectable and the maximum amount for a generous look.

French or pinch pleat: This tape gives regular, fanned, triple pleats at intervals across the drapery. They produce a handsome, tailored look for formal lined draperies and are available in several depths. When pulling up the tape, match the pleats evenly across both panels if there is a pair. This tape requires fabric twice the length of the rod and should be sewn ⅛ inch (3mm) from the top of the drapery.

Shirred: This tape produces a neat row of gathers (sometimes called "pencil pleats"). Suitable for most drapery, it is available in several widths and requires a fabric width of 2¼ to 2½ times the length of the rod. There are three rows of pockets, to offer a choice of hanging heights. The tape should be sewn ⅛ inch (3mm) from the top edge.

Heading tapes

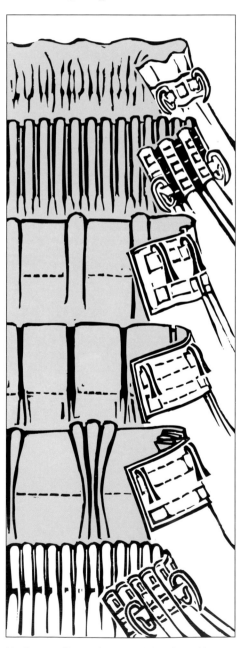

Heading tape (from top): gathered, shirred, cartridge pleat, box pleat, French/pinch pleat, and net pleat.

▶ *The pinch pleat heading, also known as a French or triple pleat, is fixed in place on this small window, giving the draperies a handsome finish. Stationary draperies are a practical choice in this situation, as there is no space on the right into which the drapery could be drawn back.*

Using heading tape

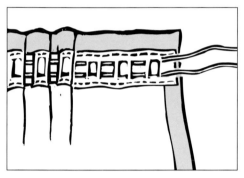

1 Turn under the heading allowance, position the tape on the drapery, and knot the strings under the cord.

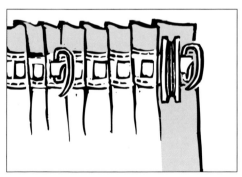

2 Hold the free cords in one hand and push the heading along until it is pleated by the required amount.

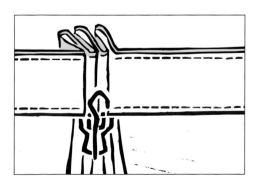

3 Insert hooks at each end and space the rest evenly along the drapery; tie the cords around a cord tidy.

4 For French pleats, insert one prong of a pleater hook in each of four pockets. Skip one pocket, then repeat.

Cartridge pleat: Cartridge pleats are single, large, regular, rounded pleats spaced between flat stretches of fabric. They give draperies sophistication, especially heavy floor-length ones. When pulling up the tape, match the pleats across both panels if there is a pair. Avoid having a pleat at either leading or outside edge; these should hang flat. Cartridge pleats require a width of 2½ times the length of the rod. The tape should be sewn ⅛ inch (3mm) from the top of the curtain.

Box pleat: Like cartridge pleat tape, this tape gives regular, tailored pleats, but these are flat and tucked behind the flat fabric rather than in front of it. Box pleats are suitable for all types of draperies, especially heavy, lined ones. When pulling up the tape, match the pleats evenly across both curtains if there is a pair. Box pleats require 3 times the length of the rod, and the tape should be sewn ⅛ inch (3mm) from the top of the drapery.

Net: This is a discreet, lightweight tape for sheer fabrics, combining pockets for hooks and loops for wire. It can be sewn to the top of the drapery, either way up, depending on how much of the drapery you want to stand up above the hooks. Alternatively, a rod can be threaded through the loops. Net tape can take a fabric width 2 to 3 three times the length of the rod.

Gathered: This tape gives a shallow, gently gathered heading suitable for informal, unlined draperies. Depending on how full the draperies are to be, the fabric width required is 1½ to 2 times the length of the rod. The tape should be sewn 1 inch (2.5cm) from the top of the drape— so the curtain will cover the traverse rod or rings—or it can be sewn closer to the top to allow it to hang below the rings.

Attaching heading tape

These instructions are based on the cord-type tape. The pleater hook tape is attached in a similar way. Heading tape is sewn to the top of the wrong side of the drapery, once the drapery has been made. Lay the tape over the

▲ *An otherwise plain French pleat drapery heading has been given the added decorative detail of a self-covered button on each of the pleats. This accentuates the pleats, but in a restrained way. The narrow decorative rod is carefully placed above the window so that it does not mask the charming plaster roses on the cove.*

raw edge of the turnback (see left for position) and pin and baste it in place. At the inside edge of the drapery, unthread the cords for about 1 inch (2.5cm), then knot them underneath. Fold the tape end under to cover the knots; baste in place. Repeat on the outside edge of the drapery, but leave the cords free and on top of the tape. Machine stitch the tape in the same direction along both edges. Machine stitch over both the tape ends, making sure the needle doesn't pass through the strings at the outside edge.

Pleating with a cord tape

Pleat the drapery by holding the loose cords and pushing the heading along until it is sufficiently pleated to measure the length of the rod (for a single panel) or half the length (for a pair). If your rod has an overlap, allow for this. Coil then knot the loose cords or wrap them around a cord tidy (a small plastic shape which is tucked into one of the pockets in the tape). Insert the hooks at equal intervals, one at each end of the drapery with others spaced evenly between them.

Curtain headings

Curtains can be gathered up and hung in a variety of ways from poles without using a heading tape. These include pierced headings, looped, tie-on, and cased headings. Except for cased headings, each of the headings described below needs to have a loop, eyelet, or tie at or very near each top corner to prevent the ends from drooping. When buying fabric for a curtain with looped headings you will need the same width of fabric as the length of the rod, and for pierced and tied headings, approximately twice the length of the rod, depending on the fabric and the way you wish the folds to hang. If in doubt, ask for advice from the salesperson.

Pierced heading

Pierced curtains have metal-rimmed eyelets inserted along the top of the curtain through which a thin pole is threaded. Use an inexpensive eyelet kit bought from a D.I.Y. or hardware store. The eyelets should be positioned on the wrong side of the hem, approximately 4 inches (10cm) apart.

If you are using an eyelet kit, practice on a spare piece of fabric before making the holes in the curtains. Place the fabric over the die provided with the kit and, using the narrow end of the tool and a hammer, punch a small hole in it. Assemble both parts of the eyelet around the hole. The washer part should be uppermost, on the wrong side of the material, with its closed side upward. Using the wide end of the tool, hit the washer sharply with a hammer. When you feel confident enough to make the eyelets in the curtain, use the position marks you have made on the curtain to line up the eyelet tool. To avoid later ripping of the fabric, the top of the curtain can be reinforced first with binding, cotton tape, or ribbon.

Looped heading

A looped heading has lined fabric tabs sewn into the top of the curtain, through which the rod is slotted. Bearing in mind the total width of the curtain, determine how many tabs you want and their width. The finished width of each should be approximately 2 inches (5cm), so to make them, double the width and add 1¼ inches (3cm) for a seam.

▲ Cheerful, cottagey sunshine-yellow gingham curtains, unlined to let through the light, have been given an interesting heading. There is an integral valance to give the heading some weight, and the fabric ties that attach the curtain to its pole are extra long so that they hang down, looking a little like ribbons.

To establish how long the tabs need to be, measure the circumference of the rod and then add 2 inches (5cm) for ease, plus 1¼ inches (3cm) for seams.

Cut out the strips of fabric; fold them in half lengthwise, right sides together, and sew ⅝-inch (1.5cm) seams. Turn the tubes right side out and press them flat with the seam in the middle of one side. Loop the tabs and sew them together with a ⅝-inch (1.5cm) seam. Sew them to the right side of the fabric, ⅝ inch (1.5cm) from the top and with the loops hanging down.

Cut a strip of fabric for the facing 3 inches (7.5cm) deep and the same width as the curtain, plus 1¼ inches (3cm). Sew a small hem along one long edge of this. With right sides facing, pin the other, unhemmed edge to the curtain, along the attachment line of the loops, ⅝ inch (1.5cm) from the top edge. Baste and then stitch this strip in place along the top edge, catching in the loop bases as you go. Sew small hems at each end of the strip so that the strip aligns perfectly with the curtain.

Headings without tapes

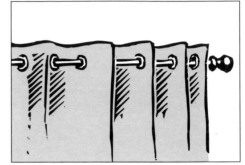

1 A pierced curtain has metal eyelets spaced along the top, and the curtain is threaded onto a narrow rod.

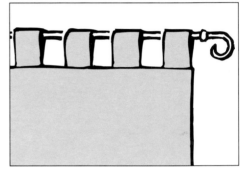

2 Tabs of fabric are looped over and sewn onto the top of the curtain. A facing strip covers the seamline.

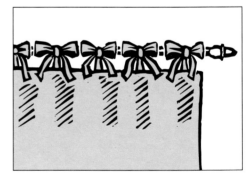

3 A variation on the looped heading is the tied-on curtain, in which fabric strips are tied into bows.

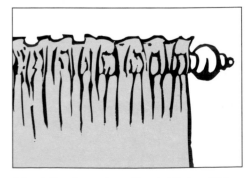

4 A cased heading can be positioned at the top of the curtain or slightly lower to form a ruffle.

Making the headings

1 Using an eyelet kit, place the fabric over the die, and hit the narrow end of the tool with a hammer.

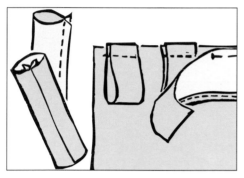

2 Fold strips of fabric in half and seam. Place along top of curtain, stitch in place, then cover with facing strip.

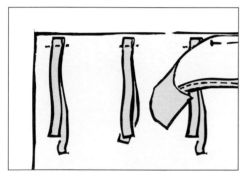

3 Stitch pairs of ties evenly across the curtain top, then cover with a facing strip as for the looped heading.

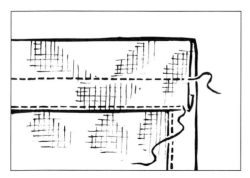

4 Fold a double hem deep enough for the slot and ruffle (if desired) and stitch on either side of the casing.

Fold the facing strip over to the back of the curtain, wrong sides together. Press so that the loops stand up. Slipstitch along the bottom edge and sides of the facing.

Tie-on curtains

Ties can be sewn into the top of the curtain in the same manner as the tabs of a looped heading and tied around a pole. Loose ties—made of ribbon, raffia, string, or "invisible" fishing line—could be inserted through the eyelets of a pierced curtain instead of a pole.

Cased heading

A cased heading, or casing, is made by forming a channel or slot to take the curtain

▲ *These stunning gauzy linen curtains have been given texture and interest by making horizontal pleats throughout their length. The pleats, which hang loose, are quite narrow at the top and increasingly wide as they approach the bottom. The curtains have cased headings at the top and drape on the floor.*

rod. At its simplest this can be made at the very top of the curtain heading; or it can be placed just down from the top of the curtain so that a ruffle stands up above it. For this, fold a double hem deep enough for the slot and any ruffle, baste, and then machine stitch along either side of the slot, in the same direction. The size of the slot is dictated by the diameter of the pole, which should fit easily, without the fabric being too tight or slack. You need a total fabric width of up to 2½ times the length of the pole, plus side hems. Curtains with cased headings are not intended to be drawn back, so they are suited to sheer fabrics that are intended to hang down permanently or be draped to one side.

Other headings

For lightweight curtains, make a double hem at the top edge and simply sew small brass rings at intervals along it for threading onto a rod. Alternatively, you can buy special curtain clips—essentially rings with decorative clips at the bottom—which clip onto the top of the curtain (see pages 232–233).

No-sew curtains

It is possible to make curtains without sewing a single stitch. All you need are tools and materials such as fabric glue, pinking shears, hammer and nails, or a staple gun and staples, an eyelet tool, or curtain clips. For curtains that make use of either of the latter two items, fold and glue a wide ribbon or tape over the raw edge at the top of the fabric to finish and reinforce it.

For all these curtains, use a fabric that is wide enough to cover the window without needing seams and, if possible, one that has a self-colored selvage. You can leave the edges plain or you can cut, turn back, and glue decorative borders such as zigzags, scallops, or castellated patterns.

Draped fabric

A simple curtain style consists of a length of fabric, twice the height of the window, just thrown over a rod, with one or both layers draped to one side. To prevent the curtain from sliding along the rod, reinforce and nail or staple the fabric at intervals to it.

Unlined and sheer draperies

Although they are not appropriate for many situations, unlined draperies are among the most versatile, and in the right setting they can be beautiful. A single thickness of light-weight fabric will not excel at excluding light or drafts, but it has its own positive qualities. It will drape easily over a hold-back or on the floor. It can diffuse sunshine, creating privacy without blocking the light, and it can make an important contribution to a layered window treatment.

Simple glass curtains, made with a casing, may serve these purposes admirably.

Natural fabrics

Linen, cotton twill, slub cotton, and even unbleached muslin all work well when made into unlined draperies, as do lightweight, purpose-made textiles such as striped cotton sheets, Indian hand-printed cotton bedspreads, and saris with glittering woven borders (but remember that pure silk fades and even rots in sunlight). You can create your own decoration on an unlined cotton drapery by painting or drawing on it with special fabric paints or pens.

Sheers

Net, voile, lace, and muslin are not intended to be lined, so they can be used to veil a window rather than to cover it up. They can be difficult to handle, especially if they are made from certain man-made fibers. If you find they are slippery, try placing strips of

▶▶ Two layers of muslin, each a different brilliant color, are sewn together across the top to create a magical drapery that drapes and billows beautifully. Natural fibers such as cotton can be dyed colorfast at home in a washing machine with fabric dyes.

▶ The single, flat, white unlined drapery that masks this window can be draped back to either side during the day. Braid strung with ornaments, laid flat across the top, adds visual interest and reduces the drapery's starkness and severity.

tissue paper between the two layers you are sewing together and the bed of the sewing machine; you just tear the paper away afterwards. Use lightweight thread with sheers.

Washing unlined draperies

Depending on the fabric, unlined draperies can often be washed, a process not advised for lined curtains because the different fabrics shrink at different rates. Moreover the weight and bulk of such draperies often preclude washing. A sensible idea is to pre-wash the

Making the draperies

Unlined draperiess are the easiest kind to make yourself, especially if you have chosen a fabric that is easy to handle. With sufficiently wide fabric you may not even have to join drops, just hem around the edges, and sew on heading tape or rings. If you do have to join drops, remember that the seams will be seen on the back of the curtain. You can use an open flat seam, but a French or flat fell seam, which encloses the raw edges, will give a much neater finish.

Once the widths are joined and any excess at the sides trimmed, turn in and press a double ¾-inch (2cm) hem on each side of the drapery and a double 2-inch (5cm) hem along the bottom, inserting leadweight tape (special weighted tape) if you want to give the fabric a bit of added weight.

To miter the corners (which gives a neat, short diagonal seam where the side and bottom hems meet), unfold one turn of both the bottom and side hems, but mark the limit of the double turns with pins on the edge. Fold the corner up diagonally, through the corner point of the drapery and the points marked with a pin. Refold the bottom and side hems to form a neat miter. Finish these hems and the diagonal folded edges with slipstitch. Do not cut the fabric across the corner, as it's possible that you will want to alter the drapery in the future.

Measure the finished curtain length up from the hem and mark the line with pins. Turn over the excess at the top, folding in the sides at a slight angle as you do so to form a neat edge. Press it and then trim back the fabric if necessary so that the heading tape will cover the raw edge. Snip the hems at each side on the fold line to ease the material. Attach the heading tape and pleat the curtains (see pages 244–245).

You are now ready to hang the drapery panel on its rod. The outermost hook on each curtain goes into a fixed hole to anchor it in place. This is either an eyelet screwed into the mounting board or into a wall-mounted wooden block, or the end hole in a traverse rod; alternatively, on a simple pole, it is the ring on the pole between the end bracket and the finial.

fabric so that any shrinkage happens before you make the draperies. The disadvantage of this is that you remove the finish or dressing that helps protect it from gathering dust.

An alternative to pre-washing is to cut the draperies extra wide and long, so that they drape on the floor, gather or pleat the fabric tightly at the top when you first hang the draperies, and wash them only when necessary. Any shrinkage will be absorbed by the billowing bottom, and you can gather the width less tightly across the top.

Making unlined draperies

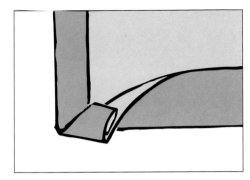

1 Turn a double ¾-in. (2cm) hem at each side and a double 2-in. (5cm) hem along the bottom. Press.

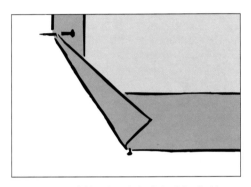

2 Open out one fold and mark the limit of the double hems with pins. Fold diagonally through both pins.

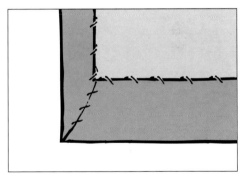

3 Refold the edges to form a miter, and slipstitch the diagonal join and both hems.

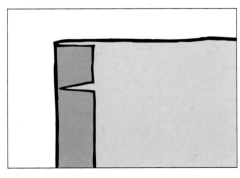

4 Finally, hem the top of the drapery, snipping into the hem along both sides of the fold line to ease the material.

Loose-lined draperies

Making the draperies

In these loose-lined draperies, the lining is attached to the main fabric at the top and sides only and so hangs loose, rather than the front and lining fabrics being sewn to each other as in locked-in lined draperies. The easiest way to make loose-lined draperies is by the "tube method"—so called because a tube is made with the main and lining fabrics. These are the easiest type of lined drapery to make. (To make draperies with a locked-in lining, follow the instructions on pages 252–253.)

Join drops and press seams open on both the main and the lining fabrics (see pages 242–243). The lining fabric should be about 4 inches (10cm) narrower than the front fabric and 3¼ inches (8cm) shorter. Finish the bottom of the lining by machine stitching a double 2-inch (5cm) hem. Then lay the fabrics right sides together, with the bottom edge of the lining 7 inches (18cm) short of the bottom raw edge of the main fabric. Machine stitch the sides of the drapery, taking a ⅝-inch (1.5cm) seam allowance, with the edges of the lining and main fabric aligned, stopping well short of the top and bottom to allow for mitering.

You now have a tube of fabric. Turn it right side out, and press the sides so that the main fabric comes around to the back an equal amount at each edge. One way of doing this is to mark the middle of the wrong side of both the main fabric and the lining with tailor's chalk, then match the marks when pressing the edges. Make a double 3¼-inch (8cm) hem on the main fabric, which will sit behind and just be covered by the lining, sewing in leadweight tape or weights, and miter the corners (see pages 248–249). If you are a perfectionist or there is any doubt about the rod or floor being exactly level, you might prefer to baste the hem and hang the draperies; then, after several days, make any necessary adjustments to the hem, and finish with slipstitching.

To finish the top of the drapery, measure the finished length from the hem and mark the line with pins. Turn down the main fabric along this line. If necessary, trim back any excess main fabric and trim the lining so

that it fits neatly underneath it. Turn in the sides of the turnback (see pages 248–249) and attach the heading tape (see pages 244–245). Gather or pleat the heading to the required width, using the cords or pleater hooks. Finally, hang the draperies.

If the draperies are designed to hang straight, fix the folds by a process known as "training" them. Pull the curtain closed and arrange the fabric into even folds. Do this by tugging the hem in line with the pleats at the top of the drapery panel, and then running your fingers down the length of the drapery to create full-length pleats. Keeping these in place, carefully draw the draperies back. Using woven tape, ribbons, or scarves, gently

▲ *These luxurious, heavy draperies are fixed at the top, but are looped back during the day to reveal their contrasting lime-green lining. Colored lining can be made in any fabric, plain or patterned, so long as it has sufficient body to support the front fabric and is colorfast in sunlight.*

▶ *The plain lining of these striped draperies has been extended around to the front, to make a contrasting edging along the top and down the sides. Each panel is hung from its own iron rod, and the rods are placed at different heights on the wall, which cleverly allows a considerable draft-excluding overlap.*

Lined draperies

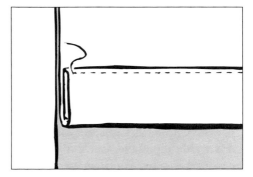

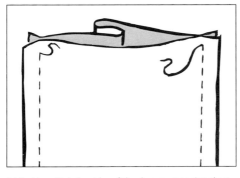

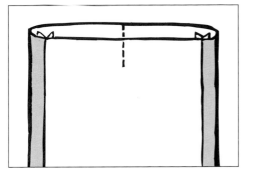

1 Machine stitch a double hem on the lining, then place it on the main fabric, 7 in. (18cm) up from the bottom.

2 Machine stitch the sides of the drapery, stopping short of the top and bottom to leave room for mitering.

3 Turn the fabric tube right side out, and press the sides, matching the center points of both fabrics.

tie each drapery in several places up its length, starting near the bottom. Leave the tapes tied for as long as possible, a few days at the least, to fix the folds.

Detachable linings

Detachable linings can be removed in summer or for cleaning. Make the draperies and the lining as for two separate unlined draperies (see pages 248–249). The lining does not need to be so fully gathered as the drapery itself. Sew the top of the lining into special tape designed for the top of detachable linings. The raw top edge of the lining fabric is inserted within the open bottom section of the tape and sewn along its bottom. Drapery hooks are then looped through the top of this tape, before being hooked through the heading tape at the top of the main drapery fabric, and into rings or runners on the rod.

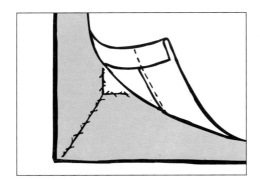

4 Unfold the hem and refold the hem and side seam into a miter. Slipstitch the diagonal join and the hem.

5 Close the draperies and use your hands to arrange the folds. Tie them in place and leave for a few days.

Detachable linings

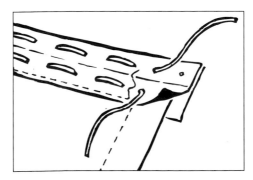

Place the edge of the lining between the two halves of the lining tape, overlapping and turning under the ends.

Valances

▲ *This shaped valance with a zigzag lower edge makes a dramatic impact when the draperies are open and the points are outlined against daylight. Covered in the same fabric as the draperies, the valance is deep enough not to look skimpy, while still permitting plenty of light to enter from the window.*

The space above draperies offers plenty of scope for decorative interest. If you choose a conventional traverse rod, rather than a decorative rod, a world of ornamental toppings, including swags and elegant cascades, opens up.

Valances

Valances can be made in many different styles. Some are, in effect, a mini-drapery, pleated to match the draperies themselves and hung from a rod in front of it. Flat valances are made of stiffened fabric and resemble a cornice (which is constructed of board and either painted or covered with fabric). They can be hung either from a rod or from a valance shelf. The simplest type of flat valance is rectangular when looked at face-on, and is covered with the same fabric as the draperies. More exciting alternatives might have a shaped lower edge, such as scallops, zigzags, or notches. Some valances have a shaped upper edge too. A valance can be decorated with trimmings such as ribbon, braid, tassels, or fringe, while a large window can be made grand with a valance of magnificent swags and cascades.

Making the valance in a contrasting fabric will give it added prominence and is an opportunity to use a more expensive fabric than you could afford for the draperies themselves. It could have similar colors but a bolder pattern, perhaps, or a pattern that will be shown off to greater effect when flat on the valance rather than lost in drapery folds.

Flat valances

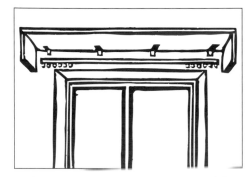

1 A flat valance can be hung from a shelf mounted above the window, over the rod for the draperies.

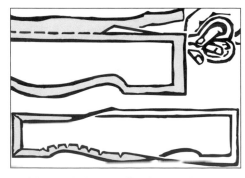

2 Fabric is attached to the stiffened valance shape and the edges are turned to the wrong side.

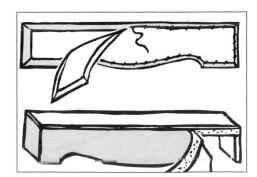

3 Lining is slipstitched to the back, then the valance fixed around three sides of the board with hook-and-loop tape.

Valance creator

1 Feed fabric through the spiral hooks from back to front, pull into a loop and secure the fabric ends behind.

2 The puffs of fabric hide the supporting hooks, and the whole result gives a "swag and cascade" effect.

Checks give definition to striped draperies, while stripes give a refreshing finish to floral printed draperies. Or, use a solid-colored fabric with a contrasting edging, or create your own fabric design, using appliqué, embroidery, or paints.

A wooden cornice can be made from solid wood, plywood, or MDF (medium-density fiberboard), which is easier to saw into interesting shapes than wood. It can be painted, or it can be decorated with glued objects around the edges or in patterns: shells, rope, or beads, for example.

Making a stiffened valance

Cut a 4-inch (10cm)-deep mounting board from ½-in (12mm)-thick plywood, making it the length of the rod plus 5 inches (12cm) to give 2½ inches (6cm) clearance at each end. Glue and screw end pieces to form returns. Mount the board on the wall just above the window and track using angle brackets fixed at 8 inches (20cm) intervals, making sure it will hide the drapery heading.

Cut out the valance shape from stiff interfacing making it long enough to fit around the sides and front of the mounting board. The traditional stiffener is buckram, which can be sewn to a piece of interlining. Iron-on buckram is also available.

Cut out the same shape from the main fabric, adding 1¼ inches (3cm) for turning under all around. Attach the stiffener to the wrong side of the fabric. Turn the fabric edges over, clipping into the curves and corners so that the fabric lies flat.

Cut lining fabric ⅝ inch (1.5cm) larger all around than the valance shape. Turn and press this allowance under and attach the lining to the back of the valance, slipstitching it to the main fabric. Attach the valance to the top edge of the board using hook-and-loop tape—where necessary, either gluing on,

▲ Unsewn fabric, draped in an elegant curve across the top of this narrow window and finished with a puff at each corner, makes a charming unstructured swag. Such an effect is easy to achieve with a "valance creator" and is an appealing alternative to the elaborate folds of some more sophisticated window headings.

or stapling, or tacking the hooked half to the board and the soft half to the back of the valance.

Swags and cascades

Hung from a mounting board, swags and cascades create an illusion of continuous drapery. They are made in many forms, ranging in complexity from one swag to many and from pleated ones cut from several pieces of fabric to gathered ones made from a single piece of cloth. Swags and cascades are best suited to full-length draperies on large windows.

Lambrequins

A lambrequin is the name given to a flat fabric shape that frames the window. Usually hanging down at the sides, it can go over a shade or a simple lace curtain, or it can stand alone at a window where no other covering is necessary.

Other styles of valances

Besides being made into stiff valances and lambrequins, fabric can be gathered or sculpted into folds or pleats, making a variety of soft valances, from tailored to flowing and dramatic. An integral valance consists of a fold of the drapery fabric which hangs down from the top of the drapery itself, giving you the best of both worlds as you have a handsome drapery heading and you can hang the draperies from a decorative rod.

Fabric can also be simply draped across the top of the window, with or without draperies or shades. It should be lined to give it extra body and support, and can then be arranged over and attached to a wooden pole (separate from the rod if there is one), wooden or metal drapery hold-backs, or some other prop.

A "valance creator" is a curly-ended bracket around which fabric can be wrapped. It is mounted on the wall above and to each side of the window. Feed the fabric through from the back of the spiral to the front, in a loop, with the ends of the fabric secured to the back, hanging down. The loops of fabric create gathers, thus hiding the brackets of the valance creator.

Tiebacks and hold-backs

▶ *A pair of original and amusing fabric tiebacks have been created by making ordinary tiebacks and sewing mother-of-pearl buttons all over them. These twinkle in the light from the window, echoing the spots of glitter on the draperies themselves.*

During the day, opaque draperies are drawn back to let as much light as possible into a room or to reveal other layers of a window treatment such as a lace curtain or a light-diffusing shade. The draperies can either hang down or be restrained by tiebacks or hold-backs attached to the wall at the sides of the window. Tiebacks are made of fabric, cord, or any soft material that can be tied, and hold-backs are made of metal or wood.

A tieback can be decorated with anything that can be sewn or glued to a suitable backing, threaded onto cord, or braided into a rope, and which is sufficiently resilient to withstand the daily business of being undone and done up again. Beads, for instance, can be sewn or threaded; a fringe of corks can be threaded together; roses and leaves made from brilliantly colored velvet or polished cotton can look stunning; a braid of burlap rope looks rugged and is well suited to fabrics such as unbleached muslin or natural linen.

Fabric tiebacks

A fabric tieback consists of two shaped pieces of material sewn together with a layer of buckram or other stiffener sandwiched in between. This is fastened to a hook or loop on the wall by means of brass rings or ties sewn into each end. The fabric could be the same as for the drapery or the valance, or a contrasting fabric. Edges of tiebacks can be defined by binding them with a contrasting fabric, known as bound-edge binding, or edging them with braid or piping.

Making a fabric tieback

Frist find the length of the tieback by looping a flexible tape measure around the drapery, then drawing it open, and holding the ends next to the wall where it will be fixed. Decide how wide it is to be. Make a rectangular paper pattern to the length and depth you want. Fold this in half along the length and if you want the ends to be rounded or curved, draw these in on one half. Cut through both thicknesses of paper around your shape and unfold the pattern. Pin it around the drapery to check it is the right size, and make any adjustments as necessary.

Use the pattern to cut out four pieces of fabric (two for each tieback), adding ⅝ inch (1.5cm) all around for seam allowances. For each tieback also cut out a piece of stiffener without the seam allowance. Attach one

Tiebacks

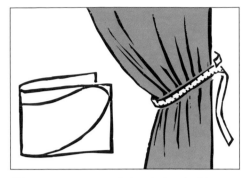

1 *Use a tape measure to calculate the length of the tieback then make a paper pattern of the exact shape.*

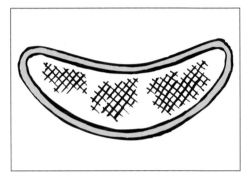

2 *Cut two pieces of stiffener and four pieces of fabric, adding a seam allowance. Iron on the stiffener.*

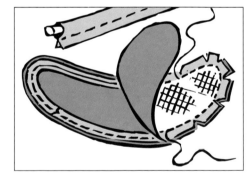

3 *Stitch on piping, if used, then join both pieces, right side together, leaving an opening for turning.*

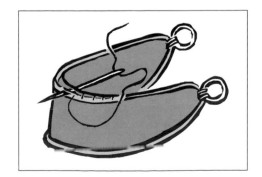

4 *Right sides out, slipstitch the opening, then sew on rings at each end, or in far enough that they are hidden.*

piece of stiffener in the center of the wrong side of one piece of fabric. The simplest to use is iron-on stiffener.

Place the fabric pieces together with right sides facing and machine stitch along the seamline, leaving an opening for turning the tieback ride side out. Trim the edges, clip the curves or corners, and turn the tieback right side out through the gap. Press flat.

Turn in the open edges and slipstitch together. Rings can be sewn at each end, or farther in, so that they are hidden when the tieback is in use.

Piping on a tieback

Piping is made by enclosing piping cord in a strip of fabric cut on the bias. The length of fabric strip must allow for piping to go right around the shape, plus an extra 1¼ inch (3cm) for overlapping the ends. You may find it necessary to join strips in order to achieve the right length. The width of the fabric strip needs to be the circumference of the piping cord plus 1¼ inch (3cm), i.e. twice the seam allowance. The strip of fabric is folded in half and the cord enclosed within it. The cord should be stitched in as close to the fold as possible, and the raw edges of the seam allowance left untrimmed.

If using piping on a tieback, attach it just before sewing the two main fabric pieces together. It is stitched to the right side of one fabric piece, along the seamline with raw edges even. When the piping turns a corner, a section will need to be clipped out of the seam allowance at that point to prevent the fabric from kinking.

To complete the tieback, join the piped fabric piece to the other piece as for an unpiped tieback. Turn right side out and sew up the gap with slipstitch.

Bound edges on a tieback

You can use readymade bias binding, but to get just the binding you want, cut strips of contrasting fabric on the bias. Binding strips need to be twice the width of the binding, plus 1¼ inch (3cm) for seam allowances.

When making bound edges, cut out the fabric pieces for the tieback to the required size and attach the stiffener, as described above, to the wrong side of one piece. Place the wrong sides of the tieback pieces together and machine stitch around the edge.

Fold over ⅝ inch (1.5cm) along each edge of the binding strip and press, then fold the strip in half lengthwise and press again. Open out the last fold and align the raw edge of the binding with the raw edge of the tieback, right sides together. Sew a ⅝ inch (1.5cm) seam. Bring the edging over the raw edges of the tieback and slipstitch the seam on the reverse side along the stitching line, trimming the enclosed edges if necessary. Turn under at the ends to finish them.

Hold-backs

Hold-backs made of wood are generally shaped something like a mushroom, with a

▲ Hold-backs are an ideal opportunity for extra decoration and unusual touches. This leaf in thin gilded metal dresses up the simplest of draperies made in inexpensive fabric. It is attached to a thick shank that is then mounted on the wall, providing space in which to fit the drapery so the leaf can be seen to full advantage.

base, a stalk, and a round head decorated with carving or gilding, behind which the drapery is looped when drawn open. You can paint or stain a wooden hold-back to match or complement the drapery fabric or the finish of other surfaces in the room.

Metal hold-backs are either fixed or hinged. A fixed one curls out from the wall like an arm, embracing the drapery when it is drawn back behind it. It can look odd when the draperies are closed and it has nothing to hold. This problem can be overcome if the draperies hang well out from the wall and hide it when drawn closed, so that it does not create a bulge in the fabric.

A hinged, hook-shaped metal hold-back has a hinge or ring near the wall which allows it to hang down flat when it is not holding back the drapery. When the drapery is drawn open the hold-back is lifted up and the fullness of the drapery looped into it, so that it stands out from the wall.

Bound-edge tieback

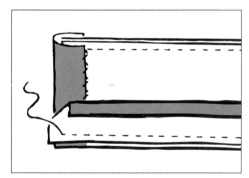

1 Machine stitch the binding to the right side of the tieback, raw edges aligned, with a ⅝-inch (1.5cm) seam.

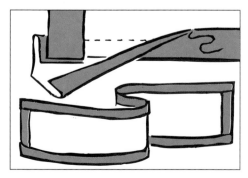

2 Turn the binding over to the wrong side and slipstitch in place, turning under the ends where necessary.

Shades and blinds

For many windows in the home, shades or blinds are the
simple, stylish solution. Where a room is small and
space is important, or where there is little room at the
sides of a window, it may be far more appropriate
to fit a flat roller or Roman shade neatly within the
window frame than to hang draperies from a raised rod.
Flat shades will show off fabric well, can be an
inexpensive choice, and if sized correctly and lined,
can provide excellent insulation.

There are shades to suit most practical and decorative requirements, ranging from the very basic to the flamboyant. They can be left unlined—the lighter fabrics useful for allowing light to pass through, but hiding an uninspiring view or giving privacy—or they can be lined to improve their light-blocking and insulating capabilities.

Depending on their design, shades can be hung in almost any room or situation. Crooked windows in old houses are probably the one exception, because shades do need to be hung absolutely straight and will look odd at a window that is out of true. For a window that is wider than it is long, two or more shades side by side work better than a single wide shade which may be too large to operate well.

The most basic of all shades is a piece of flat, lightweight fabric permanently fixed over a window to block out an unpleasant view but allow light into the room. A little more versatile than this, but still simple, is the tie shade, which should be used only where it will not need to be raised and lowered frequently—perhaps in a bathroom. It consists of a piece of unlined fabric to which are attached four ribbons or fabric strips. Sewn to the top of the shade, about a quarter of the way in from either edge, these hang down—two to the front and two to the back—and are tied together at each side under the shade's bottom edge. The drop of the shade is adjusted as required by re-tying the ties at different heights. The shade itself can be attached to a heading board using hook-and-loop tape. A dowel can be sewn into the bottom hem to ensure that the shade hangs with a straight bottom edge.

Roller shades incorporate a sprung roller which facilitates the raising of the shade and takes up very little space above the window. They are useful for any situation where as much light as possible is required when the shade is up, but where they need to be pulled down frequently. They are also practical for windows that are set at an angle, such as in an attic conversion, since the batten at the bottom of the shade can be restrained beneath the window by hooks, while the shade itself follows the slope of the roof.

◄ *An unusual arrangement of translucent white roller shades in a minimalist interior. One is set into the window recess and pulls down, while the other, larger shade pulls up from a box on the floor and covers the entire window, with a wide margin on each side.*

◄ *An impressively lofty kitchen-cum-dining room in a modern building has louvered blinds built into the windows, in keeping with the uncluttered interior. The great advantage of louvered blinds is that the amount of light admitted can be regulated when the shade is let down, or the blind can be pulled up completely.*

▲ *Slatted wooden blinds like these, which roll up inside the pull-up string, can be used as inexpensive room dividers as well as shade and privacy providers. Here they conceal the kitchen in one corner of the living room, when let down. They are also a good choice to tone in with the cane furniture and wood-slat doors.*

▲ *A single huge shade for this large window space would be too cumbersome to pull up; instead, there are three elegant Roman shades. The center one is wider, conforming in size to the window behind, and made from the same green linen as the left-hand chair, while the others are white to match the right-hand chair.*

Roller shades offer little in the way of insulation, however, although they will filter bright light and create privacy at night. Because they can be made of spongeable fabric, they are useful in frequently damp rooms such as kitchens and bathrooms. Specially stiffened fabric is readily available for making roller shades, but ordinary fabrics (except very loosely woven ones) can be used as long as they are sprayed with, or dipped into, a stiffener before being made up.

The Roman shade is the smartest, most tailored of shades. When pulled up, it folds away neatly in pleats tucked under each other. The regularity and crispness of these pleats are the result of narrow strips of wood, usually lath or doweling, slotted into a series of horizontal fabric pockets on the back of the shade and creating ridges. When the shade is pulled up by the cords, which run through small brass or plastic rings that are sewn to the edge of each pocket, the ridges

are hoisted up to fold the shade into its neat pleats. Many people prefer the appearance of Roman shades to curtains or draperies because, while they look equally luxurious (especially if padded with lightweight interlining), they are unfussy.

When drawn up, a Roman shade blocks out more light than a roller shade does, but if it is lined, it is as good as curtains or draperies for excluding drafts and light, especially if it fits the window well or hangs so that the edges overlap the architrave or window frame. Because of the reinforced folds stacking up at the back of it when drawn up, the Roman shade requires a certain depth of window in which to operate; also, part of the window at the top will always be covered.

Gathered shades: balloon, pull-up, and Austrian

Quite different from the simple appearance of flat shades are the various gathered shades which all involve festoons of fabric, some also ruched. The more extravagant of these are suited to a certain type of lavishly decorated interior rather than a room requiring a fresh, contemporary feel; they are generally better for large rooms than small ones.

The balloon shade is pulled up by means of cords and rings like a Roman shade but has a gathered or pleated heading and bunches up into a series of puffs or swags, rather than pleats. Like the Roman shade, it can provide good insulation and light exclusion. In certain situations—in simply furnished rooms with tall ceilings and windows, for example—it can be used successfully if care is taken to avoid making a place feel claustrophobic. This is especially true if the shade looks like a drapery when let down, falling straight to the floor (or windowsill) with no ruches at the bottom. Some people call this type of shade a "pull-up curtain."

Similar to a balloon shade, an Austrian shade has swags down its entire length when let down. A further variation is known as a tailed balloon shade; cords are omitted at the edges of the shade allowing the sides to trail and flop down.

▲ *A series of loosely hanging, narrow Roman shades, made from natural textured linen, make a strong and witty impact on these folding half-glass doors. Each shade is knotted at the bottom and covers a pane of glass, emphasizing the door's shape and the number of panels.*

Fabrics and finishes

Fabrics for shades need to be chosen with some care. Because a balloon shade makes an impact through its puffed-up fullness, it should be made with an unfussy pattern, such as stripes.

The simplicity of the roller shade and the tailored form of the Roman shade also call for fabrics that are plain, either with an interesting texture or patterned in a graphic style. Before deciding on a particular fabric, imagine, for instance, how a Roman shade would look once pulled up into its pleats. Alternatively, a scenic fabric is fun on a roller shade in a bathroom or kitchen, and fresh patterns like stripes and checks look good on any type of shade. Flat shades are better for large patterns than shades with lots of folds.

The fabric used for making any type of shade must be cut absolutely straight or it will look shoddy once it is finished and hung. If there is any sort of pattern on the fabric, make sure it is arranged symmetrically across the shade. It must also be printed true. Examine your chosen fabric carefully before starting to make the shade, and if it is faulty in this or any other respect, return it immediately to the store.

Interest and definition can be added to a shade with a band of contrasting fabric or trimming set back from the edges. If this trimming is to be continued across the bottom of a Roman shade, the lowest flap of fabric has to be made extra deep so that the bottom border is not hidden when the shade is pulled up.

A roller shade can be made more interesting if it has a shaped bottom edge, coming down at an angle, for example, or cut in a pattern of points or "crenellations." The shaped part hangs below the bottom batten, and the string should be attached to the batten rather than the shape below it.

Blinds

Blinds are made from materials other than fabric. They can be constructed from cane, bamboo, wooden slats, paper, and even metal, and are widely available in many styles, designs and colors (see pages 268–269).

First steps to making shades

▶ *A neat and restrained use of a Roman shade. This one is tucked inside the window frame and is made from plain white linen, which allows sunlight to glow through it, making it appear almost luminous. The fabric also matches the pure white paint on the window and the restrained pattern of the walls.*

Measuring for shades

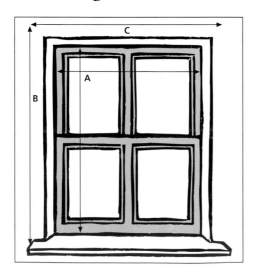

Measure the height and width of the window, either inside the recess or to cover the architrave.

Measuring and estimating quantities

Decide exactly where the shade is to hang, then measure the window, as follows, to find the finished dimensions and the amount of fabric you will need for your shade.

For a recessed shade, measure the height and width of the recess (A). For roller shade fabric, deduct 1¼ inches (3cm) from the width to allow for the ends of the mechanism within the window frame.

For a face-fixed shade, measure from the top of the hanging system at the chosen height to the sill for the drop (B), and for the width add 2 inches (5cm) either side of the opening (C) so that the light will be blocked out. Get extra fabric if you plan to wrap the mounting board with the same fabric in order to disguise it.

Roman shade construction

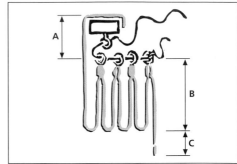

A fully pulled-up Roman shade. A = hanging allowance; B = depth of pleats; C = lower flap.

Roller shade

For a roller shade add an extra 12 inches (30cm) to the length for a hem at the bottom and to cover the roller at the top.

Balloon shade or pull-up curtain

For a balloon shade allow an extra 2 inches (5cm) for the hem at the top and 8 inches (20cm) for a double hem at the bottom. The width of fabric you need is two and a half times the length of the mounting board plus 1½ inches (4cm) for hems at the sides. If you are lining the shade, you will need roughly the same amount of lining fabric.

To make the shade look like a curtain when it is lowered, make the finished length equal to the distance from the window top to the sill. If you want to retain the swagged look at the bottom when the shade is down, make it about 18 inches (45cm) longer.

Roman shade

Estimating quantities for a Roman shade needs careful working out so make sure you check your calculation. Make a clearly drawn sketch and mark all the measurements on it so that you can refer to them when making the shade. When measuring for the shade, allow an extra 2¼ inches (6cm) for the hem and ridge pocket at the bottom and 2¼ inches (6cm) to wrap over a 2 x 1-inch (5 x 2.5cm) mounting board at the top. You will also need to allow 2¼ inches (6cm) for a 1¼-inch (3cm) turnback at each side.

For the lining allow an extra 2¼ inches (6cm) for each ridge pocket for laths about 1 x ¼ inch (25 x 5mm), and cut it to the same

Tools and equipment

To make a shade you will need the following materials and equipment. If you are sewing a Roman shade (see pages 264–265) or a balloon shade (see pages 266–267), you will also need almost all the materials and equipment required for sewing draperies (see pages 240– 241) to create the fabric part of the shade. Roman and balloon shades are suspended from a batten, approximately 2 x 1 inch (5 x 2.5cm) by the width of the shade, which is fixed to the wall with screws and plugs as necessary and can be painted to match the frame or the fabric.

For measuring up and fixing

- Yardstick and a right-angled triangle or T-square: to make sure that marked lines are perpendicular to the edges.
- Carpenter's level, a drill, screws, plastic shields, a hammer and tacks or staple gun and staples: for mounting the batten on the wall.
- Saw: for cutting a roller to size.
- Hammer: for the fitting.

For a roller shade

- A roller shade kit: consisting of a roller with spring, brackets, end cap and pin, wooden slat, cord holder, and shade pull (or these items bought separately).
- Pencil and masking tape.
- Fusible backing for untreated fabric.

For Roman and balloon shades/ pull-up curtains

- Cord, drop weight, and awning cleat: for pulling up and lowering the shade.
- Brass or plastic rings: through which to thread the cords on the back of the shade.
- Screw eyes, as many as there are cords at the back of the shade, plus one through which all cords go.
- Sewing machine with zipper foot.
- ¼, ⅜, or ½inch (6, 10, or 12mm) doweling or lath, maximum 1 x ¼ inch (25 x 5mm): enough for all the pocket ridges in the shade (Roman).
- Hook-and-loop heading tape or shirring heading tape (balloon).
- Leadweight tape (optional) (balloon).
- Fringe or edging material (optional) (balloon).

◀ *A carefully orchestrated scheme of white and washed-out blues, distressed plaster, metal, and wood called for an understated window treatment: balloon shades in their simplest form, unadorned by fringe or other trimmings, in a crisply striped fabric.*

width as the main fabric. For wood of different dimensions or doweling, calculate the amount of fabric needed for each ridge pocket, adding a little extra so that the wood slides in easily.

To work out how many ridges you need, first decide how deep the piece of fabric at the top of the shade will be. This will usually extend above the last pleat by about 1½–4inches (4–10cm) and will cover the screw eyes and give room for the pleats to lie evenly. The deeper this hanging allowance, the more light is cut out when the shade is pulled up.

Also decide if the lower flap at the bottom of the shade will hang down below the rest of the pleats when the shade is closed to allow the edge of the border, if you have one, to show. Subtract the hanging allowance and the bottom border allowance from the shade's finished length to give the folding length.

Decide how many pleats would be right for the proportions of the shade. A pleat is usually 8–12 inches (20–30cm) deep. To check that your pleats will fall within this range and to establish their actual measurement, divide the shade's folding length by the number of pleats you want, plus an additional half-pleat. A full pleat is the complete fold of fabric between two ridges. The extra half-pleat is taken up by the fabric that falls from the last ridge to the bottom edge of the gathered-up pleats.

Having established the number and depth of pleats, you have finally arrived at the number of ridges and ridge pockets you need, which will, in turn, enable you to calculate the length of lining fabric you need.

Roller and balloon shades

Making a roller shade

To make a roller shade it is easiest to buy ready-stiffened fabric and a special kit (see pages 260–261). (If you choose to use your own fabric, you will need to apply a fusible backing to the wrong side first. Iron the fabric before you do this.) The roller has a spring pin fitted into one end and is sawed to length. Then the other pin is inserted in the other end. The kit also includes two brackets designed to take each end of the roller, which can be fixed either to the wall above the window or to the sides of a recess.

Screw the brackets to the wall, the slotted bracket to the left, 1¼ inches (3cm) down from the top of a recess to allow for the thickness of the rolled-up shade. When fitting outside a recess, or to a window without one, position it 2 inches (5cm) above and out to each side.

Cut the fabric to the width of the roller, excluding hardware. Use a right-angled triangle and a yardstick to make sure that cutting is perpendicular to the sides, and cut the fabric perfectly straight, with the weave.

Assuming that the batten for the bottom of the shade is 1 x ¼ inch (25 x 5mm) thick, make a 1½-inch (4 cm) hem on the wrong side of the fabric and sew this in place with zigzag stitch to create a pocket for the batten. Cut the batten to the correct length: it needs to be slightly shorter than the width of the shade, by approximately ⅜ inch (1cm), so that it does not show. Slide the batten into the pocket and slipstitch the ends. Attach the pull-cord holder to the wrong side of the batten (the same side as the hem).

Cut the roller to fit the brackets, and hammer the other fitting into the sawed end. Draw a guideline along the length of roller, perpendicular to the ends, if it does not already have one. Position the fabric right side up and place the roller on top with the spring to the left so that the top edge meets the guideline on the roller. Tape it to the roller to keep it steady, and tack or staple the fabric to the roller.

Roll up the shade by hand and slot into the brackets, right-hand end first. Pull it down to check the spring tension; rewind by hand if necessary to increase the tension.

Making a balloon shade or pull-up curtain

A balloon shade is made like a conventional drapery panel, except for the finish to the heading and the system of rings and screw eyes fixed at the back. For a list of requirements see pages 262–263. The description here is for separate rings but ring tape can be used instead.

The shade's heading is attached to a hanging batten (also known as a mounting board) with either hook-and-loop tape or special balloon shade track. The track has cord holders which line up above the cords.

For lightweight shades, use a hanging batten and hook-and-loop tape. Peel apart the tape and attach the stiff half across the front of the mounting board with tacks or staples. Special hook-and-loop heading tape, which gathers up in the same way as normal heading tape, but has hook-and-loop tape instead of pockets, is also available.

For measuring up and determining fabric quantity, see pages 262–263. Make the shade as for an unlined drapery (see pages 248–249), with leadweight tape in the hem if you want, and attach a fringe or other edging, if you are having one, to the back of the hem. The bottom edge looks more finished with a substantial trimming, like a deep fringe. When the shade is pulled up, this looks pretty against the light; when let down, it gives the bottom edge weight and definition.

To make a lined shade, sew the fabric and lining together with right sides facing around three sides, catching in any fringe or trim between the layers as you stitch. Trim and turn right side out, press, and sew up the fourth side.

If not using special hook-and-loop heading tape, sew on any cord-type heading tape to the top. Most types are suitable, but two-cord shirring tape is recommended. Next, fold the shade vertically at evenly spaced intervals, about 2 feet (60cm), to mark off the scallops. The folds mark the positions for the rings. Bear in mind that a balloon shade looks better with an odd number of swags rather than an even number, and the rings along each side should be placed about 2 inches (5cm) from the edges.

Making a roller shade

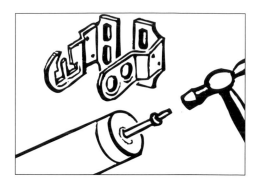

1 A roller shade kit comes with two brackets. Trim the roller to length and insert one of the pins into the cut end.

2 Make a hem along the bottom and sew with a zigzag stitch. Insert the batten and slipstitch the ends closed.

3 The shade-pull holder is attached to the wrong side of the hem with two small screws.

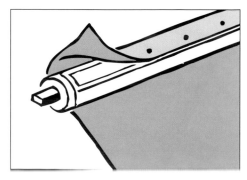

4 The top edge of the shade is fixed to the roller with tacks or staples, so that it hangs completely straight.

Sew the small rings at intervals on the back, making sure the rings are aligned horizontally. Note that when attaching the rings to a lined shade, you will need to catch in some of the threads from the front fabric as well as the lining. If you are making a shade that retains its ruching when down, you will also have to attach a ring to the cords in the pulley system in order to stop the shade dropping fully at a certain point.

Sew the other half of the hook-and-loop tape to a strip of matching fabric, or lining fabric, a little larger than the heading. Gather up the heading to the width of the finished shade, and attach the back of this tape/fabric strip over the heading tape, turning in the edges. Make sure when sewing the tape to the fabric back that it will be at the correct height to attach to the tape on the mounting board, i.e. at or near the top of the shade.

Insert the screw eyes into the bottom of the mounting board, one corresponding to each row of rings on the back of the shade plus an extra one on the side where the cords will hang down, as for a Roman shade. Secure the board above the window, checking the horizontal with a carpenter's level. Fix a cleat to the window frame or the wall.

Tie long cords to each of the bottom rings in each row and thread them through the rest of the rings above. Attach the shade to the mounting board, and thread all the cords up through the screw eyes and along to one side. Cut the cords to the same length, thread them through a drop weight, and knot them.

▲ *This pull-up shade combines some of the features of a Roman shade and some of a balloon shade: it is stiffened at the bottom, which means the shade lifts straight, not in festoons, but the folds are not sharpened with battens or doweling, so it folds and crumples softly as it is pulled up.*

Making a balloon shade

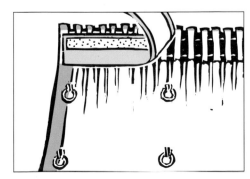

1 *Sew the rings to the shade, aligning them in both directions. Slipstitch hook-and-loop tape to the heading.*

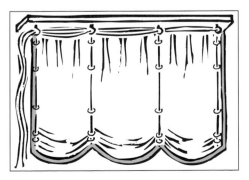

2 *Fix the shade to the mounting board, and thread the cords through the rings and screw eyes.*

3 *Ring tape is a neat way of attaching rings and cords to the wrong side of the shade.*

Blinds

▶ *Rattan blinds, slung across the glass roof of a sunroom, give welcome shade and echo the natural texture and color of the braided grass rug on the floor beneath.*

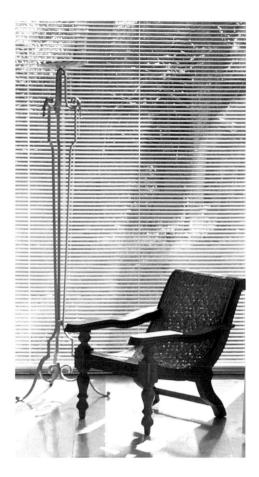

▲ *A large louvered Venetian blind, made from aluminum alloy strips, filters the bright sunlight at a huge plate-glass window and provides a geometric background for an uncluttered space. The blind's neutrality and plain lines allow the interesting items of furniture, both traditional and modern, to feature without distraction.*

Blinds are made in a great variety of materials. Bamboo, wooden slats, paper, metal, and plastic blinds are available to suit all types of interior design styles. Some work on a simple roll-up principle, which means they can be a little bulky when rolled up. Others are variations of the Venetian blind mechanism which pulls up neatly to the top of the window. The great advantage of this type of blind is that when down they can be adjusted to allow different amounts of light through at the touch of a cord.

Readymade blinds are sold in a number of standard sizes, and in addition many types can be made by suppliers to particular measurements and in different colors. Prices vary according to the materials used and the amount of work involved in making them. Pleated paper, for example, can be among the cheapest, while metal Venetian blinds or those made with wooden slats can cost as much as lined draperies.

Paper
Made from pleated paper, these blinds keep their folds even when they are let down. They fit into the window reveal and so can be used in combination with draperies. They are easy to dust. Some have holes punched through them. Paper blinds are inexpensive and are available in a wide range of colors.

Cane
Blinds made from whole or split cane either roll up or fold in pleats. They do not screen light completely but are useful in rooms where strong sunlight needs to be moderated, creating a pleasing filtered effect. At night, when a light is switched on, they are virtually see-through from outside. Privacy can be improved, however, by lining them with a panel of plain fabric. Make it slightly shorter than the blind and an inch or two (several centimeters) narrower on each side, then glue or sew it to the cane across the top at the back. The lining will roll or fold up with the blind when the cord is pulled.

Wood
Traditionally Venetian blinds were made of wood, and in recent years this material has once again been used for this purpose. The slats, which can be as narrow as 1 inch (2.5cm) or as wide as 2 inches (5cm), are held equal distances apart and controlled by tapes or—in more modern styles—by thin cords. Adjusting the angle of the slats controls the amount of light admitted. The wood may be left natural or stained or painted in any color.

Wood is also used in woven blinds, or shades, in which wooden slats form the weft and yarns form a patterned warp.

Plastic
Plastic strips can be used in the same ways as wooden slats. Available in a wide range of colors, they are extremely easy to wipe clean and therefore useful for rooms that attract dust or grease, such as kitchens.

Metal
Aluminum alloy is used to make slats for metal Venetian blinds. The slats are normally curved and come in several widths, the narrow ones being ideal for a sleek, modern look.

Vertical louver blinds
Vertical louver blinds are suspended vertically from a track and linked at the bottom by a chain. They may be made of wood or synthetic flexible strips but are most commonly made of stiffened strips of fabric, often with a textured weave and generally 3½–5 inches (9–13cm) wide. Usually falling from ceiling to floor, they are drawn like draperies and are useful for shielding large picture windows or patio doors. The amount of light they let through is controlled by adjusting the angle of the louvers.

▲ *This blind is made from primed canvas bought at a theatrical supplier, rolled around a length of wooden doweling, but it could just as well be made from paper, with the edges reinforced against tearing. The rope is made of natural fibers and similar types are available at any good D.I.Y. store.*

FURNITURE & FURNISHINGS

Whatever the decoration on a room's walls, ceiling, and floor, it is the style and coverings of the furniture within that will give the room its definitive character. At its simplest, a room with white walls and white floor, filled with furniture that has been upholstered in sumptuous velvets and bright, glassy colored silks, will present a very strong, vivid style in which color is king. The eye will be drawn to the forms of the furniture, set off by the neutral, clean background.

The same room can be completely changed by the introduction of a different style of furniture. To achieve warmth and texture in the same room, the emphasis shifts to creamy bleached wood furniture with cream-on-cream textured cushion fabrics and loosely draped white cottons over sofas and chairs, with perhaps a few warm red and terra-cotta touches—ties for the cushions or a painted chair.

When undertaking the decoration of a room, one inevitably tackles the walls and perhaps the floors first. And when time, effort, and money have gone into major refurbishment, attention to re-covering or redecorating the furniture may not be considered a priority for quite a while. This is a shame, for in addition to contributing in a major way to the final "look" of a room, the pieces on or in which we sit, sleep, rest, eat, work, and store things figure as vital practical elements in our lives. It is important to account for these elements, not just in terms of budget and practicality, but also for the impact they make in the room.

Fabric is perhaps the most exciting and versatile way of covering and decorating the surfaces of furniture. Upholstering, wrapping, draping, cushioning—fabric comes alive when used imaginatively. From the finest, softest linen to the most textured brocaded velvet, the potential of fabric for decorating and transforming furniture is limitless. In addition to the fabric, there are braids, buttons, and other trimmings to jazz up a piece of fabric, define the curve of a sofa, or accentuate the folds of draperies.

Fabric can also be decorated very successfully with paint or dye, in either a fairly controlled way, as with stenciling, or by using

▲ The bold use of color creates a dramatic, Middle Eastern effect in this room. The varnished floor provides a neutral background for the rich, jewel-like fabrics draped on the sofa. A contrast is provided by the deep blue of the wall, which is also used around the door frame and featured in the tiles to help link the room together.

▶ The strongest features in this room are light and space, which have been accentuated throughout. Furniture is grouped around the room to divide it into functional areas. The use of faded fabrics, the distressed paint effect on the armoire, and evidence of junk-shop finds add a nostalgic, tranquil feel to the room.

the more random method of hand-painted applications. Paint is also suitable for directly applying to the surfaces of furniture. Natural effects can be imitated or instant "aging" techniques applied for those who want a more battered, lived-in feel to their furniture. You can opt for the quick approach by using paint in a very loose way, such as color-washing where layers are applied and reapplied to create the desired effect. The

finish can be changed easily to suit the mood of the rest of the room, by altering the surface paint color or "texture" as easily as changing a pillow cover. Other paint techniques require more time and precision and because of this have a more permanent, perhaps less relaxed feel to them—the difference between a scrubbed pine table and an antique mahogany desk. Each has its place—it all depends on the effect you want to achieve.

Balance in all of this is crucial. Avoid over-doing a paint technique or using the same patterned fabric on every item in the room. Less is more. One beautifully colorwashed chair among a collection of pared-down fabrics can often be more effective than half a dozen of them, although, in the right place, this too could be wonderful.

The position of furniture within a room is also very important. Don't feel that all large items of furniture should hug the walls—placing them on the diagonal and juxtapos-ing them can give unexpectedly pleasing results. In large rooms with numerous pieces of furniture, it helps to think in terms of group arrangements so that there are islands of furniture throughout the room, rather than many individual but slightly lost-looking pieces. Using the same color, paint, and fabric helps to link unrelated items throughout the room. Try different mat-erials, be imaginative—but keep a balance.

▲ *Bleached cream, pale stone, and stark white are relieved by a honey-toned floor in this harmoniously elegant room. Fabrics are the dominant feature of the room, together with the abundance of natural light that floods through the window.s The light reflects off the various surfaces to create a sophisticated and relaxing environment.*

Decorative finishes for furniture

Painting the walls of a room in a neutral color or shade allows
the furniture free rein to make powerful color statements. Using
different painting or varnishing techniques, furniture can be
transformed, creating dramatic visual effects within a room.
Wood, with its ability to transform itself with the application of
paint, varnish, or wax, is extremely versatile and can be treated
in various different ways within the same room. Metal furniture,
too, can be enhanced with the application of different coverings
and the use of different paint application techniques.

The choice of paint effects is vast: on the one hand, finishes such as fake rust or verdigris (see pages 280–281) on wood or metal can add texture and "weight," while a simple coat of varnish or beeswax may be applied purely to bring out the natural color, grain, and character of wood. For a subtle coloring effect somewhere in the middle, both varnish and wax come into their own when first mixed with a little powdered color or stain, and paint can produce a superb look when applied as a colorwash.

Built-in furniture, such as alcove book-cases or cabinets, is often painted along with the rest of the wood in the room—usually in an unadventurous, light off-white. Try giving such pieces an alternative finish, such as a light colorwash or an antiqued finish, for a different effect.

Interesting surface decoration can transform a piece of furniture. A simple, plain chair could be painted in hot terra-cottas and a wild patterning of bright and bold stenciled borders, or in cool gray—worthy of an eighteenth-century Swedish interior—or in faded cream, russet and gold—befitting a nineteenth-century French salon.

Sometimes it is unwise to give single items of furniture, such as tables or chairs, a dramatic color treatment if it makes them stand out in awkward isolation; you can, for example, achieve a stylish and harmonious look by simply painting a series of pieces in varying shades of cream.

Colorwashing is a wonderfully versatile way of putting paint onto a wood surface. On bare, untreated wood, diluted latex flat paint sinks in, lightly coloring the wood and allowing its natural qualities and grain to show through. The more diluted the paint, the more the character of the wood will come through. Two colors, one over the other, will give a richer finish. Light colors, especially on pale woods such as pine or light oak, can be used to give slight hints of color, while a strong wash of inky black on a darker, grainier wood can be equally effective but a bit more dramatic. Rough and quite dark oak boards, for example, can take a fairly dark colorwash. The wash needs to be worked into the surface and, after a few

minutes, rubbed a little with a cloth. The deep browns of the wood will show through. A pale, chalky-white color also creates a beautiful finish on more textured wood. The beauty of colorwashing is that the result is immediate and the technique easy.

With simple variations, attractive and widely different effects can be achieved using colorwashes. Paint narrow checkerboard borders along edges of, or panels in, the furniture. Alternate colors in wide bands across larger pieces. The advantage of this kind of painting is that it provides the opportunity for great adventure and experimentation with color and texture. Create smart, chic pieces

in combinations of subtle chalky whites and bleached blues, or go wild with vibrant orange, mint green, and deep indigo.

Metallic paints, if "textured" a little, can give a wonderfully rich and exciting surface to furniture. Apply silver metallic paint to the prepared surface. Dilute black latex flat with water and a little detergent and, using a damp cloth, dab it over the surface, into moldings or along edges, to build up a rich patina for dramatic effect. The silver-gray color looks splendid against rich jewel colors—emerald, orange, or deep burgundy. Try painting the legs of upholstered stools in this finish in combination with rich velvets.

◀ *With a little imagination a tired piece of furniture can be given a magical transformation. The two chests of drawers, one wild, bright, and abstract, the other more restrained with its seashore motifs and touches of gold, are lively and fun. They blend happily in this bright room—where even the flowerpots are decorated with paint.*

▲ *The beauty and warmth of polished wood show up well in the honey-gold long refectory table. The natural grain and patina of the wood are drawn out with waxing or varnishing and contrast with the bleached-wood effect of the flooring. Against the neutral walls, the table's richness of texture and color contrasts well.*

Preparing surfaces for decorative finishes

▶ *The worn-out surface of this little cabinet may be the result of age, or it may have been decorated to imitate this state. In either case the effect is very appealing; but should such a piece require repainting or a new decorative effect, the old paint would need to be thoroughly removed and the surface rubbed down and washed.*

Make sure the surface you are to paint has been properly prepared beforehand, otherwise the effort of painting will be wasted. Unless you require a rough, unsanded surface with some of the imperfections that build up with time. You will find the effort of good preparation well worth while: essential for a professional, smooth-looking finish.

Preparing and priming wood

For both wood and metal furniture it is important to remove all old paint and any varnish. Wearing rubber gloves, apply liquid or gel paint stripper with an old paintbrush, following the manufacturer's directions. When the layers of paint begin to soften and bubble up, you can use a scraper to remove them from the surface—but take care not to scratch or gouge the surface of the wood. Stubborn areas can be rubbed with wire wool. Wash the surface down with either water or mineral spirits, depending on what type of stripper you have used.

It is possible to go to a professional wood-stripping company to have the item dipped in a caustic solution. It is not a bad idea to use this kind of service where appropriate: for example, to treat a large piece of furniture or an item with many layers of old paint,

for apart from the convenience, the fumes from the caustic solutions used in the stripping process can be overpowering.

Caustic solutions often leave the wood surface discolored and slightly raised and rough, although a fine-grade sandpaper will restore the surface after several rubbings over. Either use sandpaper directly on the surface, applying pressure with your fingertips, or wrap it around a block. For simple curved mouldings, wrap it around a length of dowel. Before applying a finish, you should seal any knots in the surface, as they produce resin

and can cause discoloring of the finished paint surfaces. Apply one or two coats of stain-blocking sealer over any knots, according to the manufacturer's directions. If the surface needs some filling before applying a finish, lightly sand and apply a proprietary wood filler to match the grain of the wood. When dry, rub it down again until smooth.

Once the surface has been prepared it is not always necessary to prime it. Some finishes first require a layer of shellac and should not be primed. However, if you are going to paint it then it will need priming. This can be done using an oil-based wood primer, which is available in pink or white. Dilute the primer by using three parts primer to one part mineral spirits. Then, with a wide brush, apply it liberally over the surface. The next step is to apply undercoat using a clean brush. The surface is then ready for painting.

Preparing and priming metal

The preparation and priming of metal are approached in much the same way as for wood, using specific solvents to remove the paint.

Spray paint can be removed with acetone; oil-based paints and varnishes with turpentine or mineral spirits; and French enamel varnish with denatured alcohol. Use wire wool or a firm wire brush to remove the old paint layers and rust. Continue to rub the surface until it is completely smooth and clean. There are special zinc-based metal primers available for preparing the surface of metal for painting. A base coat of red iron

Preparing wood

1 Apply liquid or gel stripper with an old brush and wait for the surface to bubble. Scrape off the softened paint.

2 Sand down the stripped surface. Use your fingertips to apply pressure for light sanding or for curved areas.

oxide inhibits rust and protects metal, so it is ideal for treating garden furniture. Always remember to wear rubber gloves when using red iron oxide. Apply the primer in a single, even coat and leave it to dry for 24 hours.

Preparing and priming plastic

Wash the plastic surfaces down with a clean cloth and a solution of warm water and household detergent. Rinse the surface thoroughly with clean water, and dry it off completely before painting.

Preparing and priming metal

1 Use wire wool or a wire brush to remove old paint layers and rust from the surface.

2 Prime the metal before painting by applying a zinc-based metal primer to the surface. Allow 24 hours to dry.

Tools and equipment

For preparing and priming wood

- **Sandpaper:** in various grades from fine to rough, for removing old finishes and smoothing back wood filler.
- **Overalls, paper mask, and rubber gloves:** for protection where the job is dusty and messy and may involve the use of solvents.
- **Flat scraper:** for removing paint.
- **Sponge with rough side, steel wool, and small pointed knives:** for removing paint, including paint stuck into deep cracks.
- **Denatured alcohol:** for removing shellac.
- **Paint stripper:** for removing other varnishes and paint.
- **Old paintbrush:** for applying paint stripper.
- **Stain-blocking sealer:** to seal knots before priming.
- **Wood filler:** where wood requires filling and smoothing.
- **Undercoat.**
- **Primer.**
- **Sheets of plastic:** to protect the floor.

For preparing and priming metal

- **Denatured alcohol:** for removing French enamel varnish.
- **Acetone:** for removing spray paint.
- **Turpentine or mineral spirits:** for removing oil-based paints and varnishes.
- **Wire wool:** for removing old paint layers and rust.
- **Metal primer.**

▲ *The magnificent red on the tub and curved metal washstand provides splashes of warmth in this cool gray-blue room. Metal furniture, especially if flaked with old paint and rust, requires some attention before painting. The rough surface of the tub was smoothed out after being rubbed, primed, undercoated, and then covered with several layers of gloss paint.*

Applying varnish, glaze, and stain

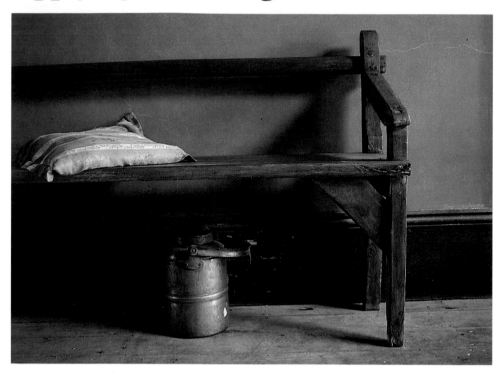

▲ *The natural color of wood can be enhanced with an application of wax polish. If a bit more color is required, you could try staining or glazing the wood. This rather battle-scarred bench has come up beautifully after being stained a rich chestnut color. The intensity of the wall color helps strengthen the wood's tones.*

Varnishes

Varnishes fall into different categories, depending on the solvent with which they can be diluted. These are: oil-based polyurethane (diluted with turpentine), water-based acrylic (diluted with water), and alcohol-based (diluted with denatured alcohol). Oil-based varnishes are available in matte, satin, or gloss finish, so choose carefully.

If you are using varnish simply to give a painted surface a good protective finishing coat, there are many household varnishes to choose from. However, polyurethane varnish has a tendency to go yellow. On many finished surfaces this will not matter, but on a pale colorwashed wooden table, for example, it is important not to ruin the effect of the subtle paint color with the wrong varnish. Oil-based varnishes can be tinted with tinting colors or artist's oil paints.

Another alternative is to use acrylic (water-based) varnish or those known as "copal" varnishes. These are more pleasant

to work with, being quick-drying and having one-quarter the toxicity of oil-based varnishes. White glue is also a useful varnish—white when liquid and clear once dry. It gives a good protective finish to most surfaces, particularly when using paper.

Shellac is a yellowish-brownish liquid which is not as tough as varnish but can be a useful sealant. French enamel varnish, made from bleached and chemically dyed shellac, looks much the same and can be dabbed onto bright brass to dull it down and give it an aged look. Originally brown, it comes ready-colored in a wide range of shades and can be successfully diluted with denatured alcohol. The liquid can stain and varnish wood in one application, but it dries very quickly so you have to work fast.

Applying varnish

Varnish should be applied with care to any finished surface. To facilitate drying, the air should not be damp, so, ideally, you should varnish on a dry, warm day. Make sure the

area you are working in is well ventilated, and protect all surrounding surfaces with plastic sheeting before starting work.

Many types of brush may be used, including a standard paintbrush, and it is a good idea to experiment with various different types until you feel comfortable with one. "Glider" brushes, made of hog bristles, are used for applying thin light varnishes; pointed brushes are best for using with shellac; while a chisel-headed lily-bristle brush is suitable for most other types of varnish application (other than shellac). Treat yourself to a good brush and look after it, cleaning it after every use. Never use varnish brushes for painting.

Coat the lower third of the bristles with varnish. Take care not to wipe the brush against the rim of the can as this causes bubbles. Transfer the loaded brush straight to the surface of the piece, brushing the varnish from the center outward. Remove any excess with a clean rag. Apply several coats of varnish, as necessary, brushing each one in a different direction. The final coat, especially if using a gloss varnish, will need a light rubbing down with fine wet-or-dry paper or fine steel wool.

Craquelure

To achieve a crackled surface effect, "aging" and "crackle" varnish can be bought at art stores. The first is a slow-drying oil-based varnish and the other, applied on top, a quick-drying water-based varnish. These work against each other to create the decorative cracked finish.

First paint the surface of the furniture in a pale oil-based paint. When the base coat is completely dry, apply the oil-based varnish, according to the directions, to the whole of the area you wish to "crackle." Use a soft fitch to insure that the layer is thin and smooth. Leave this to dry for about 45 minutes or until it is tacky to the touch. Apply the second varnish, also over the whole area. This can be left to dry naturally or aided with hot air from a hair dryer. As the top varnish dries, a network of cracks will form. After about an hour, when this process is complete and the varnish thoroughly dry, artist's oil paints or tinted oil glazes can be

Craquelure

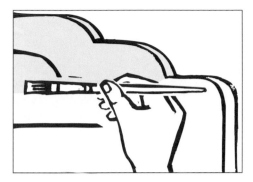

1 When the oil-based base coat is dry, apply the crackle varnish with a fitch. Once dried, apply the second coat.

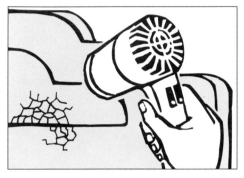

2 As soon as the varnish has dried the crackle will appear. Using a hair dryer will speed up the drying process.

3 When the varnish is completely dry, rub tinted oil glaze into the surface of the cracks with a soft cloth.

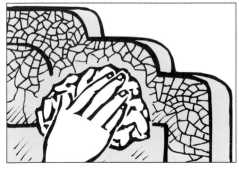

4 Rub off excess glaze with a clean cloth to leave dark cracks on a light background. Seal by applying a varnish.

rubbed into the surface with a soft cloth so that the tint lodges in the cracks and accentuates them. When you are happy with the degree of color and overall effect, rub off any excess glaze or oil paint not in the cracks and leave to dry for several days. Once dry, coat the area with shellac and/or an oil-based varnish.

Glazes

Oil glaze (also called glazing liquid) is an extremely versatile substance over paper or wood. It can be tinted with artist's oil paints and, when dry, will be translucent and smooth. Oil glaze behaves like a filmy translucent layer which, even if colored slightly, will still allow color beneath it to come through.

Creating an antiqued finish with oil glaze

Mix one part artist's oil paint to eight parts transparent oil glaze to create a murky tint. Antiquing glazes are best applied over a roughened surface so that the color will sit in the wood grain and in any surface scratches and cracks. If you have newly painted wood, you should sand or wire-brush it first to give

it a cracked appearance. Apply the glaze, brushing it out in different directions into a thin layer. Then use a rag to gently rub it off in patches, leaving the glaze in the cracks of the surface to create a mottled effect.

Besides being applied to plain or painted wood, tinted oil glaze can be applied over photocopied images and newspapers that have been glued onto furniture such as screens. This will make paper look as if it is old parchment. Finish with a coat of clear varnish to give lasting protection.

Stains

Wood stains will color wood, but, unlike varnish, they will not seal it. Wood stains can be used as a solid color or, more decoratively, painted on surfaces in geometric patterns to imitate marquetry. Look at tile patterns in historic houses or church interiors for inspiration. To stain wood, first mark out the pattern by lightly scoring the wood with a knife. This helps to prevent the different colored stains from seeping into their neighboring sections. Apply the stain with a brush and allow to dry. Finish with several coats of varnish to seal the wood.

◀ *A painted surface that looks cracked and aged by both time and use can be achieved using the craquelure technique. The gently broken surface it produces, especially when used with paints in pale colors, can be given a further aging effect with the addition of a colored antiquing glaze rubbed gently into the surface.*

Applying paint and wax

Paint on wood

Colorwashing

Exactly as its name implies, colorwashing involves the application of a "wash" of water-based paint onto a wood surface to create thin, transparent layers of color.

Build up color and texture bit by bit, painting over previous layers and moving the paint around with the brush. The application of the paint can be quite rough and uneven to give a lively, "loose" effect. If, however, you want the finish to be quite even, apply a final coat in a paler color. Take care to "contain" the unevenness by setting the finished piece of painted furniture against a clean-looking background. Colorwashing with three colors achieves a rich, intense depth.

Colorwash with a wax resist

Painted or colorwashed furniture can be given a slightly beaten-up, weathered look using a wax resist. Wax resists the paint and can be rubbed off at the end of the process to reveal the base layer—whether it be the original wood, or a painted or enamel-varnished surface.

Beeswax polish, or rubber cement that can be removed easily, should be applied over the base coat with a small brush in streaks or blobs. The more worn-out the finish you require, the more wax or glue you should apply. Once dry, paint on a layer of latex flat paint and allow this to dry overnight. Then apply subsequent diluted layers. When the last coat has dried, use an old rag and a scraper to remove the wax or glue, exposing the base and other layers of paint. Finally give the whole piece a light sanding.

Wax on wood

Liming

Liming (or pickling) is an effective technique used to enhance the beauty of the wood, leaving a white residue in the grain and cracks and a subtle white sheen over its surface. Choose a wood that has a noticeable, attractive, "open" grain. Oak and ash are two good examples of woods and will take the white liming paste or wax particularly well. However, if you are prepared to thoroughly wire-brush the surface of a piece of pine furniture (pine has a closed grain), the white waxy residue will be equally effective. All wood surfaces should be lightly wire-brushed first to open the grain. Work the brush in the direction of the grain.

Readymade liming wax is the easiest to use, and it should be applied using a fairly stiff brush. The idea is to coat the wood and allow the wax to settle in its cracks, splits, and grain. Once the wax has dried, smooth over the surface with a cloth, taking care not to lift the wax out.

▶ The wonderful patina and character of weathered slabs of old wood have been enhanced by using a liming technique. The creamy white wash sits in the grainy surface of the wood, but still allows the original color of the wood to show through. The white color scheme of this room is accentuated by the use of this technique.

Colorwash with wax resist

1 Apply the beeswax polish or rubber cement to the surface of the furniture. Brush it on in streaks with a small brush.

2 When dry, paint a layer of latex flat over the surface. Allow to dry again, then apply additional diluted layers.

3 After the final layer has dried, use an old rag and scraper to expose the base and other layers of paint.

▲ *This truly majestic piece of furniture has intricate metalwork encrusted with old peeling paint and rust, which wonderfully complement the rich textures of the kilim and the velvet of the pillows and upholstery. Aged paintwork can be re-created effectively with paint techniques that imitate rusted, bleached, or otherwise battered surfaces.*

Verdigris

1 A few small patches of yellow ocher are dabbed across the table's finished paintwork using a thin artist's brush.

2 Gently pour water over the surface of the table to expose some of the under layers of paint.

3 Sprinkle whiting powder over the damp surface of the table and press onto the surface and into the moldings.

4 When almost dry, use an old rag to rub off some of the whiting. When dry, seal with diluted white glue.

Paint on metal

Verdigris

Pale-green-topped buildings are a common site in many towns and cities. The sea-green color is the naturally occurring corrosion of copper, brass, or bronze. Verdigris, as the effect is called, takes time to develop, and although items can be left outside for the weather to do its work, it is possible to cheat and achieve authentic-looking verdigris by using paint and paste.

The technique is suitable for metal or plastic items such as picture frames, candlesticks and lamp bases, and furniture, but it has to be worked onto a horizontal surface, as the paste will not stick to a vertical one. If you are working on a metal-framed table, for example, you will need to do each part of the frame separately, turning the table so that the painted surface is always horizontal.

The base for the work should be a bronze-brown color, so first paint the item with a suitable shade of paint, French enamel varnish, or shellac and allow this to dry. Apply a wash of deep-green latex flat paint (diluted one part paint to four parts water) and leave this to dry. If necessary, apply a

second coat. You now need to make up two verdigris pastes, one using mint-green latex flat and the other a pale blue. Mix denatured alcohol into each of the paints (one part alcohol to two parts paint). Using a sieve, mix in plaster powder or whiting until you have smooth and fairly stiff pastes.

The two pastes should be applied to the painted surface randomly, building up varying degrees of texture. Don't be too precise about applying the paste and leave some areas of the basecoat showing through. While this is drying, use a thin artist's brush to apply a little well-diluted yellow ocher acrylic paint in small random patches across the surface. When dry, gently pour water over the whole surface, to expose some of the layers beneath.

Sprinkle some whiting or powder over the damp surface, pressing it into the surface and into any moldings. When almost dry, use a cloth to rub off some of the powder so that the layers underneath show. The finished result should look like the patinated metal it is imitating. When dry, seal with diluted white glue. For a really hard-wearing surface, apply a matte polyurethane varnish. Creating a look of rusted metal can be achieved in a similar way, using brown and red paints.

Using unusual materials

▲ *Bold and whimsical, these plastic blown-up pillows with their emphatic rows of brightly colored circles are a throwback to the 1960s, but they work surprisingly well in this otherwise deliberately restrained interior. Balance unusual materials with something more familiar to create maximum impact.*

such diversity, it is to be hoped that the days when almost every surface was covered in a floral chintz fabric are dim and distant.

While working with such unusual materials will not be to everyone's taste, it is undoubtedly true that using metal, plastic, and paper, for example, as materials for furnishings, will be a challenge to your imagination and perspective. Imagine a glass-topped table draped in a shimmering, gauze-like, finely meshed metal. It would make a wonderful and unusual backdrop for a collection of glass objects. Put a swath of silk beneath the metal and you have a stunning combination. Ribbons or tassels can be tied to sheets of wire mesh for added texture. Metal-framed chairs wound with jute fiber or twisted straw fronds provide fabulous textural contrast.

Mixing and experimenting are the keys to success when using any material with which you are unfamiliar. Some of these, and their applications, are by no means new: mosaic, for example. And although paper is a familiar material, using it as a covering for furniture opens up a new dimension.

We are continually drawing on past styles and themes in attempts to find new ways of decorating surfaces. While few of us have the inclination or ability to re-create the splendid mosaic masterpieces of the ancient Roman artisans, we may well consider and be influenced by their use of pattern and color in our own more modest creations.

Classic, timeless pieces can be given a twist in new materials. For example, the familiar shape of an upholstered club armchair, with its solid proportions, is retained yet transformed if sculpted from twisted metal or corrugated cardboard.

Wit and a hint of mischief may occasionally take over from practicality—and why not, if one is weary of mass-production and safe, "coordinating" schemes? For most of us, plastic inflatable pillows may look best floating on the shimmering surface of a swimming pool, but we are already being introduced to countertops made from plastic waste. So, in pride of place—perhaps on the *chaise longue* crafted from recycled plastic containers—why not a plastic inflatable bolster?

This section salutes a small but exciting selection of surprising and unlikely materials that can stunningly alter the surface of a piece of furniture. Neither fabric nor paint, they do not fall into any general category, but include such diverse materials as paper, plastic, jute fiber, wire mesh, glass, and ceramic, but used individually or even together they break the boundaries of what is both familiar and predictable in interior furnishing.

Contrast and texture and the interplay between them are the keys to using these materials with style and verve. Keep in mind balance and symmetry—a small amount of something unexpected usually goes a long way! Consider hard and soft surfaces together and juxtapose matte opacity with cool glassy light-reflecting surfaces. Imagine, for example, shiny plastic or metal gauze against a smooth rubber or linoleum floor. With

◄ *The surprising use of solid glass to make this "tablecloth" and matching stool, together with the stunning color, provides a dramatic focal point in the room. The large expanse of glass in the uncurtained window and the equally unusual orange-yellow light fixture over the table contribute to the glass theme.*

Paper

Although it is more usually found on the walls of a room, paper is a very exciting medium to use on furniture—whether wood, metal, or plastic. In its many forms, it transfers particularly easily to flat, smooth surfaces such as table tops, drawer fronts, cabinet panels, and even wooden chairs. Other than glue to paste it to the surface, the only requirement is a top coat or two of clear varnish, to prevent it from tearing.

Paper can be matte and rough like newsprint, smooth and shiny as on a magazine cover, printed, embossed, plain, silver, thin, transparent, and much more besides. Once you begin to identify the different types available—even those in everyday use—its versatility becomes instantly evident. It offers numerous decorative possibilities, for while it can, of course, be cut with a knife or pair of scissors, torn, folded or scrunched, it can also be stitched, and even woven.

Do not assume that paper cannot be a sturdy material. The Lloyd Loom chairs, popular in the 1920s, are made from twisted paper woven together, resulting in a form that is very strong and hard-wearing. In addition, some types of cardboard—corrugated, for example—are sufficiently rigid to make freestanding pieces, or "cut-out" cases that may be dropped over or applied to a wood frame—as seating, for example. To achieve a lighthearted decorative element you could also explore the technique of trompe l'oeil by painting yourself a magnificent carved wood table or a whimsical chair on a free-standing silhouette of illustration board.

Lay cut or torn pieces of paper on a flat surface under sheets of glass, or perhaps overlay fine black-and-white newsprint with tiny pieces of colored metallic foil from candy wrappers in a mosaic pattern. Try weaving strips of multicolored images from magazine pages between strips of solid-colored paper to create a flat checkered surface which can be laid or pasted, like a mat, on tables or cabinets. Folded strips of newspaper could be woven in the same way—and complemented by brown paper. Such a monotone surface lends itself to cool, clear interiors in which natural materials, such as wood, stone, or terra-cotta, feature.

▲ Painted and decorated paper has been used to cover the structure and drawer fronts of this unusual chest of drawers. This effect is easy to achieve and works particularly well on flat surfaces, as it is easier to manipulate the paper and achieve neat folds and edges. Another advantage is that if you don't like it, you can rip it off and try something else.

Textured paper

For a smart and sophisticated surface use simple embossed letters or motifs on a beautifully hand-crafted sheet of paper. You can order an embossing press with your own initials or customized image, and the advantage of heavy handmade paper is that it has some texture and thickness. Another simple method of adding texture to paper is to use a sewing machine to punch lines across its surface—but take the thread out of the machine first! The results resemble punched metalwork and can be cut to fit areas such as cabinet door panels.

There are numerous types of specialist handmade paper on the market, many of which have beautiful and unusual textures; while others resemble stone, such as marble, or granite. Some are made from recycled paper, often with a scattering of plant pieces, flower petals, or onion skins. Some are really lovely, and make wonderful decorative material. Although they appear fragile, they are actually quite strong. For protection on a table surface, however, the sheets would need to be laid under glass.

Pleating paper

Pleated or folded paper can be used behind glass cabinet doors as an inexpensive alternative to fabric. Use a crisp, smooth paper or thin artist's board and mark with tiny dots along the top and back edge of the paper. The dots need not be equally spaced but must line up on both edges. Fold on alternate sides, following the marked fold lines. Use a bone letter opener to crease the fold lines. Attach the folded sheets to the wooden frame of a glass door using thumbtacks.

◀ *Paper is an extremely versatile material available in a huge range of different colors, textures, and weights. Here, reproduced antique type-printed paper has been used to cover the lampshade and the wallpaper. Be bold and create unusual effects by experimenting with various different types of paper on different surfaces.*

Paper can be applied directly to a smooth, clean surface using white glue, diluted 1:1 with water. A large sheet of newsprint or printed wallpaper could be used across a tabletop, for example; or if you don't wish to paste directly onto the table, cut a piece of plywood or MDF (medium density fiberboard) to the same size and wrap it in the paper. Seal the finished surface with the glue solution. Alternatively, assemble smaller pieces of plywood, cut to the size of a standard ceramic tile, each covered in a different colored or printed paper, and lay the paper-covered "tiles" together on a recessed tabletop. Protect the surface with a sheet of glass.

Maps are fun to use on or over furniture. Look for old examples in secondhand bookstores, or huge, brand-new, brightly colored world maps. These are great for children's rooms or more informal, relaxed spaces. Again, use diluted white glue, both to attach the paper and to seal its surface.

Plain papers can be dyed, painted, stained, marbled, or printed on before being used. Children's paintings, pasted onto the sides and base of a simple wooden box and then sealed, would make a fun addition to a playroom. Use acrylic paints on the paper, as they will not mix with the glue.

The inside of plain pine chests can be given a lift by using a lining paper inside the lid and in the box itself. Wallpapers with old or contemporary designs are excellent, as the paper is quite tough and the selection of patterns available is wide.

A clever way of brightening up and completely transforming a fairly dull chest of drawers or small seed chest would be to cover all the drawer fronts with paper. Take a pictorial scene—*toile de Jouy* wallpaper would be a good start—and cut the pattern into a grid, one for each drawer. You will need to allow sufficient paper to turn around the sides of each drawer front. Stripes or plaid papers would be equally effective. For a children's room, for example, alternate different bold colors. Remove drawer knobs first. Apply the paper using white glue and make sure the surface is smooth and wrinkle-free. After leaving the paper enough time to dry, carefully screw the knobs back on again.

Decoupage

This technique is the decoration of surfaces with paper cut-outs. Interesting effects can be achieved by photocopying single images, enlarging or reducing them according to the size of the item you plan to cover, and cutting them out. Almost any printed paper that you can cut and paste can be used: look for old engravings of flowers or fruit, or architectural details for a classical theme, pieces of newspaper, playing cards, old documents, glossy magazine covers, wallpaper borders, or elements of more intricate patterns such as old fabric or wallpaper designs. For traditionalists, multicolored floral designs and fat little cherubs will follow the Victorian style—they used decoupage on just about everything. Also interesting—for a kitchen

▲ *This is a delightful and original way to make a feature of a dull hallway or a dreary corner. Every surface is covered with an unusual paper. The toning base colors of the floor, baseboard and wallpaper unite the effect, allowing the printed paper on the table and the pattern on the wallpaper to really stand out.*

surface perhaps—are hardware catalogs illustrating pots, pans, and other culinary gadgets. Cabinet handles and moldings can be photocopied, painted, or stained if required, and then pasted in place on the flat surface of a plain cabinet front. When assembled, the effect is that of a fake dresser or cabinet.

Letters or numbers also make interesting decoration. Use varying styles and sizes cut out from magazines, newspapers, or posters, and dot them all over a surface such as a large desk. A background of plain brown parcel paper can be used for contrast. Sheets of different typeface styles also look good when pasted together.

How to decoupage

Use an X-Acto knife to cut out the paper or photocopied images, and a 1:1 dilution of white glue and water for pasting and varnishing. Also useful is a decorator's brush for pasting and a smaller artist's brush and diluted latex flat paints (or acrylics) for coloring black-and-white photocopies.

Cut out the images on a hard, flat surface, ideally a cutting board, using the X-Acto knife. Prepare the background: for example, newspaper, brown paper, or a painted surface. Coat the paper cut-outs on both sides with the diluted glue. Position the pasted paper and brush over. When it dries the paper will shrink a little. Paint the image with diluted paint or "antique" it (see pages 278–279) if this is in keeping with the effect you want.

▲ *Scraps of old letters and music scores have been layered and pasted directly onto the newly painted cream surface of this chest of drawers to provide an unusual but very effective and imaginative look. The overall effect, linked by the neutral color of the chest's background and the fireplace, creates a harmonious blend.*

Decoupage

1 Select various images from newspapers or magazines and, using an X-Acto knife, carefully cut them out.

2 With a paintbrush, coat both sides of the cut-out shapes with a 1:1 mix of water and white glue.

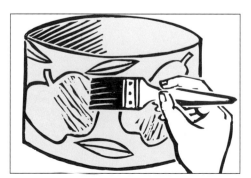

3 Position the pasted cut-outs on the surface you are covering and then brush the shapes with the mix.

Mosaic

As a decorative art form, mosaic has been around for thousands of years. Little bits of stone, pebble, glass, and even shell have been used to embellish walls, floors, and other surfaces, both inside and outside, in all sorts of buildings that range from the humblest of dwellings to the grandest of cathedrals. Throughout history, from the time of the ancient Greeks and Romans, mosaics have depicted figurative scenes as detailed as paintings or tapestries. Huge areas were covered in fragments of ceramic or precious or semi-precious stones which had borders of intricate abstract patterns running around the central image. As a purely abstract art form, mosaic ran riot during the Art Nouveau period in Europe, with roofs, courtyards, columns, and almost every available surface covered in startlingly bold and detailed designs by skilled practitioners who embraced its versatility and vibrancy.

In contemporary interiors mosaic is being re-employed as a means of decorating surfaces. On furniture it can be used to embellish tabletops, mirror frames, headboards, and even chairs. The pieces that traditionally formed mosaic are known as

▶ *Mosaic is an old tradition in most cultures. Here, a lovely pattern has been made from mosaic and set into the top of the round table. The mosaic effect is echoed in the background in the tiles placed around the kitchen area.*

Mosaic

1 Break up the pieces for your mosaic into small chips. You may need to cut them again to fit into the edges.

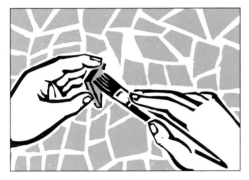

2 Once the pattern has been devised, apply glue to the back of the mosaic pieces and position them.

3 Apply grout across the surface of the mosaic. Spread evenly, filling in the gaps between each piece of mosaic.

4 Before it dries, wipe off any excess grout smeared across the surface of the mosaic with a clean cloth.

tesserae or "smalti"—small colored glass or enamel blocks. Tesserae can be bought from specialist suppliers, but it is possible to use a whole variety of materials in mosaic work: interesting effects can be achieved using broken pieces of household ceramic tiles or dishes, glass, perspex, or even mirror.

Most surfaces, if prepared correctly, can take mosaic. You may need to score some surfaces, such as metal, in order for glue or cement to take; and wood, plywood or MDF (medium density fiberboard) must be sealed first with a 1:1 solution of water to white glue. Hardboard for a tabletop, for example, can be bought to your specifications from some hardware stores. However, you can apply mosaic directly to the surface of furniture. Keeping the work horizontal until the grout has dried is important. If you have ever tiled a floor or wall, you'll find the approach is much the same, but simpler.

Arranging the tiles

Designs, abstract or figurative, can be first mapped out on the base, or you can piece the pattern together as you go along, creating a kaleidoscope of color. For a random design, begin by playing with the segments on the surface of the table or board, moving them around until a pleasing pattern forms. For thicker tiles you may need to score and snap some of the segments that are to edge the board; for thinner tiles and tesserae, use tile nippers to create curves for your pattern.

Pottery or larger tiles can be broken and subsequently cut into more refined shapes. Alternatively, you can use the randomly broken segments in a loose, abstract arrangement; but be prepared to use more grout between each piece. Should you wish to embark on more adventurous mosaic projects, with harder materials such as marble or smalti, it is worth investing in a hammer and a special small anvil, against which the piece is held while the hammer is used to break it.

Gluing and grouting

Once the pattern has been decided and the pieces cut, apply glue to the back of each piece and stick them down onto your hard-

▲ *This is a wonderful use of mosaic—insetting random and regular patterns within the paneled sections of this wooden bed frame. The decoration is pleasingly restrained and quite beautiful in its simplicity. Small ceramic tiles in neat rows perfectly balance the irregular pieces of broken tile in the center.*

board or other surface. Leave to dry. Then mix up the grout, following the instructions, or use ready-mixed grout. Grout can be colored, if desired, using acrylic paints, which should be added in small amounts to the dry powder type of grout.

Apply the grout across the surface of the mosaic, and spread evenly, filling all the gaps between the sections of tile or glass. Before it dries, wipe off the excess with a damp cloth. The piece should be left to dry for at least 24 hours and then the surface cleaned and polished with a clean cloth.

Fabric

Everyone for whom fabrics are a real passion
will find the excitement of handling textiles and
the exploration of their potential—both practical
and decorative—absolutely all-embracing. From
earthy-colored wool plaids to shimmery, lustrous
silks, the inspiration and fascination are the same.
This has, perhaps, something to do with the tactile
qualities of cloth, with its origins and history, and
with its many and varied forms.

Weave

Both the structure of a weave and the choice of yarn affect the final character of the cloth. Different weave structures used on the same yarn will produce significantly different finished fabrics. Smooth cotton sateen, for example, looks nothing like muslin, although both are made of cotton. This is almost entirely because of the way each is woven.

Plain weave—also called common weave—is the simplest and most obvious method of weaving a length of cloth. The weft threads (those traveling widthwise across the loom) go under and over alternate warp threads (those traveling lengthwise across the loom). On the next row, the warp thread travels over the weft thread where previously it went under, and vice versa. This pattern alternates row by row.

In most woven cloths, the warp threads are assembled on a loom first (in a variety of forms) and then the weft threads are woven through them. In some cloths, however—Jacquard cloth, for example—the weave is very much more complex. Indeed, Jacquard cloth is produced on its own special loom, from which the cloth takes its name.

Yarn

Different yarns—of cotton, linen, wool, silk, or synthetic fibers—give particular characteristics to fabrics. Yarns may be mixed in one cloth for various reasons: to add more strength or luster, or for economic reasons.

Cloth may be dyed once woven (piece-dyed), or the yarn may be colored before the weaving process begins. In addition, an infinite variety of pattern can be achieved by printing on cloth. Complex modern printing methods can achieve stunning effects: computer-generated imagery is used to print holograms onto cloth, for instance, and computers are also used in weaving.

Fabric for decorating

Applying fabrics to furniture and using them for furnishings are endlessly rewarding; they are so versatile. There are many reasons for wanting to cover a sofa with new fabric, for instance: perhaps for mundane practical reasons, or for a change of mood

◀ *Long, seemingly never-ending streams of billowy fabric in gorgeous, jewel-like colors flow down from the ceiling and demonstrate how a bold use of fabric can create a stunning effect. Just visible is another light shining through the material, illustrating how fabric, when used in this way, can add dimensions to a room.*

▲ *Combinations of different textures in the blue and white pillows mingle happily together when they are thrown into an attractive heap in the corner of this day bed. The blues are matched in the stripes of the seat cover, while the intricately woven white pillow covers create a link with the white-painted bedstead.*

Printing

To achieve a more controlled pattern on fabric, it is better to print, using a lino(leum) cut or stamp. Simple borders can be run around the edge of a fabric using this quick and easy method, and it can be cleverly utilized for small items like pillow covers.

Obviously, the more professional you want your finish to be, the more likely you are to need proper tools; there are special lino-cutting tools, for example. But whether you use a potato, lino, or a sponge, the principle is the same: the areas not cut away are those that are inked and printed. A version of this method uses dishwashing sponges—the kind that are rectangular and have a stiff scouring base. Use a fiber-tip pen to mark a grid on the soft side of the sponge. Divide it into squares with ¼-inch (6mm) gutters between the squares. Cut along the lines and hollow

out the channels. Squeeze acrylic paint onto a plate and thin it with water to the consistency of light cream, or use fabric paints. Do not make it so thin and wet that it drips. Press the cut face of the sponge into the paint.

Make sure that your fabric is stretched out flat, either using weights or, preferably, pinning it to a board. Then, carefully and lightly, press the sponge onto the surface of the fabric; you will achieve a kind of mosaic pattern. You may want to test the technique first on a piece of paper to insure that you have the paint at the correct consistency and so that you can decide how much paint you actually need on the sponge; be careful not to smudge prints you have already made as you print more.

You can make a checkerboard pattern using two sponge "tiles" and two colors. Print one color first, filling in the missing squares with the other only when it is dry.

Combining fabrics

This is the fabric equivalent of "distressed" paint finishes! By breaking down and re-assembling related or contrasting fabrics in one item—a throw or bed hanging, perhaps—you can create both unexpected and wonderful combinations and a distinctly original "fabric." The idea extends and develops the idea of the patchwork quilt. As in all decoration, however, there has to be a balance: the two, three, or many more different fabrics that work pleasingly together must result in a piece that is more than just the sum of its parts.

Pile more than half a dozen fabrics together on a table and you will see some kind of link. Maybe it is simply a red line from a tartan which jumps to a silk damask of the same hue, or the creaminess of old bleached linen against a rough jute, which in

▶ These pillows would have been fairly anonymous without their embroidered daisy details and deliberately rough-and-ready stitching. Customizing household accessories can lift them out of the ordinary. It is also cost effective, enabling you to put scraps of old dress material and leftover snippets of upholstery fabric to good use.

Printing fabric

1 Mark a grid with fiber pen on the sponge's soft face; cut channels along the lines to make a pad of squares.

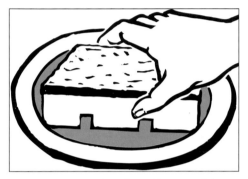

2 Squeeze paint onto plate; dilute with water to light-cream consistency; press cut face of sponge into paint.

3 Test technique on paper to avoid smudging and drips; then press sponge carefully and lightly onto flat fabric.

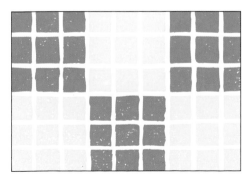

4 Print all the first color of a checkerboard effect and allow to dry then fill in second-color squares.

▲ *These fabrics have been painted and resist-dyed in colors of jewel-like intensity. Their inspiration ranges from batik fabrics and Indian saris to the boldly striped walls and furnishings of Regency salons. Simple trimmings can enhance furnishing fabrics still further; here, a gold-braid edging gives the shimmering sapphire-colored pillow an ornate finish.*

turn lies against a cream and black striped cotton. Occasionally, a cornucopia of pink, lime green, purple, and orange, although not to everyone's taste, just simply works.

If the color links in some way, you can mix your fabrics. Equally, mix different textures—silk, poplin, canvas, damask, and velvet, for example.

It is also interesting to use fabrics of varying weights together in one piece: such as thin muslin and velvet, or burlap and silk. You then have a fabric that moves in a different way, and demands that it be hung or displayed more cleverly, or suggests new uses.

Stitching small circles of frayed, different-colored cloth randomly across the surface of another fabric—like mattress tufts—is another exciting method of customizing; as is stitching itself, which can transform fabric by adding color and texture.

Work out the quantity of fabric you wish to use fairly carefully, allowing extra for hems and seams. The keys to the success of the final piece are both planning and accurate cutting. Fabrics for piping should be cut on the bias and therefore more fabric is required for this purpose. Use faint pencil lines as a cutting guide.

Seating

Seating is all about comfort and style—and balancing the right amount of each. How this is achieved will depend on where in the house, garden, or office the seating is to be and, more crucially, the part it is to play. Whether we are working at a desk or flopping down at the end of a busy day, comfort is paramount. A set of chairs able to withstand day-to-day use at family mealtimes will need a more practical design than the more stylish dining room chairs used only on special days and holidays.

It does not trouble us if wooden furniture for the garden is allowed to mellow and take on a rough, weathered patina, but we treat an antique mahogany dining chair with tender loving care, polishing it reverently and making sure it receives no damage.

Different rooms and living spaces will, naturally, have varying styles of seating. Individual items are far more likely to make an impact—and be chosen for that purpose—in areas where they can be surrounded by considerable space. For example, an intricately carved old church pew or a tall, elegant wing armchair, whose upholstered sections are each covered in different fabrics, could be viewed as a decorative object when placed individually, and would provide a strong focal point for an interior. Their comfort appeal would be secondary to their looks.

Specific items will undoubtedly influence the addition of others. Selection should, though, be based on what you like and feel good about rather than on trying to "match" a set of furniture. In areas such as living rooms, where several items of seating often mingle together, overall cohesion is important, although individual items may clash dramatically. This is where balance is essential.

The uses of fabric

Fabric can be used to link or group seating elements together with covers, throws, or pillows. By choosing one color, such as oatmeal, and covering all seating in that color, whether upholstered armchairs, sofas, or dining chair seats, you can create an interior that is instantly calming and uncluttered. However, it would be dramatically livened up if different-colored fabrics or other surfaces—wood, metal, leather, or glass, for example—were allowed in. A riot of different patterns on printed or woven fabrics can coexist provided that there is a strong color link running through them and given that there are also areas of calm, such as plain walls and floors, to anchor them.

In addition, fabric appeals to our tactile sense, creating a feeling of warmth and comfort. More than any other material, it completely transforms a surface. By introducing a cushion on a painted wooden

◀ A large kilim anchors the seating area in this wonderfully lively and colorful room. The sofa, upholstered in a plain cream fabric, offsets the riot of color going on around it. The alcove, with a built-in covered seat, provides a place to escape, while multicolored pillows occupy every available surface.

▲ Furniture has been carefully placed to fill out—but not clutter—this area of a large converted warehouse. The daybed, sited in the middle of the room rather than predictably hugging a wall, affords dual seating. The position of the lamp next to the sofa and of the large floor rug by the day-bed anchors the furniture.

window seat or a thick wool throw over the back of a plain sofa, you can change the style and character of seating surfaces—and the room—with relative ease.

Designing your seating

How seating is arranged in a room or living space is pivotal to the success of the room, from both practical and style viewpoints. In small or awkward spaces such as those under stairs, housing a freestanding piece of seating furniture would be difficult, but a built-in wooden box structure covered with loose cushions would make good use of this kind of space, transforming it into a wonderful "cubbyhole" seating area for quiet reading. Give the box seat a lid and, of course, you have storage space too!

Long, narrow living rooms need careful planning, with groups of items strategically placed so that the entire room can be used, especially if different activities have to take place in the same space. If the entire living space is one room—whether in a vast loft apartment or a more modest abode—an element of flexibility is important. Mix smaller items such as stools and side chairs with larger, more imposing pieces. Combine period-inspired furniture with a modern piece or a simple item found in a junk shop. Don't be intimidated at the thought of larger items, such as sofas, being positioned in the middle of the floor. Set chairs at interesting diagonals to "break up" space. And if the key to your space is a good desk, a chair, and a computer, then put them center stage!

Basic cushions and pillows

Cushions can be roughly divided into two types: those that fit a given space and those, normally called pillows, that lead a more nomadic existence—the ubiquitous scatter pillow. Box cushions are made to a specific size, dictated by the space between the arms and back of a sofa or chair, or the dimensions of a flat wooden bench top or window seat. Pillows can be of all shapes and sizes and their domain is infinitely varied. These padded, plumped disks and squares of piped, fringed, and braided color can sometimes, surprisingly, be the single element that gives balance and focus to a room or piece of furniture. The eye darts about in a room, settling on pattern, texture, and color, so a small pillow or pile of pillows can attract and become a link between otherwise unrelated items.

Mixing different surfaces, materials, and textiles in one space is exciting. For example, adding a pair of square pillows in a fake leopardskin against a cool backdrop of neutral off-white and beige linen may inspire a flight of fantasy that could make bringing ornate gilt and black lacquer furniture into the room acceptable, whereas it might otherwise have been rejected. Against the same backdrop, imagine a pile of pillows made of rich tapestries, old tangled fringes, and near-faded silks in a warm mix of red, ocher, and terra-cotta, and you achieve a completely different atmosphere.

Pillow styles

Basic square, rectangular, or round pillow covers have two sides of fabric, stitched together. The opening for the pillow form can be fastened by simple slipstitches or by way of a zipper, buttons, or ties (see pages 304–305, 310–313). The two sides need not be of the same fabric—each side could be a combination of fabrics joined before the cushion cover is constructed. Piping or decorative cord can add definition, while braids, fringe, and buttons lend texture. Pillow covers can be made so that the stitching line hugs the edge of the form and is surrounded by a flat border, or flange. The border, usually about 2 inches (5cm) wide, might be in the same fabric as the pillow, or in a contrast.

For a smart tailored look, combine crisp white linen for the main part of the pillow with a fine cotton shirting in a white and colored stripe for a piping detail, and for the surrounding border use a check of hound's- or dog's-tooth. Use the same three fabrics on other pillows in the same group but switch the focus. Borders can be extended, and for a rectangular pillow, like a bed pillow, a large border at the open end secured by buttons is particularly smart.

For a totally different style, take as your inspiration the rich contrast between a wool blanket and the silky band edging it and make a cover that combines smart wool

► *This beautiful wooden bench needs only the simplest of decoration. A box cushion covering the upholstered base offers softer seating, and a row of substantial square pillows in cool, creamy white fabric makes a simple, uncluttered, and stylish addition to the piece as well as providing extra comfort.*

suiting with a surround of brightly colored silk. Another idea is to mix a multitude of stripes or checks or even different scale floral patterns—printed or woven—but bear in mind that a color link should bind them. One of the attractive aspects of making pillow covers is that they take only a small amount of fabric and are therefore relatively inexpensive decorative touches.

Making a square pillow cover

To make a plain, square pillow cover without piping, first you need to decide on the finished pillow size. Cut two squares of fabric to the size of the pillow plus a ⅝ inch (1.5cm) seam allowance all around.

With right sides facing and raw edges aligned, pin and baste the two pieces together, then remove the pins. Working a few reverse stitches at each end of the seam, machine stitch around the edge, leaving an opening along one side for turning and

inserting the pillow form. Remove the basting, trim the seam allowances, and cut the corners to reduce bulk, leaving a gap of approximately ¼in (6mm) to avoid fraying. Press the seams.

Turn the cover right side out through the opening and push out the corners so that they are sharp. Press the cover and then insert the pillow form. Finally, turn under the seam allowances along the opening, pin, and slipstitch closed.

Making a round pillow cover

If made without a boxing strip between the top and bottom sides, round pillows are simply made from two circular fabric pieces sewn together with or without a line of piping, or cording, between the two. Cord or a small shallow fringe can be hand sewn around the finished pillow.

For variety, cut two halves of different, contrasting fabrics for each side. Join them together and then proceed as if for one piece.

Making a square pillow

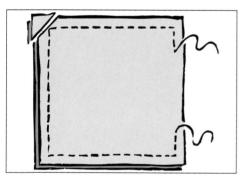

1 With right sides facing, stitch the back and front together, leaving an opening. Trim corners diagonally.

2 Press the seams open. Turn the cover right side out, insert the pillow and slipstitch the opening edges.

▲ *Layer upon layer of simple pillows provide a comfortable back for the daybed. A pile of the same pillows, secured with tied tabs around an inner cover concealing the pad, are strategically positioned to form the arms. A mixture of warm terra-cotta, charcoal, and ocher, offset by the occasional black and white stripe, makes a bold combination.*

To make a paper pattern for the pillow cover, draw around a suitably sized object such as a large plate, then add a ⅝ inch (1.5cm) seam allowance all around. Alternatively, cut a paper square with dimensions matching the diameter of the required finished circle plus extra for seam allowances. Fold the square into quarters and lay it on a flat surface. Tie a pencil onto the end of a piece of string, then pin the other end of the string to the center of the folded square so that the string between the pencil and the pin measures the radius of the required circle, plus a ⅝ inch (1.5cm) seam allowance. Draw a quarter-circle arc on the paper and cut along it.

Open out the paper circle and, using this as your pattern, cut out one fabric piece for the front of the cover and one for the back. Pin and baste the two pieces together, with right sides facing and raw edges aligned. Remove the pins. Working a few reverse stitches at each end of the seam, machine stitch around the cover, leaving an opening for turning and for inserting the pillow form. Remove the basting, then trim and notch the seam allowance to reduce bulk. Press the seam open. Turn the cover right side out and press again, turning the seam allowances to the wrong side along the opening. Insert the pillow form. Pin and sew the opening closed.

Tie-on cushions

Square or round cushions that are to be used as seat pads for a wooden or wicker chair or bench sometimes need anchoring so that they don't slip off. Ties looped around the back of the frame are the answer.

Simple covers for seat pads can be made in the same way as a basic pillow cover but with a pair of ties inserted into the back edge of the cushion between the two pieces of fabric. Tie-on cushions may be made square or round, and with or without piping. Or they can be made as flattish box cushions with a gusset or boxing strip of 2 inches (5cm) or less (see pages 306–307).

The ties can serve a decorative as well as a functional purpose. For example, unyielding wooden chairs, such as old school desk chairs, benefit from having a cushion tied onto the seat to add comfort and color.

▲ *Made to fit the seats of these metal-framed chairs, these round cushions add style as well as comfort. The two on the chair in the foreground both have depth given to them by means of a boxing strip, or gusset, but the one leaning against the back of the other chair has been made with just two circles of fabric joined together with piping.*

Making a round pillow

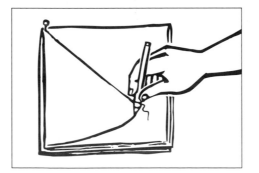

1 To make a paper pattern, fold a square of paper into quarters, draw a quarter-circle, and cut out.

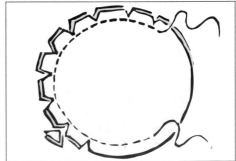

2 Cut two fabric circles. Stitch as for the square pillow (see pages 302–303), but notch the seam allowance.

Making a tie-on cushion cover

To make the ties, cut strips of fabric in either the same or a contrasting fabric (the two fabrics should be the same composition and weight) to a length that will allow for a reasonable knot or bow around the back of the chair frame. The width of the finished tie should be no more than about 1¼ inches (3cm). Cut the fabric to twice the width of the finished tie, plus a seam allowance of ½ inch (1.2cm) on each side and at each short end.

Fold the fabric strip in half lengthwise, right sides together, and press. Machine stitch, ½ inch (1.2cm) from the raw edge, across one short end and all along the length of the strip. Turn the tube right side out with the aid of a knitting needle or narrow ruler, pushing through from the stitched short end. Another way to make the tie is by topstitching the edges together. To do this, first press the ½ inch (1.2cm) seam allowances to the wrong side along both long edges and one short end. Then fold the strip in half lengthwise with the wrong sides together, and machine stitch close to the aligned folded edges. Set the finished ties aside.

Next, make a paper pattern of the required finished size and shape of the cushion cover, plus a ⅝ inch (1.5cm) seam allowance all around. Using this pattern, cut out the top and bottom of the cushion cover. Mark the chair leg (or chair back) positions on the bottom section of the cover, and pin two finished ties to each of the marked positions, with the short raw edges aligned with

Making a tie-on cushion

Make as for the square pillow (see pages 302–303) but insert the ties into the seam allowance.

the raw edges of the cover piece and the ties lying on the center of the piece. Pin the top of the cover to the bottom, with right sides together and raw edges aligned. Baste, catching in the ends of the ties in the seam. Remove the pins. Machine stitch around the edge, leaving an opening for turning and for inserting the cushion. Remove the basting, trim, clip and notch the seam allowance to reduce bulk. Press the seam open. Turn the cover right side out and press. Insert the pillow form. Pin and slipstitch the opening closed, as for the square pillow.

Other cushion and pillow ideas

Pillow covers can be interchanged to suit the mood of the interior. One cover inside another, with the outer one with contrasting ties, is a less formal, more fun approach, great for children's rooms. Big square pillows look good with button fastenings. Choose plain, unfussy buttons for matte fabrics such as cotton tickings, linens, or ginghams, delicate little mother-of-pearl buttons for finer fabrics, and big, bold, brassy ones for heavy brocades, silks, or damasks. Work thread loops if your machine doesn't do buttonholes.

Stitching applied to the surface of plain fabrics lends texture and pattern. Embroidery stitches can be used to great effect. Create spidery latticework, or a riot of multicolored dots or crosses, or copy formal motifs. Appliqué stars or other shapes using a bold blanket stitch. Cut out images from printed fabrics, such as farm animals, in bold silhouettes for children's rooms, and sew them onto plain fabrics.

Try constructing a pillow cover from a knitted square. Use creamy, soft string – the kind you find in a kitchen drawer or that ties parcels. Trim the edges with thick cotton cord in place of piping and hand sew the opening or use buttons. In bathrooms, or for outside in the summer, when all you want is to relax with a pillow beneath your head, use waterproof canvas for easy cleaning.

◄ Heavy, comfortable seat cushions on this intriguingly designed sofa and chairs are covered with bright citrus fabrics. Each cover has a row of fabric tabs attached to the cover opening which are tied together, with the knots adding a decorative finish to the back of the cushions.

Box cushions

Cushions used for seating are constructed with a tailored shape, more like a box than a flat pad. The cover for it, which has a gusset or boxing strip between the upper and lower sections, has six sides, like a box. A box cushion should be fairly solid so that the required shape is kept. The cushion itself is generally cut from foam. A layer of batting gives a softer look.

Box cushions are usually seen on the seat of an upholstered armchair, or two or three may be used snugly side by side on the base of a sofa. Wooden chairs, in which a loose seat pad of some kind is required for comfort, also rely on a sturdy box cushion.

Depending on the design of the chair or sofa, there may also be a box cushion to lean against, made in the same way but positioned roughly at right angles to the base cushion.

Making a box cushion cover

To make your box cushion cover, begin by cutting two pieces of material the same size as the top and bottom of the pad, adding 1.5cm (⅝in) all around for a seam allowance.

The gusset or boxing strip (also called a welt) is made up of five pieces. Cut one piece to fit the front of the cushion, allowing for a seam allowance all around. Then cut two pieces long enough to fit across the back of the cushion, plus 2 inches (5cm) extra at each end so that the back cushion will extend around the two back corners. Cut these pieces one-half the width of the front piece; add a seam allowance all around each piece. Lastly, cut one piece for each side of the cushion to fit between the front and back gussets.

Insert the zipper between the two back gusset pieces (see pages 312–313). With right sides facing, now pin and stitch the gusset pieces together, leaving ⅝inch (1.5cm) open at each end of the two front seams. Press the seams open. If you are using piping, stitch it to the top and bottom pieces (see pages 314–315). Next, pin and baste the gusset to the bottom piece, with right sides together and front corners matching. Clip the seam allowance on the gusset at each of the two back corners. Remove the pins and stitch in place. Open the zipper and attach the gusset

▲ *A simple wooden structure creates a clever seating area and transforms an otherwise featureless window space. Thick, heavy cushions, with their edges rolled rather than piped, align to form a padded, bench-like seat against the three walls. The cushions are buttoned to prevent the covers from moving.*

▶ *Piped edgings give shape and definition to furnishings, and here they are used to great effect in highlighting the deliberately overstuffed box cushion seat of this ample Victorian wing chair. Using the same russet and gold damask for the piping as for the cover adds a simple touch of refinement.*

to the top piece in the same way. Trim the seam allowances and corners and press. Turn the cover right side out through the zipper and press. (Hook-and-loop tape can be used instead of a zipper.)

Decorative effects for box cushions

This type of cushion looks best with piping or cord added along the seams between the top, the base sections, and the gusset. This emphasizes the distinctive box shape of the cushion, but it can also be a decorative feature, particularly if it is made in a fabric contrasting with the main fabric.

The art of tufting or buttoning, although best left to the professional upholsterer, can give the surface of the cushion both texture and a rich, almost quilted look. For this effect, buttons are secured on either side of the cushion with a linking cord or strong thread pulled right through the cushion, pad and all, and thus cause the top of the cushion to undulate, like a mattress. Use fabric-covered buttons or, for a real sense of luxury, small pompoms (little tufts of cotton, wool, or silk thread) or small circles or squares of fabric.

To brighten up a rather plain club armchair, choose four different-colored fabrics from the same family: for example, a striped velvet in a peacock blue, a plain dark navy velvet, a deep scarlet, and one in tangerine. With the main part of the chair upholstered in a combination of the different fabrics – you might have the tangerine on one arm and the red on the other with the navy blue between—make up the box cushion with each visible facet in a different color.

Other ideas for box cushions

Long, thin box cushions, constructed with a narrow gusset, can be used to make the top of a wooden box or bench a comfortable seat. Simply constructed wooden boxes with lids make excellent storage spaces and can double up as seats around an informal kitchen table. Box cushions can also be shaped to fit a window seat. Measure the seat carefully and cut a template from newspaper to insure that the cushion fits neatly, as sometimes, especially in old houses, the shape may not be symmetrical.

Making a box cushion cover

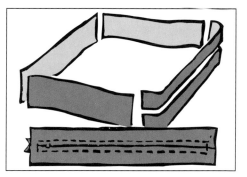

1 Cut out the top and bottom cover pieces and the five gusset pieces. Insert the zipper between the back pieces.

2 Stitch the gusset strips together, leaving ⅝ inch (1.5cm) open at each end of the front seams. Check the fit.

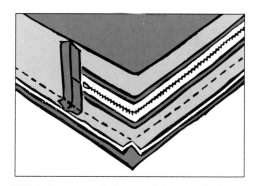

3 Stitch the gusset to the bottom of the cover, clipping the gusset seam allowance at the two back corners.

4 Open the zipper. Stitch the gusset to the top of the cover. Trim the corners diagonally and turn right side out.

Bolsters

As their name suggests, bolsters offer a means of support for other pillows. They are long or short rolls that lie along the end or sides of a daybed or on certain types of sofa. On bench sofas, with one long mattress-type seat cushion, it would not be unusual to see a short bolster at each end. Small bolsters, known as neck rolls, are used on beds.

Open-ended bolster covers

For a bed that has to double up as a sofa by day, an open-ended bolster cover can store rolled bedding quite neatly. A quick knot in the fabric at each end of the cover keeps everything in place. Alternatively, a length of cord in a casing or a specially made band with a button and buttonhole would do just as well to close the cover, and would add a note of sophistication.

For this type of versatile cover, a long cylinder of fabric is all that is needed. It should be longer than the rolled comforter that will be inside it. The surplus fabric at each end, once it has been tied or secured, can fall attractively over the edges of the bed. The width of the cover should be the same as the circumference of the rolled stuffing. Long fabric ties, sewn to the ends of the cover, secure them.

Closed-end bolster covers

The simplest way to make a bolster cover with closed ends is to sew a tube of fabric and gather each end neatly together so it meets in the center of the end like a drawstring bag.

▲ Two bolsters lined up across the back of this sofa bring a touch of formality, as does the use of the same fabric for all its elements. However, the use of tailored slipcovers and the different finishes made to each end of the bolsters—flat against the inside arms but bunched and tied at the center—create a pleasingly relaxed contrast.

Making a basic bolster cover

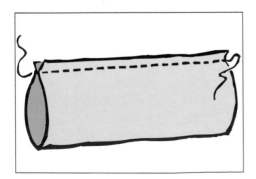

1 Cut the bolster cover piece long enough to exceed the ends and stitch the two long sides together to form a tube.

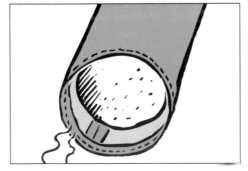

2 Turn right side out, then turn in the seam allowances at each end. Make a row of gathering stitches along the fold.

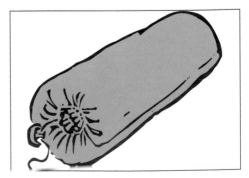

3 Gather the ends of the cover. Sew a large button or a pompom over each gathered center.

On this type of cover, the shape of the bolster can be defined by adding strips of contrasting fabric to the main fabric at each end; then, when the ends of the cover are drawn together, these appear as attractive concentric circles. Ribbons can create a similar effect but need to be applied to the fabric – that is, sewn onto the surface like appliqué.

Making a basic bolster cover

To determine the length of the cover piece, add the length of the bolster to the diameter of the end, plus a ¾ inch (2cm) seam allowance at each end. For the width, add 1¼ inches (3cm) for the two seam allowances to the circumference of the bolster. Cut a piece of fabric to this size. Fold it in half lengthwise, with right sides together and raw edges aligned, and pin. Machine stitch ⅝ inch (1.5cm) from the raw edge. (If a zipper is required, leave a gap in this seam and insert the zipper at this stage.) Press the seam open. Turn the cover right side out. Turn ¾ inch (2cm) to the wrong side at each end and press. Using a strong thread doubled, handsew a line of running stitches close to the folded edge at each end. Insert the bolster into the center of the fabric tube. Gather the ends of the cover, tying the thread ends together and securing them inside the center of the gathers.

▲ *Some clever examples of the ways in which bolster covers can be finished. While a simple, flat end is very functional, a random gathering of surplus fabric at each end of a rolled-up cylinder can be tied into bunches with a piece of ribbon. This is one of the simplest and most effective of finishing techniques, requiring no sewing.*

Making a fitted bolster cover

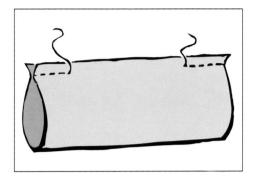

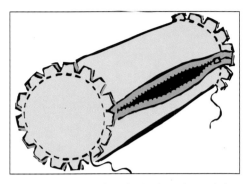

1 Cut the main cover piece and stitch together to form a tube, leaving a gap for the zipper. Press the seam open.

2 Insert the zipper. Stitch on the circular ends. Notch the seam allowances and press. Turn right side out.

Adding piping to a bolster cover

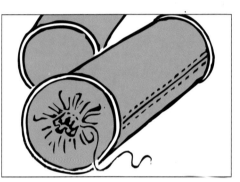

1 Make the main cover piece as for the fitted cover. Stitch the piping to the ends, then add an extra strip of fabric.

2 Turn right side out and gather the ends. For a fitted cover, simply attach the piping before the circular end.

Fitted bolster covers

For a more tailored look, the bolster end can be a separately inserted circular piece of fabric. The center of the circle can be further embellished with a whirl of cord, a dangling tassel, a brass or chrome ring, or a button.

Making a fitted bolster cover

Cut the main cover piece as long as the bolster and as wide as the circumference of the bolster plus a ⅝ inch (1.5cm) seam allowance all around. Fold in half lengthwise, with right sides together and raw edges aligned, and pin. Baste and then machine stitch, leaving a gap for the zipper. Press the seam open. Turn the cover right side out and insert the zipper (see pages 312–313). Open the zipper and turn the tube wrong side out. Pin, baste, and stitch the circular ends to the tube. Trim and notch the seam allowances. Press the seams open and then turn the cover right side out.

Adding piping to the ends

To attach piping around the circular ends of the bolster, cut and assemble the main cover piece as for a fitted bolster cover. Stitch the piping to the right side of the ends. On a basic bolster cover, add an extra tube of fabric at each end that is long enough to cover the end, and turn the cover right side out. Gather the ends as for the basic cover. On a fitted cover, stitch on the circular ends after attaching the piping to the main piece.

Decorative effects for the bolsters

For a more sophisticated bolster, combine fabrics and cord in one cover. For a touch of flamboyance, mix fake leopardskin, dramatic ink-blue silk, and a shiny gold cord and tassel. Hand-stitched braid or other passementerie teams well with all kinds of fabric: a rough burlap looks surprisingly good with an elegant woven trim, for example.

Directory of fastenings and trimmings

There is a wide range of decorative trimmings available for use on cushion covers, tablecloths, placemats, and bed linen. They can be chosen in a contrasting color, pattern, or texture to serve as a bold foil to accessories or can be in a solid, matching color to create a subtle but striking detail.

Fastenings on your pillow covers, slipcovers, or pillowcases serve a practical purpose but can also be a design focus, as becomes obvious with the use of ties or bold buttons.

Edgings

Bias binding

Bias binding is a strip of fabric, cut on the bias (diagonally across the grain) and used for enclosing piping cord or for covering raw edges—for example, around the edges of placemats.

Bias binding can be handmade from any lightweight fabric—patterned, solid-colored, or striped. It can also be bought readymade in various widths and in a range of solid colors.

Braid

Decorative braid is a narrow, woven strip, often handmade, with a raised texture and fancy patterning. It can be applied to fabric to edge pillows, or

sewn onto slipcovers to emphasize their color or shape. Often it is used to decorate lampshades.

Two especially effective types of braid are gimp, which is a braided woven trim shaped like a close, continuous "S," and picot braid, which is a ribbed trimming.

Cords and piping

Cords and piping are used to edge cushions, slipcovers, and upholstery and are often positioned to hide seams. Readymade decorative cords are usually made from twisted strands of silk, cotton, jute, or wool. Cord comes in varying

thicknesses and can be one color or multicolored. Some cord comes with a flange for inserting into the seam.

Piping, also called cording, is a fabric-covered cord. It can be bought readymade or can be handmade by covering a filler cord with a narrow strip of fabric (see pages 314–315). Double piping is a double row of covered cord (or piping) also used to edge upholstery. **3**

Fringe

Fringe is a loose-hanging trim usually made from wool, silk, or cotton. It can be fine or thick, and is often encrusted with knots or beads for added decoration. Bullion fringe is a more elaborate, thick twisted fringe, often containing gold or metallic threads.

Other trims

Rosettes

These small, circular, woven decorations can be sewn to the surface of covers on the front arms of chairs or sofas. They imitate the shape of a rose and can often be quite ornate.

Studs

Metal or brass upholstery studs can be either flat or dome-headed and are nailed into the edges of upholstered chairs, footstools, and sofas, particularly Chesterfield sofas, on which they form an integral part of the style. They hold the fabric in place, act as a decorative trim, or help to conceal raw edges. Some can be quite decorative, with the surfaces "antiqued" or carved. **4**

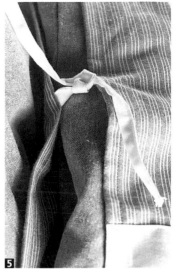

Tapestry strips

Firm, narrow woven bands, resembling needlepoint, the strips are applied to the edges of covers or cushions or embellish chair and sofa seats. Designs are usually traditional and often echo architectural moldings.

Tassels

These dangling decorative trims are made of bunched yarn or cord. They may be attached to rope (for example, to hold back draperies) or joined to small rosettes (key tassels) for attaching to keys on doors or drawers. They are used to decorate pillows and bolsters. **1**

Fastenings

Buttons

Available in any number of shapes and sizes and made from brass, glass, bone, or mother-of-pearl, to name but a few materials. Buttons are used to fasten all kinds of edges on accessories. Buttons can also be used without buttonholes to make unusual decorative patterns. **2**

Eyelets

Metal eyelet kits come with a punch and die to cut holes in fabric and then to secure a brass or chrome ring to

hold together the raw edges of the hole. Eyelets are corded or roped together to join two edges of fabric.

Fabric ties and ribbons

Silk, cotton, or synthetic ribbons and handmade fabric ties have many uses in furnishings. They can be tied in bows to hold two open edges together or can simply be tied or knotted to edges for decoration. **5**

Snap fasteners

A useful fastening device, but one intended to be hidden, snaps are small metal fasteners that are sewn to either

side of an opening and then pressed shut to close the opening. They can be used to close pillow covers.

Hook-and-loop tape

Much disliked by traditionalists, hook-and-loop tape (also known as "touch-and-close" fastening) is a quick and simple method of holding fabric in place. It consists of two pieces of nylon tape, one with a soft, furry, looped surface and the other with a rougher surface which is actually made of rows of tiny hooks. When the two tapes are pressed together, the hooks grasp the soft, looped surface and a fairly strong bond results. The tapes are sewn to the edges of the fabric—for example, the underside of the open edges of a duvet cover. Hook-and-loop tape comes in a variety of widths and several colors, and can be sewn to fabric or glued to a harder surface.

Zippers

The most practical of fastenings, a zipper consists of two fabric tapes edged with metal teeth or a plastic coil. The teeth or coils interlock when the slider is pulled between the two halves of the zipper. Usually hidden from view behind the fabric, zippers are inserted in pillow covers and slipcovers so that they can be easily removed for cleaning.

Simple fastenings and zippers

▲ *Pillows and cushions are marvelous accessories – nothing can more easily transform a space. They can be made in all shapes and sizes and from various different fabrics. The cushions and pillows shown above are all of different shapes but are linked into a Chinese porcelain theme of blue and white to complement other objects in the room.*

Pillow covers, duvet covers, and slipcovers that require frequent washing will all require fastenings that are hardwearing and practical. Hook-and-loop tape, snaps, and zippers meet these requirements and are the most frequently used fastenings. They are easy to conceal so that they do not detract from the main effect of the object.

Hook-and-loop tape
Unlike other fastenings for fabrics, this can also be used to attach fabrics to a solid surface. For instance, it could be used to attach removable fabric panels to a room screen or to attach a skirt to a wooden bed frame. In these instances and for openings that may be subjected to strain, such as duvet covers and box cushions, it is best to attach strips of hook-and-loop tape. For smaller openings that do not need to be so hardwearing, such as small scatter-pillow covers, dots of the same material are more suitable.

Snaps
Simple to attach, snaps work well along the inside edge of a cushion or duvet cover opening. They can be bought as single fastenings or already attached to a fabric strip. A strip of snaps is ideal for the opening of a pillow or duvet cover.

Attaching simple fastenings to a pillow cover
To make a pillow cover to be closed with hook-and-loop dots or snaps, first cut two pieces of fabric as for a basic square pillow

(see pages 302–303), but allow for a hem allowance of 3 inches (7.5cm) along the opening edge of each piece.

Pin a double hem in place along the opening edge on each piece by turning 1 inch (2.5cm) to the wrong side twice. Slipstitch or machine stitch the hem and then press. With the right sides facing, machine stitch the two pillow pieces together along the other three sides. Then at each end of the opening edge, stitch 2 inches (5cm), close to the double hem to strengthen the sides.

Sew hook-and-loop dots, snaps, or even a strip of snaps along each side of the opening on the double hem in corresponding positions. Trim the seam allowances of the cover and clip the two outside corners diagonally to reduce the bulk.

Turn the cover right side out and press. Insert the pillow form and fasten the dots or snaps. When the cover is closed, the fastenings should not be visible.

Simple fastenings

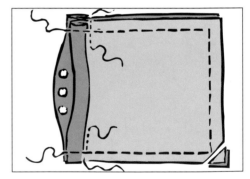

1 Attach hook-and-loop dots or snaps to the double hems along the opening edge of the cover.

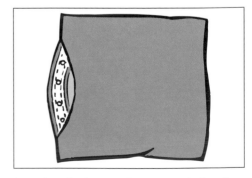

2 Attach a strip of snaps in the same way. The fastenings will be invisible on the right side.

Zippers

Zips can be bought to an individual size or as one continuous strip of uncut teeth. The latter is used off the spool as required and individually bought sliders are applied to it. Choose a color that suits the item it is to be attached to.

Zippers can be inserted and neatly concealed in the seam of a cushion cover or duvet cover. On a square scatter pillow the zipper can be inserted either in the seam at the base of the pillow or in a center seam on the cover back, as for a round cushion.

Inserting a zipper in a pillow's side seam

Cut two pieces of fabric as for a basic square pillow cover (see pages 302–303). With right sides facing, stitch the two pieces together for 2 inches (5cm) at each end of the opening edge, leaving an opening for the zipper. Baste the opening together along the seamline and press the seam open. Pin and baste the zipper along the seamline, with the right side of the zipper facing the wrong side of the seam. Stitch around the zipper (using the zipper foot on the machine) from the right side close to the basting. Remove the basting.

Open the zipper. Then, with right sides facing, pin, baste, and stitch the remaining three sides together. Remove the basting. Trim the seam allowances, clip the corners diagonally, and press the seam open. Turn the cover right side out and press again.

Inserting a zipper in a pillow's back

Cut out the front of the cover as for a basic square pillow cover (see pages 302–303). Cut another piece 1¼ inches (3cm) wider than the first (to allow extra for the zipper seam), then cut it in half widthwise.

With right sides facing, stitch the two back pieces together for 2 inches (5cm) at each end of the opening edge, leaving an opening for the zipper. Baste the opening together along the seamline and press the seam open. Insert the zipper as for the zipper in a side seam. Open the zipper and, with right sides together, pin, baste, and stitch the back of the cover to the front and complete as for the zip in a side seam.

Inserting a zipper in a round pillow

Make a paper pattern as for a basic round pillow cover (see pages 302–305). Cut out the cover front using the pattern. Then cut straight across the paper pattern one third of the way from one edge. Using the two paper pieces, cut out the two pieces for the cover back, adding a seam allowance along each opening edge. Stitch the two back pieces together and insert the zipper as for the square pillow (see pages 302–303). Then join the back to the front with right sides together. Notch the seam allowance, turn right side out, and press.

Pillow side seam

1 Stitch cover pieces together along one edge, leaving an opening for zipper. Baste opening together and insert zipper.

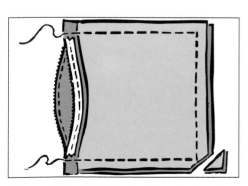

2 Remove basting. Stitch the other three sides together. Trim and turn the cover right side out through the zipper.

Pillow back

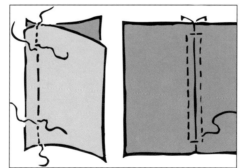

1 Stitch the back pieces together, leaving an opening. Baste opening together, press seam open, and insert zipper.

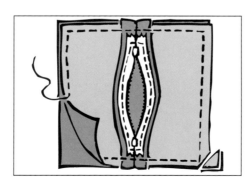

2 Remove basting. With zipper open, stitch the back to the front. Trim and turn the cover right side out.

Round pillow

1 Using a paper pattern, cut one piece for cover front. Cut two pieces for back and insert zipper in back seam.

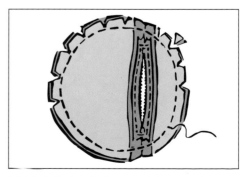

2 Stitch the back to the front; notch the seam allowance. Turn the cover right side out through the zipper.

Piping and trims

▶ *Piping can add decoration and definition to a piece of furniture or a pillow. It also serves to strengthen the seams of structured items. Here, a probably unintentional contrast occurs between the formal primness of the cream-upholstered chair and the faded old-gold velvet cover. This contrast is emphasized by the piping.*

Nothing finishes off upholstery and accessories better than edging. Using either piping, fringing, tassels, or cord—available in a huge range of materials, colors, and textures—you can create a very professional touch and add interest and style.

Piping

Piping is a means of adding decoration and definition to items such as a cushion, an upholstered chair, or a duvet cover. It can be made in the same fabric as the main piece to which it is attached (called self-piping) or it can be made from a contrasting fabric to highlight shape or add texture.

Piping is made by enclosing a length of filler cord in a narrow strip of fabric. The covered cord is then inserted between two layers of fabric and stitched, so that it is visible along the seam on the right side. The filler cord itself is made of twisted strands of (usually) cotton, bleached or unbleached. It

Piping a pillow cover

1 Cut the fabric strips to cover the piping on the bias. Join the strips end to end on the straight grain and trim.

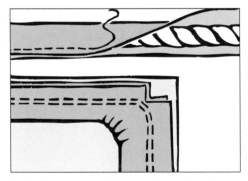

2 Stitch the strip around the cord, using a zipper foot. Stitch the piping to the cover front and trim the corners.

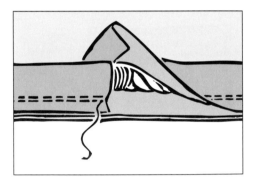

3 Trim the cord so that the ends butt together. Turn in one end of the fabric strip and lap it over the other end.

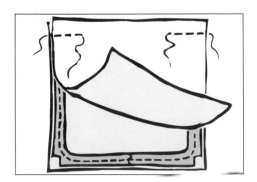

4 Stitch the cover together along one side, sandwiching the piping between the layers and leaving an opening.

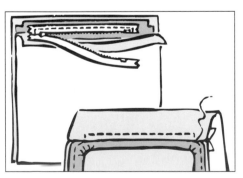

5 With the zipper open, stitch the zipper to the piped edge, then close it and stitch it from the front to the other edge.

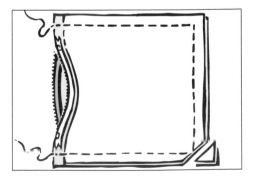

6 Open the zipper and stitch the other three sides of the cover together. Trim and turn right side out.

comes in a variety of thicknesses. It is best to use pre-shrunk cord for anything that will be laundered or dry-cleaned; if you are in doubt, immerse it for a few minutes in hand-hot water.

The strips of fabric used to cover the cord are generally cut on the bias of the fabric to give it more flexibility for easing around corners and curves. However, this is not essential. It may be that the pattern of the fabric is such that you want to cut along the width or length of the fabric.

Piping a pillow cover

For covering the filler cord, measure the amount of piping you think you will need and add about 4 inches (10cm) to allow for joins. For narrow cord, the strips should be about 2 inches (5cm) wide so that when folded in half lengthwise around cord, the resulting width is about 1 inch (2.5cm). Increase the width for thicker cord.

Find the bias of the fabric by folding diagonally so that the selvage is parallel with the adjacent edge. Mark strips of the required width parallel to the diagonal fold, and cut out the strips. To make one long strip, pin the strips together, end to end with right sides facing, and stitch along the straight grain. Press seams open and trim the seam allowances flush with the strip edge.

Lay the cord along the center on the wrong side of the strip, then fold the fabric around it so that the raw edges are brought together. Stitch by machine, close to the cord, using a special piping foot or a zipper foot. Trim the seam to ⅝ inch (1.5cm).

Cut out a front and a back pillow cover piece. Align the raw edges, pin and baste the piping to the right side of the cover front. Clip the piping seam allowance at the corners, leaving a 2 inch (5cm) overlap where the piping ends meet. Stitch around the edges. To join the piping ends, pull back the fabric strip and trim both ends of filler cord so that they butt together. Trim the fabric so that one end turns under and overlaps the other to give a neat finished edge. Complete the stitching of the seam.

Leaving an opening for the zipper and placing right sides together, stitch the back of the cover to the front along the opening

edge so that the piping is sandwiched between the layers. Press the seam open. Stitch the zipper in place one side at a time. Complete the cover as for a pillow cover with a zipper in the seam (see pages 312–313).

Cord

Readymade decorative cords come in all kinds of thicknesses and colors and can be made from cotton, wool, silk, or a mixture of fibers. Some cords have gold or other metallic thread running through them which adds sparkle and a touch of luxury. It is also possible to find wonderful antique cords. Cords designed for inserting as piping come with a flange attached which is usually a piece of cotton webbing. These can be used exactly as you would a length of covered piping. Cords without flanges have to be hand sewn after the pillow cover is made.

Attaching cord to a pillow cover

Leave a small opening in the seam when making the cover. Hand sew the cord over the seamline around the edge of a finished pillow cover. Insert each end into the opening in the seam and sew it in place. Or wrap each end of the cord with a matching thread and butt the ends together neatly where they join. Cord can be looped to make a bow at each corner and sewn in place with overcasting.

Tassels and fringes

Fringes make interesting finishes for pillow covers and these are hand sewn to the completed pillow cover as for cords. Some fringes also come with a flange webbing and can be inserted in a seamline like piping. Tassels add an ornate touch to cushions and bolsters. They are available in a wide range of shapes, sizes, and colors, but can also be made by hand.

Attaching a flanged fringe to a pillow cover

Stitch the fringe to the right side of the front of the cover along the seamline, with the fringed edge lying toward the center of the cover. Make the cover as for a cover with piping, sandwiching the fringe between the two sides of the cover.

Cord and braid

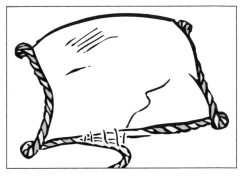

Hand sew cord over the seamline, forming loops at each corner if desired. Secure the ends inside the cover.

Fringes and tassels

As for a piped cover, stitch the fringe to the right side of the front before attaching the back of the cover.

▲ *The fluffy, colorful fringe perfectly complements the printed Manolo Blahnik shoe drawings on the pillows. Fringes such as that shown here have a flange and can be machine stitched between the two sides of fabric when the pillow is being assembled. Fringes can be specially dyed for particular projects.*

Borders

Both flat borders, or flanges, and ruffles add an extra touch of luxury to what would otherwise be an unexceptional pillow. They are worth taking extra trouble over, as they help enhance the pillow fabric.

Flanges

Flanges around the edges of a pillow stand out like a flap. The pillow is encased within a stitched line and made accessible by a zipped or buttoned opening. A flange can be made either from the same fabric as the rest of the cover or in contrasting fabric. A double flange is essentially two single flanges, the lower one slightly larger than the top one.

Making a single-flanged pillow cover

Make a pillow cover as for a cover with a zipper across the back (see pages 312–313), but allowing extra fabric on all four sides for the flange, as well as the usual seam allowance

all around the edge. A standard flange or flap is 2 inches (5cm) deep. Once all the edges of the cover are stitched together, trim the seam allowances and clip the corners diagonally. Press the seam open and turn right side out. Press flat, keeping the seams exactly on the edge and making the corners sharp.

On the back of the cover (zipper side), baste the front and back together along the border line and machine stitch. Alternatively, work satin stitch along the border line and then, if desired, work a second line of satin stitch outside the first. Remove the basting.

To make a cover with a contrasting single flange, cut the pillow cover pieces to the size of a cover without a flange and insert the zipper in the center of the back piece (see pages 312–313). Then cut the flanges. The size should be a length of fabric to the

finished width of the flange, plus two seam allowances, by the length of the side, plus two seam allowances. It is a good idea to cut more than you need so that the flange strips can be trimmed down later.

Stitch, right sides together, the lengths of flange to the pillow fabric, leaving the ends at each corner to trail. Join the border strips at the corner by mitering (see pages 340–341) or butt the ends together, stitching straight across the adjacent flange (right sides together), trimming the surplus and pressing the seam flat. By abutting the strips you should finish up with two parallel strips the length of the finished pillow, with the other two set between them. Once the flange is joined to the front and back of the cover, complete the cover as for a single flange.

Single border

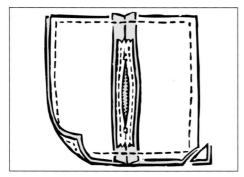

1 Make the cover with a zipper across the back, adding extra all around for the flange. Trim and press seam open.

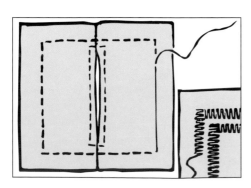

2 Turn the cover right side out and press flat. Stitch along the flange line, using straight stitch or satin stitch.

▲ These simple linen pillows use the stripe in the fabric as a flange which is set outside the edge of the pillow. The stripe is cut and sewn to each side of the central panel before the pillow cover is assembled. Each corner is mitered, with the stripe carefully matched for a neat, geometric finish.

Double flange

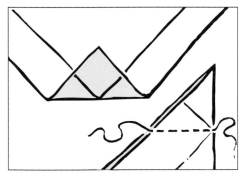

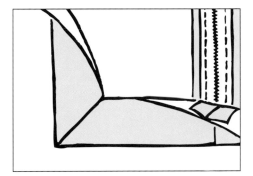

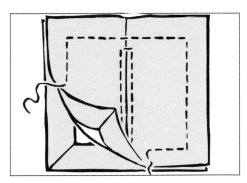

1 Double the depth of the required flange all around. Press the flange to the wrong side and miter the corners.

2 Trim the miter seam allowances and press the seam open. Turn the corners right side out.

3 Determine the final depth of the flange. Join the front of the cover to the back and stitch along the flange lines.

Ruffles

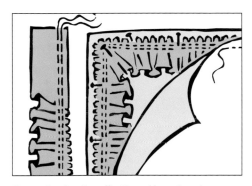

Piece and gather the ruffle. Pin and baste it to the cushion cover front before stitching on the back.

◄ *Two contrasting finishing techniques combine to make a pleasing effect. The cord piping of the chair is very linear, enhanced still more by the use of striped fabric. Meanwhile, the floral-print pillow cover is finished with a generous ruffle.*

Making a double-flanged cover

A pillow cover with a double flange is made in the same way as one with a single flange, but double the depth of the required finished flange must be added on to the lengths, plus the seam allowances. Assemble the back section as for a cover with a zipper across the back (see pages 312–313). Fold the flanges to the wrong side and press. With right sides together, miter each corner (see pages 340–341). Trim the mitered corners, turn right side out, and press. Lay the two sides together, wrong sides facing, and baste along the flange line, catching the raw edge of the flange inside the cover. Machine stitch closed.

Ruffles

Ruffles add a softening touch to pillows and other accessories, and are generally made from light, filmy fabrics or informal prints. With imagination and a bold choice of color, however, ruffles need not be restricted to the boudoir; they can be used to make a strong impact anywhere.

Attaching a ruffle to a cover

Make a ruffle twice the circumference of the required finished pillow cover. The ruffle can either have a narrow hem or be doubled over so that the raw edges of both layers are aligned. Run a gathering stitch around the raw edges of the length of the ruffle. Pull the thread to gather the ruffle, then pin and baste it to the right side of the front piece of the cover, aligning the raw edges. Complete the pillow cover in the usual way, catching the ruffle seam allowance in between the front and back sections of the cover.

Covers for seating

The possibilities of covering furniture with fabric are as exciting as they are endless. Do you go for loosely draped, unstructured sheets of cloth that billow like dust covers over an old sofa? Or do you prefer smart, tailored little numbers with tucks and pleats and artfully placed buttons, which might disguise the awfulness of a battered dining chair?

The art of adding fabric to furniture opens up a wealth of decorative possibilities. Small seats can be tightly covered, whereas long, low benches look stunning when loosely dressed; deck chair frames can be given a new lease on life covered in a different fabric, or natty little folding stools can be sharpened up with new, slung canvas.

Fine detailing adds sophistication to the disguise. Use eyelets, buttons, loops and ties, tassels, and trims. Invent new ways of using old materials. However, don't lose sight of the practicalities and the function of the piece, even if your own ingenuity takes over.

Deck and director's chairs

Deck chairs are a simple combination of fabric and wood, a construction that folds neatly away. They have a timeless quality and a modest structure that have endured for many years. It is difficult to disassociate them from their exterior environments of beach, garden, or shipboard, although they can look wonderful in a large children's room or a bathroom.

A director's chair has much the same feel as a deck chair, but because of its higher seat and more obvious "chair-like" qualities, it is useful in informal settings in the home. For deck chairs, director's chairs, and other folding chairs, the seat and back are made from pieces of fabric slung between two bars, and attaching it to the frame could not be simpler. The method for fitting new fabric depends on the design of the chair and whether the frame needs to be, or can be, taken apart. Where "sleeves" of fabric can be made, these are ideal for sheathing the bars of the frame for seat and back, but where the design does not allow for this, fabric can be attached by stretching it around the bars on either side of the seat or back, and then stapling it to the outer edges with a heavy-duty

◀ *Traditional striped canvas can provide a whole new lease on life for ancient deck chair frames. In this example, mixing the colors of the canvases, which both have the same design, creates a sense of continuity, while also providing a pleasing contrast and more visual interest.*

▲ *While pastel cottons and delicate chintzes make attractive upholstery fabrics, they are difficult to keep clean and are vulnerable to wear and tear. A sensible choice for hardworking kitchen or dining room chairs is the tough and durable finish shown here, achieved by tightly binding thin rope over a metal chair frame.*

staple gun. A sleeve consists of a loop of fabric, secured down the inner side of each frame bar with a line of machine stitching. If the chair design requires the sleeve to fit over a place where the frame is joined, holes can be punched in the fabric and large eyelet holes secured before reassembling. Choose strong fabrics that are not going to tear. Try unusual material such as imitation suede or tartan.

Folding stools

Small, low, X-frame stools, made from wood or metal, work well in interior settings. They make useful "occasional" seating, doubling up as small tables for lightweight items such as books or newspapers. A few of them, dotted around a room filled with other styles of furniture, help to punctuate space. For a more minimalist interior, try a row of them using bright-colored fabrics against a plain white wall, or mix different patterns on the same theme: for example, children's prints of animals or cowboys to make a perfect ensemble for a young child's bedroom.

The methods of attaching the fabric, whether a sleeve is made or the fabric is stapled, are the same as for deck chairs.

Drop-in seats

▶ *These blue and white checked dining room drop-in seats complement the nineteenth-century Swedish-style table and chairs. The seats provide bursts of color to contrast against the many different wooden textures of this typically Scandinavian setting.*

The tricky art of upholstering a sofa, chair, or daybed is generally best left to a professional, for when done properly it is worth the investment. However, it is relatively simple to re-cover the upholstered drop-in seat of a dining chair.

A chair with a drop-in seat is usually a dining chair, and the seat lifts right out. It consists of a simple wooden frame covered in padding (horsehair and batting) which rests on and is supported by strips of webbing pulled taut across the frame. An unbleached muslin covering is stretched tightly over the padding and fixed to the underside of the frame by tacks. The top fabric is applied over the muslin and fixed in the same way. The underside is finished off with a piece of burlap with its edges turned under for neatness. If the webbing is still good, and the padding is in reasonable condition—it may need some building up—you should not need to strip everything off.

Re-covering a drop-in seat

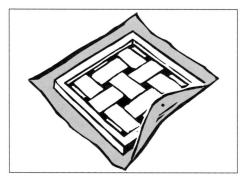

1 Bring the sides of the new muslin to the underside of the frame. Secure with a tack at the center of each side.

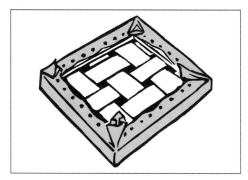

2 Smoothing the muslin as you proceed, continue to add tacks along each side of the frame.

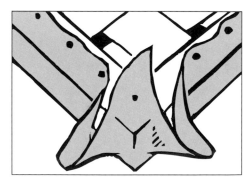

3 Pull the muslin taut over the corners and tack. Fold a pleat to each side of the tack and secure.

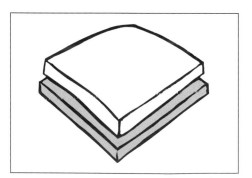

4 Turn the seat over. Lay in place a new piece of batting the same size as the top of the seat.

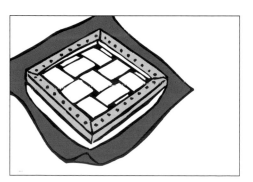

5 Keeping the batting in place, lay the seat upside down on the new outer covering, centering it carefully.

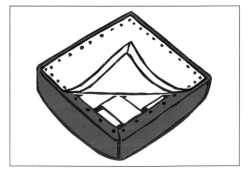

6 Cut out a fresh piece of burlap. Turn under the hem and tack the burlap to the underside of the frame.

For the fabric covering of a drop-in seat, customized fabric is always more challenging than simply using fabric as it is purchased. Two strongly contrasting colors could be stitched together and the joined fabric could be positioned over the seat so that the seam runs centrally across the chair—front to back or side to side. A pair of chairs with a weathered patina (see pages 280–281) would be a stunning focal point with covered seats in burgundy and indigo silk.

Re-covering a drop-in seat

The only tools you will need are a pair of scissors, a tape measure, a hammer, a mallet, and a chisel. The materials needed to cover the padded seat are a sheet of batting big enough to cover the top of the seat, a piece of unbleached muslin to fit over the seat, a piece of upholstery fabric for the outer covering of the seat (big enough to go over the top of the seat and the underside of the frame), ⅜ inch (1cm) fine tacks, and black upholstery linen or burlap for finishing the underside of the seat.

With the seat upside down and using the mallet and chisel, remove the tacks securing the old burlap. In the same way remove the tacks that hold the old outer fabric covering in place. Open out the burlap and the old fabric and use them to make paper patterns for the new pieces, making sure that the pattern allows for an extra 2 inches (5cm) all around for turning under the seat and stretching over the underside of the frame.

Remove the old top layer of batting and discard it. Beneath this should be a layer of muslin, under which is the horsehair. If necessary, remove the old muslin, but if it is sufficiently intact, keep it in place. Cut a new piece of muslin using the paper pattern made from the old outer cover. Lay the seat upside down on the muslin and bring the sides up and over the edge of the frame. Using the hammer, secure the muslin with a tack at the center of each side. Smoothing the muslin as you go, add tacks along each side of the frame. Pull the muslin taut over the corners and tack. Fold a pleat to each side of the tack and trim away the excess fabric. Turn the seat over. Cut a new piece of batting to exactly

the same size as the top of the seat. This is a soft layer that prevents the wiry horsehair from coming through the fabric. Lay the batting on top of the seat.

Using the paper pattern made from the old outer fabric, cut out a piece of fabric large enough to go over the seat to the underside of the frame. Lay the seat (with the batting on top) upside down on the new outer covering. Tack the fabric to the frame.

Using the paper pattern made from the old burlap, cut out a fresh piece of burlap. Turn under the hem and fasten the burlap to the underside of the frame, tacking at 1 inch (2.5cm) intervals.

Woven webbing

For a natural, textured look try using upholsterer's webbing tape about 2 inches (5cm) wide, woven across the frame of a stool or perhaps on a simple dining chair where the seat has gone, leaving an empty frame. A very stylish effect can be achieved by this relatively simple method. You will need enough webbing to be divided equally into short

strips that will be fixed side by side across the frame to create the "warp" and the same quantity to use as the "weft," the layer that weaves in and out of the fixed layer. The length of each strip (warp or weft) will be the distance across the top of the frame from edge to edge, plus an amount that can wrap around to the underside of the frame for securing (with tacks or a staple gun) out of sight. If you want the fixing to be a feature, and therefore to be seen, you could use various types of upholsterer's decorative studs.

Cut and fasten the first layer of webbing, making sure each piece is pulled very taut before fixing. The seat will be bound to sag a little as body weight is put on it, so bear this in mind and perhaps allow some excess that can be unrolled for retightening. Weave the second layer of strips between the first, again fixing each end in the same way.

Webbing tape, commonly made of jute, can be dyed so that a colorful, contrasting checkerboard effect can be achieved with relative ease. It is also possible to buy colored webbing of the kind used to edge carpets.

◀ *Webbing can make for an extremely comfortable chair. It is very versatile and can be easily replaced with a different colored webbing to suit any decor. Neutral webbing can be dyed in vibrant, colorful shades and two or more colors can be interwoven to achieve interesting designs.*

Slipcovers

▶ *Like 1950s summer dresses out to tea, these linen chair covers in ice-cream colors look spruce and elegant. Against the bleached wood floor, their sharp colors stand out and perfectly contrast with the white tablecloth. A row of buttons is a witty addition. These are fabric-covered but they could be just as effective in white or colored glass—or even brass.*

As their name implies, slipcovers are not attached to the furniture they cover. They might have ties or zippers, or even button fastenings, but their essential character is removability. The fabric for such a cover must be practical and easily cleaned. It can be used to glorious decorative effect with stitching, folding, pleats, knots—or it can simply be thrown over the chair.

Designs for slipcovers

The shape of the furniture dictates the look of the slipcover, whether it has a tailored look, in which the cover resembles formal upholstery, or a more casual, unstructured effect. The furniture is the mannequin, around which the fabric is pinned, tucked, pleated, and stitched, and through experiment the cover will take shape.

Squarish arms on a sofa, for example, can be made more attractive with an un-expected pleat here and there, and with double pleating a highly textured look can be achieved. Try using a contrasting fabric inside a pleat for further emphasis.

Detail is the all-important thing. Take a tip from *haute couture* and add exquisite touches that will transform a plain cover, such as punched eyelets along the base of a skirt, or rows of hand-worked buttons in glorious glassy colors. Fringe and tassels add texture and give a more luxurious feel. To the front of a pleat add a tab of fabric or tape and a bright bold button to fasten. Along the base attach a band of grosgrain ribbon to a solid-colored fabric for definition and added color, or hand-embroider bold crisscrosses or dots using tapestry yarn. A row of small pearly buttons down the back of a white linen cover – quite a tailored affair over an upright dining chair – would look very impressive.

Most slipcovers have a skirt of some kind- which runs around the base and is a separately made piece that extends to the floor. Use double, overlapping layers in the same cloth, or contrast fabrics with different textures. Fold wide box pleats around the front edge of a long sofa; for the two shorter sides, run tiny little pleats or use different-colored fabrics for a striped effect.

The beauty of making slipcovers as opposed to upholstery covers is that they allow you to play around with the shape a little. Take the skirt from the seat height or

Making a slipcover for a dining chair

1 Pin the two back pieces of fabric together with right sides facing. Remove from the chair, baste, and stitch.

2 Cut out the skirt piece and a piece the same size for the lining. Stitch together with right sides facing.

3 Turn the skirt right side out and pin it to the chair seat piece with right sides facing. Stitch.

make a pleat in the center at the back. By taking this idea further you can disguise the shape of a sofa or chair quite considerably.

Making a slipcover for a chair

Measure the front of the chair back from the top of the chair to the seat and then across the width of the back, allowing for the thickness of the frame. Cut out a piece of fabric to these dimensions, plus a 2 inches (5cm) seam allowance all around. Measure the back of the chair from the top to the floor, then measure the back of the chair across the widest part (usually at the base of the chair), again allowing for the thickness of the frame. Cut out a piece of fabric to these dimensions, plus a 1¼ inch (3cm) seam allowance.

With the wrong sides facing, pin these two fabric pieces together over the back of the chair, making sure that the cover will slip off easily and keeping the proposed seamlines symmetrical. Remove the cover, baste along the proposed seamline, and remove the pins. With the cover still wrong side out, try it on the chair again and adjust, if necessary, making sure that the basting stops precisely at the level of the chair seat. Remove, and machine stitch. Trim the seam allowances. Set this piece aside.

Measure from the seat of the chair to the floor and then around the legs of the chair at the base, from one back leg around the front legs and the other back leg. Cut out a piece of fabric to these dimensions, allowing for a 3-inch (7.5cm) overlap at each side

of the back and adding a ⅝-inch (1.5cm) seam allowance all around. Cut a lining piece exactly the same size from the same fabric. With right sides together and raw edges aligned, stitch these two pieces together, leaving the edge that will fit around the chair seat opening. Trim the seam allowances and then clip the two corners diagonally. Press the seam open. Turn right side out and press flat with the seam aligned along the edge. Baste the raw edges together. Set this skirt piece aside.

Cut a piece of fabric to fit the chair seat exactly, with a ⅝ inch (1.5cm) seam allowance all around. Lay this piece wrong side uppermost on the chair seat, then pin the skirt to the chair seat with right sides together and raw edges aligned, leaving the extended portion at the back free. Take the pinned pieces off the chair, baste, and remove the pins. Stitch, and then slip the back section of the cover back onto the chair (still wrong side out). Pin it to the chair seat section where the two sections meet at the back of the seat. Remove, baste, and stitch.

Trim the seam allowances around the chair seat. Then cut the two front corners of the chair seat section diagonally and notch the corresponding corners on the skirt section. Press the seam open and then toward the center of the seat.

Cut four lengths of ribbon or make four fabric ties (see pages 342–343). Then cut a piece of fabric to line the back valance drop, including a ⅝ inch (1.5cm) seam allowance

all around. Put the cover on the chair wrong side out and pin the lining to the back skirt, with right sides together. Remove and then position the ties along the seam. Baste and stitch, catching the ends of the ties in the seam. Trim the seam allowances and corners and press the seam open.

Remove all the basting. Turn the whole cover right side out and press. If desired, line the underside of the seat area to enclose the raw edges, slipstitching the lining in place.

Put the cover on the chair right side out. Hand sew ties to the front skirt to correspond to the ties at the back.

Covering furniture with throws

Just throwing a length of fabric over a chair and allowing it to fall naturally into folds or gathers is the simplest way of covering furniture. Blankets, shawls, or quilts can be mixed with each other and displayed against a backdrop of bleached white cotton first draped over the furniture. Large pieces of cloth can be handkerchief-knotted on their corners or around the legs of a chair.

To make a very simple throw, sew together two pieces of fabric, as though you were making a pillow cover, add a layer of batting or interlining between them, turn it right side out, and secure the opening by hand. You will have a lightly padded square or rectangle. Sew flat buttons or small loops of cord across the surface for decoration, and hang the whole thing over the back or arm of a sofa or daybed.

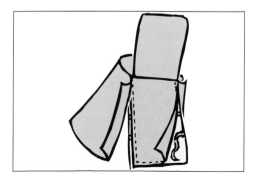

4 Pin the chair seat section to the back cover section along the back of the chair seat, and stitch.

5 With the cover wrong side out on the chair, pin a lining to the back skirt. Stitch, catching in the ties.

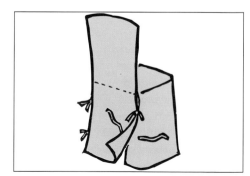

6 Turn right side out. Line the seat if desired. Then stitch ties to the front skirt section to match the back ties.

Pillow shams, skirts, and throws

The vast range of bedding and bed linen now available makes the bed the key element in the bedroom's design. How the bed is "dressed" makes the ultimate design statement.

Pillowcases and shams

The days when pillows were invariably concealed under a bedspread are gone. Today, the bed is more likely to be covered with a quilt or duvet, and the pillows are on show—often augmented by a number of scatter pillows. Bed pillows, in their pillowcases, are slipped into a sham, made of some decorative fabric to coordinate with the bed cover.

At its plainest, the pillow sham consists simply of a top piece and a longer bottom piece, which is folded under the top to form a pocket to hold in the pillow. A slightly more elegant sham has a flat border, or flange, around all four edges. This can be in the same fabric or a contrasting fabric. Solid colors can be combined with stripes, checks, plaids, or other prints.

Embroidery is another means of embellishing a pillow sham. A line of blanket stitch along the open edge is an attractive detail. A cross-stitched border is another possibility.

For an instant monogram, try stenciling bold letters or motifs, using a permanent fabric dye. Other stenciled motifs could be used instead. If you are making a patchwork quilt or duvet cover, the obvious solution for the pillows is to make the top of the sham from the same pieced fabric as used for the bed cover.

▲ The key to bed linen is to keep it simple—but that does not mean it always has to be white. Here, although white is the basic color, the crisp blue and green ginghams dominate and there are similar colors in the bed cover to provide a harmonious link. The bedstead, with its simple curved iron frame, accentuates the cool, clean overall effect.

Making a pillow sham

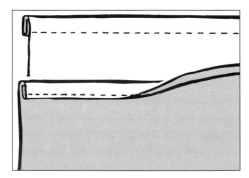

1 Cut out a single piece of fabric for the sham and stitch a double hem along each short edge.

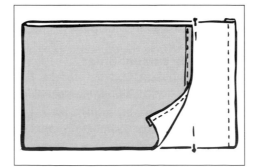

2 Fold the fabric so the right sides are together and the flap extends 6 in (15cm) past the end. Pin in place.

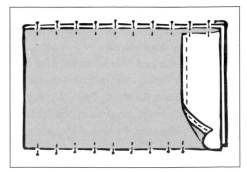

3 Turn the sham over and fold the flap back so the folded edge aligns with the hemmed edge. Pin into place.

Old cottons and linens, once they have been thoroughly washed, make beautiful pillow shams. Smart checks and stripes in cool colors can be added as flanges, flaps, or edgings.

Making a pillow sham

Pillow shams should be made from cotton, poplin, or linen. Cut a single piece of fabric twice the length of the pillow plus a total of 8 inches (20cm) for the inside flap and for the double hem allowances, by the width of the pillow sham, plus an extra 1¼ inches (3cm) for seam allowances.

Along each short side, turn under and stitch a ½-inch (1.2cm) double hem (see pages 340–341). Fold the fabric right side together, the length of the pillow from one end, so that the flap extends 6 inches (15cm) past the doubled-over pillow sham. Pin the raw edges together. Then turn the sham over and fold the flap back on the sham so that the folded edge aligns with the hemmed edge. Pin the raw edges of the flap to the other layers and baste. Remove the pins and machine stitch through all the layers ⅝ inch (1.5cm) from the edges. Pink the raw edges or zigzag stitch them and trim. Turn right side out. The flap will now be on the inside of the finished pillow sham.

Dust ruffles

These bed dressings consist of a skirt between the base of the mattress and the floor. The skirt is attached to a flat piece of fabric,

usually some inexpensive lining, which sits between the mattress and the bed base. The skirt can be flat, with tailored inverted pleats at each corner, or, if the bed has a footboard, the corner pleats are split to fall to either side of the bed leg.

Box pleats, although taking a considerable amount of fabric—three times that required for a flat skirt—are smart and simple, and using a contrasting fabric in the pleats can give a striking effect. For a more sculptural finish, instead of pleats at the corners, simply join the fabric using punched eyelets and tied cord. Or, if you prefer a softer effect, gather the skirt into rich folds of crumpled linen, muslin, or silk taffeta.

Whichever style you choose to make, careful measuring and estimating of the amount of fabric required are essential; a dust ruffle will not work if there is not enough material in it. Because dust ruffles tend not to be washed as often as covers and pillow shams, a less robust fabric can be used.

Throws

A throw suggests casualness and spontaneity. It is intended to go over all other bedding and provides an extra layer for additional warmth, perhaps used only occasionally and otherwise kept at the foot of the bed. Throws can also be a useful device for concealing a mixture of bedding beneath and thus "tidying" a bed that perhaps by day becomes a sofa.

Throws are generally made from a rectangle of fabric, cut large enough to cover the bed end to end and to fall to the floor on both sides. They are then hemmed and possibly lined as well. Throws can be used with valances, in which case the fabric is cut to fall only part of the way down each side of the bed in order to reveal the valance beneath. Throws may be plain or quilted, with additional borders or edgings that add color or texture. As the throw is intended to be folded down once the bed is in use, a heavier fabric can be used.

◄ *Cool blue and cream combine as the dominant theme here. The wonderful midnight-blue backdrop behind the ice-cream swirls of the bed frame is picked up in the checks and stripes and toile de Jouy patterns of the various items of bed linen. The top quilt is reversible, using the three different fabrics to great effect.*

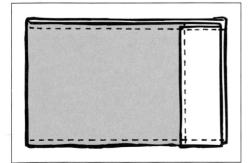

4 *Baste and machine stitch through all the layers. Pink the raw edges or zigzag stitch them and turn right side out.*

Duvet covers

▲ *This is an inspired use of an awkward space—the bed does not attempt to look small. Understated cream and white cotton bed linen is combined with a minimal use of black and white mattress ticking to create an elegant interior. Subtly stitched motifs crisscross the duvet cover and a simple line of stitching runs around the edge of it.*

In many homes, duvets, or down comforters, have largely replaced sheets and blankets. They are used with special covers, which are essentially two pieces of rectangular fabric joined on three sides. A large pocket can be made at the open end, to keep the duvet neatly enclosed, just like the pocket on a pillow sham.

Alternatively, the duvet cover opening can be fastened with ties or buttons. Both these devices can be used to bring contrast and color, such as checked red and white ties on a plain cover or bold tartan ribbons to fasten one in striped ticking. Buttons can be bold

and eyecatching, while the buttonholes can be made using brightly contrasting thread. If you prefer to keep things simple, just use snaps or hook–and–loop tape or dots.

For a more subtle approach, add piping along the seam between the two layers of fabric. On a bed that is covered entirely in white, a piped line of blue and white gingham or multicolored floral print adds just a hint of detail and color, perhaps picking up another fabric in the room.

For children's bedding, a duvet cover with one fabric on the top and another beneath is fun and can transform a space simply by

Making a simple duvet cover

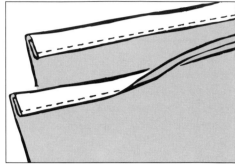

1 *Cut two pieces for the cover. Along the opening edge of each piece, stitch a 1¼ in. (3cm) double hem.*

2 *Stitch the two pieces together with wrong sides facing, leaving the hemmed edges open. Trim.*

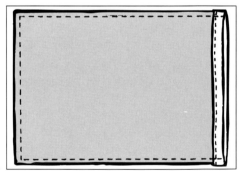

3 *Press the seam open, then turn the cover wrong side out and press flat. Stitch again and turn right side out.*

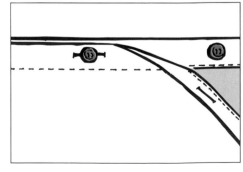

4 *Make buttonholes along the opening edge about 10 inches (25cm) apart and sew on the buttons to match.*

being reversed. Another way of adding interest is to mimic a patchwork quilt and use large squares to create a checkerboard pattern of two or three bold colors, or a combination of different sizes of stripes.

Cotton or a cotton-polyester blend is the best fabric to consider for duvet covers, as it is easy to wash and is comfortable to touch. It should not be too heavy. For a double duvet cover, you may not be able to find wide enough fabric, so you will have to join pieces together before cutting out your first pieces to size. Always join with a full width of fabric in the center, flanked by two seams.

To make the seams more interesting, add a strip of fabric between the two pieces you are joining together on either side. Press seams toward the inserts and then assemble as described opposite.

Making a simple duvet cover

Cut two pieces of fabric, each a little longer than the duvet itself, plus a total of 4 inches (10cm) for hems and seam allowance, by the width of the duvet, plus 3 inches (8cm) for the seam allowances. Along the opening edge of each piece, machine stitch a double 1¼ inches (3cm) hem (see pages 340–341).

To join the two pieces with a French seam, first pin them together with wrong sides facing and raw edges aligned, leaving the hemmed edges open. Stitch ¾ inch (2cm) from the edge. Trim the seam allowances to ⅝ inch (1.5cm) and then clip off the two seam allowance corners diagonally. Press the seam

open and turn the cover wrong side out so that the right sides are together. Press the seam flat, aligning the seamline along the fold. Stitch ¾ inch (2cm) from the edge. Turn right side out and press.

Making the buttonholes on the cover

Mark the positions for the buttonholes along one edge of the opening about 10 inches (25cm) apart. Use a button to mark the length of the buttonholes, allowing for the button thickness. If you are making the buttonholes by machine, follow the directions in your sewing machine manual.

If you are sewing the buttonholes by hand, use a pair of small scissors to cut the buttonhole. Start by overcasting the cut at one end several times. Buttonhole stitch down one side of the slit, overcast the other end, turn

the fabric around, and buttonhole stitch up the other side. Fasten the thread end into the end of the buttonhole on the wrong side. Sew on the buttons opposite the buttonholes.

Making tie fastenings for the cover

The simple duvet cover can be fastened with ties instead of buttonholes. Use lengths of ribbon with the raw edge slipstitched over, and secure them to each side of the duvet opening in pairs.

Or ties can be made from strips of fabric, either the same as the cover or from a contrasting fabric. Cut strips about 12 inches (30cm) long by 2½ inches (6cm) wide, fold over and press a ½ inch (1.2cm) hem on all sides. Fold the strips in half so that the long sides meet, wrong sides together. Topstitch all around and stitch in place as for ribbons.

Making the buttonholes

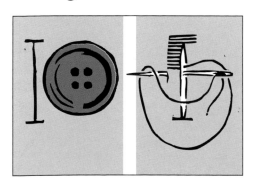

Use a button to mark the length of the buttonholes, and buttonhole stitch around the slit, overcasting at each end.

◀ *A blue and white checked gingham duvet cover and buttoned pillows lie comfortably crumpled against the white linen sheet on this simple bed. The room is cool and understated, with neutral background colors that allow the bed covers to dominate. The gingham is echoed in the frame on the cabinet and helps to unify the theme.*

Bed hangings

▲ *An all-white decorative scheme is often the most striking. Here the choice of bed drapery was influenced by the distressed plaster walls and wooden shutters; the pillows and bedspread, with their unusual leaf-shaped edging, and the swaths of white fabric suspended from a half-corona would not look out of place in a medieval bedchamber.*

Extending the decoration of a bed up into its surrounding space, by hanging fabrics around it or over it, can transform an ordinary bed into something extraordinary and magical.

Imagine climbing into a sleeping bunk on a train and closing the curtains to create your own private space, or lying beneath tented canvas, peering out at the stars. These two effects can be easily recreated in your bedroom with a little forethought and planning.

Curtains can become walls, to surround a bed completely, either hung from a frame such as a traditional four-poster, or as a screen, between ceiling and floor. This is effective, for example, in a wide alcove, where a bed might be positioned sideways to the wall.

Fabric hangings to divide or create a space may either hang like curtains, whether from poles or from a support such as a wooden canopy, or be stretched like a screen between a support frame or fixed hooks.

Curtain-style bed hangings

If bed hangings are treated as curtains and hung from a rectangular framework that leaves the heading exposed, it is best to choose a simple heading such as eyelets, buttons, ties, or tabs.

Tabs made from bands of fabric (see pages 342–343) loop around the pole support. Consider making these in a fabric that contrasts in color or pattern with the curtains themselves.

For a dramatic effect, use alternate colored bands of fabric, such as pink and orange velvet atop a teal-colored velvet curtain. Add brass buttons to the tabs, and to hold the curtains open, heavy rope tie-bands, and you have a wonderfully rich and dramatic bed arrangement.

Eyelets punched through the top of the curtains are another effective and stylish method of hanging fabric around a bed, either from a pole or from hooks suspended from a low ceiling.

The beauty of bed hangings is that they have an inside and an outside, making an ideal opportunity to use two layers of completely contrasting fabrics. Imagine a crisp white linen on the inside and a heavy brocade on the outside, or a wide striped cotton lining a *toile de Jouy*. Obviously, the fullness of the fabric would depend on the effect required and the type of fabric you were using.

Swaths of gathered fabric can be hung from traditional wooden cornices as part of a four-poster, half-tester, or corona. Usually these headings, which are not really seen except from inside the bed, are gathered with tape, like drapery headings.

Screen-style bed hangings

A flatter, screen-like effect can be achieved by sewing a sleeve at the top and base of a piece of fabric—a strong canvas works well, for instance—and stretching it between a tubular frame. A side and an end, with a bed positioned sideways to the wall, create a simple enclosure for a child's bunk bed, for example. Sew pockets onto the side of the fabric that faces the bed, for pajamas or stuffed toys.

The premise of using stretched fabric can be further extended to make a complete pitched roof for a bed. Try using sewn sleeves to slot over three horizontal poles, two parallel on either side of the bed, and one higher up, centered over the middle section of the bed.

A flap, hanging partway down each side, can cleverly mimic a tent. For added detail, shape the edges or hang small tassels from it. Similarly, a pole hanging above and across each end of the bed can support a length of fabric which, at the head end, can fall behind the pillows, thus creating a backdrop.

If you also cut the fabric long at the foot end, and attach strips of fabric or ribbon to either side, it will allow the fabric to be rolled up and tied to the poles like a rolled-up tent flap.

▶ *This sleeping area, little more than an alcove, could have had a rather claustrophobic atmosphere. Instead, a suspended canopy draws the eye up and across the ceiling, exaggerating the tiny space. A candle sconce and painted wall design provide interesting Gothic detail.*

Table settings

How you choose to decorate a table will depend on a
number of factors: the table's style and shape, the material
from which it is made, its setting, and its particular role.
Some tables, for example, may be covered by day to
protect their surfaces and then uncovered in the evening
for meals. Conversely, a large wooden refectory table in
a kitchen might be left uncovered during the day
and used as a work surface, then covered with a
tablecloth in the evening for dining.

◄ *An attractive striped tablecloth in a heavy woven fabric is contrasted with the whisper-thin table napkins, which have matching brown tassels.*

▲ *A massive, long table such as the one above can, depending on the finish, be left uncovered for meals. Here, the points of color are provided by the ceramic plates.*

A temporary cover, such as a sheet of thick plywood, can help enlarge a table and make it more sturdy. A plywood sheet can also be placed over a series of sawhorses to make a table large enough for a dinner party.

Every sit-down meal requires a table setting. Even the most informal, impromptu snack calls for plates, flatware, and glasses, arranged in some kind of order. For sophisticated dinner parties, Sunday brunches, or children's birthday parties, the table can be set and decorated to create a particular atmosphere or theme. Start with a color scheme, then add decorative details in the form of flowers, berries, fruit, shells, or ribbons. Take care, however, not to overload the table with too many objects. It may be better to provide a focus in the form of a single, striking flower arrangement or a coordinated set of colored glassware.

Starched white linen napkins, the bigger the better, are hard to beat. Look for them on antique stalls or in flea markets—they don't have to match. Roll them into napkin rings (antique silver ones if you're fortunate enough to own them) or secure them with wide satin ribbons tied into rough knots. Ribbons edged with wire can be twisted into marvelous ornamental bows. To reflect a particular celebration or anniversary, ribbons with printed motifs can be found. Similarly, try to find napkin rings to suit the occasion. For instance, for a glamorous dinner party, pierce small squares of brightly colored silk with pieces of wire and twist the wire around plain white napkins. Plain wooden napkin rings can be brightly painted, while inexpensive clear plastic ones are available for those who favor the minimalist look.

Candles provide the best light for evening suppers or dinner parties. Use thick church candles of different heights or tiny votives, one for each table setting. Home-made candles in small glass jars are attractive, or, for an alfresco table setting on a metal or wooden garden table, substitute terra-cotta holders or containers: look for old miniature flower pots and group them together for maximum effect. Spiky metal candlesticks of varying shapes look good grouped together, and cast atmospheric shadows on the walls.

Tables that are not particularly attractive, such as functional trestles or basic particleboard models, may require a permanent disguise, such as a casually draped cream dust sheet or a pair of old velvet draperies, while a beautiful table that is reserved for special dinner parties might be used at other times as a display area for decorative objects such as pots or vases of flowers, arrangements of shells and driftwood, or ornaments and curios.

Tablecloths

Tablecloths can be used purely for decoration or they can have a practical role—protecting a polished top, for instance, or covering up a less-than-attractive surface. They are easy to make. For the simplest of cloths, take a square of fabric—perhaps with country-style checks or deckchair stripes—and simply machine stitch a hem around the edges. Jazz up a plain cloth by sewing on a central panel of fabric, adding a wide border and mitering the corners. Punched eyelets in the corners of a cloth add detail and have an added bonus in that they can be anchored to the ground with pegs if you want to use the cloth for alfresco meals or picnics.

Although there is probably nothing to beat a fine white linen tablecloth for formal settings, a less expensive version in white mattress ticking with a fine herringbone weave can be just as effective—especially if it is starched. A rough-textured linen cloth in beige or taupe is equally attractive and creates a good neutral backdrop for colorful table settings. Many fabrics can be painted with relative ease. Stick to simple stenciled shapes, applied sparingly across the cloth, such as large, bold letters or images in keeping with a particular theme, be it Halloween, Thanksgiving, or Christmas. Keep the design uncomplicated, and don't use too many colors or the finished result will look muddled and messy.

A combination of cloths in different sizes, placed one over the other, is both attractive and practical. Choose fabrics in contrasting textures (white linen over gray wool suiting or tweed) or contrasting colors (shiny silks in deep orange and purple). On a round table a square cloth draped over a circular one provides more visual interest than a single, large area of fabric. Always let the fabric trail on the ground a little. Heavier fabrics, such as chenille (a traditional covering for protecting polished dining tables when they are not in use) in a dark, rich crimson or moss green, can be trimmed with a rope fringe or edged with shimmering taffeta for elegant, candlelit settings. For long, oblong tables, a fitted cloth with pleated corners that falls to the floor (see pages 336–337) is particularly effective.

Table linen

▲ *A plain wooden table tucked away in a corner of a room can all too easily fade into the background. Lit by incoming sunlight, this cheerful blue and white gingham cloth has a fresh, country-style appeal that makes the table a real focus of the room, as well as complementing the checkered china and upholstery.*

Round tablecloths are usually decorative, often found covering an occasional table in the corner or at either side of a bed. Because of this they do not have to fulfill a very practical function, so you can have fun with choosing different fabrics for the cloths.

Round tablecloths

Because round tablecloths are very wide, especially those that fall right down to the floor, it is unlikely that you will find a large enough piece of fabric to cut the circle in one piece, so several widths may need to be joined. They should never be joined down the middle, as this would look unsightly on the table, but a full width of fabric should be centered and the extra widths added on either side of this central panel.

Making a round tablecloth

To calculate the amount of fabric required, first measure the table's diameter and height. The basic width (diameter) of the finished cloth will equal twice the height of the table, plus the diameter of the tabletop. To this measurement, add 2–4 inches (5–10cm) to give some draping on the floor, plus an extra 1¼ inches (3cm) for the seam allowance around the circular edge. (Adjust if you want a shorter drop.) This gives the final width and

Round tablecloth

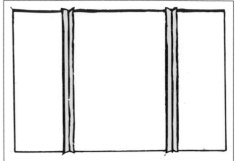

1 *Join the fabric pieces, positioning a full width in the center. Join lining pieces in same way. Press seams open.*

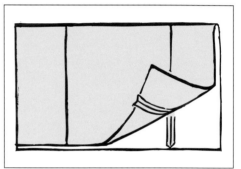

2 *Fold the fabric in half, aligning the seams. The width along the fold measures the full diameter of the circle.*

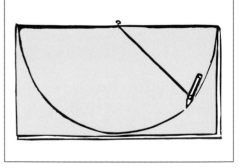

3 *Mark a half-circle on folded fabric, using a pencil and a length of string. Cut lining to same shape.*

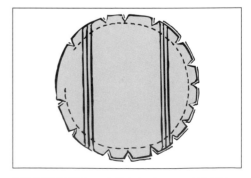

4 *Pin lining to fabric and stitch, leaving an opening for turning. Trim, notch, and turn right side out.*

length of fabric needed. The lining will be the same size. Join the main fabric pieces into a square wide enough to make up the required diameter of the tablecloth, positioning a full fabric width in the center and remembering to allow extra for seams. Press the seams open. Next, fold the fabric in half, lining up the seams. Mark the center point along the folded edge with a pin. Tie a pencil on the end of a length of string. Measure the length of the required radius (half the diameter) from the pencil along the string and pin the string at this point to the marked center point. Mark the circumference of half the circle. Cut along this half-circle through the two layers. Unfold the fabric and use it to cut a lining of the same size. (Cut an interlining if desired.)

If using interlining, attach this first to the wrong side of the fabric, using large loose stitches (see pages 342–343). With right sides together, pin the circle of fabric to the lining circle. Machine stitch, ⅝ inches (1.5cm) from the edge, leaving an opening of about 10 inches (25cm) for turning the cloth right side out. Trim and notch the seam allowances and press the seam open. Turn right side out. Press under the seam allowances along the opening and slipstitch closed. Press.

Rectangular tablecloths

Plain rectangular tablecloths are the most versatile and are very easy to make. For an interesting variation, two covers can be made for one table—one that sits across the table widthwise only and the other over the top of it lengthwise only, with each cloth falling to the floor. Use contrasting colors or patterns for maximum effect—two sizes of blue check, for example.

Determining the size of a simple rectangular tablecloth couldn't be easier. All you have to do is measure the length and width of the table, and the desired drop. The length of cloth required is the length of the table plus two times the drop, plus hem allowances. The width of cloth required is calculated in the same way. For neatness, hems can be hand sewn, but this can obviously be quite time-consuming, and machine stitching is more practical.

Rectangular tablecloths with skirts

"Fitted" tablecloths can be made by adding a skirt, in much the same way that a fitted bedspread is made.

Before embarking on purchasing fabric for this type of tablecloth, you should carefully consider how the skirt will be constructed. The height of the table (that is, the drop of the skirt) is likely to be less than the standard width of fabric. Therefore, if you are using plain fabric or a pattern that can be used either horizontally or vertically, you can do what is termed "railroading"—using the width of the fabric as the drop. However, if you are using a stripe or other vertical pattern, you may have to join fabric widths in order to achieve the total length that goes around the table. Plan where your seams will be, and adjust the quantity of fabric required accordingly to avoid asymmetrically placed seams.

One way to hide any necessary seams in the skirt is to position them inside the box pleats at the corners. A pleat can also be added in the center of each long side for this purpose. An interesting detail is achieved if the pleats are cut separately and made from a contrasting fabric. If you are attempting this, be sure to position the joining seams just inside the pleat so that they do not show on the pleat folds.

▲ *With each color given equal weight, fresh citrus yellow and white marry perfectly in this kitchen. Because of the large size of the table, the yellow drape used on its own would have appeared too overpowering, upsetting the color balance. Breaking up the mass of yellow with a smaller, white rectangular cloth has restored a sense of harmony.*

▲ *A combination of tablecloths can be practical as well as decorative. This fringed green and white pin-striped throw is thick and hard-wearing, which makes it ideal for daytime use. For formal evening meals or entertaining, this protective layer can be removed to reveal the fine white linen tablecloth beneath.*

Making a rectangular tablecloth with a skirt

To calculate the amount of fabric needed, first measure the flat surface area of the table top and add a ⅝ inch (1.5cm) seam allowance all around. These are the dimensions for the top piece. For the skirt (which will have an inverted pleat in each corner), measure each side of the table. At each corner add 8 inches (20cm) extra to fold into the pleat. The total length of the sides plus the pleat allowances and any necessary seam allowances is the required length of the skirt piece (or pieces) for both fabric and lining. For the width of the skirt piece, measure the drop of the skirt from the edge of the tabletop to the floor, and add 2–4 inches (5–10cm) to drape on the ground, plus seam allowances at both sides.

You will need enough main fabric for the top piece and the skirt and the same amount of lining fabric. Cut the table-top piece and the skirt piece (or pieces) from the main fabric and from the lining. Begin by making the skirt. If you have several pieces of fabric for the skirt, pin and stitch them right sides together to make a large loop of fabric. Press the seams open. Do the same for the lining. With the right sides together, pin and stitch the lining to the fabric along one long edge. Press the seam open, then turn right side out. Press, aligning the seam along the fold. Pin the raw edges together (with wrong sides facing).

Next, pin and baste the pleats in place. The pleats must be placed precisely so that when the skirt is attached to the top of the cloth they fall exactly at each corner (and in the middle of a long side if additional pleats are to be made). Baste the skirt to the top panel, right sides together and raw edges aligned. Machine stitch all around, making sure the pleats do not lose their position. Trim the seam allowance. Clip the seam allowance corners of the top panel piece diagonally, and notch the skirt section corners. Press the seam open, then toward the center of the top.

Turn the seam allowance of the top panel lining to the wrong side and press. Pin the folded edge along the seamline where the skirt joins the top panel and handsew it in place, using slipstitch. Turn the cloth right side out and press.

Rectangular tablecloth with skirt

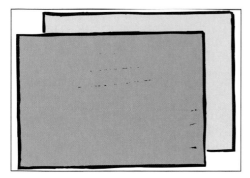

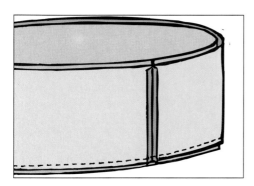

1 Cut one piece of main fabric and one piece of lining to size of tabletop plus seam allowances all around.

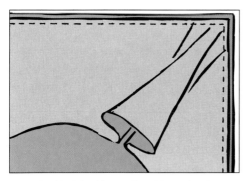

2 Cut the skirt piece (or pieces) and join into a loop. Make the skirt lining; join it to the skirt along one edge.

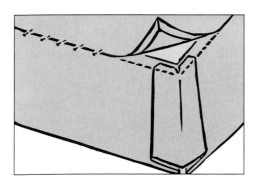

3 Turn the skirt right side out. Pin and baste the pleats at the corner positions and stitch the skirt to the top panel.

4 Press under the seam allowance on the top panel lining. Slipstitch the lining to the wrong side of the tablecloth.

Decorative square tablecloths

Arranged so that their points hang over the sides of a rectangular or square table, square tablecloths make effective covers. They are made in the same way as simple rectangular cloths, but to determine the size you want, you will have to measure the fabric in a slightly different way. Start by deciding how far down each side of the table you wish the top cover cloth to fall. From this point, which will be the corner of the cloth, to the center of the tabletop, doubled, is the width/length of each side of the cloth.

There are many simple ways to embellish a square cloth. The hem around the cover can be made with two rows of parallel stitching to add more detail. Using contrasting sewing thread will give the cloth more definition. To embellish the corners of the top cloth, if desired, attach small tassels.

Other decorative details that can liven up plain cloths, such as fringe or braid, should be attached to the edges of the cloth by hand after the cloth is made. A fringe should always overlap the base edge of the cloth by most of its length, allowing about 1½ inches (4cm) to trail on the ground. A braid applied to the edge of the cloth should line up with the finished edge. Flat braids or ribbons can also run across a square or rectangular cloth, parallel to the sides, set in about 4 inches (10cm) or so, and crossing at the corners to create a small square at each corner.

◄ *Napkins, placemats, and flower arrangements are the finer details that can give a meal a real sense of occasion. A classic scheme of delicate white china on a white linen tablecloth has been given a twist with the addition of roughly stitched, bold scarlet napkins tied with raffia coils.*

Sewing guide

Machine stitched seams

Basic flat seam

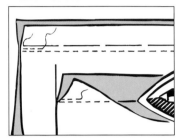

Place the two pieces of fabric together with raw edges aligned and right sides facing. Pin and baste along the edges. Remove the pins. Stitch ⅝ inch (1.5cm) in from the edges, working a few stitches in reverse at both ends to secure the thread. Remove the basting and then press the seam open.

French seam

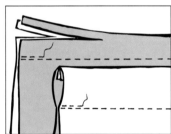

A self-finishing seam suitable for joining lightweight fabrics and for joining straight edges, French seams are ideal for items where both sides are to be visible, as no additional line of stitching will be seen. To make a French seam, place the two pieces of fabric together, with wrong sides facing, and machine stitch a single seam ¼ inch (6mm) from the edge. Trim the seam allowances to ⅛ inch (3mm) and press the seam. Turn the fabric so the right sides are together and press along the seam line. Baste a line of stitching close to the folded edge and sew a second seam ⅜ inch (1cm) from the folded edge. When completed, turn the fabric right side out; finally press the seam allowance flat to one side of the finished seam.

Flat fell seam

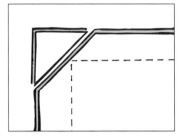

This self-finishing seam is extremely useful where strength is important. With right sides together, stitch ⅝ inch (1.5cm) from the aligned raw edges. Press the seam open. Trim one seam allowance to ¼ inch (6mm), fold the wide allowance over the narrow allowance, and press. Fold under the edge of the wide allowance to enclose both raw edges, and topstitch close to the fold through all the layers. Press. The additional line of stitching will be visible on both sides of the fabric.

Finishing curves and corners

Clipping straight seam allowances

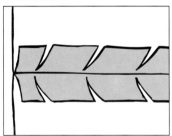

To ease tight selvages, cut into the seam allowance at approx. 2 inch (5cm) intervals, diagonally to the seam line and pointing downward.

Trimming corners

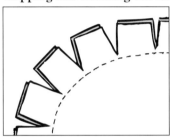

After stitching the seam, trim any corners on the diagonal, making sure you leave approx. ¼ inch (6mm) of the seam allowance to avoid any subsequent raveling of the fabric.

Clipping and notching curves

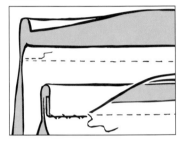

To enable curved seams to lie flat when pressed open, you should clip or notch the seam allowances. On inward curves, make straight clips at intervals to allow the seam allowance to open out. On outward curves, cut out tiny wedges (called "notches") at short intervals to remove the excess bulk of the fabric.

Finishing raw edges

Pinking

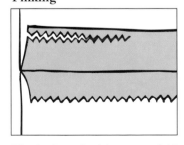

The simplest and quickest way to finish raw edges is to use a pair of pinking shears, although it is not the most hardwearing of methods.

Zigzag stitching

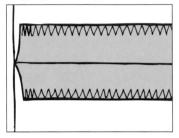

Using the zigzag setting on your machine, make a line of stitching as close to the raw edge as possible.

Self-binding (overlocking) seam

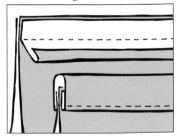

Useful where there is extra bulk—when attaching a gathered edge to a flat edge, for example. Leave seam allowances of about 1¼ inches (3cm) and trim one edge to ¼ inch (6mm). Folding the wide edge over the narrow edge, tuck the raw edge underneath. Pin and then slipstitch along the fold.

Bias binding

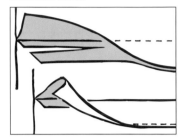

Align one unfolded edge of the bias binding along the edge of the fabric and pin, baste, and machine stitch along the fold of the binding. Fold the binding over the edge to the other side of the fabric, and either machine stitch through all layers or slipstitch the binding in place along the stitching line. This is also a way of finishing the raw edges of fabric—the edges of tablecloths, napkins, or place mats, for example—in which case, the seam is made with wrong sides facing. If you do not want the stitches to show, slip-stitch along the folded edge instead, as for a self-bound (overlocked) seam.

Overcasting by hand

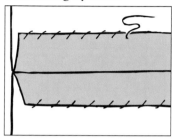

Overcasting is the best way to finish raw edges by hand to prevent raveling. Take equally spaced, equal-length diagonal stitches over the raw edge(s), working against the grain of the fabric.

Hems and mitering

Hems

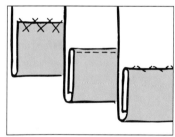

Single hems: For thick, heavy fabric, turn under the required amount of hem and press. Using herringbone stitch, sew along the edge so as to attach it to the back of the main fabric.

Double hem: A double hem secures a firm edge and is particularly suitable for sheer fabrics. Simply fold over half the hem allowance and then fold over again along the hemline. Pin, baste, and finally slipstitch the hem in place.

Slipstitched hem: This hem uses less fabric than the double hem and is useful for medium-weight fabric. Turn ¼ inch (6mm) to the wrong side along

the raw edge and press. Fold the hem allowance to the wrong side along the hemline. Pin and baste. Finish by slip-stitching the hem in place.

Mitered corners

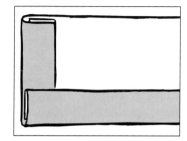

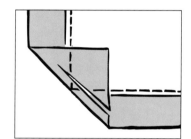

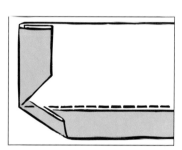

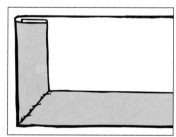

Mitered corners are used where neat corners are required. They can be made on single or double hems, and those of equal or varying widths. For single hems of equal width, turn up both side and bottom hems and press. Open out the hems, then fold in the corner of the fabric at the point where the two pressed lines cross. Check that the pressed lines on the triangle align

with those on the fabric. Turn in the hems again, so that they meet smoothly, then slipstitch the folded edges and herringbone stitch the hems in place. For double hems of equal width, simply turn up both hems twice, unfold once, then turn in the triangle and continue as described above. Both the diagonal folds and the hems can be slipstitched.

When side and bottom hems are of different widths, turn in single hems and press. Unfold the hems, but mark the limit of the turns with pins. Fold up a corner through the point where the pressed lines meet and the points marked with pins. Refold the hems to form a neat miter; stitch as before. For double hems of this kind, simply turn in double hems, unfold to single and mark the limit of the double turns.

Hand stitches

Running stitch

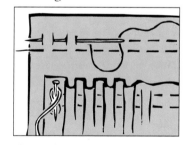

This stitch is used for simple sewing and gathering. It is worked from right to left, and consists of small stitches of equal length. To gather fabric, begin on the right side of the fabric and sew two parallel lines of large running stitch. Finish each line by winding the thread end around a pin. Pull both threads by applying even pressure to both ends of the line of sewing.

Backstitch

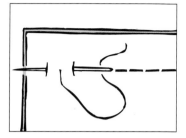

Backstitch is useful for seams or tight corners where it is awkward to use a machine. Working from right to left, bring the needle out of the fabric and insert it a little way behind where the thread came out, then bring the needle forward the same distance in front of that point. The forward stitch will be double the length of the back-ward stitch. Continue in this way, making sure that you always insert the needle into the end of the last stitch so that there are no gaps in the stitching.

Ladder stitch (slip basting)

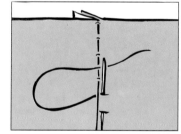

Ladder stitch, also known as slip basting, is useful for matching pat-terned fabric exactly and is worked on the right side of the fabric. Press the seam allowance to the wrong side of one piece of fabric, then with right sides upward, place this over the unfolded seam allowance of the other piece. Pin firmly in place. Starting with a knot under the fold, stitch up through the fabric and across the seamline into the other piece. Next, take the needle under the fabric for a little way, then back up and across the seamline into the folded edge again, between the two layers of fabric. Repeat these small stitches across the seamline for the length of the fabric.

Slipstitch

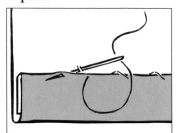

Slipstitch is used to sew down a folded edge, such as a hem, or to join two folded edges, as in a mitered corner. In one continuous movement, working from right to left, take a tiny stitch in the main fabric, close to the previous stitch; insert the needle into the fold—about ¼ inch (6mm) to the left—and bring it out to the front. Continue, alternately making a tiny stitch in the main fabric and a larger stitch inside the folded edge.

Lock stitch

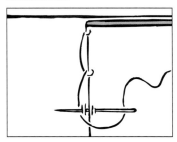

This loose stitch secures layers of fabric together—for example, holding a drapery lining in place. With wrong sides together, place the lining over the main fabric. Pin down the complete length of the fabric in the center. Fold the fabric back against the pins.

Using matching thread, make a horizontal stitch through the folded edge and the main fabric, picking up only one or two threads of the fabric. Work at 2-inch (5cm) intervals down the fabric, keeping the thread very loose between the stitches. Work additional rows of lock stitch as required.

Herringbone stitch

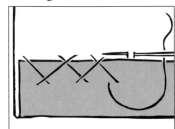

This firm stitch, worked from left to right, is generally used for hemming a single thickness of heavy fabric. Fasten the thread in the hem. Work over the edge diagonally, taking small stitches in the hem and just above it alternately. This stitch is often used to hem draperies; it is also used as an embroidery stitch.

Blanket stitch

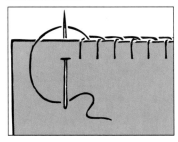

Blanket stitch can be used to finish the edge of the fabric or as a decorative stitch when worked in a contrasting color. Insert the needle down through the fabric at the appropriate distance from the edge. Holding the thread under the needle point, pull the needle through at the edge, forming a loop along the edge of the fabric.

Prick stitch

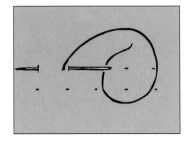

Prick stitch is used for inserting zippers and for other places where the sewing must be unobtrusive. It is sewn in the same way as backstitch, but the top stitches are smaller and should appear as pricks in the fabric. Working on the right side, take the needle back a couple of threads behind where the thread came out and then take a stitch a little way in front of that point.

Ruffles and pleats

Ruffles

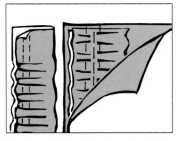

Single ruffles: Calculate the depth of the ruffle and add a hem and seam allowance. Cut the strip. Turn up the hem and stitch. Stitch two parallel rows of long, straight machine stitch and gather to the required length. Pin and baste to the main fabric with right sides together. Remove the pins. Machine stitch in place along the seam line and remove the basting. Finish the edges using zigzag stitch and press upward.

Double ruffles: To produce a full ruffle, cut double the depth of the fabric and allow twice the required top seam allowance. Fold the material in half lengthwise and gather the top, as for a single ruffle.

Pleats

For each pleat allow three times the required width, and remember to cut parallel to the weft of the fabric to insure that the pleats hang straight.

Knife pleats

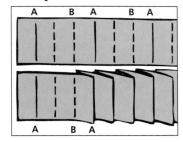

Having decided upon the required pleat width, calculate the number of pleats by measuring the edge to which the pleats will be attached and dividing by the width of the pleat. Multiply this number by three to calculate the width of fabric needed, and add the seam allowances. Calculate the depth required, and add seam allowances. Join the widths with flat fell seams, and pin and stitch the hems. Mark the pleats on the fabric at right angles to the edge of the fabric. Mark the pleat line (A) and then measure twice the pleat width and mark on the placement line (B). Alternate (A) and (B) markings and measurements along the fabric. Fold the fabric on the first pleat line (A) and bring to line (B); repeat to the end of the fabric. Baste along the top of the fabric and press. Stitch in place as for ruffles.

Box pleats

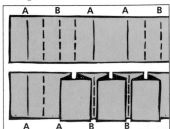

Box pleats consist of two pleats folded in such a way as to turn toward each other. Begin in the same way as for knife pleats. Mark pleat line (A), measure twice the width, and mark placement line (B). Then measure twice the pleat width again, to mark the next pleat line (A), then twice the width again, to the beginning of the next sequence, pleat line (A). To pleat the fabric, simply fold the two pleat lines (A) outward to meet over the placement line. Inverted box pleats are assembled in the same way except that the pleat lines are folded inward to meet over the placement lines.

Trimming

Piping

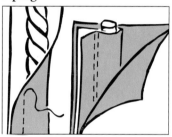

Join bias strips until they are the same length as the required length of piping cord. Place the cord on the wrong side of the strip, fold the strip over, align the edges. First baste and then machine stitch, close to the cord, using a zipper foot attachment. Pin the piping to the edge of the main fabric along the previous stitching line. Baste and stitch the piping in place.

Fastenings

Buttons, hooks, and studs

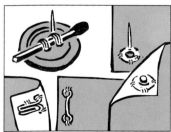

Buttons: Mark the position for the button, and secure the thread. Slide the button over the needle and place a matchstick over the top of the button. Work stitches through the holes of the button and over the matchstick. Remove the matchstick and pull the button up, so the slack threads are under the button. Finish by winding the working thread around the slack to make a shank; secure the thread end inside the shank.

Hooks and eyes: Fix the eye part of the fastener every 2–4 inches (5–10cm) along the fabric by sewing a few stitches through each hoop. Insure that the hooks are correctly aligned, then fix to the other side of the fabric by stitching over the neck.

Snaps: Mark the positions of the snaps by measuring every 2–4 inches (5–10cm) along the fabric and ¼ inch (6mm) from the edge. Mark the positions with pins. Sew the socket part on the seam underlap by working a few stitches through each hole. Place the ball half on the overlapping fabric and check its alignment with the socket half; then sew it in place.

Fastening tapes

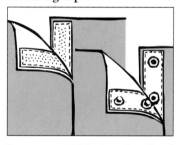

Snap tape: This is a length of tape that has snaps fixed at set intervals along the tape. It is available in several widths.

To attach the tape, simply separate the two layers and sew the socket strip to the lower layer of fabric and the ball part to the top layer of fabric. Stitch down the long edges of the strips, using a zipper foot.

Hook-and-loop tape: This consists of two strips of fabric, one of which has tiny hooks and the other, tiny loops. These strips stick together when pressure is applied. Separate the two layers, and stitch in place down the long edges.

Zippers

Useful for pillow and cushion covers, zippers are available with either metal or nylon teeth and in a full range of colors, lengths, and weights.

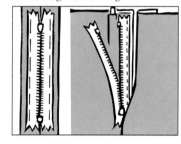

Centered zipper: Stitch the seam up to the zipper opening. Then baste the seam along the opening and press it open. Lay the zip downward on the wrong side of the fabric, exactly along the seamline, then pin and baste it in place. Turn the fabric right side up, and sew the zipper in place, just inside the basting lines, using a zipper foot. Fasten the threads and remove the basting from the opening.

Zipper inserted in a piped seam: Open the zipper and lay one side, right side down, on the right side of the piped seam with the zipper tape in the seam allowance and the zipper teeth aligned with the piping. Baste and then stitch in place ⅛ inch (3mm) from the teeth, using the zipper foot. Close the zipper and fold back the seam allowances of both edges. Lay the plain edge on the zipper, aligning it with the piping; pin, baste, and stitch in place.

Fabric ties

Flat fabric ties make a wonderful alternative to other fastenings and are useful for bed linen and scatter pillows. Tubing strips—tubes made from bias strips—can be attached as loops and used instead of buttonholes.

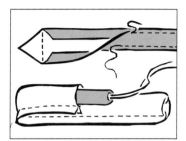

Flat ties: Cut a piece of fabric to the desired length and twice the width, adding ⅜ inch (1cm) all around. Folding the edges of the length to the wrong side by ⅜ inch (1cm), press and cut the corners at a diagonal, then fold and press the width ends down to the wrong side. Fold the fabric in half lengthwise and stitch all the sides, ⅛ inch (3mm) from the edge.

Tubing ties: Fold the desired length of a 1–1¼ inch (2.5–3cm) bias strip in half, and sew the long edges together, ¼ inch (6mm) from the edge. Push a blunt-ended needle threaded with strong thread through the tube, having first secured it to one end, working along the length until it emerges at the other end. Pull the thread, and the tubing will be turned right side out. Finish by tucking the ends into the tube and then overcasting them.

Sources

Major suppliers and manufacturers are listed here to provide a starting point when sourcing materials. Many of those listed have toll-free information lines and will supply catalogs on request. The addresses listed give the headquarters or main showroom of a company, from whom you should be able to get a contact address for your nearest stockist.

Architectural moldings

Design Toscano
15 East Campbell St.
Arlington Heights, IL 60005

Driwood Molding Company
P.O. Box 1729
Florence, SC 29503

Old World Molding and Finishing, Inc.
115 Allen Boulevard
Farmingdale, NY 11735

Fabric

Ainsworth Noah & Associates
351 Peachtree Hills Avenue
Suite 518
Atlanta, GA 30305

B & J Fabrics
263 West 40th Street
New York, NY 10018

Bergamo Fabrics
D & D Building, 979 Third Avenue
New York, NY 10022

Clarence House
211 East 58th Street
New York, NY 10022

Covington Fabrics
15 East 26th Streeet
New York, NY 10010

Kravet Fabrics
225 Central Avenue South
Bethpage, NY 11714

Lace Country
21 West 38th Street
New York, NY 10018

Ralph Lauren Home Collection
867 Madison Avenue
New York, NY 10021

Manuel Canovas
D & D Building, 979 Third Avenue
New York, NY 10022

Mitchel Fabrics
637 Main Street
Winnipeg
Manitoba R3B 1E3

Osborne & Little
90 Commerce Road
Stamford, CT 06902

Paron Fabrics
206 West 40th Street
New York, NY 10018

Quadrille
D & D Building, 979 Third Avenue
New York, NY 10022

Randolph & Hein, Inc.
Pacific Design Center
Suite G790, 8687 Melrose Avenue
Los Angeles, CA 90069
and
Galleria Design Center
Suite 101, 101 Henry Adams Street
San Francisco, CA 94103

J. Robert Scott
8737 Melrose Avenue
Los Angeles, CA 90069

Silk Surplus
235 East 58th Street
New York, NY 10022

Eileen West
525 Brannan Street
San Francisco, CA 94107

Flooring

Resilient

Armstrong Vinyl Flooring
P.O. Box 3001
Lancaster, PA 17604

Dodge-Regupol, Inc.
P.O. Box 989
Lancaster, PA 17608
Cork tile.

Forbo Industries, Inc.
Humboldt Industrial Park
Maple wood Drive
P.O. Box 667
Hazleton, PA 18201
Linoleum.

Johnsonite (A division of Duramex, Inc.)
16910 Munn Road
Chagrin Falls, OH 44023
Rubber and vinyl.

Decorative wood

Hardwood Manufacturers Association
400 Penn Center Blvd.
Suite 530
Pittsburgh, PA 15235

National Oak Flooring Manufacturers Association
22 North Front St.
660 Falls Building
Memphis, TN 38103

Bruce Hardwood Floors
16803 Dallas Parkway
Dallas, TX 75248

Eco Hardwood Floors
P.O. Box 882461
San Francisco, CA 94188

Kentucky Wood Floors
P.O. Box 33276
Louisville, KY 40213

Sheoga Hardwood Inc.
15320 Burton Windsor Road
Middlefield, OH 44062

Hard

Ceramic Tile Institute of America
12061 Jefferson Boulevard
Culver City, CA 90230

Country Floors
15 East 16th Street
New York, NY 10003
and
8735 Melrose Avenue
Los Angeles, CA 90069
Ceramic tile, terra-cotta and stone

Paris Ceramics
151 Greenwich Avenue
Greenwich, CT 06830

Ann Sacks Tile & Stone
115 Steward Street
Seattle, WA 98101

Soft

The Carpet and Rug Institute
P.O. Box 2048
Dalton, GA 30722

Larsen Inc.
232 East 59th Street
New York, NY 10022
Natural fiber, including coir, sisal and wood

Paint

Ashley House Wallcoverings, Inc.
1838 West Broadway, Vancouver
British Columbia V6J 1Y9

Coast Decorating Centre
4464 Main Street, Vancouver
British Columbia V5V 3R3

Crown Berger
Bentley Brothers
2709 South Park Road
Louisville, KY 40219

Eco-Design
1365 Rufina Circle
Santa Fe, NM 87505
Natural paints and stains

Glidden Paint Co.
925 Euclid Avenue
Cleveland, OH 44115

Benjamin Moore & Co.
51 Chestnut Ridge Road
Montvale, NJ 07645

The Old Fashioned Milk Paint Company
P.O. Box 222
436 Main Street
Groton, MA 01450

Plaid Enterprises
1649 International Court
Norcross, GA 30091

Rust-Oleum
11 Hawthorn Parkway
Vernon Hills, IL 60061

Sherwin-Williams Co.
101 Prospect Avenue NW
#10 Midland Building
Cleveland, OH 44115

Walls Alive
1328 17th Avenue SW
Calgary
Alberta T2T 0C3

Western Paint and Wallcovering Co.
521 Hargrave Street
Winnipeg
Manitoba R3A 0Y1

Tiles

Dal Tile International
1000 Cannon Avenue
Lansdale, PA 19446

Florida Tile Industries, Inc.
Lakeland, FL 33802

Italian Tile Center
A division of the Italian Trade Commission
499 Park Avenue
New York, NY 10022

Laufen International
4942 East 66th Street North
Tulsa, OK 74156

Monarch Tile, Inc.
834 Rickwood Road
Florence, AL 35631

Summitville Tiles
P.O. Box 73
Summitville, OH 43962

Tiles de Sante Fe, Inc.
P.O. Box 3767
Sante Fe, NM 87501

Wallpaper

Agnes Bourne
2 Henry Adams Street, #220
San Francisco, CA 94103

Bradbury & Bradbury Art Wallpapers
P.O. Box 155
Benicia, CA 94510

Eisenhart Wallcoverings Co.
P.O. Box 464
Hanover, PA 17331

Imperial Wallcoverings
23645 Mercantile Road
Cleveland, OH 44122

F. Schumacher & Co.
939 Third Avenue
New York, NY 10022

Waverly
939 Third Avenue
New York, NY 10022

York Wallcovering and Fabric
201 Carlisle
York, PA 17404

Index

Acknowledgments

1 Ray Main; 2 Hans Zeegers/Ariadne; 4–5 Richard Waite (Designer: Louise Cotier)/Arcaid; 6 Hotze Eisma/In Huis; 8–9 Todd Eberle; 10 Hotze Eisma; 11–12 Mads Mogensen; 13 James Merrell/Options/Robert Harding Syndication; 14–15 Todd Eberle (Designer: Michael Formika); 16 Verne Fotografie; 17 *above* Richard Glover; 17 *below* Eduard Hueber (Whitney Powers); 18–19 Rob van Uchelen/Ariadne; 19 John Hall; 20 Eduard Hueber (Dean Wolf); 20–1 Jerome Darblay; 21 Fritz von der Schulenburg (Architect: Nico Rensch)/The Interior Archive; 22 Polly Wreford/Homes & Gardens/Robert Harding Syndication; 24 Paul Ryan/International Interiors; 25 Jerome Darblay; 26 *left* Henry Bourne/World of Interiors; 26 *right* David Phelps; 27 *above* Richard Felber; 27 *below* Chris Drake/Country Homes & Interiors/Robert Harding Syndication; 28 Ray Main; 29 *above* Paul Ryan/International Interiors; 29 *below* Antoine Rozes; 30 *above* Jean Pierre Godeaut (Yuri Kuper); 30 *below* Verne Fotografie; 31 *above* Dominique Vorillion (Arch: B. Urquietta)/Stock Image Production; 31 *below* A. Bailhache (Stylist: M.Gibert)/Marie Claire Maison; 32 Eduard Hueber (Dean Wolf); 33 Fritz von der Schulenburg (Paula Navone)/The Interior Archive; 34 *above* Hotze Eisma (Ron Jagger); 34 *below* Scott Frances/Esto; 34–5 Peter Cook; 36 *above* John Hall; 36 *below* Todd Eberle (Designer:Michael Formika); 37 *above* Scott Frances/Esto; 37 *below* Marie-Pierre Morel (Stylist: C. Peuch)/Marie Claire Maison; 38 Todd Eberle; 39 Fritz von der Schulenburg (Adelheid Gowrie)/The Interior Archive; 40 *above* Simon Brown (Justin Meath Baker); 40 *below* Christopher Drake/Options/Robert Harding Syndication; 41 Fritz von der Schulenburg/Country Homes & Interiors/Robert Harding Syndication; 42 Francis Hammond; 42–3 Jean-Francois Jaussaud; 43 Antoine Bootz; 44 *above* John Hall; 44 *below* Christian Sarramon; 45 *above* Henry Wilson (Mazzuchi)/The Interior Archive; 45 *below* Francis Hammond; 46 Simon McBride; 46–7

Verne Fotografie; 47 Jerome Darblay; 48–9 Fritz von der Schulenburg (Richard Mudditt)/The Interior Archive; 50 Simon Kenny/Belle Magazine; 51 *above* Earl Carter/Belle Magazine; 51 *below* Simon Kenny/Belle Magazine; 52 Schoner Wohnen/Camera Press; 53 Verne Fotografie; 54 *above* Hannah Lewis (Sue Parker)/Elle Decoration; 54 *below* Pascal Chevalier (Michel Klein)/Agence Top; 54–55 Paul Ryan/International Interiors; 55 *above* Christophe Drake/Homes & Gardens/Robert Harding Syndication; 55 *below* Paul Ryan/International Interiors; 56 Henry Wilson (Ian Dew)/The Interior Archive; 58 David Churchill/Arcaid; 61 Christophe Dugied/Marie Claire Maison; 62 Henry Wilson (Celia Lyttleton)/The Interior Archive; 63 *left* Henry Wilson (Celia Lyttleton)/The Interior Archive; 63 *right* Jacqui Hurst; 64 Jean-Pierre Godeaut (Designer: Manuel Mestre); 66 Huntley Hedworth/Elizabeth Whiting & Associates; 66–7 Simon Brown / The Interior Archive; 67 Simon Brown / The Interior Archive; 68 Henry Wilson (Giola Rossi)/The Interior Archive; 69 Crown Paints; 70–1 Mads Mogensen; 72 English Stamp Company; 73 Alberto Piovano (Architect: Mariano Boggia)/Arcaid; 74 Schoner Wohnen/Camera Press; 75 Simon McBride; 76 Tim Beddow/The Interior Archive; 77 Jacques Dirand; 78 Henry Bourne (Melissa North)/Elle Decoration; 78–9 *above* Anaglypta Wallcoverings; 78–9 *below* Cole & Son/Michael Dyer Associates; 79 *Above* Anna French; 79 *below* David Barrett/Homes & Gardens/Robert Harding Syndication; 80 Christopher Drake/Country Homes & Interiors/Robert Harding Syndication; 82 Sanderson Design Archive; 83 Ray Main; 86 *above* Ari Ashley/Interior Archive; 86 *below* Hotze Eisma; 89 *above & below* Ian Parry/Abode; 90 Schoner Wohnen/Camera Press; 91 Christopher Drake/Homes & Gardens/Robert Harding Syndication; 92 Paul Ryan/International Interiors; 92 *below* James Merrell/Country Homes & Interiors/Robert Harding Syndication; 94 Jerome Darblay;

95 Laura Ashley; 96 Dolf Straatemeier/V.T. Wonen; 98 Christopher Simon Sykes/The Interior Archive; 99 Mike Parsons; 100 Scott Frances/Esto; 100–1 Homes & Gardens/Robert Harding Syndication; 101 *above* Muraspec Wallcoverings; 101 *below* Henry Wilson (Christopher Davies)/The Interior Archive; 102 Nadia Mackenzie; 103 Lucinda Symons/Country Homes & Interiors/Robert Harding Syndication; 104 Simon Brown; 105 *above* Henry Wilson (Ian Dew)/The Interior Archive; 105 *below* Dominque Vorillon; 106 *left & right* Richard Glover; 106 *below* Paul Warchol; 106–7 Fritz von der Schulenburg (Mimmi O'Connell)/The Interior Archive; 107 Hotze Eisma/V.T. Wonen; 108 Trevor Mein/Belle Magazine; 109 Fritz von der Schulenburg (Paula Navone)/The Interior Archive; 110 Ray Main; 111 Eric Morin; 112 Ray Main; 113 Ross Honeysett (Architect: Ian Moore); 114 Mark Darley/Esto; 115 David Simmonds/ Elle Decoration; 116 Simon Kenny/Belle Magazine; 118 James Merrell/Options/Robert Harding Syndication; 120 John Hall; 121 Dominque Vorillon; 122–3 Verne Fotografie; 124 *above* Ray Main; 124 *below* Sølvi Dos Santos; 125 *left & right* Ray Main; 126 Ken Adlard; 127 *above* Eduard Hueber (Whitney Powers); 127 *below* Antoine Rozes; 128 *above* Scott Frances/Esto; 128 *below* Andreas von Einsiedel/Country Homes & Interiors/Robert Harding Syndication; 129 Hotze Eisma (Karen Butler); 130 *above* Jean–Pierre Godeaut (J.Prisca); 130–1 *above* David Phelps; 130–1 *below* James Mortimer/The Interior Archive; 131 *above right* Ingalill Snitt; 131 *below right* Fritz von der Schulenburg (Architect:Nico Rensch)/The Interior Archive; 132 John Miller; 133 Ianthe Ruthven; 134 Peter Cook (Sergison Bates); 135 Gilles de Chabaneix (Stylist: Fasoli)/Marie Claire Maison; 136 John Hall; 137 Eric Morin; 138 *above* Simon McBride; 138 *below* Rodney Hyett/Elizabeth Whiting & Associates; 139 Richard Waite; 140 David Cripps/ Elizabeth Whiting & Associates;

142 T. Jeanson (Maison McCoy)/Stock Image Production; 143 Nina Ewald/Abode; 144 Thomas Lane; 146 Michel Claus; 147 Fritz von der Schulenburg (Dot Spikings)/The Interior Archive; 148 Scott Frances/Esto; 149 Tim Street-Porter (Designer: Barbara Barry); 150 Fritz von der Schulenburg (Architect: Nico Rensch)/The Interior Archive; 150–1 Peter Cook (Jonathon Woolf)/Hilary Coe; 151–2 Verne Fotografie; 154 Otto Baitz/Esto; 155 Michel Claus; 156 Deidi von Schaewen; 158 Hotze Eisma; 159 *above* John Heseltine; 159 *below* Christopher Simon Sykes/The Interior Archive; 160 *above* Neil Lorimer/Elizabeth Whiting & Associates; 160 *below* Nadia Mackenzie; 160–1 Paul Warchol; 161 *above* David Parmiter; 161 *below* Jean Pierre Godeaut (Dimitri Xanthdolis); 162 *above* Mads Mogensen; 162 *below* Jean Pierre Godeaut; 164 *left* Michael Freeman; 164 *right* Fritz von der Schulenburg/The Interior Archive; 166 Ray Main; 167 Paul Warchol; 168–9 Michel Claus; 168 *above* Georgia Glynn-Smith; 168 *below* Verne Fotografie; 169 Tim Street-Porter (Daniel Sachs); 170 Richard Felber; 172 David Phelps; 173 Ari Ashley/Interior Archive; 174 *above* John Hall (Faulkner); 174 *below* John Hall; 176 Todd Eberle; 177 Alexander van Berge/V.T. Wonen; 178 Hotze Eisma; 178–9 John Hall; 179 *above left* Eduard Hueber (M. Burger); 179 *above right* Sinclair Till; 179 *below* Deidi von Schaewen; 180 Neil Lorimer/Elizabeth Whiting & Associates; 182 John Hall; 183 Fritz von der Schulenburg (Adelheid Gowrie)/The Interior Archive; 184 Sinclair Till; 184–5 Paul Warchol; 185 *above left & right & below* Sinclair Till; 187 Fritz von der Schulenburg (Mimmi O'Connell)/The Interior Archive; 188 James Merrell/Woman's Journal/ Robert Harding Syndication; 190 Alexander van Berge; 191 Fritz von der Schulenburg/ The World of Interiors; 192 *left* Nina Ewald/ Abode; 192 *above right* Vaughan; 192 *below right* Jean-Paul Bonhommet/Elizabeth Whiting & Associates; 193 *left* Simon Brown

(John Stefanidis)/The Interior Archive; **193** Simon McBride; **194** Henry Wilson (Sophie Saren)/The Interior Archive; **195** Ken Adlard; **196–7** John Hall; **198** Jan Baldwin (Andrew Mortada); **198–9** Simon McBride; **199** *above* Sølvi Dos Santos; **199** *below* Simon McBride; **200** Paul Ryan/International Interiors; **200–1** Albert Roosenburg/V.T. Wonen; **201** Nicolas Tosi (Stylist: C. Ardouin) / Marie Claire Maison; **202** John Miller; **203** Hotze Eisma; **204** Albert Roosenburg; **205** Hotze Eisma; **206** Polly Wreford/Homes & Gardens/Robert Harding Syndication; **206–7** Trevor Richards/Homes & Gardens/Robert Harding Syndication; **208** Francis Hammond; **209** Michael Mundy (Wilkinson); **210** Fritz von der Schulenburg / (Adelheid Gowrie) The Interior Archive; **211** Hotze Eisma; **212** Richard Felber; **213** John Hall; **214** Henry Wilson (Celia Lyttleton)/The Interior Archive; **215** Richard Bryant/Arcaid; **216** Albert Roosenburg; **217** Jean Pierre Godeaut (Lisa Lovatt Smith); **218–9** David Phelps; **219** Dominque Vorillon; **220** *above* Simon Brown (Justin Meath Baker); **220** *below* Eric Morin; **221** Fritz von der Schulenburg/The Interior Archive; **222** John Hall; **223** Henry Wilson (Ian Dew)/The Interior Archive; **224** John Miller; **225** Albert Roosenburg/V.T. Wonen; **226** *above* Gilles de Chabaneix (Stylist: M.Kalt)/Marie Claire Maison; **226** *below* Alexander van Berge; **226–7** Peter Woloszynski/The Interior Archive; **227** *above* Fritz von der Schulenburg/The Interior Archive; **227** *below* Marie-Pierre Morel (Stylist: J. Borgeaud)/Marie Claire Maison; **228** Marie-Pierre Morel (Stylist: C. Peuch)/Marie Claire Maison; **229** Ray Main; **230** *above* Henry Wilson (Ian Dew)/The Interior Archive; **230** *below* Nicolas Tosi (Stylist: J.Borgeaud)/ Marie Claire Maison; **231** Polly Wreford/ Homes & Gardens/Robert Harding Syndication; **232** *above* James Merrell/Homes & Gardens/Robert Harding Syndication; **232** *below* Henry Wilson (Ashley Hicks)/The Interior Archive; **232–3** Gavin Kingcome/

Homes & Gardens/Robert Harding Syndication; **233** *above* Nicolas Tosi (Stylist: J. Borgeaud)/Marie Claire Maison; **233** *below* Ray Main; **234** Tim Clinch/The Interior Archive; **235** Polly Wreford/Country Homes & Interiors/Robert Harding Syndication; **236** *above* Marie-Pierre Morel (Stylist: C. Peuch)/Marie Claire Maison; **236** *below* Jacques Dirand/Maison & Jardin; **236–7** Tevor Richards/Homes & Gardens/Robert Harding Syndication; **237** *above* Sanderson; **237** *below* Henry Wilson (Stephan Ryan)/The Interior Archive; **238** Fritz von der Schulenburg (David Bennett)/The Interior Archive; **238–9** *above* Christopher Drake/Country Homes & Interiors/Robert Harding Syndication; **238–9** *below* Jacques Dirand/Maison & Jardin; **239** Trevor Richards/Homes & Gardens/ Robert Harding Syndication; **240** Paul Warchol; **241** *above* Jan Baldwin/Options/ Robert Harding Syndication; **241** *below* Todd Eberle; **242** Jacques Dirand/Maison & Jardin; **243** Andreas von Einsiedel/Homes & Gardens/Robert Harding Syndication; **244** Christopher Drake/Homes & Gardens/ Robert Harding Syndication; **245** Jacques Dirand/Maison & Jardin; **246** Christopher Drake/Country Homes & Interiors/Robert Harding Syndication; **247** Brigitte/Camera Press; **248** Fritz von der Schulenburg (Paula Navone)/The Interior Archive; **248–9** Debi Treloar/Homes & Gardens/Robert Harding Syndication; **250** Tom Leighton/Elizabeth Whiting & Associates; **251** Fritz von der Schulenburg (Mimmi O'Connell)/The Interior Archive; **252** Ray Main; **253** Jacques Dirand/ Maison & Jardin; **254** Christopher Drake/ Homes & Gardens/Robert Harding Syndication; **255** Hotze Eisma; **256** A. Gelberger/ Maison Francaise/Agence Top; **257** John Hall; **258** Otto Baitz/Esto; **259** *above* Fritz von der Schulenburg (Architect: Nico Rensch)/The Interior Archive; **259** *below* Christian Sarramon; **260** Laura Ashley; **261** Peter Woloszynski (A.Parlance)/ The Interior Archive; **262** John Hall; **263** Henry Bourne/

World of Interiors; **264** James Mortimer/The Interior Archive; **265** Christophe Dugied (Stylist: M.Bayle)/Marie Claire Maison; **267** Dominque Vorillon; **268** Henry Wilson (Christopher Davies)/The Interior Archive; **269** *above* Jean-Francois Jaussaud; **269** *below* Trevor Richards/Homes & Gardens/Robert Harding Syndication; **270** Fritz von der Schulenburg (Mimmi O'Connell/Painter: Juliette Mole)/The Interior Archive; **272** Ray Main; **273** *above* Henry Bourne/The World of Interiors; **273** *below* Scott Frances/Esto; **274** Trevor Richards/Abode; **275** Mark Luscombe–Whyte/Elizabeth Whiting & Associates; **276** Mads Mogensen; **277** Fritz von der Schulenburg/The Interior Archive; **278** Mads Mogensen; **279** Hotze Eisma; **280** Fritz von der Schulenburg (Dot Spikings)/The Interior Archive; **281** Marie-Pierre Morel (Stylist: G. Le Signe)/Marie Claire Maison; **282–3** Gilles de Chabaneix (Stylist: D. Rozensztroch)/Marie Claire Maison; **284** Trevor Richards/Country Homes & Interiors/Robert Harding Syndication; **285** Pierre Hussenot (Roy-Comte)/ Marie Claire Maison; **286** Hugh Johnson/ Homes & Gardens/Robert Harding Syndication; **287** David Parmiter; **288** Geoffrey Frosh/ Homes & Gardens/Robert Harding Syndication; **289** Marie-Pierre Morel (Stylist: C. Puech/G.Le Signe)/Marie Claire Maison; **290** Marie-Pierre Morel (Stylist: J. Postic)/ Marie Claire Maison; **291** Dominic Blackmore/ Ideal Home / Robert Harding Syndication; **292** James Merrell/Options/ Robert Harding Syndication; **293** Jan Baldwin/Options/ Robert Harding Syndication; **294** *above* Nadia Mackenzie; **294** *below* Trevor Richards/Homes & Gardens/Robert Harding Syndication; **294–5** Solvi Dos Santos; **295** *above* Nadia Mackenzie; **295** *below* Designers Guild; **296** Gilles de Chabaneix (Stylist: C de Chabaneix/ V. Mery)/Marie Claire Idees; **297** Christophe Dugied/Marine Archang; **298** Sandra Lane/ Homes & Gardens/Robert Harding Syndication; **299** Francis Hammond; **300** Spike Powell/Elizabeth Whiting & Associates;

301 Hotze Eisma; **302** Paul Ryan/International Interiors; **303** Tim Beddow (Kelly Hoppen)/The Interior Archive; **304** Simon Brown; **305** Todd Eberle; **306** Fritz von der Schulenburg (Architect:Nico Rensch) The Interior Archive; **306–7** Kiloran Howard/ Homes & Gardens/Robert Harding Syndication; **308** Jerome Darblay; **309** Christophe Dugied (Stylist: J. Postic)/Marie Claire Maison; **310** *left* Paul Ryan/International Interiors; **310** *right* Paul Warchol; **310** *below* Ariadne; **311** *left* Nadia Mackenzie; **311** *right* Ariadne; **312** Ianthe Ruthven; **314** John Hall; **315** Todd Eberle; **316** Simon Brown/Homes & Gardens/ Robert Harding Syndication; **317** Hotze Eisma; **318–9** Christophe Dugied (Stylist: J.Postic)/Marie Claire Maison; **319** James Merrell/Country Homes & Interiors/Robert Harding Syndication; **320** Alexander van Berge; **321** Marie-Pierre Morel (Stylist: C. Puech)/Marie Claire Maison; **322** Laura Ashley; **324** Tom Leighton / Wedding & Home/Robert Harding Syndication; **325** Henry Wilson (Ian Dew)/The Interior Archive; **326** Tom Leighton/Wedding & Home/Robert Harding Syndication; **327** Hotze Eisma; **328** Tim Beddow (Kelly Hoppen)/The Interior Archive; **329** Hotze Eisma/V.T. Wonen; **330–1** Marie-Pierre Morel (Stylist: M. Bayle)/Marie Claire Maison; **332** Christophe Dugied (Stylist: J. Postic)/ Marie Claire Maison; **333** Louis Gaillard (Stylist: C. Puech)/Marie Claire Maison; **334** Christophe Dugied (Stylist: J.Postic)/ Marie Claire Maison; **335** Simon McBride; **336** Simon Brown; **337** Simon Upton/ Options/Robert Harding Syndication; **338** Hotze Eisma; **339** Sandra Lane/Homes & Gardens/Robert Harding Syndication

Authors' acknowledgments

Anoop Parikh

Many of the ideas in the Design and Detailing chapter were unashamedly stolen from the homes show-cased in magazines such as *Elle Decoration* (UK and USA editions), *Marie Claire Maison* (France) and *Martha Stewart Living* (USA). My greatest thanks therefore go to the many designers and home-owners featured during 1995 and 1996, and to the editors for producing such consistently inspiring titles.

Several books were also invaluable sources of practical information on materials and construction. These were Terence Conran's *The Essential House Book*, Albert Jackson and David Day's *How to Store Just About Anything*, and *The Reader's Digest Complete Guide to DIY* — my thanks to them all. Shops and manufacturers mentioned in the list of suppliers were a mine of useful product and technical information, but I am particularly grateful to both The Newson Group, and to the Department of the Environment's Energy Efficiency Office for their useful leaflets on energy-saving lighting.

Debora Robertson

At *Homes & Ideas*, I would like to thank my colleagues Virginia Hiller and Amanda Cochrane for their support, advice and good humour. And without the highly professional team at Conran Octopus, producing this chapter would have been far less enjoyable than it was. In particular I would like to thank Catriona Woodburn, whose calm demeanour, persistence and attention to detail are truly awe inspiring.

Thomas Lane

With thanks to all the individuals and companies who gave me their help while I was researching the finer points of flooring, and in particular to Adrian Smart for his advice on tiling. With thanks to Joanna for her patience and support, and all the staff at Conran Octopus.

Elizabeth Hilliard

I would like to thank: Felicity Bryan and Michele Topham, Georgina Cardew, Karen Hill, William Selka, Jan Walker, and Deborah Walter.

Melanie Paine

Heartfelt thanks to my colleague Joanne Outram for all her hard work and for holding the fort so admirably whilst I was working on the book.

Publisher's acknowledgments

The publishers would like to thank the following people for their invaluable assistance with the production of this book:

Alison Bolus, Tessa Clayton, Lesley Craig, Mollie Gillard, Helen Green, Karen Howes, Margot Richardson.